THE EVIL EYE

THE

Clarence Maloney, editor

EVIL EYE

Columbia University Press ❁ New York

1976

LIBRARY OF CONGRESS CATALOGING IN PUBLICATION DATA
Main entry under title:
The Evil eye.

  Outgrowth of a symposium on the evil eye belief held at the
1972 meeting of the American Anthropological Association.
  Includes bibliographies and index.
  1. *Evil eye—Congresses.* I. *Maloney, Clarence.*
GN475.6.E94   133.4'25   76-16861   ISBN 0-231-04006-7

Columbia University Press New York Guildford, Surrey
Copyright © 1976 Columbia University Press
All rights reserved Printed in the United States of America

CLARENCE MALONEY

INTRODUCTION

THE EVIL EYE BELIEF—primarily the belief that someone can project harm by looking at another's property or person—is found in many parts of the world, though not in all of it.

Some people might think of this belief as simply a superstition, or classify it among the occult; but what is one person's superstition or occult idea is another person's belief or religion. In recent years, the general public has gained a renewed interest in diverse beliefs and religions, and so have social scientists. We have put together a book on the evil eye phenomenon that we think will be of general interest. At the same time we hope it will help us to understand how such apparently strange or outdated ''superstitions'' arose, how they fit into social and cultural systems, and why they persist in so many parts of the world to this day.

The first twelve chapters represent the major parts of the world where the evil eye exists as a clearly recognized belief with associated behavior. Chapter 13 is an important chapter, surveying the traits associated with this belief in a large number of cultures and arriving at certain conclusions based on the data. Chapters 14 and 15, the concluding essays, delve even further into the meaning of this belief and its associated behavior.

The contributors of all fifteen chapters are anthropologists. The book grew out of a symposium on the evil eye belief held at the 1972 meeting of the American Anthropological Association. Most of the chapters were written expressly for this volume,[1] and all the authors have had long experience of living among the various people whose beliefs and practices they describe and analyze.

We have a plethora of information here, seemingly confused and conflicting. As anthropologists we want to make some sense of it. Several of the authors strive heroically to understand the deeper meanings of the belief and to see its role in society. And they have achieved this, in varying ways, to a considerable extent.

The first problem is to know what is meant by the evil eye belief. Who casts the evil eye, who or what can it strike, and what is the nature of the ascribed power? These questions are answered differently in various chapters. In one region (Philippines) the power emanates only from the person who casts it, through his eye or mouth. But in another (the Mediterranean) it may be an avenging, righteous power of a deity, or even (in ancient Egypt) the power of a god emanating from his eyes. The evil eye may be (in Italy) a pervasive malevolent force like a virus or plague, to be staved off with charms made nowadays of plastic, or it may be (in Mexico) the effect of bad "air" over the land, or it may be (among Slovak-Americans) a "chronic but low-grade" evil eye. It may be thought of (in the Mediterranean) as the embodiment of the source of evil, maybe the Devil himself, or even (in the Near East) as a sort of deity in its own right on occasion. But elsewhere (in India) there is no such dichotomy of good and evil rending the world asunder, and the evil eye is only an emanation from the mind behind the eye of the person who casts it. Yet elsewhere (in Guatemala) it is the name of a sickness, not just the cause of sickness.

All these are variations and scenarios around the simple belief that one's eye-power can cause sudden harm to another's property or person.

In different parts of the world, different kinds of people can cast it. In one country (Ethiopia) it is cast by people of a certain low caste, in another (Mexico) mainly by strangers, in another (Tunisia) by marginal people but not by kin, and in yet another (Iran) [2] mainly by kin. Elsewhere (in India) it may be cast by any being—one's own mother or other kin, neighbors, strangers, gods, or even animals. In some places (ancient Israel, Italy) it has at times been cast by high ecclesiastical officials, while in another place (Greece) it is often thought of as cast by witches who can bewitch people, and among yet another ethnic group (Slovak-Americans) it is a spell thought to be cast by those who as babies returned to the mother's breast after weaning.

And in different countries different kinds of objects can be struck with it. In some (Mexico, Philippines) it mainly strikes babies or children, while elsewhere (the Mediterranean) it attacks people of any age, women and the weak being especially susceptible. In most regions the wealthy or the handsome are considered susceptible because they are the objects of envy. But there is an ambivalence between this and the thought that it is the weak who are attacked. In one chapter (Italian-Americans) the belief is described principally as something people avoid by wielding charms if they want to be successful, while in another (Ethiopia) the people of the dominant ethnic group are susceptible. In some places (Ethiopia, Mexico) it is principally regarded as causing illness, while in others (Guatemala, Philippines) it may also cause disease in fruits or vegetables, and over a wide area (Europe, Near East, South Asia) it may affect one's domestic animals, crops, houses, and possessions by inflicting sudden destruction or harm. In one country (Tunisia) it does not strike inanimate objects unless they belong to someone, but in another (India) instances are cited where unowned objects have been attacked.

The force of the evil eye in two countries described here (India, Ethiopia) may be an expression of the personal ritual impurity of the attacker, but this is not so everywhere. In one place (Mexico) it is likened to electricity, but among other folk (Slovak-Americans) the power is produced in one by certain treatment that symbolizes a whole set of psychodynamic characteristics. While the power coming from the eye is commonly regarded as harmful, there may also be (in Nepal and Tibet, and sometimes in India and the Near East), a loving, benevolent, protective, or watchful eye.

This belief also gets mixed up with the mystique of the eye, with mythology (as Maclagan shows for Scotland), and with beliefs in various saints, deities, and religions. In pulling together this book with data from so many cultures we had hoped to be able to readily define and hypothesize the meaning of the evil eye belief, but instead we have turned up a whole cluster of evil eye beliefs and practices. Now we have to search for the core of this complex in cultural evolutionary terms, and the essential meaning of it in behavioral terms.

Potential Theoretical Approaches

The common features found in the descriptions of the belief in the twelve world regions (or ethnic groups) described in this book seem to be limited to the following: (1) power emanates from the eye (or mouth) and strikes some object or person; (2) the stricken object is of value, and its destruction or injury is sudden; (3) the one casting the evil eye may not know he has the power; (4) the one affected may not be able to identify the source of the power; (5) the evil eye can be deflected or its effects modified or cured by particular devices, rituals, and symbols; (6) the belief helps to explain or rationalize sickness, misfortune, or loss of possessions such as animals or crops; and (7) in at least some functioning of the belief everywhere, envy is a factor. The three final chapters of this book suggest some further features common to the core of the belief, based on hypotheses of its functions in social interaction.

Our first twelve authors discuss the evil eye belief variously in terms of world-view systems, social structure, psychological interpretations, and history, or in terms of several of these. For the Mediterranean Moss and Cappannari put it in the context of world view or religion, as an elaboration of the dichotomy of good and evil characteristic of the theology of that part of the world. For Guatemala, Cosminsky puts it in the context of another dichotomy, the hot-cold classification system applied to foods and body humors, and also to social behavior. This hot-cold dichotomy is also a subsidiary factor in discussion of the belief in Mexico by Kearney and in the Philippines by Flores-Meiser. The latter author refers to the belief principally as an explanation of illness and suggests that the power imputed to the one who casts it is an expression of personal power like mana. For India too I have shown that the elaboration of the belief arises in part from the world-view system, especially the notion that each person has an inner energizing force which interacts with the world about him, so that the psychic power of the mind can be projected. And for Italy, Appel has also invoked in part the world-view system, stressing relation of the belief to historic dynamics, for the belief helps to enable realignment of cultural categories otherwise not classifiable by people who consider themselves rational or modern.

As to the working of this belief in the social interaction Dionisopoulos-Mass perceives that in Greece it is a means of social control, like gossip or witchcraft, minimizing deviant behavior. For Tunisia, Teitelbaum also perceives it as a means of social control, but principally through economic leveling. For Italian-Americans, Swiderski sees evil eye charms as important markers of the identity of a minority subcultural group. For Ethiopia, Reminick thinks of the belief mostly as an expression of interaction between dominant and subordinate ethnic categories. For South Asia, too, the belief may at times be construed as supportive of social hierarchy, inasmuch as the purity-pollution system is involved, though at other times it seems to function in social leveling.

Psychological interpretations are offered by Kearney for Mexico and by Stein for Slovak-Americans. Kearney portrays Mexican *mestizos* as having a paranoid outlook on the world, both individually and collectively, giving rise to fear that generates belief in the evil eye. He carefully supports this psychological interpretation, though it is criticized by some readers as an ethnocentric one. Stein sees the evil eye belief as symptomatic of a whole range of behavior traits, which the Slovak-Americans themselves consider "jealousy." On another level, Spooner, after reviewing several interpretations of the belief, proposes in his concluding essay that the psychology of staring might be invoked to explain why the eye is central to these beliefs, and that it might have universal validity. This theme is pursued in greater detail by Garrison and Arensberg.

Each of the theoretical positions of the first twelve contributors seems particularly apt for the culture that gave rise to it. For example, the good-evil dichotomy is a workable framework for the evil eye belief in the Mediterranean but not in the Philippines. Reminick's discussion of the belief in terms of two unequally ranked ethnic categories is peculiar to Ethiopia, Teitelbaum's emphasis arises in part because he studied a limited population and documented their common and individual economic goals, and Dionisopoulos-Mass produced an interpretation suitable for an island peasant population. And it may be significant that the interpretations provided by both Dionisopoulos-Mass and Stein seem to be substantially based on data from women not much involved in economic production. The paranoid explanation might do for Mexican *mestizos,* but not for many other populations, while the endless ramifications of the belief found in India are again somewhat unique to that part of the world.

Of the twelve chapters dealing with particular cultures or world areas, those by Kearney on Mexican Amerinds and Stein on Slovak-Americans offer the most developed behavioral explanations, and thus we have placed them last among these chapters. The theories proposed—by the one that the belief is rooted in the ethos of the culture and by the other that it symbolizes and expresses the conflict between independence and dependency in the individual—are excellent contributions, but they still leave us searching for universally valid explanations for the belief.

Envy has been suggested by several authors as a universal attribute of the evil eye belief, and Roberts in his chapter has suggested that his cross-cultural study might lead to a more universally valid theory of envy. Elsewhere, Schoeck in his book about envy suggests that social scientists have repressed the concept, preferring to speak of conflict, hostility, adjustment, or adaptation, because in contemporary society we view envy as a "serious disease." [3] But while envy is indeed structurally important in the kinds of societies that have the evil eye belief, four of our contributors (Kearney,

Cosminsky, Flores-Meiser, and Maloney) suggest that envy, though perhaps present, is not even the principal motivation behind the belief. It may not be coincidental that the first three of these authors write about cultures that are the least hierarchically or socially complex among those described in this book. This is in line with Roberts' patterns of cross-cultural associations. Garrison in chapter 15 has explored the question of envy and has discovered four types of psychodynamic processes in anecdotes in this book.

Roberts' cross-cultural study, therefore, is invaluable for an understanding of the meaning of the evil eye belief. He has tabulated the presence or absence of the belief in 186 societies around the world—an effort requiring several months of work—and has shown the statistical relationship of the belief to other culture traits in these societies in 39 tables. He has isolated a cluster of traits statistically associated with the belief, and has reduced this further by factor analysis. His findings on social structure, personality type, child socialization, cultural complexity, and technology clarify for us the kinds of societies in which the belief can become elaborated. They also provide historical parameters, which anticipate and support the statements in the final chapter about the cultural matrix in which the belief developed in cultural evolutionary terms. This data must be fully taken into account in any theoretical hypothesis.

Spooner reviews four types of approaches in this book (and he also provided the concluding thoughts in our original symposium on the evil eye). But he does not find that any of these approaches exclusively explain the belief; most readers will not disagree with his findings.

Garrison and Arensberg offer a structural hypothesis of the evil eye "event" while reiterating the cultural matrix that makes such an event possible. The evil eye event is seen in essence not as a dyadic act between attacker and attacked, but as a triadic relationship. This approach, developed in the first half of chapter 15, is complemented by Garrison's further study in the second half of that chapter of reported accounts of the phenomenon, analyzed in psychological and behavioral terms. The reader may judge how well the last five chapters in the book provide the theoretical framework to understand the meaning of the evil eye belief in terms of behavior.

Potential Historical Explanations

Spooner points out that the historical explanations are the least interesting of the several possible approaches, at least to the social anthropologist. But the historical data seem more manageable and less contradictory. And for those who find that the psychodynamic hypotheses concerning the belief provide insufficient cover for the many variant and contradictory permutations, the historical approach may indeed be interesting.

The accompanying map (constructed with much reliance on Roberts' data) shows where the belief is generally found. The core area is the Near East and the Mediterranean and South Asia; the belief is also found throughout northern Europe, across North Africa, and along the sub-Saharan fringe, as well as in parts of East Africa, but there it seems to merge with witchcraft. In Southeast Asia the belief is exceedingly vague, if indeed it exists at all. As for East Asia, there are sporadic reports of it in Taiwan and among Chinese Muslims, and also perhaps in southern China and Japan. But the belief, to the extent that it even exists in East Asia, is not very clearly conceptualized by those peoples.

Decades ago Seligmann [4] produced a thorough German study of the geographical extent of the evil eye belief, citing it from Old Testament times in the Near East and in Hamitic and Arab sources, and throughout Europe: Germany, England, Scandinavia, Scotland, Brittany, Ireland, Italy, Greece, Spain, Estonia, Russia, Poland, Hungary; also in Turkey, Iran, North India, and Polynesia (?). He did not hear of its existing in Thailand, Burma, Tibet, Korea, or scarcely in Japan, and he knew of a man who had lived in China for twenty-seven years but had never heard of it there. He had no data on Central Asian Turkish or Mongol peoples—and such data are still lacking, but the belief is probably weak or absent there.

We are bound, therefore, to consider a diffusionist interpretation, which is also supported by Roberts' data: that the belief originated in the Near East with the evolution of complex peasant-urban cultures and spread in all directions. It is statistically associated today with such features as plow agriculture and dairying, as well as premodern urbanization.

A number of our contributors advance a diffusionist position. Moss takes it for granted in the Mediterranean, recently extended to Italian-Americans. I have given reasons to believe it came from the Near East into South Asia, diffusing through that subcontinent with the elaboration of complex peasant-urban cultures. Flores-Meiser also suggests that it diffused to the Philippines, though in many ways it parallels the presumably indigenous belief of the hot mouth. The question is whether it was brought to those islands by Indians, Arabs, or the Spanish, all of whom had civilizational impact. It will take research in many more parts of Southeast Asia, as well as on such associated

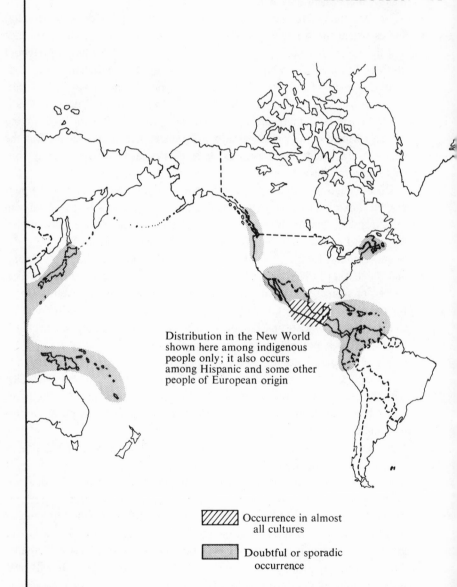

Distribution in the New World
shown here among indigenous
people only; it also occurs
among Hispanic and some other
people of European origin

Occurrence in almost
all cultures

Doubtful or sporadic
occurrence

THE EVIL EYE BELIEF

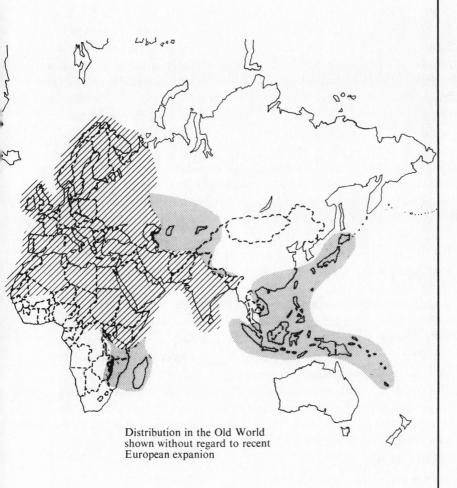

Distribution in the Old World
shown without regard to recent
European expanion

traits as the hot-cold bifurcation, to sort out the historical trends. And we do not know if its sporadic occurrence in East Asia is residual, or is indigenous to those civilizations, or if it was brought by Buddhists or Muslims.

There are so many aspects of the evil eye belief found contiguously from Scotland at one extreme of its main area of distribution to Sri Lanka at the other, that we must rely heavily on a diffusionist explanation. In Scotland, for example, where this belief was described by Maclagan at the turn of this century, cattle and milk products and the churning process were especially susceptible to evil eye attack; the eye could make a cow's udder or a woman's breasts dry up, or cause milk to be devoid of butterfat. All this is true at the other geographical extreme, in India. A charm of a knotted red thread, or of hair, may be tied on children or on a pregnant cow both in Scotland and in South Asia. A fragment of the Bible may be sewn in the clothes as a preventative in Scotland, while in South Asia a fragment of the Koran or a Hindu incantation may be put in a receptacle and tied on children. In both regions the evil eye's malevolent effects may be cured by salt, and by spitting. Also in both regions its attack can be prevented by making deprecatory remarks about one's children or possessions, or by giving to charity. In Scotland a child newly dressed may have a burning stick or peat waved over it to prevent attack, serving the same purpose as the waving of a torch before gods and dignitaries in South Asia. In the two regions the belief serves similar functions in the folk etiology, is popularly regarded as preventing too much self-praise, and is explained as suppressing envy.

The history of the diffusion of the belief must be complex. Scotland and Sri Lanka represent the extremes of the diffusion of the Indo-European linguistic phylum, while the Hamito-Semitic phylum extends across that axis well into Africa, with marginal influence in central Asia and Southeast Asia. This covers the main zone of the evil eye's Old World diffusion, though incorporated within this are other linguistic phyla such as Turkic and Dravidian where the belief is also found. It must have been spread in large measure by the expansion of Indo-European- and Semitic-speaking peoples (in contrast with speakers of Sinitic, Malay, or Bantu languages, for example), and the early dairying and herding traditions of those peoples may account for the statistical association of the belief with those features. Nonetheless, the belief apparently had an earlier origin, since it existed in Egypt before the arrival of the Semitic speakers and in Pakistan before the arrival of the Indo-European speakers.

As for the new world, the difficult historical question is whether the belief existed before Columbus. Kearney suggests that it originated only once, in the Near East. Cosminsky also thinks that it was brought to Mesoamerica by the Spanish. Other scholars are not so sure, for there was a mystique of the eyes in pre-Columbian Mesoamerican civilizations. The belief is associated both with etiology of European derivation such as the hot-cold dichotomy and with indigenous beliefs such as bad air. Roberts' survey shows that a number of Amerind groups have it, in South America and also in parts of North America not much affected by the Spanish, but probably only as a vague and poorly conceptualized idea. Then there is also the possibility of pre-Columbian diffusion from the Old World. In any case, elaboration of the evil eye belief in its present form certainly derives from the Spanish, and now is found more or less over Latin America.

There have been previous works on the evil eye, but few have been very anthropological. Gifford's book is the most useful, presenting as it does a potpourri of anecdotes from Europe and also some from other parts of the world. It is principally descriptive. An early book purportedly on this subject was written by Elworthy, but it deals with a motley of religious phenomena and refers principally to ancient civilizations. While we have no contribution in this volume representing northern Europe, there is ample detail on the evil eye belief in Maclagan's book about the belief in Scotland. More recently published is a work on the belief in Finland by Vuorela, in German, with ample detail and explanation; the belief characteristically became embedded in the interactional process of a society having dairying as an important means of subsistence, so that here, too, milk, butter, cows, and other animals are subject to attack, which may be warded off by ashes, salt, or tar. There is a useful article on the belief in a Guatemala village by Simon, and numerous lesser references in ethnographies, encyclopedias, and folklore works.

The anthropologists, of course, want to understand both historical dynamics of a trait such as this and its meaning in the structures of the societies that adopt or modify it. Foster, for example, became interested in the subject of envy and developed his theories about it after he witnessed how quietly 100 Mexican school children ate their lunch; this eating behavior is related to the evil eye belief in Mexico and as far away as India, where it is the norm. Clearly, we are not dealing with a "superstition" that can be dismissed with jokes, but with a belief important enough to diffuse over half the world, for which there must be reasons. And so we present several views of the historical matrix and the contemporary meaning of this belief.

N O T E S

1. The exceptions are: Spooner, chapter 6 on Arabs and Iran; Reminick, chapter 7 on Ethiopia; and Stein, chapter 12 on Slovak-Americans.
2. Barth, *Nomads,* as cited in chapter 15.
3. Schoeck, pp. 99–105.   4. Seligmann, *Die Zauberkraft.*

B I B L I O G R A P H Y

Adams, R., and A. Rubel. "Sickness and Social Relations," in *Handbook of Middle American Indians,* Robert Wanchope and Manning Nash, eds. Austin: University of Texas Press, 1967.

Barth, Frederick. *Nomads of South Persia.* London: Allen and Unwin, 1956.

Elworthy, Frederick. *The Evil Eye.* 1895. Reprint, New York: Macmillan, 1958.

Foster, George M. "The Anatomy of Envy: A Study in Symbolic Behavior," *Current Anthropology* 13 (1972), 165–202.

—— "Peasant Society and the Image of Limited Good," *American Anthropologist* 67, no. 2 (1965), 293–315.

Gifford, Edward S. *The Evil Eye: Studies in the Folklore of Vision.* New York: Macmillan, 1958.

Hastings, J., ed. *Encyclopaedia of Religion and Ethics.* Edinburgh: Clark, 1908.

Maclagan, R. C. *Evil Eye in Western Highlands.* London, 1902.

Meerloo, Joost A. M. *Intuition and the Evil Eye.* Wasenaar (Netherlands), 1971.

Schoeck, Helmut. *Envy: A Theory of Social Behavior.* Michael Glenny and Betty Ross, trans. New York: Harcourt, Brace, 1966.

Seligmann, Sigfried. *Der Böse Blick.* 2 vols. Berlin, 1910.

—— *Die Zauberkraft des Auges und das Berufen: Ein Kapital aus der Geschichte des Auberglaubens.* Hamburg, 1922.

Simon G. "The Evil Eye in a Guatemalan Village," *Ethnomedizin* 2, no. 3 (1973), 437–41.

Spooner, Brian. "The Evil Eye in the Middle East," in *Witchcraft Confessions and Accusations,* M. Douglas, ed. Association of Social Anthropologists Monograph no. 9. London: Tavistock, 1970.

Vuorela, Turvo. *Der böse Blick in Lichte der finnischen Überlieferung.* Helsinki, 1967.

CONTENTS

Introduction   v
CLARENCE MALONEY

1. THE MEDITERRANEAN

Mal'occhio, Ayin ha ra, Oculus Fascinus, Judenblick:
The Evil Eye Hovers Above   1
LEONARD W. MOSS AND STEPHEN C. CAPPANNARI

2. ITALY

The Myth of the Jettatura   17
WILLA APPEL

3. ITALIAN-AMERICANS

From Folk to Popular: Plastic Evil Eye Charms   28
RICHARD SWIDERSKI

4. GREECE

The Evil Eye and Bewitchment in a Peasant Village   42
REGINA DIONISOPOULOS-MASS

5. TUNISIA

The Leer and the Loom—Social Controls on Handloom
Weavers   63
JOEL M. TEITELBAUM

6. ARABS AND IRAN

The Evil Eye in the Middle East   76
BRIAN SPOONER

7. *ETHIOPIA*

The Evil Eye Belief among the Amhara   85

RONALD A. REMINICK

8. *INDIA*

Don't Say "Pretty Baby" Lest You Zap It with Your
Eye—The Evil Eye in South Asia   102

CLARENCE MALONEY

9. *PHILIPPINES*

The Hot Mouth and Evil Eye   149

ENYA FLORES-MEISER

10. *GUATEMALA*

The Evil Eye in a Quiché Community   163

SHEILA COSMINSKY

11. *MEXICO*

A World-View Explanation of the Evil Eye   175

MICHAEL KEARNEY

12. *SLOVAK-AMERICANS*

Envy and the Evil Eye: An Essay in the Psychological
Ontogeny of Belief and Ritual   193

HOWARD F. STEIN

13. *CROSS-CULTURAL*

Belief in the Evil Eye in World Perspective   223

JOHN M. ROBERTS

14. *CONCLUDING ESSAY 1*

Anthropology and the Evil Eye   279

BRIAN SPOONER

15. *CONCLUDING ESSAY 2*

The Evil Eye: Envy or Risk of Seizure? Paranoia or
Patronal Dependency?   287

VIVIAN GARRISON AND CONRAD M. ARENSBERG

Index   329

THE EVIL EYE

LEONARD W. MOSS
STEPHEN C. CAPPANNARI

1. THE MEDITERRANEAN

Mal'occhio, Ayin ha ra, Oculus fascinus, Judenblick: The Evil Eye Hovers Above

LONG BEFORE THE ADVENT of Christianity, the cosmologies of many ancient peoples of the Mediterranean spoke of the universe as a perfect and complete social order, ordained by the god(s). Yet day-to-day events demonstrated the world to be less than perfect. If the god was good, and his product, the universe, less than good, how could the difference be reconciled? In religions that had a pantheistic godhead, one could always find a mischievous or jokester god who frustrated the master plan. In monotheistic faiths the problem was more difficult. Here one would have to posit

LEONARD W. MOSS is Professor of Anthropology at Wayne State University, Detroit, Michigan. During summers he is Professor of Anthropology at the Rome campus of Trinity College. Although his primary concentration has been on contemporary peasant societies, he has also done work in pre-Roman archeology. Dr. Moss is a Knight in the Order of Merit, Republic of Italy.

His fieldwork in Italy has been supported by the Fulbright-Hays Program (1955–56, 1961–62, 1968–69), the American Council of Learned Societies, and the Wenner-Gren Foundation.

STEPHEN C. CAPPANNARI collaborated with Leonard Moss in some of the field research on which this chapter was based. When this chapter was written he was Professor of Psychiatry (Anthropology) and Director of the Division of Human Behavior, Vanderbilt University School of Medicine, Nashville, Tennessee. He did fieldwork among the Kawaiis Amerinds of California as well as in Italy. He encouraged Howard Stein to produce the exceedingly useful article on the evil eye among Slovak-Americans in this volume.

But before editing of this volume was complete, in 1974, Stephen Cappannari died of a massive coronary—an unexpected departure and a great loss. Leonard Moss wishes to express his appreciation of a twenty-two-year working relationship with Stephen Cappannari.

an anti-God, a controller of the forces of evil; or one would have to endow the godhead with a degree of capriciousness unbefitting the creator of perfection. Islamic theology accepts good and evil as the will of Allah. Both Hindu and Buddhist faiths accept karma as the reaping of that which is sown in earlier lifetimes. Man himself, though part of the perfect social order, often fell short of perfection. Made of dust or mud, imbued with original sin or motivations less than pristine, man himself could be the source or agent of evil.

The evil eye is but one embodiment of the source of evil. Magic, witchcraft, the machinations of the anti-Christ, and other sources abound in the Mediterranean world. We will not argue the causes of witchcraft in this paper—although the spirits of Lilith and Samuel hover over the same area as the evil eye. We will not debate Beatrice Whiting's thesis on the prevalence of witchcraft in the absence of superordinate authority.[1] Certainly, we will not argue that high oral anxiety is related to belief in witchcraft, not when we are concerned with cultures in which weaning from breastfeeding occurs very late.[2]

Good and Evil in the Ancient World

The eye of man and the eye of god are powerful instrumentalities. The seat of the soul and the power of evil are both to be found in the pupil; hence, the visual organ works both good and evil. In early Mediterranean mythologies—in Egypt, Babylonia, and elsewhere—the eye is symbolic of the deity: Eye of Ra, Eye of Atum, Eye of Osiris, Eye of Horus, etc. These latter two deities become important in the death-resurrection theme. Horus the king fights with Seth, losing his eye but tearing off Seth's testicle as just retribution. On his death, Horus becomes Osiris, who rescues the eye from Seth and recreates himself as Horus. This all-powerful, ever-living god brings peace to mankind when his eye is intact in his body. Loss of the eye disturbs the social order of man. The ankh (see figure 1.1) of Horus becomes symbolic of the *sol invictus,* the journey of the sun, the moon, the morning star, the kingship, creation of good and evil, and a prelude to a physician's prescription of a drug. The symbol Rx is not a contraction of the Latin *recipe,* but is another abstraction of the falcon-headed god, Horus.

Apparently as early as ancient Egypt, the eye assumed three functions in religious belief: seat of the soul (window to the soul); creation of good; and

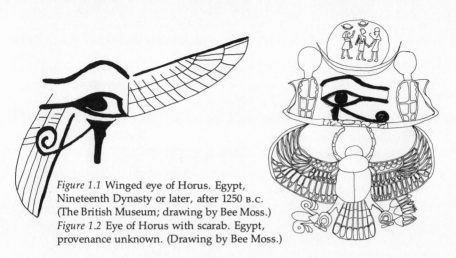

Figure 1.1 Winged eye of Horus. Egypt,
Nineteenth Dynasty or later, after 1250 B.C.
(The British Museum; drawing by Bee Moss.)
Figure 1.2 Eye of Horus with scarab. Egypt,
provenance unknown. (Drawing by Bee Moss.)

creation of evil. The Hebrew word for the pupil of the eye is *ishon,* "little man." Gaster notes similar conceptions in German, *Männlein im Auge,* and Spanish, *la niña del ojo.*[3] As a window to the body, the eye affords easy access to emanations both from within and from without. Evil spirits may enter through the eye and may be exorcised through the same organ. Andrew D. White notes a medieval prescription for a salve against "nocturnal goblin visitors" that when applied to the eyes, accompanied by censing with incense, and signed by the cross becomes an efficacious weapon against inhabitation:

> Take hop plant, wormwood, bishopwort, lupine, ash-throat, henbane, harewort, viper's bugloss, heathberry plant, cropleek, garlic, grains of hedgrife, githrife, and fennel. Put these worts into a vessel, set them under the altar, sing over them nine masses, boil them in butter and sheeps' grease, add much holy salt, strain through a cloth, throw the worts into running water.[4]

The invocation of the eye of god, in the form of an amulet, affords protection from known and unknown evils. The homeopathic use of the eye was practiced by ancient Egyptians, Etruscans, Greeks, and Jews. Such amulets are frequently found in contemporary Mediterranean cultures. However, it is the eye's function as the instrumentality of evil upon which we shall focus. The power to fascinate can be the power of social control. This force may be inadvert; one may not know that he possesses the power. A pact with Satan can knowingly give one the power to create evil. A vengeful, righteous god may empower a given individual to restructure the social order by fighting evil with evil. The force may take many forms. Jealousy, coveting, anger, destruction are all attributes of the eye.

Osiris, in a moment of anger, could destroy with a glance. Onufri, a substitute name for Osiris, later becomes syncretized as St. Onuphrius.[5] One of the judges of the dead, who sat with Osiris, was *Arti-f-em-tes*, "eyes like flint knives." [6] The eye as instrument of anger can be destructive. Indeed, the German word often used for evil eye is *Böseblick*, "angry eye." In many of the Mediterranean cultures the evil eye is associated with jealousy. This gnawing, envious emotion ultimately can create evil. Illustrative of this principle is the Judeo-Greek story that appears in *Agada*. After his conquest of "the world," Alexander began his journey to Macedonia. He washed in a stream of miraculous water that gave life to a salted fish in his knapsack. Alexander's eyes shone like stars when he realized that the stream ran from the Gates of Paradise. Following the stream to the gates, he bid them to open. The gates remained closed, but rolled forth a token, a human eyeball, as proof of his visit. Home in Macedonia, Alexander questioned his wise men about the significance of the eye. They suggested that it be placed on a scale and a gold piece be weighed against it. To Alexander's amazement, the eye outbalanced all of his gold, silver, and jewels. The wise men told the king that even his horses, chariots, and palaces would be outweighed by the eye, since the human eye is never satisfied with what it sees; it wishes to acquire more and more. Alexander demanded proof. The wise men removed the treasure from the balance pan and placed but a pinch of dust on the scale. The dust proved heavier than the eye. Alexander immediately drew the conclusion: "So long as a man is alive, his eye is never sated but no sooner does he die when he is as dust. Then his eye loses its impulse and becomes powerless. It can no longer desire." [7]

The duality of good and evil apparently plays an important role in sustaining belief in the power of the eye to cause evil. If a good and loving God has ordained a perfect world, then the seeds of evil are sown by earthly man. Man's greed, envy, malice, aggression, are concentrated in his soul and projected outward through the eye in a destructive manner. Talmudic sages have argued that man was endowed with two impulses, good and evil. God created the world and pronounced it good; hence, all things created must have a beneficial function. The impulse to evil (*yetser ha ra*), the imagination of man, is a constant test of the innate goodness of man. The mortal nature of man is the ultimate weapon of the divine to hold mankind in line.

Historic and ethnographic evidence tend to support the thesis that dualism aids in a continuation of this belief. We know little of the Etruscan patterns of belief except what is told to us by Herodotus, Livy, Cicero, Pliny the Elder, Juvenal, and others. Their language, not susceptible to understanding, gives us a vocabulary limited essentially to funerary inscriptions and boundary markers. Funerary art does reveal certain themes that are subject to interpretation. By the fifth and fourth centuries B.C., Etruscan attitudes toward death had undergone change. The scenes of happy banquets, athletic contests, and other joyous moments no longer decorated the sarcophagi and canopic jars. They were replaced by scenes of violence and battle. Themes of combat between Tinia (Jupiter) and Charun or Tuchulca dominated the art form. The Rassena people had fallen on hard times. Defeats by the Romans had profoundly altered their views of life and death. Forces of evil continued to plague one after death, and countermagic against the evil eye was invoked by horning the fingers of the figurines sculpted on the sarcophagi and cinerary urns.

Roman belief systems owed much to the Greek pantheon; yet, the impact of the *disciplina etrusca* should not be overlooked. The Romans borrowed from it far more than the rituals of divination. The *libri haruspicini* that dealt with hepatoscopy and the *libri fulgurales* that treated divination of lightning and thunder were but two aspects of the discipline. The Romans also borrowed those books dealing with regulation of interpersonal behavior (*libri rituales*), conduct of man in the afterlife (*libri acheruntici*), and the ultimate fate of men and mankind (*libri fatales*). Later incursions of belief systems from the East, not the least of which was Mithraism, further supported the growing dualism of good-evil.

Jews

The precise role of Judaism in the growth of Greek and Roman religious systems remains to be documented. It has been argued that the Hellenes conquered the Jews and were in turn conquered by Judaic modification of their philosophical systems. The ultimate impact of this filtering through Greek and Roman belief to Christianity is poorly researched. There is much, however, to be found in the biblical and talmudic literature. Evil spirits, evil impulses, and the evil eye (*ayin ha ra*) abound in the folklore of the Jews, such as the following prescription: "To see an evil spirit one should take the afterbirth of a black she-cat, roast it in a fire, pulverize the ashes, and rub them in your eyes. Then you will see the evil spirits." [8] Evil spirits may be seen in wet, dark, and unclean places. Latrines are popular places for them. These beliefs are similar to Muslim beliefs in *jinn*.

The biblical concepts of *ayin ha ra* have a twofold meaning: jealousy and hate. Involved in jealousy is both envy and greed. Illustrative of this would be such passages as: "Eat not thou the bread of him that hath an evil eye" (Prov. 23:6), and "He that hath an evil eye hasteneth after riches" (Prov. 28:22). Saul often found it difficult to conceal his envy of David. He clothed the shepherd lad in his kingly apparel before the battle with Goliath (1 Sam. 17:39). Following David's victory, Jonathan covered the lad with his armor and robe. When Saul saw this, his face went white and he flew into a towering rage as he heard the multitude extol the strength of David. An evil eye had entered into Saul (1 Sam. 18:8–12).

It is the aspect of hate, sometimes righteous hate, that gives the evil eye its ultimate destructive power. Abba Arika, founder of the Rabbinic Academy in Sura (Babylonia, third century B.C.), contended that 99 of 100 people who die do so because of the evil eye. Rabbi Eliezer ben Hyrcanus, Sage of the Mishnah, could scorch objects at a glance. Rabbi Simeon bar Yochai shared the divine instrument and, in addition, to punish one who had offended against the word of God, the good rabbi could reduce him to a heap of dry bones. Rabbi Sheshat also exercised this power, even though he was blind! Rabbi Judah observed two men throwing bread at one another and berated them: "One might infer [from this] that there is plenty in the world." He set his gaze on them and caused a famine.[9]

The evil eye required rabbinical legislation. Though work is forbidden on the Sabbath, it is permissible to utter an oath against the evil eye. A man is forbidden to stand in his neighbor's field when the grain is in full ear. Special care must be taken with firstborn males and bridegrooms; as objects of envy they are particularly susceptible. It may be argued that the ritual breaking of a glass by the bridegroom at the conclusion of the wedding ceremony is to chase away the evil that may lurk at the time. Invocation of the holy name is powerful in avoiding the impact of disaster. If one enters into a situation where the evil eye may be present, "let him take his right thumb in his left hand and his left thumb in his right hand and say the following, 'I, A son of B, come from the seed of Joseph, against whom the evil eye has no power.' If one holds the power of the evil eye and is frightened of his own eye, let him gaze upon the wing of his left nostril." [10]

When working with Mediterranean folk beliefs it becomes fruitless at times to attempt to pinpoint origins. Long-time contact will invariably lead to borrowings between cultural groups. Whether Judaic in origin or not, the belief in the evil eye exists among contemporary Jews in Italy, the United States, and elsewhere. Jewish doctrine is eminently clear on the issue of folk beliefs relating to magic. Moses Maimonedes (1135–1204) stated: "All these are false and fraudulent notions which idolators of ancient days used to mislead the ignorant masses in order to lead and exploit them. It is unfit for Jews, who are a wise and intelligent people, to succumb to such superstitions or to conceive of any value in such notions. . . ." [11] Indeed, a biblical injunction on the same theme can be cited: "For there is no enchantment with Jacob, neither is there any divination with Israel" (Num. 23:22).

Be that as it may, evidence exists that formal rituals against *ayin ha ra* are still practiced by Jews. The use of the *royte baendel* (red ribbon) as countermagic to protect an infant is still found among American-born mothers of Eastern European descent. The ribbon is attached to the undergarments of the child, used as a hair ribbon, or attached to the carriage or the crib. Among Sephardic Jews the ribbon, if used, will be blue, but most often blue beads will serve to ward off evil. When a child is complimented or when excessive praise is given, it is common for the complimenter to invoke the Hebrew-Yiddish expression: "*Kein ayin nha hora* [sic] *zol ihm nit schatten,*" "An evil eye should not befall him." If the complimenter does not provide the countermagic, the mother will quickly say: "*Unbeschrieen,*" "Without invoking ill-luck." If the admirer remains suspect, further prophylaxis might involve rapping wood or spitting three times; this latter action is most often done surreptitiously. Should a mother suspect that her child has become ill from the evil eye or other source of disease, the name of the child may be changed. The pseudonym, usually the name of an animal, provides twofold therapy: the Angel of Death becomes bewildered and cannot find the child; the child gains the strength of the lion, wolf, or bear for which he is now named.

One should never talk about possible trouble or tragedy, for then it will come to pass. ("Don't open your mouth for Satan.") At the time of *Yizkor* (memorial services), in many traditional synagogues, those with both parents living will leave the worship services. This action is most often explained as proper conduct so that those who mourn will not be distracted from concentration on their prayers. Alternatively, some identify this action with the fear of the evil eye, i.e., jealousy on the part of those who have lost their parents. [12]

Many amulets and actions to counter the evil eye have come down through the ages. Charms made of silver, gold, bronze, or amber are particularly powerful, and their power is increased through addition of the Hebrew word *Shaddai* (one of the mystic names of god). The *Magen David* (Star of David) and medallions in the shape of an open hand, a fish, or an eye are considered countermagic to fascination by Italian Jews. The gesture of the right thumb tucked between index finger and middle finger is particularly efficacious against the evil eye. Called the *feige*, this gesture is common to Jews and Christians in many parts of Europe. In Italian *fica* means vulva, derived from the Latin *ficus*, the fruit of the fig tree.

Although many Christians, including Martin Luther, gave much credence to amulets made by Cabalistic Jews, the Jewish people as a whole were viewed as the Devil incarnate and the source of the evil eye. Sanitary practices of the Jews that aided them in escaping many epidemics only helped to prove that they were in league with the Devil. The Council of Elvira (Spain, fourth century) in Canon Law 49 forbade Jews to stand among ripening crops belonging to Christians lest they cause the crops to rot and wither with their malevolent glances.[13] The Jews of England were forbidden to attend the coronation of Richard the Lion-Hearted (1189) for fear that an evil eye might harm the crown. So feared was the purported power of the Jew that the German word for evil eye remains *Judenblick* (Jew's glance).

Italy

Deeply seated in the folklore of southern Italy and Sicily is the belief in the evil eye. Perhaps no portion of the peninsula is without some conception of the malevolent organ. In central Italy, the farming family's prize possession, the Tuscan ox (*tor chianino*), wears a red ribbon between its bovine eyes. Red paint may border the windows of house and barn. Strands of garlic are draped near the entry door. A sprig of rue (*cima di ruta*) may be placed on the window sill to prevent entry of the evil eye. Farther to the south the intensity of belief increases. For much of the mainland, red is the color of countermagic. In the deepest south and in Sicily, blue becomes the color of preference. The significance of color-countermagic poses an intriguing question. Presumably, among Arabs of the Mahgreb and the Arabian Peninsula, blue eyes are infrequent; hence, it is argued, the blue-eyed stranger (devil) possesses the evil eye. This explanation is doubtful, at best; the good eye of Horus was often depicted in blue or purple. In Italy, one who has perpetu-

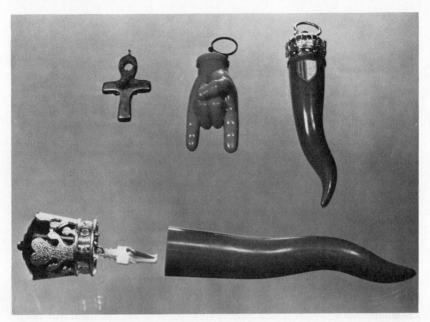

Figure 1.3 Common Italian charms against the evil eye. *Top left, ankh,* with blue bead; *center, mano cornuta,* or horned hand, of red plastic; *right, corno,* or goat's horn, also of red plastic, bearing the city seal of Catania. *Bottom, gobbo,* hunchback with red umbrella that fits inside the red plastic *corno.*

ally bloodshot eyes is strongly suspect; therefore, an association between red and the evil eye is posited. However, the power of red to repel demons and evil was established in the talmudic period. Perhaps the redness of blood is, in itself, an explanation. This is difficult to sustain for the Jews, inasmuch as there is a strong abhorrence and avoidance of blood. In any event, even in those areas of Italy where blue is the dominant color of countermagic, the red *corno* (horn) is the most prevalent amulet against the evil eye. Horns were considered powerful weapons against evil by the ancient Egyptians, Jews, Greeks, and Romans.

In a Molisan village, the authors collected considerable data in 1954–56 on folk beliefs related to health and medicine. Some hard-core ideas have changed little since that time. Between birth and death many dangers of life are encountered. The evil eye is ever present and most difficult to detect. The *corno,* "horn of the male goat," is powerful in warding off the ravages of the evil eye. Nearly everyone carries a gold or coral *cornetto* (most recently, plastic) on his person. This charm is dismissed as a *portafortuna* (a luck piece) but on probing it is admitted that the spangle serves to counter the force of *iettatura* (evil eyed one). Iron in any form (nails, keys, stakes, a horseshoe with points down, etc.) can be touched (*tocca ferro*) to avoid contamination by the evil eye. A knife blade is also valuable in chasing the *mal'occhio*. If one is menaced by an unseen force (including witches and ghosts) one may cut an "X" in the bark of a tree or a wall and say, *"io credo in Dio omnipotento,"* "I believe in God all-powerful." The "thumb in fist" or "horning fingers" are emergency measures. Should one find oneself without an iron implement, grasping one's own genitalia will work as well.

Almost anyone might have the power of the evil eye. Even a priest, a cardinal, a pope (Pius IX), or a foreign dignitary (King Alfonso XIII of Spain) might be suspect. Persons who are unusually thin are culpable (e.g., Clare Boothe Luce). Gypsies are particularly feared. On a recent visit to Rome, an American tourist was accosted by a female gypsy asking for alms. Having been refused, she attempted to pick his pocket. He deftly whipped out a *corno* affixed to his keychain. The gypsy covered her eyes and ran off.[14] One who compliments a child without adding *"Dio ti benedica"* (dialect: *Di bendet*), "God bless you," may be suspected of casting evil on the child.

The evil eye can cause loss of crops, wasting of animals, rotting of pork, souring of wine, moulding of stored foodstuffs, disease, sterility, abortion, and mental disorders. Of course, all these events may be caused by other factors as well. For example, mental disorders may be inherited, caused by grief, sunstroke, envy, jealousy, bewitching, excessive rain, or the sirocco.

The evil eye is distinguished from *malalingua,* "evil tongue." The worst that one with an evil tongue can do is spread jealous rumors. Usually the evil-tongued one casts aspersions on the virginity of a bride-to-be or on the potential of her chosen spouse.

Detecting the presence of the evil eye is not a simple task. One do-it-yourself technique, common throughout Italy, is placing a drop of oil in a bowl of water; if the oil spreads, the evil eye is present. One must immediately counter by making the sign of the cross on the forehead above the bridge of the nose.[15]

In most southern Italian villages there are practitioners of folk medicine. The *mago* (or *magaro,* etc., in various dialects) is considered to be the most highly skilled specialist in dealing with problems that stem from the evil eye. "Sorcerer" or "wizard" might be the best translation of *mago*. It is generally agreed in contemporary Italy that the best practitioners of the art are to be found in and around Eboli. Currently, these wizards offer their services through want ads in newspapers, including at least one English-language publication.

For those more inclined toward institutionalized religion, various saints may be implored for intercession to alleviate problems stemming from fascination. In the south, San Martino and Santa Lucia have achieved major reputations in healing such afflictions. Santa Lucia is particularly important in that during her lifetime she had taken a vow of chastity. To satisfy a suitor, who admired the beauty of her eyes, she plucked out her own eyeballs and handed them to him. An angel immediately restored her sight by wafting to her a new pair on a platter.

From Salerno south on the Tyrrhenean coast, prows of fishing boats are commonly decorated with the eye of Santa Lucia. Informants indicate a twofold meaning for the symbol: avoidance of the evil eye is guaranteed by countermagic, and the eye of Santa Lucia aids the crew in finding fish. In the region of Trapani (Sicily), the eye painted on the prow of a fishing boat is an aid in spotting tuna. In the northern Adriatic, the fishing port of Chioggia has many boats with a leading eye. Here, however, this symbol is identified with Santa Chiara (St. Claire of Assisi). In addition to her ability to aid victims of the evil eye, Santa Chiara demonstrated during her lifetime her capacity for being in two or more places at the same time. Little wonder that her teletransportation has earned her the role as patroness of television! A high degree of regionalism is still evidenced in Italy. Various saints, at the local level, have been implored for cures from the ravages of the evil eye. Apparently some success has been achieved by virtue of the number of silver eyes *ex voti* found in Italian village chapels.

Malta

Malta has a strategic location that has made the island a crossroads of Mediterranean culture from the time of Phoenician Carthage to the present. The apostolic church interacted with earlier belief systems and then met Islam in a head-on confrontation. The emergent syncretism utilizes both the Arabic blue and the northern Mediterranean red to ward off the ravages of the evil eye. Fishermen decorate the prows of their boats with the eye and drivers

Figure 1.4 Eye on prow of fishing boat, Island of Gobo, Malta.

paint an eye on the trunk lid or bumper of their automobiles—thus exceeding the safety standards demanded by contemporary crusaders. The sovereign military order of St. John of Jerusalem, the Knights Hospitalers, held Malta as its fiefdom from 1530 to 1798. The elaborate harbor defenses of Valletta, erected by the knights, were made all the stronger by the homeopathic use of eyes and ears sculpted into the stones of the watchtowers. The display of the goat horn, thumb in fist, and horned fingers as jewelry is as conspicuous in Malta as in southern Italy.

A number of Maltese proverbs refer to the belief, and "May God save you from the evil eye" is frequently heard. Of a person first praised and then despised, it is said, "The bone is hung to ward off the evil eye." The power of evil is suggested in the expression: "Where the evil eyes comes in, trouble comes in two measures." Fumigation is an ancient technique to ward off the ravages of the eye. "The last one will have to fumigate" is said to those who bring up the rear and to whom fall the dirty tasks of cleaning up.[16]

Figure 1.5 Horned hands on trunk of car, Valetta, Malta.

Conclusion

It is rare to find a custom that spans all the faiths that have left us a record of their existence in this part of the world. The evidence at hand leads one to think that belief in the evil eye is probably one of the oldest continuous religious constructs in the Mediterranean basin. We are tempted to paraphrase the *social fact* as enunciated by W. I. Thomas: if men believe a thing is real and act in accordance with that belief, the consequences of their actions are real.[17] Adherents to such beliefs seem to be parroting the Italian folkloristic expression: "It is not true, but I believe it."

When an individual knowingly possesses the power to fascinate, that individual has an awesome weapon of social control. Resolution of conflict is quickly achieved by invoking this God-given instrument. Use of this avenging power can eradicate evil from a world that has been ordained as whole and perfect by an ever-loving God. Social organizations can be maintained or altered, according to divine will, and group solidarity promoted through the eradication of threats.

It is a truism to note that all social relations are culturally patterned. Yet, there is an inherent ambiguity to human interactions. The multivalence of feelings can be potentially disruptive in community interrelationships. Since the evil eye is regarded as a magical and often as an involuntary threat by its bearers, anger or retaliation can be replaced by a patterned response that provides alternatives to personal confrontation. This ambivalence is the basic social-psychological theme that underlies the evil eye belief. George Foster discusses the relationship between envy and the evil eye. He notes a variety of cultural responses to control envy. Concealment and denial are systematic approaches to avoid or ward off the effects of evil.[18] An Italian peasant will never voice a prediction of his harvest. He will rarely admit that his state of health or being is any better than *meno male*—"luckily, not bad."

The evil eye offers a ready explanation for the causation of mental illness, disease, disaster, crisis, famine, and death. As in the case of mental illness, this concept not only offers an explanation but also may include a structured way to prevent or cure such a manifestation. Countermagic, exorcism, and other patterned rituals may be devised within this system of belief. It provides focus for animosity against the abuser of the great power. Clearly, emotions of jealousy, envy, and greed, which cause evil to be perpetrated, indicate that the evil eye is not always God-given. Yet, it must be noted, envy is not the sole origin of the evil eye. Many people conceive it to be the avenging, righteous power of the deity. In a less than perfect world, Satan and his forces are ever present. (Pope Paul VI, on November 15, 1972, discussed the concepts of the devil and evil. The text of his remarks appeared in *L'Osservatore Romano* and were reprinted in *The New York Times Magazine*.) [19] Expunging these powers of the netherworld is far from easy when the evil eye hovers above.

NOTES

1. Whiting, p. 90.   2. Whiting and Child.   3. Gaster, p. 216.
4. White, p. 39.   5. Gifford, p. 122.   6. Ibid., p. 30.
7. Ausubel, *Treasury of Jewish Folklore*, pp. 568–69.
8. Cohen, p. 262.   9. Ibid., p. 272.   10. Ibid., p. 374.
11. *Yad Hachazakah, Hilchoth Akum*, 11:16, as quoted in Moss and Applebaum.
12. Moss and Applebaum, pp. 7–8.
13. Ausubel, *Book of Jewish Knowledge*, p. 150.
14. Told to Moss by Seymour K. Wilhelm, M.D.

15. Moss and Cappannari, pp. 97–98.
16. Aquilina, pp. 287, 496.   17. Thomas, p. 572.
18. Foster, p. 175 ff.   19. Greeley, p. 26.

BIBLIOGRAPHY

Aquilina, Joseph. *A Comparative Dictionary of Maltese Proverbs.* Valletta: Royal University of Malta, 1972.

Ausubel, Nathan. *A Treasury of Jewish Folklore.* New York: Crown, 1948.

—— *The Book of Jewish Knowledge.* New York: Crown, 1964.

Cohen, A. *Everyman's Talmud.* New York: Dutton, 1949.

Foster, George M. "The Anatomy of Envy: A Study in Symbolic Behavior," *Current Anthropology* 13 (1972), 165–202.

Gaster, Theodor H., ed. *The New Golden Bough: A New Abridgement of the Classic Work by Sir James George Frazer.* New York: Criterion, 1959.

Gifford, Edward S. *The Evil Eye.* New York: Macmillan, 1958.

Greeley, Andrew M. "The Devil You Say," *The New York Times Magazine,* Feb. 4, 1973, pp. 15–28.

Moss, Leonard W., and Emanuel Applebaum. "Folklore among Detroit Jews," *Michigan Jewish History* 3 (1963), 1–9.

—— and Stephen C. Cappannari. "Folklore and Medicine in an Italian Village," *Journal of American Folklore* 73 (1960), 95–102.

Thomas, William I. *The Child in America.* New York: Alfred A. Knopf, 1928.

White, Andrew D. *A History of the Warfare of Science with Theology in Christendom.* New York: George Braziller, 1955.

Whiting, Beatrice, *Paiute Sorcery.* Viking Fund Publications in Anthropology, no. 15. New York: Viking, 1950.

Whiting, John W. M., and Irvin Child. *Child Training and Personality.* New Haven: Yale University Press, 1953.

WILLA APPEL

2. ITALY

The Myth of the *Jettatura*

DRIVING ALONG the Adriatic coast of southern Italy, between
Bari and Brindisi, you will see a ridge of hills on your right covered with
gnarled olive trees. Cross that ridge and you are suddenly plunged into a
mythical landscape, the land of the *trulli*. The *trulli* are stone beehive-
shaped houses and field shelters. As field shelters, they stand out as single
cones, but they are grouped in a seemingly haphazard manner as houses and
farms. The *trulli* sit flat on the ground, their patios fanning out like broad
tongues from simple arched doorways. The earth is rust brown. Olive trees
and vineyards surround the *trulli*, and stone walls surround everything—the
houses, the plots of land, the roads, and even individual olive trees.

In this visually strange world, even the psychological fears and obsessions
of the inhabitants take a graphic form. On the grey *trulli* diverse symbols,
whitewashed and up to six feet tall, protect the homes and their inhabitants
from the evil eye.

Attack and Therapy

Near the doorways of the *trulli*, you will usually see a metal object: a horseshoe or an old key hung up on a nail. These, too, protect against the evil
eye, and quite explicitly against the envy of neighbors. Metal, and iron specifically, is a recurring prophylactic against the evil eye, probably because

WILLA APPEL is presently a guest teacher in anthropology at Sarah Lawrence College. She
received her Ph.D. in anthropology from Cornell University and specializes in religio-symbolic
systems and in historical-economic aspects of anthropology.

This paper derives from three years of fieldwork in southern Italy from 1970–73, concentrat-
ing on the world-view system.

of its ability, as a magnet, to attract other substances. It is considered not only to attract but also to absorb the power of the evil eye: if, in a conversation, some allusion is made to the evil eye or to some unfortunate event, the common reaction is to reach for a metal object.

But even horseshoes, painted symbols, the cross, or a saint's medal worn around the neck are not enough protection against the malign forces of the evil eye. A *borsa,* or small pouch in which consecrated objects are placed, is also worn around the neck for additional protection. Despite all this caution, people still fall under the eye's spell.

The evil eye in some respects is like a virus, and the village lies in constant threat of an imminent plague. Evil eye is a continuing presence in village life. It is called by several names: *affascino* is the "fascination," the unknown and malign power that ensnares its victims; *attacatura* means the same thing, but implies, too, the binding of one thing or substance to another. When the fascination takes a human form, it is called *mal' occhio,* "evil eye" or *invidia,* "envy."

"Fascination" in no way implies the deliberate intent to harm; it is rather an unwitting, arbitrary force. The term *fattura,* which in Italian means a receipt (like a store receipt), in dialect refers to a contract made with a magician with the intent to bewitch, infatuate, or kill a victim.

Essential in all these terms is the sense of domination: the victims of the evil eye are helpless in the grip of an overpowering occult force.

It is almost impossible to determine the source of this dread force. Even the carriers of *mal' occhio* are often unaware of their destructive power.

The advice that I received from virtually everyone in the village where I conducted fieldwork was to trust no one. One informant told me that Italians were "malevolent and shrewd," that her mother had taught her to trust no one, not even her own shadow. Others told me never to tell anyone anything about my affairs, nor the hour when I usually retired. "There is an expression here," another informant told me, "be friends with everyone, but trust no one." She then added for emphasis, "I don't trust anyone, not even the sun!"

The sicknesses associated with *mal' occhio* fall along a continuum, headaches, sleepiness, exhaustion, depression, and hypochondria being the milder forms, and spirit possession being the extreme example. All these illnesses are associated with the sense of being *acted upon* by powerful and unknown forces. The cure initially entails the attempt to determine whether

Figure 2.1 Stone-roofed houses, or *trulli*, common to the Adriatic coast of southern Italy. Cross painted on cupola gives protection from the evil eye.

the sickness is, for example, just a mundane headache—i.e., whether it is organically based—or whether it is caused by the fascination.

There are special curers for the evil eye. These women have learned from other curers, the skill generally being passed on through kin. Each curer can teach two others, but no more—if she teaches more than two, she will lose her own power to cure. The recurrence of the theme of the Trinity is evident not only in the actual cure but also in the method and training of the curers.

This is the "standard" cure in the village: Take a bowl of water, drop three drops of oil into it, cross yourself and say:

> *Two eyes have looked at you,*
> *Two saints have enjoyed you,*
> *Father, Son, Holy Ghost;*
> *Enemies run away!*

This is repeated three times, three drops of oil being allowed to drip into the water each time. If the oil coagulates, it means the patient is afflicted with the evil eye; if the oil "disappears," his sickness is not due to the evil eye.

In this example the religious symbolism is quite clear. Water represents holiness and is identified with the Holy Trinity, as in baptism. In the rite of extreme unction the sign of the cross is made with oil on the forehead of the dying person to absolve him of his sins. There is thus an association of water with purity and cleansing, and of oil with sin. The stickiness of oil, too, is like the *attacatura* that attaches itself or sticks to its victims. This interpretation is reinforced by the conclusions drawn in the cure: if the oil remains or "coagulates," this is proof of the fascination; if the oil disappears into the "holy" water, there has been no fascination.

The words of the cure, and the sign of the cross that accompanies them, are effective because they repeat and reaffirm the rite of baptism, which is the chief protection against the evil eye: "I baptise you . . . in the name of the Father, Son, and Holy Ghost." In this ritual, the forces of the Trinity are explicitly balanced against the force of evil. Although the details of this ritual vary from place to place, the basic formula remains essentially unchanged. Here is an example from Viggiano.

> *Who has fascinated you?*
> *The eye, the thought, and the evil desire.*
> *Who will remove the fascination?*
> *The Father, the Son, and the Holy Ghost.*[1]

These words are repeated three times, accompanied by the immersion into water each time of three drops of oil. (In some areas salt or hot coals are used instead of oil.)

In this example the evil eye, evil thought, and evil desire are counterbalanced by the three-pronged force of the Trinity. The balance is perfectly symmetrical: three versus three. In the earlier example cited, two groups of two are balanced against the Trinity. The sense of balancing evil against good does not depend on a literal symmetry. The forces of good generally occur in numbers, such as three and seven, that are significant in Roman Catholic ritual.

The notion of balancing is explicit in these rituals where evil, tangibly represented by the evil eye, is combated by the Holy Trinity. This quality of a tenuous and constantly threatened social equilibrium is certainly consistent with the nature of actual social relations in peasant communities. Society can never be purged of the evil eye—it is a latent and inevitable part of life. The scales are tipped in favor of evil when an individual falls prey to the fascination. The cure consists in neutralizing its power and reestablishing a balance, at least in the afflicted individual. Often the therapy involves passing the evil on to someone else.

After it has been determined by the means of the divination with water and oil that someone is, in fact, the victim of the evil eye, the water is tossed out the door. The next passerby will then "absorb" the evil force, thereby ridding the first victim of its effect.

The ideas of absorption and of "passing the buck" are frequently expressed in cures for *mal'occhio*. Here is another example from Ferrandina:

> To undo the *attacatura* that has caused nettle rash, the afflicted person wears his clothing inside out for three days. This indicates the expulsion of the malevolent power. The curer, while reciting the magical formula, rubs the victim's body with holy water, all the while repeating:
>
> > *Evil cursed wind,*
> > *go drown yourself in the sea.*
> > *This is consecrated flesh and*
> > *you have nothing to do with it.*
>
> The clothing of the fascinated person is then removed and placed at a crossroads, where the first passerby absorbs the evil in which they were impregnated.[2]

Another common theme in these cures is the attempt to use the same methods employed by the fascination. Here is an exorcism against the evil wind that goes around searching for victims:

> *. . . Go away, evil wind,*
> *go away in the guise of wind.*
> *You are banished by the Holy Trinity.*
> *All of you go away.*
> *Mother Mary banishes you.*
>
> *Evil wind, ugly beast,*
> *get off this person.*
> *Go away, disorder.*
> *San Antonio banishes you. . . .*

In this example, the fascinated person must take off his clothes and put them on inside out. Then, walking backwards, he must leave the house and place the clothes outside the door in the open. The next morning, still walking backwards, he must pick them up and finally must put them on normally. He must be careful to repeat both the verbal formula and the expelling procedure for three consecutive evenings.[3]

The procedure described above attempts to counter the effects of disorder by replicating what are conceived to be the methods of disorder. It is almost like playing a tape recording backwards in order to erase the tape back to the beginning.

Still other rituals attempt to outwit the fascination. In Collobaro, to avoid *mal'occhio,* the bed of a bride is littered with scraps of newspapers. The fascination is considered to be half-literate, and thus will lose time and energy reading all the scraps. Similarly, outside the newlywed couple's door a broom is placed. The fascination will be forced to count all the straws in the broom and become so tired that he will lose enthusiasm for his work.[4]

Saints and Cults

The recurrent problem, in dealing with the evil eye, is how can man combat the destructive power of the unknown? Forces act on man, dominate him, and he becomes transformed into something "other" than his ordinary self. Spirit possession is the extreme form of being acted upon: the victim is actually possessed.

In southern Italy, many of the saints are associated with a particular illness or syndrome. Cults develop around these saints and around the sanctuaries dedicated to them. The followers of a particular saint feel themselves to be afflicted with "his" sickness and pay homage to him on the day dedicated to him. In exchange for his protection they offer everything they possess: money, food, precious objects, and often even hair and cigarettes.

The majority of the rural population does not participate in these devotional pilgrimages. The participants in these cults are mostly drawn from among a particular group of especially marginal people. Their ranks include the poorest, the social misfits, spinsters, widowers, the emotionally disturbed, and in general, the most deprived members of society. These are people who no longer have an active, positively defined social role. They have been left at the wayside of social and cultural change, and suffer from an inextricable tangle of social and physical ills. They appeal to the saints, whom they deem not only their protectors and saviors from a particular evil but also the perpetrators of it.

The cult of San Donato, for example, is especially widespread in the area around the city of Salento in Puglia. San Donato is associated with epilepsy and various other nervous disorders, though not all cult members actually suffer from these ailments. Epilepsy is not considered to be a physical sickness in this area, but rather a magical *male* sent by San Donato, who is the protector of epileptics. To be afflicted with the *"male* of San Donato" also means to have received a "call" from this saint. In the words of a man whose wife was thus afflicted, "The sickness of San Donato is sent by our own saint; he sends it and he removes it. He wants it this way—he chooses someone and he sends him his sickness. He sends it to us poor people to make us suffer on earth, and he repays us then in Paradise. We are poor, but we are also fortunate." [5]

Those afflicted with the *male* of San Donato often suffer seizures of an epileptic nature not all of which are caused by any physical disorder. They are understood to be caused by the possession of the victim by the *male* itself. This *male* is inflicted on its victims much as God afflicted Job with trials and tribulations.

The cultural ideology of the *male* of San Donato provides, in the Salento area, a ready-made framework into which a variety of disorders can be placed. It also provides a stylistic idiom, possession, with which to express these disorders. This framework confers a distinct identity upon the cult participants as members in a magico-religious community. The annual pilgrimages, each of which lasts for a few days, create not only a sense of communitas among the participants but also an actual community differentiated from that of normal society. For people who are marginal to the existing social structure, the cults provide an alternative structure in which they are fully participating members.

Even this cursory examination of saints' cults and their composition sheds light on the social causes of the sense of impotence involved in being "acted upon." The cult followers are among the most deprived and impotent members of Italian society. Although nominally the cult followers are members of the larger society, in effect they have been more or less permanently excluded from active, positive, participation in it. The helplessness experienced by peasants suffering the milder forms of evil eye sicknesses is more transitory. The illnesses of the evil eye are all, however, illnesses of impotence that reflect the existing social relations of peasants both among themselves and with the outside world.

The particular evil eye belief that exists today among Italian peasants is the product of a specific social and historical situation in southern Italy, which I shall now attempt to describe.

Conflict of Ideas in the Period of Illuminism

In the second half of the 1600s, the ideas of the French and English Enlightenment were introduced into the Kingdom of Naples. Because of the lack of a strong bourgeoisie, such as existed in both France and England, the ideas of Enlightenment, or Illuminism as it was called in Italy, could not really affect the bases of social and economic life in the kingdom.

From the sixteenth to the eighteenth century, Naples was a kingdom ruled by a dynasty of Spanish Hapsburgs and Bourbons and divided into many small baronies. The royal administration was not strong enough to control these feudal barons, and the result was chaos. Various attempts at reforming the unwieldy feudal structure were made with no great success. Even the 1806 reforms of Bonaparte and Murat, which destroyed the surviving feudal laws, had a limited effect. The nominal abolition of feudalism did not signify a real break with the feudal system, especially in regard to production and property. The situation was especially backward in the countryside, where up until the Second World War the feudal system remained virtually intact.

The English and French movement of Enlightenment opposed feudalism both spiritually and materially: it opposed the reliance on authority in religious matters, and the restrictions on trade in economic enterprise. The movement was populated by the new and rising bourgeois class, which opposed the old order of authority, the aristocrats and the clergy.

Without a strong bourgeoisie the ideas of Illuminism, which had been predicated on the rationalization of society, were unable to take a real hold in Neapolitan life. Naples itself was a city in perpetual chaos; social institutions did not function, and the city was governed by the spirit of litigation.[6] In all sectors of society, both in the capital and in the countryside, the sense of impotence to act, to rationally determine the events of the future, was predominant.

Although the ideas of Illuminism could not affect the social or economic structure of the Kingdom of Naples, they did find fertile soil in certain sectors of the Neapolitan intellectual class. Not only did the intellectuals advocate real social reform, but their belief in the Enlightenment took on a literary form and focused on the notion of *jettatura*—the ancient belief in the evil eye. The transformation of this belief seems to embody in a single myth many of the contradictions created by the introduction and assimilation of

Illuministic ideas into the old feudal order. The new version of the myth was the symbolic compromise between two conflicting world views: first, the medieval, which saw man as being directed from the outside, and second, Illuminism, which saw man as having a rational consciousness capable of ordering his world and fate.

The evil eye belief, which originated in the ancient notion of the fascination, of evil resulting from deliberate pacts made with devils, could not be completely dismissed by the enlightened intellectuals. They were forced to reconcile their Illuministic ideas with the reality of social life in Naples. Life was seemingly arbitrary, argued the intellectuals, and man was continually made subject to unexpected twists of fate, not because man was inherently irrational but because there existed certain men, *jettatore*, who unwittingly made everything go wrong. The word *jettatore* derives from the verb *gettare*, which means "to cast off" or "to throw out." The *jettatore* is the personification of *mal' occhio*, the person whose cast look brings harm. But this new version of the evil eye belief differed substantially from its predecessor. The *jettatore* was no longer believed to obtain his destructive power from contracts made with demons but rather from the power of human passions themselves. Furthermore, he did not act with the deliberate intent to harm but was instead the involuntary bringer of harm. He, too, was often a victim of the destructive force he unknowingly carried. He, too, was acted upon.[7]

The transformed myth of the *jettatura* embodied the conflicting views of the medieval and enlightened worlds. The ambivalent character of the myth is reflected in its style, which is simultaneously comic and serious.

> The narrations of Neapolitan *jettatori* and their victims come to us at times in a comic atmosphere that is born from the calculated contrast between the conscience which is at the center of civilized life, which sees man as a rational operator, and the scandal of a world in which everything goes cockeyed with predictable regularity, only because certain individuals are unknowingly and involuntarily instruments of a blind destructive force.[8]

A vivid illustration of the ambivalent tone of the myth is contained in a book entitled, *Cicalata: sul fascino volgarmente detto Jettatura (Idle talk on the fascination called "Jettatura")*, written by Nicola Valletta in 1787. Valletta writes most seriously about the history of the *jettatura* belief and how wise men have learned to avoid it. His seriousness in certain passages of the book contrasts with others that are downright facetious. His book ends with the following list of questions that, claims the author, still need to be answered in regard to the *jettatura:*

1) Is the *jettatura* more commonly carried by men or women?
2) Is it more commonly carried by wig-wearers?
3) Is it more commonly carried by people who wear glasses?
4) Is it more commonly carried by pregnant women?
5) Is it more commonly carried by monks, and if so, of what order? [9]

Despite Valletta's tongue-in-cheek prose style, it is apparent that he believes in the *jettatura*. It is as though he cannot quite reconcile his continuing belief in this "superstition" with his more enlightened views.

The eighteenth-century accounts of *jettatura* were always embodied in a literary form. Alexander Dumas' journal of 1841–43 contains a fictional biography based on the life of a well-known reputed *jettatore* of a noble family. The biography relates a series of misfortunes created by this unnamed prince.

His mother died giving birth to him. A nanny nursed him and consequently lost her milk. A simultaneous misfortune struck when his father was dismissed as Ambassador to Tuscany because he had abandoned his post without authorization and had run to Naples at the news of the birth of his son and the death of his wife. The prince continued to create misfortune within his family circle, but his dark activities also extended to society at large. The day he entered the religious seminary, all the boys in the class contracted convulsive coughing. . . . Nor were the monks of the Camaldoli convent saved from his dread influence. The day after the prince entered the convent to serve his novitiate, an ordinance of the Partenopean Republic suppressed religious communities. . . .[10]

The content and style of the *jettatura* stories reflect the unresolved character of the myth, which attempts to accommodate two contradictory world views. It expresses the ambivalent position of at least a certain segment of Neapolitan society that is not yet fully modernized, but that has rejected many of the principles of the old feudal order. The sense of social disorder and impotence experienced by Neapolitan intellectuals resulted from their exposure to the ideas of the Enlightenment. By embracing these new ideas they had become marginal members in their own society.

The figure of the *jettatore* symbolizes this ambivalence. He is both human and superhuman: although he appears to be an ordinary person, he possesses extraordinary powers. He is a mediator between the sacred and the profane, between the world of ordinary men and the divine world of gods, demigods, and demons. The *jettatore* is "the individual who unknowingly and systematically introduces disorder into the moral, social, and natural spheres of reality, and is the one who, as an agent of destiny, makes things always go wrong." [11] It is appropriate that in the early versions of the myth, the *jettatore* was invariably a member of the upper class. The figure of the *jettatore* was modeled after the intellectuals themselves.

Peasant Ambivalence in Modern Society

In time, when the modernization of Italian society has advanced, at least among the upper classes, the myth drops from usage by these classes. It is picked up and retained by the class of society that to this day occupies an ambivalent position in Italian society.

Italian peasants have been exposed to the goods and values of modern Italy. Television, radio, newspapers, and magazines have penetrated to even the most isolated peasant hamlets. Yet peasants traditionally have been denied access to goods and possibilities. The combination of exposure and denied access to another, preferred way of life creates among peasants, as among the intellectuals before them, a sense of impotence and social confusion.

The contemporary *jettatori,* fittingly enough, are modeled after peasants. They appear not in literary accounts but in the rituals directed against the evil eye. In one of the rituals described earlier, the attempt is made to outtrick the *jettatore* or fascination by forcing him to read scraps of newspapers. Being only half-literate, like peasants themselves, he is distracted by this task from his malicious work. Here we find, symbolized on a magical plane, one of the key differences between peasants and other social classes in Italy. Literacy allows for the social domination of peasants by landowners, bureaucrats, clergy, and bourgeoisie. Some curing rituals make the symbolic identification of *jettatori* with peasants more explicit: ridding oneself of the evil eye often entails passing it on to someone else by, for example, throwing contaminated water out the door so that the next passerby absorbs it. Here the original victim of the evil eye becomes the next *jettatore.*

The helplessness in the face of one's destiny that characterizes the myth also characterizes the sicknesses attributed to the evil eye. The degree of affliction depends on the degree of marginality or ambivalence experienced by the peasant. Most of the sicknesses reflect the sense of impotence normally experienced by peasants. The cures for these illnesses aim at reintegrating the afflicted person back into society. Peasants who are marginal even to peasant society suffer chronically. For these people, the participants in the saints' cults, reintegration is not possible. Rather, the cults represent a more permanent way out of society through the formation of communitas, and can be compared to protomillenarian movements.

The impotence experienced in evil eye sicknesses reflects the relationship of peasants to the predominant social structure. But the evil eye belief is politically conservative; it provides an explanation of social disorder based on the nature of the human condition. Disorder is not attributed to a particular set of historical and economic conditions, and consequently there is no way to alter the situation. Man must resign himself to his fate and can only try to protect himself against the evil eye.

NOTES

1. DeMartino, p. 15.   2. Ibid., p. 23.   3. Ibid., p. 24.
4. Ibid., p. 20.   5. Rossi, *Le Feste dei poveri,* p. 25.
6. Villari, p. 50.   7. DeMartino, p. 123.   8. Ibid., p. 117.
9. Valletta, p. 69.
10. A. Dumas as quoted in DeMartino, pp. 122–24.
11. DeMartino, p. 10.

BIBLIOGRAPHY

Croce, B. *Storia del regno di Napoli.* Bari: Laterza, 1944.
DeMartino, E. *Sud e magia.* Milan, 1959.
Douglas, M. *Purity and Danger.* New York: Praeger, 1966.
Garin, E. *Medioevo e rinascimento.* Bari, 1961.
Rossi, A. *Le Feste dei poveri.* Bari: Laterza, 1969.
—— *Lettere da una tarantata.* Bari: DeDonato, 1970.
Turner, V. *The Forest of Symbols.* Ithaca, N.Y.: Cornell University Press, 1967.
Valletta, Nicola. *Cicalata sul fascino volgarmente detto Jettatura.* 1787. Naples: Societa Typografica, 1814.
Villari, R. *Il sud nella storia d'Italia.* Bari: Laterza, 1971.

RICHARD SWIDERSKI

3. ITALIAN-AMERICANS

From Folk to Popular: Plastic Evil Eye Charms

THE ITALIAN IMMIGRANTS who arrived on American shores in the mid-nineteenth century were persecuted by a multitude of supernatural troubles. Witches bewitched them, devils bedeviled them and practitioners of the evil eye, capriciously or by design, subjected them to the wasting effects of their malign glances. The immigrants did not recoil, unaided, before these forces. They were sustained by an armament of incantations, potions, gestures, and charms tried through centuries of village life in the native country. The high degree of continuity between the old country and the new in magical beliefs and practices was noted by those having close contact with the newly settled Italian immigrants.[1]

One especially fearsome magic power was the *mal'occhio* or *jettatura*— the evil eye. Ever since Roman times the evil eye, under a variety of names, has troubled and intrigued the Italian people. Horace, in a letter, described his rustic idyll as undisturbed by the *obliquus oculus,* the unlucky glance that poisons.[2] Mascagni, the composer, and Cesare Lombroso, the positivist philosopher, both gave credence to the evil eye, Mascagni fearing it to the point of surrounding himself with a mass of protective amulets.[3] Various writers and poets have elevated the evil eye to allegorical, metaphoric, and ultimately mystic heights.[4] The richest level of tradition regarding the evil

RICHARD SWIDERSKI teaches in the Department of Anthropology in Richmond College of the City University of New York. After studying Near Eastern languages and Chinese, he shifted to anthropology and received his Ph.D. from Princeton University. He has made a study of an Italian-American fishermen's festival.

The data on which this paper was based were obtained in New York, Philadelphia, and Boston.

eye exists in the folklore of Italy and Sicily, and it is this folklore that was borne more or less intact to America by the immigrants.

In the folk tradition the evil eye is sometimes a vague but vast miasma, afflicting animals, disposing children to ill behavior, and retarding the progress of carriages or, today, of automobiles. More frequently it is a property attributed to the glance of some particular individual, who may cast it with deliberate malice upon others or who may be unaware of or unable to control his unhappy talent. The wielder of the evil eye, the *jettatore,*[5] is described as having a striking facial appearance, high arching brows with a stark stare that leaps from his black eyes.[6] He often has a reputation for clandestine involvement with dark powers and is the object of gossip about dealings in magic and other forbidden practices. Successful men having tremendous personal magnetism quickly gain notoriety as *jettatori.* Pope Pius IX was dreaded for his evil eye, and a whole cycle of stories about the disasters that happened in his wake were current in Rome during the latter decades of the nineteenth century.[7] Public figures of every type, from poets to gangsters, have had their specialized abilities attributed to the power of their eyes.

Exposure to the evil eye either would cause a serious accident or would draw a long, wasting illness upon the victim. Few remedies could provide a certain cure once the symptoms appeared. Perhaps the *jettatore* might be cornered and bullied into retracting his spell. But he might be a *strega,* or witch, and take a still more lethal revenge. Perhaps an incantation, an herbal decoction, a prayer to a saint might help. But then they might not. The best assault against the terrifying force of the evil eye was preventative. Protective gestures could be made, clandestinely if need be, in the presence of a known *jettatore.* Talismans worn about the person might ward off known and unknown assaults of the evil eye.

These talismans have the force of many incantations continually uttered. They are gestures constantly held against the evil eye and all the unnatural powers surrounding it. Along with fear of the evil eye the Italian immigrants to the United States brought a great variety of talismans and continued to import them from Italy once they were settled. As time passed, the Italians became Italian-Americans, and their folk beliefs underwent considerable modification. Varying traditions from different parts of Italy merged into a mainstream, and many details were lost altogether. Parallel to these changes in ideology there came changes in notions about the evil eye and the ways of forestalling it. The evil eye became a threat whose precise nature was decreasingly clear from one generation to the next. The shift in evil eye belief is reflected by changes in the talismans used against the evil eye. In recent years a whole range of cheap plastic evil eye charms has been mass-produced in Italy and marketed in America. Standard, familiar talisman forms have been duplicated in plastic, along with hybrid forms never before encountered in the folk tradition.

For the purposes of this paper I shall distinguish between the talisman, the original form used in native Italian folk culture, and the charm, cast in plastic and employed in the context of contemporary urban popular culture. These new popular charms, which have gained wide use and acceptance, represent the emergence of popular evil eye tradition out of the transplanted folk tradition of the immigrants. The charms, when compared with the folk forms from which they are derived, reflect a fundamental change in beliefs about the evil eye. They are material evidence of a shift in supernatural ideology that marks the acculturation of Italians in America. The modifications in evil eye beliefs are only part of massive cultural changes, and the new charms form a microcosm of these changes. In the following pages I shall examine some folk talisman forms and the beliefs surrounding them. With each talisman I shall consider the charm or charms it has fostered in the popular milieu, and the ideas attached to the charm. The modification and hybridization connecting talisman to charm, folklore to popular belief, will receive attention. I shall especially seek to discern any patterns in the change from folk to popular, and the ways in which changes in material form parallel changes in belief.

My data concerning the popular notions about the efficacy and use of charms is drawn from research on Italian-American groups resident on the East Coast of the United States, primarily in the cities of Boston, New York, and Philadelphia. Though the charms are made in Italy, they are made, it seems, for export, for their use and sale are not nearly as conspicuous or widespread in Italy as they are in these American cities.

Chili-*Corno*

The *corno* is one of the most powerful talismans against the evil eye. Though, strictly defined, the word refers only to the horns of animals—rams, bulls, and oxen—other pointed natural objects such as pigs' teeth, roosters' spurs, and crab claws were, by their horn-like quality, held to be serviceable substitutes for real horns and were also called *corni*. Ornate *corni* were wrought from gold, silver, or coral, and real horns were fit into silver or gold settings to be carried on chains both for protection and to proclaim the wearer's affluence. The precious materials added a magic, that of value, to the already potent *corno* form. So effective a talisman was the *corno* that the word came to be applied generically to all evil eye talismans in some parts of Italy. The very mention of the *corno* was deemed adequate to provide some measure of protection against the evil eye.[8]

The pointed horn could, it was believed, "pierce" the evil eye and render it powerless. Worn about the person, suspended by a chain around the neck, or carried in a pocket, the *corno* might be held against the gaze of an approaching *jettatore*. Mounted on the wall of a shop or other building, it could avert damage caused by any envious stares directed that way.

Pointed vegetable forms were also esteemed in folk tradition as evil eye talismans. The fruit of the native Italian black "pepper" plant has a long, thin shape and serves as a readily available talisman in many parts of Italy. The color black has some magical significance but, according to the Sicilian folklorist Pitrè, red is the sacred color "par excellence." [9] It is hardly astonishing, then, that the chili or red pepper, when introduced into Italy from South America, was quickly adopted as protection against the evil eye. The chili itself became a favorite condiment, and a fair portion of the crop, dried or fresh, found use as talismans. The chilies were hung, singly or in masses, in the house or in a special part of a shop to discourage the evil eye.

One of the first plastic charms to appear, and one of the most frequently encountered in use, is a form that combines qualities of the *corno* with those of the chili. The two forms are clearly distinguished in the folk tradition, despite their similarity of shape. The plastic charm, however, resembles both. It is made of bright red plastic and has a stubby body that curves toward the end and comes to a point. It often comes mounted in a gold- or silver-colored plastic setting, with a metal key ring attached by a metal or plastic cord. Sometimes a city crest is affixed to the top of the chili for buyers who identify themselves with a specific city in Italy. The charm is usually called a "pepper" in English, but a *"corno"* or a "pepper" in Italian. It has the color of a chili, the shape of a chili or a *corno,* and a gold or silver crown setting like those used for *corni*. It is usually thought of as a chili. Detached animal horns are uncommon in urban settings and the chili is the one common object to which the plastic charm bears significant resemblance. The connection of the charm with the traditional *corno* has become obscure, especially to children. In one interesting occurrence some children placed a plastic charm among some real chilies their mother had purchased, hoping to deceive her into attempting to cut the charm.

The plastic charm is not a strict copy of either *corno* or chili, but is an idealized vehicle for the most effective magical properties of both. It is a biologically unreal form, but culturally quite real and quite valuable. It is a cultural improvement upon nature; the plastic charm is more like an animal horn than a chili could be and more like a chili than an animal horn could be.

The chili-*corno* charm is used in all the ways *corni* and chilies were used and has tended to supplant both. It is not perishable like the chili or expensive and difficult to procure like the *corno*. In its various forms the charm finds employment as a watch fob and a key ring holder. Tiny versions are worn on chains around the neck or on bracelets. It is hung up in shops, in the windows or over the doors, along with real horns and other evil eye talismans. The most conspicuous display of the charm is when it is hung from the rearview mirror of a car, often in the company of a rabbit's foot, a horseshoe, dice, or similar items.

This last use is the most diagnostic of the beliefs that surround the plastic charm, for the chili-*corno* is regarded quite simply as a good luck charm in the same category as the horseshoes and rabbit's feet accompanying it. There is a limited awareness of the charm's specific power to ward off the evil eye, but this power is considered subsidiary to its capacity for bringing good luck. The warding-off of evil eye affliction is a concomitant of the fortune promised by the charm. In fact, the absence of the evil eye is one of the essential conditions of good luck. The charm, in providing for the one, assures the other, though its users are not especially cognizant of this rationale. Gamblers have recourse to the charm, rubbing it before rolling dice or drawing a card. Truck drivers claim that it assures them of a faster run with few traffic or weather hazards. One woman, an excellent cook, felt that her bread always rose properly because of the charm's influence. There is little devotion of a fanatical sort to the charm. It is a good thing to have around, it aids people in their work, but it is not a necessity. Those who understand its specific use against the evil eye concede its value in promoting business enterprises or in guaranteeing the accuracy of a bet. An educated man who ac-

Figure 3.1 The most popular plastic evil eye charms.
Left to right: large red plastic chili with tiny *gobbo* inside; small white *gobbo* holding a chili; small red chili used as a key ring; white plastic *mano cornuta;* white *gobbo* with red chili-like tail holding a horseshoe in one hand and making a mano cornuta with the other; gold plastic horseshoe with *gobbo* suspended from the arc, a composite charm.

Figure 3.2 Gold crown removed from large chili, revealing little *gobbo* inside.

Figure 3.3 Mano cornuta in white plastic, with key ring.

cepted the use of the charm explained that most people could succeed and be healthy if others did not envy them and bring about their ruin. The charm, he said, takes this into account: in reminding people of the destructive power of envy it promotes good luck, the usual result of envy's absence. His sharply reasoned statement is a justification of the charm's good luck uses by one who is aware of its origins.

The merging of the chili and *corno* into a single charm accords with a generalization of beliefs. The generalization of forms into an artificial ideal form is parallel to a generalization in beliefs about magical effectiveness. The talismans change from evil eye specifics to good luck charms of a global nature. The widespread vagueness about the charm's nature matches the senses in which it is used. There exist plastic replicas of the native black Italian "pepper." Their distribution is quite limited, and they are used as evil eye charms only, by those having considerable knowledge of evil eye lore. The chili-*corno* charm has acquired its good luck mystique because it does not make specific reference to either chili or *corno,* but embodies the essential form of both, the curved, pointed shape, and the color red. It is, for the Italian-Americans, an abstraction that fits current popular belief more comfortably than either of the talismans from which it is derived.

While losing the specific folk meanings of its two constituent talismans, the plastic charm has acquired a new popular meaning in the multiethnic world of American cities. It is regarded as an Italian-American identity symbol. It is displayed in conjunction with Italian and American flags, pictures of Garibaldi, Lincoln, or Washington, saints' pictures, and other paraphernalia. It is "uniquely Italian" to the point that it is difficult for a non-Italian to purchase a plastic charm. It is available only in the Italian sections of cities, and in stores generally not frequented by outsiders. The charm's use as a representation of the Italian-American culture of which it is a part does not conflict with its good luck value, but rather enhances it: since Italian-Americans use it, the argument goes, they are luckier than other people. The plastic chili-*corno* charm, one of the most distinctive features of Italian-American culture, is an apt symbol for the culture as a whole.

Mano Cornuta

The *mano cornuta,* or horned hand, is a gestural equivalent of the animal horn. The sign is made by extending the index and little fingers, bending in the two middle fingers and enclosing them with the thumb. The sign suggests the head of a horned creature. It can be made and unmade rapidly and clandestinely at the approach of a *jettatore.* The *mano cornuta* was reproduced in metal, wood, and shell at an early date. The wearing of these talismans has the effect of making the gesture continually and thus affords constant protection against the evil eye. A darker aspect of the *mano cornuta* is its use as a sign of the Devil: with two fingers open and three closed, it "affirms the Two and denies the Three." As the Hand of Glory, the *mano cornuta* has been used by both Old and New World criminals to insure success in illicit enterprises and to frighten victims.[10]

A plastic replica of the *mano cornuta* is produced today, and is found in use and for sale almost as often as the plastic chili-*corno.* The *mano cornuta* charm is bright red or reddish orange in color and is a fairly precise model of a human hand making the gesture. Unlike the traditional folk talismans, most of which are flat with a little relief, the plastic charm is three-dimensional and quite realistic. The plastic *mani cornute* are all left-handed, in deference to traditions that the left-handed gesture is more potent, since the Devil is thought to rule the left side of the body.

With the *mano,* as with the *corno,* the color red is absorbed into the popular charm, creating a form not encountered in nature or in earlier folk versions. The modeling is anatomically detailed, and the plastic *mano cornuta* bears a close resemblance to a real hand, or to the gruesome version of the Hand of Glory wherein the mummified hand of an executed criminal was contorted into the *cornuta* gesture. The plastic *mano cornuta* is an improvement upon the folk talismans themselves, thanks to ability of plastic to receive detailed modeling in mass production.

Though the plastic hand is a new form and, with the red color, a hybrid, it retains a fairly specific function as an evil-eye measure. It has some repute as a good luck charm but not to the exclusion of awareness of its evil eye properties. In this case the popular charm is a readaptation rather than a generalization of the folk talisman. The *mano cornuta* charm is employed by those who wish an evil eye deterrent specifically fashioned in the popular milieu, by those aware of the particulars of the evil eye threat but unwilling to use the old-fashioned folk talismans, or unable to obtain them. The *mano cornuta* in its popular version retains its force as a folk talisman while gaining magical sophistication and acceptability. The plastic hand is a popular concession to those who adhere to folk tradition but wish it rephrased in a popular idiom.

Horseshoe

The horseshoe has long been an American popular image of good fortune, frequently joining the rabbit's foot and the four-leaf clover in the American lore of fortune. Traditionally, the horseshoe possessed, in Italy as well as in other countries throughout the world, a capacity to ward off evil spirits. The evil eye was but one category of malignant forces against which it was held to be effective, its resemblance to the horned head of an animal or the lunar crescent providing sufficient rationalization for this use.[11]

Even after the demise of the horse as a major form of urban transportation, metal horseshoes were produced in America for use as charms. Plastic horseshoe charms entered the popular market long before the advent of the mass-produced Italian evil eye charms. The horseshoe, as a form, presented somewhat of a problem, then. Unlike the *corno* and the *mano cornuta,* which were too specific in their meanings for inclusion in Italian-American popular culture and had to be generalized, the horseshoe was too vague and general a form to serve a specifically Italian-American population. It was not "Italian" enough to act within a cultural milieu that involves great sensitivity to its own uniqueness. The horseshoe had to be absorbed into Italian-American culture while retaining the magical virtues inherent in its form.

The interpretation of the horseshoe in the popular milieu is a simple compromise. It is a red plastic horseshoe with a small red plastic chili-*corno* suspended from the center of its arch. Thus the horseshoe is marked as an *Italian*-American charm and its benefits are channeled to the group who use the charm, the Italian-Americans. This composite charm, a completely new invention, brings two extremes together by the addition of a specifier—one might even say an ethnic adjective—to a symbol whose indifferent generality and prevalence among non-Italians would otherwise disqualify it from a place among plastic charms. The chili-*corno* contextualizes the horseshoe.

Here is a process of particularization running counter to the process of generalization that transformed the *corno* and the *mano cornuta* into popular charms. Though opposed in action, both processes, particularization and generalization, have resulted in charms on the same level of meaning, an Italian-American level more general than folk tradition but less general than American popular culture. The formal development of the horseshoe charm draws on both the native folk tradition and the pluralistic urban culture and represents the convergence of the two in magical material culture.

The horseshoe charm is too large to be worn in any fashion, so often it is found hung on a wall or dangling from a car mirror. The horseshoe is clearly differentiated from the common horseshoe charms by those who use it. It is "better" or "stronger" than other horseshoe charms, and supposedly it is only effective for those of Italian ancestry. It brings good luck in the same fashion as the chili-*corno* does. In fact, this horseshoe, in being a composite of a common good luck charm and an evil eye talisman, implies that good luck is to some extent a consequence of being free of the evil eye and its ravages. The charm makes both positive and negative contributions to the luck of the user. It gives protection to houses, and is at times hung near the bed of a sick person or a child to provide a cloak of protection. The plastic horseshoe has also found favor with truck drivers making long runs. The horseshoe marks another area of popular belief in which folk tradition has been transformed into form and sentiment more befitting the syncretic state of culture. It, too, is an identity symbol, for besides procuring the horseshoe's good luck for Italians, it marks a single ethnic use of a common charm and draws that charm into the Italian-American milieu. Hence the assertion that it is "better" than other forms of the horseshoe charm is a statement of ethnic pride as much as an evaluation of efficacy.

Gobbo

At this point a curious little figure enters into our account. He is the *gobbo,* or hunchback. A clown or a jester in much of European tradition (for example, the character Lancelot Gobbo and his father in Shakespeare's *Merchant of Venice*), the *gobbo* has a more mystical aspect for native Italians. A male hunchback was, in Italy, supposed to be very fortunate, in contrast to the female hunchback, who endured much misfortune.[12] Tiny hunchback figures of the Egyptian god Bes are matched by similar figurines from Peru.[13] Though the use of these ancient models is unknown, the manufacture and sale of hunchback figures for good luck charms in gold, silver, ivory, and other precious materials has been a continuous tradition in Italy and other Mediterranean countries for some time. Italian gamblers are quite fond of the *gobbo,* for they feel that the hand that has stroked a hunchback's hump will be favored at the gaming tables. Small *gobbo* figures substitute for a real hunchback and can be held in the hand and rubbed before every crucial throw.

In some areas of Italy the hunchback's hump is thought to be the result of an evil eye attack in youth.[14] The protruding hump, however, more often appears as a protection against the evil eye, on the same principle as the *corno* and the chili. The *gobbo* therefore appears occasionally among evil eye talismans, but his main use is among gamblers, and in certain regions.

Perhaps, then, it is strange to encounter him cast in white plastic, with a leering, almost demonic little face and bulging eyes with pupils marked, dapper in tuxedo and top hat. His presence in plastic is better explained by what he holds between his extended hands: the top of a red chili-*corno* that goes from his waist along his legs to the soles of his shoes. This *gobbo* charm is met with fairly often, as a key chain and in the other uses described for the chili-*corno*. In tradition he serves a special function, but, accompanied by the chili-*corno,* he is inducted into the popular, general usage. The *gobbo* is not so common a charm as the horseshoe. His gift is good luck, but a certain kind of good luck. The chili-*corno* harnesses that good luck on a popular level, bringing the *gobbo* into congress with the chili and the *mano cornuta*. The *gobbo* draws good fortune and the chili repels bad fortune. They complement each other, and together are meaningful on a level more general than either. The chili serves the same purpose with the *gobbo* as it does with the horseshoe. It contextualizes the *gobbo,* making him more than an idiosyncratic talisman and gambler's ornament. A new popular charm is again created from diverse traditional materials. The charm does find favor among contemporary gamblers, but it also has use as a luck charm helpful in business enterprise or in sport. The *gobbo-*chili composite reaches popular culture by generalization from more particular forms, in a manner opposite the one behind the composite horseshoe. In the final form, however, there is, as with the horseshoe, the notion that good luck is partially contingent upon evil eye protection, embodied in the pepper. Though the charm's specific reference to the evil eye is vague in use, and though those actually carrying or displaying the *gobbo* rarely associate him with the evil eye, yet the makeup of the charm signalizes the contribution of evil eye protection to the good luck promised by the charm. The appearance of the charm reveals the nature of its power.

Sirena

La sirena, the mermaid, has undergone changes similar to the *gobbo*'s transformation. Like the *gobbo* she has appeared in a range of folk talismans designed to bring good luck, and having some marginal application to the evil eye. She is frequently depicted with two tails, parted at the waist and curling up on opposite sides, often to be held in her hands.[15] She is a comely figure—bare-breasted, buxom, smiling. This enticing image is preserved in a white plastic version, only here she has but one tail, and it is a red plastic chili-*corno*. In this peculiar substitution there is a triple metaphor: the chili resembles an animal horn and the mermaid's fish tail is shaped like a chili—all three are evoked in one piece.

This is the most complete and ingenious material syncretism of talismans yet encountered. In popular culture the mermaid becomes an effective charm when possessing a chili tail. What is absurd physically is quite reasonable culturally. The nature of belief offers a rationale for the presence of the chili. Both mermaid and chili are joined literally as they are figuratively in the assurance of good luck, which seems invariably to include protection against the evil eye.

The mermaid-chili translates another aspect of popular culture into a peculiarly Italian idiom: this is the level of "girlie" magazines and suggestive, though not obscene, dolls and figures. Though the traditional mermaid talisman was generally worn by women, the plastic mermaid, admittedly of infrequent occurrence, is always in the possession of men. It is taken and treated much more lightly than the other charms mentioned, having more the role of a curio than that of a charm with definite assigned powers. By connection with this level of popular culture the mermaid has lost its association with the evil eye and, in fact, with good luck in general. It does, in its form and use, represent an interesting modification of tradition to produce a singular ethnic variant on a theme in popular culture.

Variant and Conglomerate Charms

The *gobbo,* as if not to be outdone by his sister talisman, appears in another plastic charm. His top hat is black and his head is cocked to the right. In his tuxedo lapel there is a carnation, and in place of his legs there is a red plastic chili-*corno.* His right hand makes the *mano cornuta* straight out from the chest, while the right hand carries a horseshoe. He is the quintessence of a successful man surrounded by the appurtenances of his success. Indeed, he might seem to be the product of his own powers as a charm, for the *gobbo*-mermaid-*corno*-chili-horseshoe-*mano* is a good luck charm of a very general sort. He combines in his person all of the charms and talismans discussed so far. He is well provided with good luck and with power against the evil eye. In the conglomerate *gobbo* is seen both particularization and generalization of talismans, adhering around the central core of the chili-*corno.* The chili-*corno* appears to be the axis of the charm, for each of the other charms has appeared in plastic form associated with it in some way. The conglomerate draws forms from Italian folk tradition and American popular culture and, through whatever process takes place, assimilates them into Italian-American popular culture. An even more extreme conglomeration occurs when the *gobbo* described here is suspended from the arch of a plastic horseshoe, which is usually cast in gold-colored plastic. This is the ultimate abstraction, the syncretism of all the main talismans into one unbelievable composite, centering around the chili-*corno* and the horseshoe. Neither this form nor the conglomerate *gobbo* is monstrous in its context. Both are end products of a motion in material-culture form that reflects a change in beliefs. Like the material forms, the beliefs exhibit generalization and particularization into a system where the conglomerate *gobbo* and the horseshoe are understandable and acceptable.

In these two final figures lies the essence of the shift from folk to popular culture among the Italian-Americans. Both are used much as the plastic chili-*corno* and have similar sense as identity symbols. In folk culture the evil eye was a specific danger met by specific talismans. It was enough just to avoid it and remain adequately healthy. Popular culture has given rise to a concept of good luck that presupposes freedom from evil eye affliction and that incorporates avoidance of the evil eye without giving the evil eye much explicit attention. The old folk talismans against the evil eye, with their negative quality of piercing the evil eye, become participants in positive good luck charms. They acquire ethnic value in bringing general good luck charms into Italian-American culture, and are themselves made more general in doing so. The folk talismans make certain that good luck is good luck according to the implicit Italian-American definition: a discrete absence of evil eye threat. The talismans are merged and blended to spawn a whole new series of mythical beings in the chili-mermaid and the chili-*gobbo*. The popular charms that results are not used actively, unlike the folk talismans. Their presence has no note of urgency about it, and this is reflected in their toylike form. They are carried, displayed, or hung somewhere, open encouragement to good fortune, secret forestalling of wicked forces. They are significant decorations, more reassuring than vital, the ideological furniture of a new, temporary, and unique culture.

NOTES

1. E.g., Williams, *South Italian Folkways*.   2. *Epistles*, 48.
3. Seligmann, p. 55.   4. See Valetta.
5. According to a technical distinction, the wielder of the *mal'occhio* applies his powers deliberately, through spite or desire for revenge. The *jettatore*, on the other hand, cannot help himself, though his power is equally destructive. The distinction is rarely made today.
6. A picture of a typical *jettatore* appears in Seligmann, opposite p. 56.
7. Elworthy, pp. 24–26.   8. Ibid., p. 260.   9. Pitrè, p. 204.
10. Cavendish, pp. 278–79.   11. Elworthy, pp. 216–20.
12. Seligmann, p. 253.   13. Elworthy, p. 331.
14. Seligmann, p. 330.   15. Elworthy, pp. 356–57.

BIBLIOGRAPHY

Cavendish, Richard. *The Black Arts*. New York: Capricorn, 1967.

Elworthy, Frederick. *The Evil Eye*. 1895. Reprint, New York: Collier, 1967.

Pitrè, Giuseppe. *La famiglia, la vida, la casa del popolo siciliano*. Palermo: Libreria Internazionale, 1913.

Seligmann, S. *Die Zauberkraft des Auges*. Hamburg: L. Friederichsen, 1922.

Valetta, Nicola. *Cicalata sul fascino volgarmente detto Jettatura*. 1787. Naples: Societa Typografica, 1814.

Williams, Phyllis. *South Italian Folkways in Europe and America*. New Haven: Yale University Press, 1938.

REGINA DIONISOPOULOS-MASS

4. GREECE

The Evil Eye and Bewitchment in a Peasant Village

"NISI" IS A SMALL rocky island, barely rising out of the Aegean. It is barren in comparison with other islands, and during the summer it is a burnt brown color, sparsely covered with dried brush. There are two villages on the island, a little more than an hour's walk apart. Hora, the island capital, is a tiny village of only 750 people, and it is an endogamous community. As part of an ethnographic team, I spent a year in this village.[1]

The village's whitewashed houses reflect the blinding Greek sun, so that the appearance from a distance is striking. The houses are charmingly built one against the other, a conglomeration of flat roofs, stairs, right angles, and arches. The streets are narrow paths winding through the town like a labyrinth; some are so narrow that people must walk single file. Even the streets are whitewashed in places, with patterns encircling the cobblestones, or with shapes of fish, ships, and flowers in flat places. There are three religious feasts during the year at which times the houses are whitewashed: Easter, Assumption, and Christmas. The women also touch up their houses every Saturday, making them spotless for Sunday. The window sills and doors of the houses are a bright blue, a fact that may be significant, since blue is a color affording protection from the evil eye.

REGINA DIONISOPOULOS-MASS lectures in anthropology at Texas A and M University. She studied anthropology at Northern Illinois University, De Kalb, Illinois. She has participated in archeological work in England, and has also had training in Egyptology.

This chapter is based on fieldwork on the demography and ethnology of an island Greek village in 1970 and again in 1971–72. The research was supported by grants from the Dean's Fund and from the Department of Anthropology at Northern Illinois University.

Dynamics of Power

The village is compact and people say laughingly that what happens in upper Hora is discussed in lower Hora within a matter of minutes. And because of the proximity of the houses, each person in Hora knows what material goods his neighbor possesses. One's every action is easily observed by one's neighbors, and privacy is almost unknown.

This intimacy allows three dynamics of power to function in the village: the evil eye, gossip, and magic. These dynamics have been dealt with by some anthropologists in relation to witchcraft. Witchcraft and envy studies have appeared increasingly in the last forty years; scholars whose contributions in this field are well known include George Foster, who perceived "the image of limited good," Eric R. Wolf, who referred to institutionalized envy among Latin American peasants, and Clyde Kluckhohn, whose work on Navaho witchcraft is considered to be a classic. Foster and Wolf dealt with the evil eye, gossip, and witchcraft as manifestations of envy, and each discussed the functions of institutionalized envy as methods of social control. Kluckhohn treated witchcraft as a form of social control, and he illustrated how it was used to maintain stability in Navaho society. Kluckhohn described the manner in which persons became witches. "Persons become witches in order to wreak vengeance, in order to gain wealth, or simply to injure wantonly—most often motivated by envy." [2] Wolf stated that

> witchcraft, as well as milder forms of institutionalized envy, [has] an integrative effect in restraining non-traditional behavior, as long as social relationships suffer no serious disruption. It minimizes disruptive phenomena such as economic mobility, abuse of ascribed power or individual conspicuous show of wealth. On the individual plane, it thus acts to maintain the individual in equilibrium with his neighbors. On the social plane, it reduces the disruptive influences of outside society. [3]

These analyses of envy can, in my opinion, correctly show the integrative function of certain aspects of institutionalized envy in peasant societies. However, not all aspects are integrative. In Hora, "the image of limited good" is very real. Daily, the people of Hora must deal with the evil eye, gossip, and magic in any one of many possible manifestations of envy. However, not all the aspects of envy are controllable and therefore useful as devices of social control. Many are quite disruptive, both to the individual and to the society.

For the purpose of this paper, witchcraft is defined as potentially harmful power, yet power that has a socially acceptable role and works to promote some type of harmony in the society. The social utility stems either from the exercise of these powers or the fear that they will be exercised. Witchcraft may be present in the village, in the home, or in the fields at all times of the day or night.

In contrast to witchcraft is sorcery, here defined as intentionally evil and aggressive actions that may cause great harm to individuals and to society. Acts of this nature are more likely to happen at times of rites of passage, when there is already much anxiety and tension and when envy is rampant. It is at these times that one is more vulnerable to the effects of witchcraft and more subject to attack by sorcery. A new mother and child (especially a baby boy and his new parents), a newly engaged couple, or newlyweds must be especially careful, since the whole village is full of envious, barren women, sterile men, envious unmarried maidens and youths, and envious parents of unmarried children. Any of these people could, from envy, employ witchcraft on the fortunate person and by using the evil eye, gossip, or magic, seriously harm him. Or the envious person could employ sorcery in openly aggressive actions to destroy the good fortune of the envied one and hopefully acquire that good fortune.

I will limit this paper to discussing the witchcraft and sorcery that occurs at three particular rites of passage: the pre-engagement, the engagement, and the wedding. First, however, it will be necessary to examine the three dynamics of power, to define them, and to discuss their classification as actions of witchcraft or actions of sorcery.

Therefore, for this paper, I have constructed three continua, one for each dynamic of power. I then locate some of the aspects of the three dynamics on each of the continua according to strength of social value. The continua are then divided in half, and I label one half witchcraft and the other sorcery according to the presence or absence of social use.

The Evil Eye

The first dynamic of power is that of the evil eye. This is a power of the eye (an admiring look), the thought, or a voiced compliment. It is a clear example of Turner's definition of witchcraft, a "threatening statement accompanied by misfortune," [4] as the compliment is a threat, one expressing the envy of the complimenter for the admired one's good fortune. It is a threat covered with words of flattery and praise. It expresses the complimenter's desire, which will probably make the admired one nervous and defensive.

To form a continuum of the evil eye, we may rank the cases according to the strength of their social value. In the continuum shown in chart 4.1, the left side designates those who occasionally show "an evil eye"; some informants think that anyone can have the evil eye, since everybody is envious at some time or other. The next point on the continuum represents those who are believed to have the evil eye but who do not know they have it; therefore, they harm without intent or knowledge. They are not necessarily thought of as being bad people. There was a well-respected man named Yannis who was believed to have the evil eye. He was a good man and highly thought of, but it was said that when he looked at an animal, it immediately dropped dead from his powerful eye. People felt he did not mean to hurt the animals, but his powerful eye almost always caused instant death. These people were born with the evil eye, which is the most common way of acquiring it. Those who believe that they were born with the eye and try to employ various types of chants or customs to control their power to keep from harming anyone else may be placed a little farther to the right. These are all examples of witchcraft. People who possess the evil eye of the witchcraft category are described as being able to *matiazi* or bewitch with the eye. The verb comes from *mati,* the Greek word for eye. Nearly everyone is afflicted by this at one time or another, especially children. One who is suddenly tired or depressed, suffers headaches, or is feverish or chilled is undoubtedly suffering from the eye. The diagnosis and the cure are the same. If during diagnosis it is determined that the person was afflicted by the eye, he is instantly cured, the evil being dissolved.

CHART 4.1. *Evil Eye Continuum*

Everyone Occasionally	Possessor Does not Know	Possessor Tries to Control	Malicious and Intentional Use Rising from Envy and Greed
Matiazma			*Vascania*

There are numerous ways of becoming cured. Most rites involve oil, cloves, water, fire, and holy words. One of the more common cures involving cloves is the following. The curer takes nine (some informants say twelve) cloves, which have heads on them, in the right hand. While holding the cloves, the curer makes the sign of the cross over the afflicted person three times. Then the curer lights a candle. Some informants said it should be a candle from a church, though not all informants agreed. The curer then inserts a needle through the head of one clove and as he does this the curer says to himself, "if it is a woman who has cast the eye, then destroy her breasts. If it is a man who has cast the eye, then crush his genitals." The clove is then inserted into the candle flame to ignite it. With the burning clove, the sign of the cross is made over the afflicted one and this verse is recited:

> *Three saw you. Three bewitched you.*
> *In the name of the Father, the Son, and the Holy Spirit.*
> *From your mother you were born.*
> *By the Virgin and Christ you were baptized.*

This verse calls upon the Holy Trinity to counteract the evil that may have been cast upon one. It renews the afflicted person's bond with his religion by emphasizing the Trinity, the Virgin, and baptism, and it places him under the protection of the religion.

As the verse is being finished, the clove has burned out and is put into a cup of cold water. Then the next clove is put on the needle and the whole rite repeated. If a clove snaps from the heat, it is believed to be a clear indication that the person was afflicted. A person who jumps or flinches when the clove snaps is assured that it is the spell being broken and the evil fleeing his body that have caused him to flinch. If no clove snaps, then the person was not under the spell of an evil eye but is believed to have an organic illness and may be told to see a doctor or another type of healer. If the last of the nine (twelve) cloves snaps, then three more cloves must be burned. This is done until the last clove of a group of three does not snap. The victim at this point may be told to drink three sips of the water from three different places on the rim of the cup. The curer then dips his finger into the cup and shakes the water from his fingers into the four directions between the victim and himself. This represents the form of the cross. He does this three times. Then the curer dips his fingers again and makes three wet crosses on the forehead of the afflicted. He then passes his dampened fingers over the victim's hair from the forehead back to the nape of the neck three times as if to brush away the evil and send it far behind the person. The afflicted one gets up and moves his chair away as if to leave the evil on the spot where it left him. If a clove snaps, the curer protects himself by yawning and covering his mouth a couple of times while reciting the verse so that the evil will not set upon him.

Cloves may also be burned to learn the identity of the curser. Three cloves may be burned, one at a time, and the curer will ask questions about the afflictor's identity. "Is it a woman?" one asks. "Is it someone who lives nearby?" If the clove splits open, then a positive response to the question is assumed. As the identifying features became more numerous, the questioner may even ask specific names of people whom he feels fit the description and may have had a reason to be envious.

Olive oil is another powerful substance used in curing the evil eye. The curer fills a bowl with cold water by pouring the water into the bowl three times in the shape of the cross. While doing this, he chants three times, "Jesus Christ beats all evil into nonexistence." He recites this again three times while making the sign of the cross over the bowl with a spoon of oil. Then a drop of oil is taken from the spoon with the finger and dropped into the water. Another cross is made and another recitation performed. Then a second drop of oil is added. This rite is performed a third time. If the three drops remain on the top of the water, then the person has not been cursed but rather is sick because of a disease or natural cause. If the oil appears to dissolve by spreading out across the top of the water rather than remaining in small clusters, the person is cured of the eye. The sick person takes three drops of the oil and water with his finger and drinks them. He then dips his fingers three times into the mixture and three times runs his hand through his hair from forehead to back. The cure is then believed to be complete.

A person can cure himself by reciting the Lord's Prayer over and over if there is no one else around to take care of the victim. Numerous types of *phylactos,* charms and phylacteries, can be worn for protection against the eye. Many of these protective devices are made and sold in convents and monasteries. A cross made of wood cut from a tree of a monastery and made into a cross on the feast day of the monastery is a good *phylacto.* Other *phylactos* are made of flowers, dried and sewed into little packets at convents. Homemade *phylactos* are probably more common, however. Before the homemade and the store-bought *phylactos* can protect, they must be kept at a church for forty days and blessed to acquire power. Once a *phylacto* has been blessed, it does not automatically keep its power. Rather, it may lose its power easily. If it is carried into a house that did not have its foundation blessed by a priest at the time of construction, or if it is carried into a la-

Figure 4.1 Greek evil eye charms. *On neck cord, left to right:* blue "eye" bead, with two black eyes; double cross, having crucifixion on both sides; homemade cross, lined with little blue beads and suspended from a blue-green bead; crab's claw, a popular evil eye charm. *Bottom left:* baptismal charm of Virgin and Child. Pink ribbon is for a girl, and the inscription on the reverse side reads, "May she live." *Bottom right:* gold crucifix charm used to protect children, suspended from blue bead with swirls. The white circle enclosing the black spot is an "eye." Coin is to show scale. (Photo by Lawrence Santeford.)

trine, it will lose its powers and must be taken back to a church for forty days to regain its stength.

The baptismal charm given to each person attending a baptism is worn by many as a *phylacto*. This charm may be of the crucifix or the Virgin. It is pinned to the clothing of the attendants. Each charm has a pink or blue ribbon according to the sex of the child that is being baptized.

Homemade *phylactos* are fashioned from soil from Palestine, a piece of the "true cross" (which one informant said was rather rare to find these days), dried flowers from the Good Friday service, and palms from Palm Sunday. Anxious mothers may knit a blue cover for a clove of garlic and pin this to their children's clothing.

One method of making a *phylacto* for human or animal use is to burn the

Figure 4.2 Key ring attached to bell, with little blue bead on the chain.

flowers from the Good Friday service with six teaspoons of flour and three teaspoons of salt. The ashes are carefully collected and sewed into a cloth packet. This may be pinned to a piece of clothing or worn in a pocket. It is ineffective if carried in a purse or wallet. This type of *phylacto* may be kept to treat sick animals. It may be rubbed across a cow's belly three times to cure the cow of the eye or it may be placed on the ground and the cow led over it three times so that it passes beneath the full length of the cow.

Numerous items found in the natural environment are used as protective devices. Starfish and the crescent-shaped arm of the crab are hung in houses. Soot from a fireplace may be put behind the ear for protection. The dog-onion root is brought home on New Year's Day and hung in the house to protect the family and home throughout the New Year. Keys, garlic, palms from Palm Sunday, and mule shoes may be hung on the doors and near the windows of the houses to bar envy and evil. People wear garlic cloves in their clothing. The whole skin of a snake is considered to be a strong prophylactic device and it is carried in the clothing, hung from the rafters of a house, or put over the door of an animal shed. There are several types of store-bought *phylactos,* blue beads being the most common. A blue bead may be hidden in the wearer's clothing and provides adequate protection. Blue beads are purchased to decorate animal harnesses, and multicolored bead harnesses may also be made. People wear a variety of gold charms. A gold cross is considered to be one of the best protective devices. Unbaptized children are not allowed to wear a cross, so they are given a variety of charms and beads to wear instead. Baptized and unbaptized children have protective icons attached to their beds or just above them.

The evil eye can be aimed at people, animals, houses, bread or cheese being made, plants, and nearly anything else. The sudden death of a child is often attributed to the eye. One lady told me about her firstborn son. A beautiful child, he died in his sleep after a short, sudden illness. The mother was convinced that her child had sickened and died from the evil eye.

A tree or vine that suddenly withers is certainly the victim of the eye. Vineyards are protected from the eye by placing the skull of a long-dead but prized mule or donkey on a fence or within the field. Prized trees are protected by placing a skull in the tree. There are many tales of trees and vines that were green and strong in the morning but that had withered and died from a passing envious eye by nightfall.

Animals are protected in several ways. In the sheds, they are guarded by a whole snakeskin hung from the rafters, a crab arm hanging on the door, a mule's shoe, or garlic. The evil eye can cause a pregnant animal to abort, a milk-giving animal to go dry, or a strong animal to fall, go limp, or become weak. Although women seem to do most of the curing of afflicted people, men know how to cure and are always ready to cure a sick animal. In fact, the curing ritual and verses must be passed from man to woman to man to be effective. A person who learns from a curer of the same sex does not gain power and may endanger the power of the teacher. The finest of mules, donkeys, and cows may have blue beads and tassels on their bridles, or across their foreheads to protect them. The best sheep of a flock may have a protective device meant to protect all the sheep. However, goats and pigs are not given *phylactos,* as they are animals of the devil. More than once farmers had almost lost their finest animals because of the eye. One farmer recalled a time when he was plowing with two huge, strong, white cows. Someone passed and said, "Oh, what beautiful cows." At the end of the furrow, one of the cows went down and could not get up. The farmer immediately began to treat his cow for the eye and the cow soon got up and went back to work. The farmer felt that if it had not been treated, it would surely have died. Another farmer, long ago, went to his pasture in the morning and discovered that all of his sheep, which has been so healthy the night before, had died during the night. The villagers who told this story were sure it was the evil eye, and since he had not been there to treat his afflicted animals, they all died.

Even nonliving objects may be affected by the eye. An olive press in a village near Kalamata was admired by a passing stranger. Before he had gone sixty feet, the press split in half and the villagers agreed that this was due to the eye.

The bus that ran between Hora and the other village was owned and operated by a man of Hora who had lived in Athens for several years and believed himself to be quite sophisticated. He proclaimed quite loudly that he did not believe in the evil eye and he would freely admit that there were people who believed that his father had had it. Yet the little bus that he owned was blue and white, the Greek national colors but also the colors used against the eye. The dashboard and visors were covered with numerous

Figure 4.3 Lasagne figure carried through the village streets and honored at the carnival of the last meal before Lent, also called *lasagne*. Though grotesque, it is adorned with beads, a cross, and two garlic bulbs, evil eye charms to protect it from the "admiring" glances of villagers. Children are often told to eat all their food lest Lasagne come and eat it. (Photo by Pierre Bettez Gravel.)

protective devices against various types of evils, including the eye. Several icons, charms, and blue beads were hung prominently.

The evil eye falls into the category of sorcery when there is, first, a malicious and intentful employment of the eye, and second, a manipulation of the power to harm others, to destroy or at least damage their health, children, and property. This type of bewitchment is *vascania*. *Vascania* is such a strong force that often the cure requires the intervention of a priest, as opposed to *matiazma,* which can be cured by anyone. The priest reads a prayer against the eye in the church while the victim stoops forward in front of the priest. The priest symbolically casts his garments over the victim to place him under the power and protection of the Church (Greek Orthodox rite) and drive the evil from him. Although the victim may be cured by an experienced person, there may be a need for many repeated rites. Therefore, a strong force, such as the Church, is deemed necessary to combat sorcery.

Matiazma may be seen as having a socially acceptable role in preventing the accumulation of wealth, or at least in preventing a stress on economic and social differences in the village. This tends to unite the village, and at least to an outsider's eye, the village will appear to be fairly uniform in social and economic standing. One woman who was renowned for her ability to cure the eye said that the best protection against it is not to brag about what one has. The dog onion is brought into the house to quiet gossips. "If a gossip talks about one's possessions, then jealousy arises and the eye is tempted," she added. *Vascania,* however, is a harmful and disruptive force. Persons capable of *vascania* are simultaneously mistrusted and kindly treated, as no one wants to bring down this type of wrath on himself.

Georgia, a woman with whom I lived during the course of my fieldwork, was said to have this type of power. Her sister, the wife of a baker, was believed to have caused the illness and eventual death of the single rival baker. Both women were born in Asia Minor and had settled on Nisi with their parents, as refugees of the Balkan Wars. Although they had lived on Nisi since the 1920s, people still referred to them as outsiders. Georgia was very vindictive. She recalled wrongs done to her in the twenties and thirties and she discussed those events often. When angered she would not hesitate to recall prior incidents and soundly chastise her victim for the old and new wrongs. The village secretary, a well-educated, sophisticated girl, was so frightened of this old lady's evil eye that when Georgia went to the mayor's office for her monthly social security check, the secretary would give her the check the moment that she entered the room so that she would leave immediately, rather than become angry and vengeful at being required to wait while those ahead of her were given their checks. After I moved to another house, people told me that they had wanted to warn me not to live with her, but they were afraid of her power. Several families told me that when they heard I was leaving her house, they would have invited me to live with them. However, they were terrified of what she would do to them in retaliation for their taking me into their home.

Gossip

The second dynamic of power is gossip. Gossiping is one of the main village preoccupations. Adults gossip at all places of social interaction: the coffee house, the store, the evening promenade, the wells, and within the church during service. So important is gossip that one woman told me that although her husband had built a wash area for her in their garden, she preferred to go with the other women to the stream. There she heard gossip that she would have missed if she did her washing at home.

There are two types of gossip. Witchcraft gossip is *koutsouboulio,* and sorcery gossip is *glossofeya.* In normal conversation, Nisiotes inevitably refer to the *koutsouboulio* gossips. Witchcraft gossip may be equated with what society says. It may be harmful in that untruthful stories or incorrect interpretations of actions are attributed to individuals, but it also has a social value, that of reinforcing the norms of society. Deviations from the norm are considered something to talk about. The *koutsouboulio,* as such, are the village chorus. They not only maintain the social norms of a society but help instruct others in what these norms are; and they help keep others from deviance. Hence, gossip regulates social interaction and helps stabilize and maintain the harmony of the village. A potentially harmful force thus has a socially acceptable role in village life.

The people most often gossiped about are those who are outsiders. The policemen, the doctor, and the schoolteachers were constantly being discussed by the villagers, especially by linking them with local girls of marriageable age. There were numerous whispered stories about the police station and the clinic being used as brothels.

Everyone participates in *koutsouboulio,* and nearly everyone admits to it in a joking manner. However, no one dares to admit that he belongs to the sorcery category, and few persons were ever identified to me as *glossofeya.* These are gossipmongers, malicious gossips. They devour with the tongue (*glossa* meaning tongue and *feya* meaning eater). They may be specifically named and feared for their aggressive and malicious natures and abilities. These are people who can cause great harm by employing their powers directly. They speak, thus causing envy and jealousy to arise. They are people who slander others, starting stories about one's reputation and actions with the intention of doing harm. Although people frequently complained to me that the only thing wrong with their village was the *koutsouboulio,* and while they instructed their children to act in such a manner as to keep from being victims of the *koutsouboulio,* it is the power of the *glossofeya* that is really feared. The *glossofeya,* it was frequently claimed, employ magic with their threats and aggressive gossip, and since they speak with an intent to do harm, one cannot really protect oneself. The gossip may be calumny. The

CHART 4.2. *Gossip Continuum*

Matchmaker Gossip	Society "Says"	Individual actions Misinterpreted	Malicious and Intentional Gossipmongering
Koutsouboulio			*Glossofeya*

victim may never have committed the act of which he is accused. Nevertheless, he is tormented by the *glossofeya*. A continuum of gossip is shown in
chart 4.2.

Magic

Finally, there is the dynamic force of magic. To the left of the continuum
are people who can cure many types of evil and various diseases, and they
can also cure spells of magic and of the evil eye. They are practicing
witchcraft in that they are manipulating potentially dangerous powers. The
villagers may feel that these people, who demonstrate their powers in curing
rituals, may have the potentially dangerous powers of the sorcerer. This is
especially true of those who cure by using chants, which call for either a
painful death or disfiguration as the fate of the original afflictor. For example, in the commonly used chants against the evil eye, the evil is returned
to the possessor of the eye: "if it is a woman crush her breasts and if it is a
man crush his genitals." Certainly, the person using this chant is calling
upon a potentially violent power. It is used here for curing. On another occasion, it may be used in anger.

In general, it was extremely difficult to get anyone to talk about a *magissa,* or witch. One person said there might be witches in the next village.
Others said the only witches are the Turkoyiftes or Turkish gypsies who occasionally visit Nisi. One man said his sister who had married a man from
another island was killed by a witch who was the sister of the husband. People were somewhat reluctant even to talk about witches from elsewhere or
about cases of witchcraft that had occurred elsewhere, but it was many long
months before anyone was willing to talk about local witches. Their hesita-
tion was undoubtedly due to their fear of reprisal by the witch. By naming
the witch, they were giving life to his power and thereby evoking his wrath
and indignation.

There are numerous women on Nisi who perform curing rituals. Never in
my presence were people who cure referred to as *magissa*. While this is
usually translated as "witch," in fact it is cognate with "magician." They
were referred to as "women who know a lot" or as "doctors"; and on several occasions I heard them refer to themselves as doctors. This, of course,
makes their role socially acceptable. Greek Orthodox priests may also be
placed in the witchcraft category. They are highly religious and represent a

link between man and God. On Nisi, they also claim to have tremendous powers, which they use in serving God and in insuring good crop returns, good health, and good animals. The role of the priest is to maintain harmony between man and God and between man and man. However, the priest's powers are much feared by many of the villagers, and it is commonly believed that if the priest curses someone, that person will not die peacefully. His body will not decay, and his soul will wander the earth as a violent spirit. The priest's curse may bring much harm and grief to the villagers. I was told that the village priest on Nisi is greedy, and that he used his priestly powers to blackmail the villagers into hiring him for carpentry work, which is his other profession. When a priest employs his powers to do harmful or destructive work, he is certainly engaged in sorcery. It is said by many people that the worst eye in the village is that of the priest.

The makers of love potions may be placed in either the witchcraft or the sorcery category depending upon the intentions of the maker and the outcome of the match. The first involves those who make love potions that produce agreeable, harmonious, and happy couples. The other category includes those who make love potions that result in unhappy families, and matches that may later end in divorce. Or a love potion may lead to the jilting of a sweetheart. Therefore, a person may be referred to as the one who brought about the match and be blessed by all involved or may be blamed for this match and cursed for years. Sorcerers are those who have created a tense situation of hostility and unhappiness in the society, which would include the relatives of the two families involved, and therefore nearly the whole village may be brought directly into play.

To rank the various aspects of magic one might form a continuum such as that shown in chart 4.3.

CHART 4.3. *Magic Continuum*

Curers of Various Diseases	Priests	Makers of Love Potions	Malicious and Intentional Use of Power, Sorcery
Positive Magic			*Negative Magic*

Social Dynamics of the Evil Eye, Gossip, and Magic

The three continua are illustrated as a group in chart 4.4. I will now analyze some of the different situations in Nisi where these dynamic powers were carried out especially in regard to pre-engagement, engagement, and marriage.

CHART 4.4   *Witchcraft-Sorcery Continuum*

WITCHCRAFT			SORCERY
Potentially harmful powers. These powers have a socially acceptable function and work to promote harmony in the society. They are evident daily in all aspects of village and home life.			Intentionally evil and aggressive actions which may cause great harm to individuals physically, mentally, emotionally, and financially. These are disruptive powers and they are most evident during rites of passage.
The Evil Eye			
Everyone occasionally	Possessor does not know	Possessor knows and tries to control	Malicious and intentional use rising from envy and greed
Matiazma			*Vascania*
Gossip			
Matchmaker gossip	Society "says"	Individual actions misinterpreted	Malicious and intentional gossip-mongering and backbiting
Koutsouboulio			*Glossofeya*
Magic			
Curers of various diseases	Priests	Makers of love potions resulting in Harmonious matches Unhappy matches	Malicious and intentional use of power for destructive purposes
Positive social results			Negative social results

The village secretary once told us how difficult it was to levy taxes or take a census, as the people maintained that they had nothing. Their lands were poor and few, their animals were diseased, old, and dying, their health was so bad they were unable to work regularly. But when a peasant farmer is trying to impress another about the qualities of his children in regard to a possible marriage, he cannot praise his wealth and health enough.

While the peasant's attitude may appear to be incongruous, there is an explanation. Concern about assessments and fears about evoking the evil eye are reasons for not bragging about one's wealth and health. However, when the issue is a match, modesty is out. This, of course, makes the potential couple an object of envy, since the dowry is in order and since they are con-

sidered to be desirable. Few persons at any one time would be both of marriageable age and ready to be married, because of the considerable financial
investment; so those who are eligible are vulnerable to the evil eye, gossip,
and magic. This is especially true when they have been identified as being
desired and more so when both parties are ready and willing to marry.
Dowry linens are kept in chests with blue beads and with flowers from the
replica of the tomb of Christ used in Good Friday services. These protect the
goods from evil, as do the candle stubs from the Easter service, which are
also put into the chests. Marriageable young men and women often wear a
blue bead and a crucifix to protect themselves from the eye and magic. Particularly desirable, and hence particularly vulnerable youths may be told by
their mothers to wear a clove of garlic in their pockets or to put a spot of
soot behind their ears.

The looms on which dowry articles are woven have a blue charm hanging
from them to protect both the goods and the weaver from the eye. The finest
of the animals have blue beads and tassels on their bridles and may have
other types of charms on them as well.

The *koutsouboulio* gossips have an important role in the pre-engagement
arrangements. Gossip acts as a precurser. The villagers are aware of what is
about to happen or what has happened. One informant told me that her son
and his girlfriend wanted to marry. Now her husband would send a *proxinou*
or matchmaker to begin the subject of an alliance between the two families.
She then added that the girl's family would know the matchmaker was coming, who he was, and what his mission was because the gossips, the *koutsouboulio*, would inform them. It is my contention that one of the roles of
gossip is to allow ample opportunity for the pros and cons of a match to be
aired.

The evil eye, gossip, and magic, in regard to marriage, deal mainly with
philotimo and *dropi*. *Philotimo* is the "love of honor," which among men is
considered a love or respect for masculinity. One's masculinity is increased
by lessening that of other men, as though masculinity is in limited supply. If
one gains, someone else must lose.[5] At the coffee house, village meetings,
sports events, the evening promenade, the store, the church, and during all
periods of social interaction, each man is pitted against the others. If not
openly aggressive, he is at least on his guard to seek out every possible
chance to lower someone else's masculinity and build up his own. *Philotimo*
may be applied to women and their honor or lack of honor discussed. More

often, however, the quality of *dropi* or shame is dealt with. A woman who is not chaste, is unfaithful to her husband, or does not act as a good woman should brings shame to the men around her. Here, shame reflects upon the honor of the men—her father, her brothers, and her husband. Women are feared and censured by their male kinsmen because of the shame they can bring upon their men through their actions.

An Example of Powers of Social Control

In 1968 a young couple eloped. Manoli was 18 and his bride Katina was only 14. Manoli's family was economically and socially more prominent than Katina's. Katina had three sisters and her family was poor. Consequently, her dowry prospects were limited. Manoli's family knew he was interested in Katina. One of his aunts told me that when she heard that Manoli was planning to elope with Katina, she tried to talk both parties out of it. The *koutsouboulio* had informed Manoli's father that Manoli was considering marriage. The father also tried to persuade Manoli not to marry Katina. The father felt that his son had been bewitched. As Manoli had eaten at the girl's house, his family felt that someone there must have put a love potion in his food.

The couple ran off to the mountains for a few days. After returning to the village, they married and they lived with the groom's parents, as the bride's family, in accordance with custom, would have nothing to do with her. Although each had carried such prophylactics as blue against the evil eye, a tiny gospel to dispel evil, and scissors to "cut the magic" that someone might try to cast on them (i.e., sorcery at the wedding), it was obvious to the villagers that the couple had been bewitched during the wedding service. The groom was unable to consummate the marriage. It was believed that when the best man passed the wedding crowns over the couple's heads three times, someone present had uttered magic words and had tied three knots in a string, thereby acquiring power over the couple. The groom repeatedly tried to consummate the marriage (his testimony). In a society where the wedding sheets are publicly displayed, this became a well-known fact. The groom took ill and was bedridden for four months. He began to waste away, and the priest was summoned daily to bless him and the house. A relative suggested that a witch in Athens be consulted and he, his parents, and his wife went to Athens. The witch performed a curing ritual and instructed them to return to Nisi and be remarried at an outlying chapel. This was done. At this service, known as reversing the crowns, the magic spell was broken. Manoli became well quickly.

After two years Manoli went into service and his wife continued to live with her parents-in-law. Her parents then gave her the dowry house and goods that they had withheld for the first three years of marriage. She moved into the house and had one of her younger sisters live there also. Soon the gossip began. Many people were critical of Katina and they felt she had ulterior motives in leaving her parents-in-law's house while her husband was away in service. A new young policeman arrived and he asked her to dance often at each of the festivals. It was rumored that he daily accompanied her to her fields, which were an hour and a half away. All of these actions were discussed by the *koutsouboulio,* who were presenting social commentary on actions they felt deviant. Her father-in-law and his wife's uncle went to the police station and faced the policeman. Shortly thereafter, the policeman was called before his superiors and soon was given a transfer to another area. Manoli began divorce proceedings. Since he could not prove that Katina had committed adultery, both he and Katina agreed to a divorce on the grounds of mutual incompatibility. Manoli returned to Athens to finish his final two months of service. Katina's reputation was damaged. She was called names everywhere in the village and she was involved in a hair-pulling fist fight with one woman who called her names.

Soon the story was slightly altered. It was said that her sister who lived with her had also had an affair with a policeman. Manoli's relatives had been quite vocal in discussing his bad fortune, and many blamed his mother-in-law for the whole trouble. Indeed, both he and his brother maintained that Katina's mother had bewitched Manoli into marrying Katina. Manoli said that it must have been witchcraft. Otherwise, he would have listened to his father and waited. He added, "Why else would I have married during the best years of my life?"

Suddenly, a new rash of rumors began, initiated mainly by Katina's relatives and neighbors. They claimed that Katina was suing for divorce as her marriage had never been consummated. A few said that they thought Katina had had an affair with the policeman, but only because her husband was impotent. This was an obvious effort to rationalize her deeds and may be seen as a backlash. Katina was shamed and her reputation ruined. The most effective attack against Manoli was to ruin his reputation by condemning his masculinity.

A final rumor was passed about by Manoli's friends and relatives. They said that Katina's mother (already branded as the sorceress who had administered the love potion) had had an affair with a policeman, had a baby, and went to Athens to live, where she put the baby up for adoption. A few years later, the mother married and had four daughters. Therefore, her daughter's actions were really her own sins revisited. Manoli told me that he bore no grudge against his wife, as he felt that she had done what she did because of her mother. He also held no grudge against his father-in-law, whom he respected.

Public opinion allows us to form the following analysis. The couple was married because of a love potion, magic, which in this case was an act of sorcery, as the couple and their families were not happy with the match. The groom's family believed that the match had been due to sorcery, and they believed that the sorcerer had been Manoli's mother-in-law. At the wedding, an unidentified sorcerer had caused the groom to become impotent and ill. This magic spell was cast at a rite of passage and a time of great tension and anxiety. Later, a witch, using a curing ritual, and the priest (also a witch by our definition), using magic, were able to cure the groom and break the spell. Later, when Manoli was away in service, Katina left the home of her parents-in-law, thus leaving herself open to gossip, as she was unchaperoned. While she heard the *koutsouboulio* about herself, she did not take appropriate action to protect herself. She could have moved in with her own parents, moved back in with her parents-in-law, or at least refused to dance with the policeman. Because she did not take action to stop the *koutsouboulio* about her conduct, her reputation was ruined because of the *glossofeya*. In retaliation, her friends and relatives undermined Manoli's reputation by attacking his masculinity, an openly aggressive act of *glossofeya*. The final aspect was the gossip about Katina's mother. Said to be true, it was a story we heard only after the divorce proceedings began. It was told specifically to damage Katina's mother's reputation and Katina's.

The above cases illustrate a small portion of the variety of social functions that the evil eye, gossip, and magic, as forms of witchcraft, perform. As controlled dynamics of power, they stress the socioeconomic unity of the society and reinforce the norms. Deviant social action, including conspicuous consumption, is minimized either through fear of the exercise, as in fear of the evil eye, or through an actual attack brought on by bragging. Some aspects of these serve as face-saving devices. When the *koutsouboulio* inform a family of the intentions of a possible suitor, the family either prepares to meet him and discuss a match or counteracts with rumors to prevent his arrival. This may be seen as face saving, since possible conflicts may be eliminated if the youth realizes that he will not even be considered and need not go to the home. Also, individuals who realize that they or their families are being gossiped about because of deviant actions may take steps to end the deviant actions and thereby stop or at least minimize the gossip. The priest and curers may be known as stabilizers of village tensions and conflicts. They may be well respected for their actions. Their powers may be held in awe, as they are powers of almost unlimited possibilities. However, the very nature of these powers makes the villagers fearful of them as well. The believed maker of love potions might cause social damage or might be successful in arranging a happy match that will result in harmonious conditions among the relatives.

As long as all these powers are held in check, or at least the attempt to control them is evident, these powers will provide systems of social control in the village and help to stabilize the society. This is in accord with Wolf's, Kluckhohn's, and Foster's findings. But Kluckhohn's definition of "witch" would actually be what I call a sorcerer, and at this level we see the breakdown of family and village stability. Each of the aspects of witchcraft, if willfully employed to cause destruction, may be so intense that total village disharmony may result. It is at rites of passage, where tensions already exist, that attacks of sorcery, intentionally manipulated, and evil acts appear most frequently and do the most damage. The harm done by witchcraft may be guarded against and almost completely corrected. But the damage done by the sorcerer may be final, as some things cannot be repaired. A direct assault on one's reputation, a broken home, and a jilted sweetheart, are only a few examples of the finality of the damage caused by sorcerers.

NOTES

1. Nisi is not the real name of the island; villagers' personal names are also fictitious. The research in this village was conducted while I served as part of an ethnographic team under the direction of Professor Pierre Bettez Gravel.

I would like to thank the following for advice, comments, and criticism in writing this paper: Professors Cecil Brown, Pierre Bettez Gravel, James Gunnerson, Kenneth Honea, and Matt Solo of the Anthropology Department of Northern Illinois University, and Professor Byron Palls of the Foreign Language Department.
2. Kluckhohn, p. 26. 3. Wolf, p. 460.
4. Turner, p. 371. 5. Foster, p. 301.

BIBLIOGRAPHY

Foster, George M. "Peasant Society and the Image of Limited Good," *American Anthropologist* 67, no. 2 (1965), pp. 293–315.

Kluckhohn, Clyde. *Navaho Witchcraft.* 1944. Reprint, Boston: Beacon Press, 1970.

Turner, Paul R. "Witchcraft as Negative Charisma," *Ethnology* 9, no. 4 (1970), pp. 366–72.

Wolf, Eric R. "Types of Latin American Peasantry: A Preliminary Discussion," *American Anthropologist* 57, no. 3 (1955), pp. 452–71.

JOEL M. TEITELBAUM

5. TUNISIA

The Leer and the Loom—
Social Controls on
Handloom Weavers

TUNISIAN COASTAL VILLAGERS working as handloom weavers preserve a lively attachment to their sedentary way of life. Under the cultural veneer of what appears as a "superstition," the evil eye belief functions effectively in everyday social relations. Evil eye concepts serve as mechanisms of social and economic control in these weaving communities.[1]

Evil eye beliefs and practices are only a small part of the ethnographically interesting characteristics of this segment of Mediterranean Arabic society. These beliefs are part of a circum-Mediterranean heritage of ideas about the supernatural. The Tunisian version of the evil eye (*'ayn harsha*) belief may be traced from Berber antecedents through successive invasions and colonizations by Carthaginians (Phoenicians), Romans, Vandals, Arabs, Turks, and finally the French, whose protectorate there was established in 1883. Tunisia gained independence from France in 1956. Of the present-day inhabitants of this small North African republic, 89 percent are Arabic-speaking Sunni Muslims, numbering nearly six million people. They have selected elements of this long heritage of mixed traditions to fit their present situation. Fear of the leer is built into their culture.

JOEL M. TEITELBAUM is Associate Director, African Universities Population Dynamics Program, University of North Carolina. He formerly taught ethno-nutrition in the College of Human Development, Pennsylvania State University. He holds a Ph.D. in anthropology from the University of Manchester.

The fieldwork on which this article was based was conducted in Tunisia in 1965–66, with a subsequent visit in 1971. The author has published several articles on Tunisian weavers.

The Tunisian Version of the Evil Eye

Tunisian villagers believe that the "eye" can hurt only living things, usually animals or plants owned by humans. It cannot directly affect inanimate objects. Thus a cow, a camel, or planted crops may be stricken or killed by an evil leer even in the absence of the owner. But a machine such as a loom or an automobile cannot be destroyed directly by the eye; instead the owner or operator can be made to have an accident with it or to break it through misuse or neglect. Things and animals that are highly prized and may engender envy in others are thought particularly susceptible to the power of the eye; hence conspicuous consumption is thought to increase risks. Women and children especially must be shielded from the view of others to avoid being taken by the eye, which is thought to cause illness or accident, or even lead to death. Women are kept in a state of seclusion in the homes, and children allowed outside in plain view are dressed in rumpled old clothing or made to appear dirty and unattractive to prevent envious thoughts by others. Nicknames of a joking or unflattering nature are often substituted for their real names to avoid envy. Charms and amulets are tied on them and pious phrases uttered when speaking about them to protect them from the evil eye.[2]

As the supposed deleterious power of the glance requires actual viewing of the affected party, the eye is thought to work only at close quarters. In the village prying strangers and marginal persons or deviants are often considered possible users of the eye and hence should be avoided, especially by women and children. Such attitudes express the norms of group solidarity, conformity, role-behavior in a religious idiom, but do not imply the blaming or accusing of specific evil eye culprits. The most regularly worrisome glance is thought to be that of an envious or jealous neighbor with whom one maintains a relationship of competitive interaction unmitigated by ties of kinship or affection. As kinship derives from the mystical bond of "blood," or consanguinity, casting the evil eye is ruled out among close kindred in Islam. People who ordinarily cohabit and dine together are believed incapable of afflicing one another with the evil eye because their relationship is sanctioned by God. Thus kin, affines, and friends cannot "cause" one another misfortune; evil is the social antithesis of intimacy and co-residence.

As often noted, Tunisian folk explanations maintain that the hurtful effect of the eye results from feelings of jealousy, envy, greed, and frustration on the part of those who find themselves obliged to admire the good fortune or well-being of another; hence they project these feelings on the admired one. This concept is an indigenous perception of human nature and interpersonal conduct. It is a folk model in which each actor plays a dual role; he may inadvertently "take" others with a jealous glance or he may be "taken" by them. But he is supposed to avoid "taking" by observing proper etiquette, while shielding himself against being "taken" by use of amulets or rites known to deflect or neutralize—"take off"—the evil eye. This model enjoins prudence, moderation, and decorum in social interaction. One is expected to repeat aloud blessing of God and pious imprecations and to suppress one's own evil sentiments toward the other, while displaying self-defense charms to fend off possible jealousies of the other party. Thus, protracted greetings and what seem like quaint, unnecessary flourishes abound in social situations when people visit one another or meet in the road. An embrace of the head or hand implies sufficient affection to prevent the evil eye from penetrating the interaction; indeed, prolonged kissing is the most frequent greeting among friends and kindred.

Through subtle use of these symbols ambivalent feelings may also be communicated.[3] Lapses or unexpected avoidance behavior are quickly interpreted as signifying deterioration in the quality of interpersonal sentiments, raising the spectre of bad feelings that could lead to misfortune through the evil eye. In short, the evil eye forms part of the moral universe of the villager, assigning good and evil intentions to his relations with others. When praising someone one adds a blessing to control jealousy; rather than boast about oneself it is best simply to use customary understatement by responding to the question, "How are you? with the answer, "No pain, thanks be to God." The evil eye mystique is pervasive.

Moving from the folk view of interpersonal relations to a sociological statement about the society, we find that belief in the evil eye functions in public life as a controlling element in group dynamics, structuring ambiguous fields of association that are not subject to clear-cut rules or lines of authority but involve competing norms and activities. It remains to elucidate this social-control function in the context of the handloom weaving conditions I have observed in Tunisian villages, and to generate from it broader statements of the context in which evil eye powers are utilized.

The Setting

Several villages, of a few thousand inhabitants each, cluster within a few miles of one another amid the ruins of classical Roman cities on the east-central coast of Tunisia. Most of the men work on looms of the standard Near Eastern type with shuttles and a horizontal warp, fashioning brightly colored cloths traditionally used for wearing and bathing apparel. They inhabit a semiarid region with rocky soil and poor agricultural resources; the products include olives and olive oil, with some garden vegetables and fruits. There is a little pasture for the animals. Small boat crews draw moderate fish harvests from the adjacent waters of the Mediterranean, for seafoods are relished by the coastal dwellers.

The growing population of this area, a long-settled region of peasant agriculture, turned to handloom weaving about fifty years ago to provide a cash product for the market because of inadequate land and sea resources. After 1882, the French protectorate destroyed the city guilds that had monopolized the handicraft industry in previous centuries. From that time village weavers replaced the urban craftsmen, inhabiting spots along the coastline where temperature and humidity conditions were found suitable for efficient year-round operation of their simple looms. These places were in the Tunisian Sahel and the island of Djerba, where evil eye beliefs remain strong.

Each Sahelian village forms a small-scale community in which men compete with one another as well as cooperating. Between villages there is tension and reserve, modified by stereotyped joking relations that allow peaceable association. Several such villages strung out like beads on a necklace of roads are dependent upon a central textile market town where loom goods are bought and sold. Within a village, weavers form the majority of the able-bodied adult males, over 60 percent, and each community forms a pool for endogamous marriage. Although Islam encourages close-cousin marriage, it is practiced mainly by the higher-status, nonweaver segment. Between weaver families there are few cousin marriages and the ideal of first-cousin, patrilateral, parallel-cousin matrimony (*bint' amm*) is rarely attained. Four-fifths of the children of weavers marry within the community to non-kin, usually as a result of arranged unions between weaver families. Poorer laborer families and wealthier professional and propertied people marry outside the community more frequently than do the weavers. This makes for a complex web of affinal and diachronic kinship ties within the village that are renewed from generation to generation according to occupational status group. Despite an ostensible ideology of patrilineal descent, the community forms a tightly knit social system with shallow (three-generational) genealogical reckoning and a horizontal spread of bilateral cognatic and affinal kinship bonds.[4]

Although there has been little migration into the area since Tunisian independence in the late 1950s, a considerable number of weavers have emigrated to seek temporary manual labor in the industries of Europe; in addition, educated and highly skilled persons have settled in the cities of Tunisia and found permanent employment. This loss of the able-bodied from the community has had a profound effect on social and economic life; thus demographic factors figure in the evil eye belief in the village context.

Social pressures in the community make for uniform patterns of behavior and similar styles of life, especially among weavers. The weaver ethos entails a stable unit of man-women cooperation through the sexual division of labor. Powerful norms favor monogamy, although prior to independence Islamic laws were interpreted as encouraging polygyny. Villagers also express intense opposition to divorce despite the Muslim laws concerning repudiation of a wife, which was easily done before independence. My census shows that marriage and divorce rates correspond well with these norms of the community: only two men are polygynous—neither of them are weavers—and the divorce rate has been consistently low at about 3 percent of extant marriages. Analysis shows that a male weaver has need of a female helper to make his cloth production profitable. He delegates the ancillary tasks of thread-winding and putting preparatory and finishing touches on loom and cloth to his wife (or mother or sister). Thus, work-sharing reinforces the stability of the marriage bond; weaving makes an extra wife superfluous and an economic burden. Men ply looms together in dark, dank, street-side shops while their women perform ancillary tasks for each behind high housewells in a state of seclusion. The social segregation of the sexes coincides with the economic sexual division of labor in weaving.

Technology and Work Norms

Since a man is freed from many tasks by the help of a woman, the three major factors affecting the production of his loom are: (1) market conditions; (2) the technical capacity of the standard loom; (3) individual variations in skill and efficiency among weavers. The first two are beyond the control of an individual weaver. Market price cycles result from mass interactions of supply and demand, and the ordinary weaver is at the mercy of the textile merchants and speculators who possess sufficient capital to buy cheap and sell dear on the thread-and-cloth market in a nearby town. Also, loom parts do not operate very quickly under human power, and the handloom requires slogging patience for routine work, as well as adequate maintenance at periodic intervals. A skilled weaver maintains an average of 20 to 22 throws of the shuttle per minute and can produce on the average slightly more than one square meter of cotton cloth per hour. During an eight-hour workday, the mean amount of cloth woven was found to be 8.5 square meters, and the mode was 7.6 square meters. Since working hours are not formally regulated, each man can, in theory, operate at his own pace. However, weaving is frequently interrupted for rest breaks and refreshments, and work-rates are socially controlled.

The village-wide production norm for a day's work consists of four pieces of cloth, known as a "portion." The "portion" contains 7.6 square meters and accounts for the modal output figure above. This work quota is set in part by the market custom of selling cloth in packages of four pieces each morning at the textile town's *suq*. In reality, the range of cloth output varies from less than 4 square meters per day by slow or disabled weavers to 12 square meters per day by faster-working skilled men. Since cash income varies directly with output, this makes possible a 300 percent range in income. Such individual variation could promote great inequality in the accumulation of wealth were there no restraints on the amount of cloth a man may weave. Real status equality among weavers is achieved by production quotas. Evil eye customs reinforce these output norms.

Since the destruction of the nineteenth-century urban weaving guilds, there have been no formal regulations on working hours, output, or quality of product. Yet the quota of "a portion a day" is upheld within the community, and mean output does not greatly exceed the mode. Cloth production falls in an ambiguous area of informal regulation in which the evil eye belief operates in concert with other social controls and economic strategies.

For purposes of marginal economy and companionship, most men weave in groups of about four to a shop, sharing the costs of upkeep. They customarily begin work early in the morning and stop at noon, when the heat of the day interferes most with activity. After a heavy midday meal and a siesta, they return to their looms and weave on until darkness and the evening meal. During working hours they pass around refreshments—most often small glasses of powerfully decocted, heavily sugared tea—and smoke cigarettes during the frequent rest breaks. Co-weavers aid one another at critical moments during the preparation of a loom warp, which occurs about once each month for each man. Although a weaver usually dines at home, the men regularly spend their nightly leisure hours together in the weaving shops where they play card games, drink tea and other beverages, eat sweets and smoke while discussing the day's events, gossip and joke about others, and visit from shop to shop according to patterns of age-group and friendship networks.

Clearly, output is limited by the custom of weaving during the day only. Few men work during the evening hours; those who do are primarily slower weavers who have not finished a daily "portion" of cloth and wish to achieve this norm. Men at leisure in the shops tolerate poorly the extension of working hours. Fast workers trying to exceed their "portion" are joked with and chided for their excessive zeal and repeatedly invited to join in recreational interactions. Their work is disrupted by social pressures resulting from a tacit conspiracy to maintain the output norms of the group. This ceiling on cloth production functions to preserve economic parity among weavers as well as to prevent supplies of cloth from outstripping market demand, thus maintaining profit margins for all. Quota-breakers must act surreptitiously. A man who wishes to boost his production by night work is obliged to shut himself up alone in his shop or get together with another such moonlighter, in order to avoid the social pressure of other men in the weaving shop. In general, only by breaking his rapport with co-weavers can any weaver substantially exceed the production norm.

A number of men have closed up shops and rebuilt looms in their homes in recent years, since the profit margin on cloth has more than doubled since independence. This response emerged in the late 1960s as the exit of numerous emigrant workers lowered the total supply of cloth. The economic motive for the in-house loom, a sharp break with weaving custom and sex segregation, is clear: increased individual production. However, the explanation given by this minority of home weavers is that they withdrew from the weaving shops to avoid being "taken" by the evil eye of others; even when pressed they will not identify *which* others, but offer stories of past events in which they have had accidents or broken their looms because of the evil eye. Here the so-called fear of the evil eye is used to rationalize their persistent evasion of normative social expectations in search of economic improvement.

Such men tend to become isolated and to avoid the leisure groups of shop weavers even when not working. Should a home weaver pay a visit to a loom shop during working hours, he is not invited in; defined as a marginal person, he is considered ill-willed and antisocial. Weavers who abide by the norms explain that such persons are avoided because of their greedy, jealous natures; their leers or words are believed to bring misfortune to ordinary weavers. Thus, community-wide belief in a mystical form of abuse becomes a rationalization for ostracism of deviants. It operates to separate quota-breakers socially from the majority of weavers. Hence, the evil eye functions in a systematic feedback mechanism by associating social distance with economic differentiation within the community while reinforcing conformity to the output norms and maintaining income parity among most shop weavers.

Amuletry and Weaving

As a precaution against the eye villagers wear amulets pinned on clothing, consisting of tiny figures or writings from the Koran known to ward off evil and misfortune. The symbols of "good luck" are dominated by the image of the fish—considered the ultimate blessing that promotes well-being. To bless one another village people exclaim, "The fish upon you," or when questioned as to their movements respond with the customary evasive phrase, "I am going to get the fish." They also use invocations of God and the prophet Muhammad, as is expected in Islam. The fish symbol is used widely in art forms, and amulets of gold, silver, amber, or other precious materials are thought to be especially efficacious in warding off evil. Today plaster, cloth, and even plastic models of the fish abound. Drawings of fish are engraved on jewelry, buildings, and pottery and frequently are tattooed on the skin.[5] For greatest effect the fish image must be displayed prominently to deflect the eye. The silvery dried tails of large sea-fish are the items most openly displayed in weaving shops, hanging on threads from loom struts to "protect" the weaver and his livelihood. Few working looms go without such symbolic talismans; on some looms they occur in such profusion as to screen off the weaver from the view of the onlooker and force one's attention upon the fishtails themselves. But talismans are also social indicators that can be measured.

From my census of weavers and their looms it became apparent that inordinate use of the fishtail and other talismans against the evil eye was associated with attempts to break output norms without incurring social censure. A fast or skilled weaver often employed this device to tacitly request others *not* to interfere with his rhythm of work by making comments or distracting his attention with sociable invitations. The profusion of fish symbols signaled "Busy, do not disturb," a message that communal etiquette would not permit him to state bluntly in words. When questioned about the fishtails, their owners usually laughed at the investigator at first, trying to brush away suggestions of their significance while in the presence of other weavers. However, in private a man would explain that he had been "taken" or narrowly averted injury by the evil eye in the past; that the fishtails and other symbolic amuletry were his source of protection, as he was a good worker admired by others for the quality or quantity of his cloth, and thus open to envy.

This evidence of the functional uses of the evil eye belief was subjected to numerical analysis, based on my census of weavers performed in 1965 and again during a follow-up study in 1971. The data confirmed the social function of the evil eye amuletry. According to the 1971 census, half of 190 working weavers maintained modal production rates; they did not overembellish their looms with fishtails or other talismans. About 10 percent, fast weavers, covered their looms with fishtails and displayed personal amulets. By 1971, another 10 percent had moved their looms into their homes, where the talismans were no longer needed as the loom was shielded from public view.

Although there is some overlap in the figures due to the possession of multiple looms by certain individuals, another fourth of the weavers could be classified as slow workers who did not keep up with the production rate during the day. Several of these men performed make-up work at night in the presence of others at leisure; these night weavers, though tolerated, often surrounded their looms with talismans, thus fending off intervention by their companions. They said the fishtails improved their weaving strength; they associated the fishtails with the eating of fish, which is believed to increase one's strength and stamina. (Indeed, among these coastal weavers, fish is considered to be a better food than mutton, which is normally considered the ideal flesh in Arab Muslim society.) In all, about one-third of the weavers employed multiple anti-evil-eye talismans as open symbols of norm-breaking output or work schedules.

A dozen men—most of whom were rapid weavers—made no use of amuletry on their looms. They had acquired reputations as regular consumers of alcoholic beverages and they imbibed the drinks, a sin against Islam, discreetly in their weaving shops rather than in the presence of womenfolk and respected kin at home. (Only confirmed alcoholics drank openly regardless of locale and company in this society—drinking is viewed as shameful.) An extraordinary rationale emerged from questioning informants about drinking behavior: they believed that consumption of alcohol by weavers served both economic and mystical purposes. Drinkers felt they could work better by using wine or beer as refreshment during the workday, rather than tea, and they often exceeded the production quota. They placed their bottled spirits (wine, beer) next to their looms within sight of passersby and shared them with drinking companions. Unlike other weavers, who associated according to age groups, imbibers spanned a wide range of ages from late adolescence to late middle age. They were bound together by their shared need for the immoral beverage.

However, symbolic display of the bottle was considered by the population of the community at large to be an inverse form of anti-evil-eye amuletry. Nondrinkers explained that men who sinned by consuming alcohol conspired with the Devil. Satan gave them the strength to weave rapidly and prevented supernatural misfortune from the glance of others, since as "sons of the Devil" they were immune to the invidious or envious sentiments of ordinary men. Obviously incapable of benefiting from the blessing of God conferred by pious words or amulets such as the fish, the drinking weavers replaced this symbol of good with the bottle—a symbol of evil.

However, drinkers did not often weave at night, as they used these hours to party together, and they spent a good deal of their income on the purchase of black-market wine and beer smuggled in from a coastal town. Thus, their higher profits from weaving did not substantially improve their living standards. Indeed, their families often wanted for daily food needs, and this, too, lowered the drinkers' reputation in the community. Children were taught to avoid such families, as it was generally thought that men who drank might use the evil eye on others. In short, avoidance of the eye reinforced the social boundaries between ordinary men and drinkers, perpetuating the deviant status of the latter through ostracism, while moral values were reaffirmed by the majority opposition to alcohol. Symbolic inversion of evil eye mystique functioned to stereotype and devalue deviance and to redress economic disparity.

Conclusion

The extremes of overproduction and nonconformity, as illustrated above, have been shown to be associated with concepts of good and evil, piety and sin, or moderation and excess in Tunisian village society. The belief in the evil eye here becomes a symbolic formula for expressing notions of group solidarity and social control, as well as a rationale for deviant behavior and economic differentiation. Hence, the function of this belief in small-scale social structures may be viewed as crystallization of group norms and values to informally regulate ambiguous areas of interaction. These processes operate within a context of social and economic parity and competition that has limits externally determined by the wider economy and society. The evil eye spreads an umbrella of mystical unity over the village social entity that perpetuates itself by marriage and residence as well as by work. The work norms impose a social schedule on weaving tending to standardize quantity of output and encouraging cooperation and parity among co-weavers, despite their competitive position vis-à-vis one another on the market. For many years there has been an excess of weavers; only though the limitation of total production have most men earned sufficient profit to cover their family expenses. The daily "portion" of cloth represents a golden mean that most weavers and their wives, even the poorly skilled, can attain; because of the common belief in the evil eye, it is not usually exceeded.

However, as the labor pool melted away by emigration (nearly a 50 percent decrease from 1956 to 1971), the increased profit incentives for individuals and the loosening of the social networks capable of applying pressure led to a disintegrative process that unraveled the tight knot of weaving quotas and the male domination of handloom weaving. This accounts for a recent tendency by isolated men to move looms into the home for increased output as social interaction among weavers declined. In addition, the sexual division of labor has been disrupted by the employment of women as weavers on in-house looms. This radical breach of custom was unknown before 1965, but by 1971 had become the most important source of additional loom labor supply.[6]

Finally, there remains the problem of external domination of community weavers by market-town merchants, a persistent phenomenon that repeated attempts at cooperative organization have failed to alter. Although this topic requires more detailed analysis, it fits into the general picture of status-group conformity and community norms presented in this paper. Community weavers will permit themselves to be exploited for profit by outsiders rather than allow the sale of thread or cloth to fall into the hands of their fellow villagers. This kind of mechanical solidarity has political overtones, since it retards the process of stratification within the community by denying monopoly of productive resources to anyone. Economic parity is closely associated with mystical beliefs about power and sin and with the moral value of egalitarianism in Islam. The evil eye is a form of symbolic communication that invokes the use of amuletry to shield weavers against the leering eyes of their neighbors—a form of social control.

NOTES

1. The notion of "function" used here derives from the school of sociological analysis exemplified in Dorothy Emmet's book, *Function, Purpose and Powers*.
2. See Spooner, this volume.
3. I am indebted to Paul Rosenblatt for the notion of indirect communication by "magical" codes of messages customarily recognized as encouraging or discouraging intimacy. This interpersonal nexus also figures in traditional methods employed for "curing" illness with humoral therapy. As suggested in my article on humoral therapy in Tunisia ("Ill Humour and Bad Blood"), these two sets of beliefs may be interdependent. Cross-cultural comparison of mystical "prevention" through deflection of the evil eye should be fitted into the context of alchemical concepts of antidotes for illness and misfortune exemplified by "blood" beliefs common in the Mediterranean world and the Near East; these involve use of powerful foods, medicines, and rituals of restoration.
4. In 1965–66 I carried out detailed ethnography in one such community, Lamta, described in my doctoral thesis at the University of Manchester, 1969.
5. Amulets are worn on the person; talismans are attached to personal property. The symbols remain the same.
6. This will be the subject of subsequent publications.

BIBLIOGRAPHY

Despois, J. *La Tunisie orientale, Sahel et Basse Steppe*. Paris: Presse Universitaire de France, 1955.
Durkheim, E. *De la division du travail social*. Paris: Alain, 1893.

De Montety, H. *Femmes de Tunisie*. Paris: Mouton, 1958.

Emmet, D. *Function, Purpose and Powers*. Philadelphia: Temple University, 1972.

Evans-Pritchard, E. E. *Essays in Social Anthropology*. London: Faber, 1963.

Ferchiou, Sophie. "Differenciation sexue-le d'alimentation au Djerid (Sud Tunisien)," *l'Homme,* 1969, pp. 64–85.

Gluckman, M. *Custom and Conflict in Africa*. Oxford: Blackwells, 1955.

Malinowski, B. *Magic, Science, and Religion and Other Essays*. Glencoe, Ill.: The Free Press, 1948.

Spooner, Brian. "The Evil Eye in the Middle East," in *Witchcraft, Confessions and Accusations,* M. Douglas, ed. Association of Social Anthropologists Monograph no. 9. London: Tavistock, 1970.

Stambouli, F. "Ksar Hellal et sa region: contribution à une sociologie du changement dans les pays en voie de developpement." Unpublished thesis, Université de Paris, 1964.

Teitelbaum. J. M. "Ill Humour and Bad Blood," in *Man-Environment Relations and Health*. Washington, D. C.: American Association for the Advancement of Science, 1972.

—— "Lamta: Leadership and Social Organization of a Tunisian Community." Unpublished Ph.D. thesis, University of Manchester, 1969.

—— "The Social Perception of Illness in Some Tunisian Villages," in *Psychological Anthropology,* group 1, World Anthropology series, Sol Tax, general ed. Chicago: Aldine, 1975.

BRIAN SPOONER

6. ARABS AND IRAN

The Evil Eye
in the Middle East

THE EVIL EYE is a phenomenon familiar to all, but apparently
as little described by ethnographers as it is discussed by those who fear it.
The following notes constitute an attempt to interpret the literature that
exists in the light of my own field experience and discussions with colleagues who have recently worked in Muslim countries.[1] If the attempt
should prove abortive (which is the more possible because the scanty material available includes no detailed case studies) it is nevertheless justified by
the present context, for the concept of the evil eye is reported throughout
Europe, the Middle East, and North Africa, and in so many cultures elsewhere that it may be regarded as a widespread phenomenon.[2] Further, it is
reported in circumstances that show it to be undoubtedly of the same order
of phenomena as witchcraft. Its role in social organization is not as well defined or conspicuous (or as well studied) as that of witchcraft. For instance,
there are no public accusations. In many cases it may be dismissed as a
superstition. Generally, however, it represents a real fear of evil influence
through other people. For instance, in Persia:

BRIAN SPOONER is Associate Professor of Anthropology at the University of Pennsylvania. After
studying at Oxford, he spent six years with the British Institute of Persian Studies. His publications include *The Cultural Ecology of Pastoral Nomads* (1973) and articles on Iranian culture
and civilization, and he has edited *Population Growth: Anthropological Implications* (1972). His
major interests are human ecology and cultural adaptation in the desert areas of the Middle East
and he has done field research in Iran, Afghanistan, and Pakistan. He made the concluding
presentation at the symposium that gave rise to this book.

This chapter originally appeared as "The Evil Eye in the Middle East," in *Witchcraft, Confessions and Accusations,* Mary Douglas, ed., Association of Social Anthropologists of the
Commonwealth Monograph no. 9 (London: Tavistock, 1970), pp. 311–19, and is reprinted
here, with minor stylistic changes, by permission of the author and the publisher.

The possessor of an evil eye may or may not know that he has it. He may have been born with it. . . . It exists in various degrees of power in different people. It is said by some, however, that there are few who actually do have it, and that perhaps most of them do not realise that it is in their possession. One Shaikh expressed the opinion that most of the fear of the evil eye has been created by the imagination of the people, and that the real causes for it are not nearly so numerous as they think, but the fear of it is certainly general, and so many ills and misfortunes are ascribed to it, that most people have been suspected at some time of being the cause of calamities that have come to those with whom they have had contact. . . .[3]

The main general characteristics of the evil eye are that it relates to the fear of envy in the eye of the beholder, and that its influence is avoided or counteracted by means of devices calculated to distract its attention and by practices of sympathetic magic. Jealousy can kill via a look:

Dans une de nos caravanes un mulet de charge, très vigoureux, excita la convoitise d'un bédouin qui le regarda fixement; quelques instants après, le mulet se cassait la jambe. Le propriétaire en reconnut la cause dans le mauvais coup d'oeil du bédouin.[4]

The most common name for the evil eye is simply "the eye" (Arabic *'ayn*). Verbal forms "to eye" or "to eye-strike" are also used. In Persian it is often referred to as "the salty eye" (*cašm-e šur*). Variations such as "the narrow eye," "the bad eye," "the wounding eye," "the look," are also found. In some accounts it is an independent evil power that acts through certain people and in certain situations; in others there are simply certain people whose look is evil.

The concept existed before Islam, and is found under each of the universalistic religions represented in the area (Islam, Christianity, Judaism, and Zoroastrianism). The evidence suggests that it preexisted all of them. Particular beliefs and practices concerning the evil eye tend to be neither exclusive nor well defined: that is, generally in any situation there are other evil agents besides the evil eye that may be blamed; and some of the rites that are used to counteract it may also be practiced for other purposes. The present ethnographic situation is complicated by the fact that the belief operates within the framework of these formal universalistic religions,[5] and the spread of these religions may possibly be responsible for much of the uniformity of practices and attitudes concerning it. It is not actually mentioned anywhere in the Koran, but the following quotation—especially the last two lines—is a text commonly cited in support of the belief in Islamic countries:

In the Name of God, the Merciful, the Compassionate
Say: "I take refuge with the Lord of the Daybreak,
from the evil of what he has created,
from the evil of darkness when it gathers,
from the evil of women who blow on knots,
from the evil of an envier when he envies." [6]

It is a vague text, which obviously makes room for popular explanations of the problem of evil alongside more formal theological resolutions.

Knotting pieces of thread and blowing on objects and patients are common in black and white magic rituals throughout the area. The formal religion is made use of to ward off the evil eye, as it is also to scare away *jinn* and other evil influences. Certain verses of the Koran are particularly effective, spoken or written. On the northern side of the Mediterranean, besides the crucifix, obscenity, in a sense the opposite of religion, is much used to deflect the evil eye. However, in Islamic countries there is no reference to its use in this context (unless the origin of the Beja women's coiffure is phallic). [7] Such a general difference may perhaps be related to other general differences between Islam and Christianity, such as the different orientation of each toward sex and marriage, but there are also many minor local variations in ritual that bear no relation to the religious regime.

Variations also occur from place to place in the application of the belief, but in general the evil eye may be posited as the cause of any misfortune from the most trivial to sudden death, [8] though a gradual wasting sickness seems to be thought of as its most characteristic effect. There are examples of its influence being feared because of the visit of a particular person, invariably a stranger or someone with some unusual physical trait; and there are ritual practices for its neutralization where a particular misfortune, especially sickness, might be alleviated. In general, it is unusual people—persons who for some reason or other do not fully belong to the closely knit community, either because they are strangers or because they have some physical defect or abnormality, not necessarily of the eye or sight—who are suspected of being vehicles of the evil eye. A stranger is thought of as a temporary vehicle. A man with a physical defect is likely to be suspected of having been born with the evil eye. A cognate conception of an evil tongue is also found in some communities, and a Turkman saying states that the eye alone does no harm unless the agent also speaks envious words (*viz, wez deghmez, dil degher*). [9] In the east of Persia it is said that "the loving eye is more dangerous than the evil eye" (*cašm-e nāz az cašm šur bad-tar ast*). This warns of the dangers of, for example, the doting glance of a mother. I am inclined to interpret this as an extension of the concept of the evil eye. An outsider envies, an insider dotes. Both attitudes are forms of undue attention.[10]

Finally, it is interesting that observers of nomadic communities devote very little attention to the evil eye, and certainly much less in general than do observers of peasant communities. The concept exists among nomads, and their children are often covered with prophylactic charms, but other precautions and the find-the-culprit rituals are seldom if ever seen. This situation could be due to the much greater mobility of nomads both as herding groups and as individuals. Nomadic communities have a better-defined and more inclusive role structure than peasant communities. Among nomads there is no private life, and the stranger-guest is an integral feature in the life of the community. Among peasants, where each family jealousy guards its privacy, the guest is entertained by similar, perhaps more conspicuous rituals, but is nevertheless in most cases separated by a wall from the private life of the family.

A brief, generalized summary of the facts relating to the belief as far as they are known, and of the relevant sources of ethnography, is given below. Meanwhile, if I may hazard an interpretation at this stage: the concept of the evil eye appears to be an institutionalized psychological idiom for the personalization, or simply the personification, of misfortune, in particular insofar as misfortune, or the fear of it, may relate to the fear of outsiders [11] and their envy. The cognate idea of an "evil tongue" has been mentioned. A further cognate idea of an "evil soul," being evil that comes by way of the breath, is also reported.[12] Of the possible modes of communication, only actual physical touching is not represented. It is interesting that, concerning these four modes of communication, the influence of evil is communicated most commonly via a look, whereas the complementary influence of good (from *baraka*) is communicated by touch. Why the evil eye (and not the evil tongue or the evil breath) should be so widespread a phenomenon is probably a psychological rather than a sociological question. However, staring is an act with connotations that vary from inauspiciousness to downright rudeness, according to culture. Marçais cites "the naturally injurious power of a strange and staring look." [13]

The Attack

In the case of personalization, the suspected vehicle of the influence of the evil eye is invariably a person who is in some measure an outsider in the immediate group and could in some way be tempted to envy. Therefore, persons with obvious physical or economic defects are especially suspect, whereas pregnant women and small children are the most vulnerable. Beauty is always vulnerable, and it has been suggested that the origin of the veil is connected with the fear of the evil eye. Similarly, individuals passing through *rites de passage* are particularly vulnerable. The following are some of the more common categories and traits that may attract suspicion:

1. Women are particularly liable to suspicion. Since their social role is more strictly defined than men's, and they are at a physical and social disadvantage to start with, any unusual behaviour, or any trait that prevents them from fulfilling their women's function, may make them suspect: e.g., barrenness, brashness, unexplained visits, etc.

2. Beggars are generally suspect, and owe much of their income to the suspicion. The practice of presenting a guest with any object he admires, similarly, is very probably connected with the evil eye in origin.

3. Blue or green eyes are often cited, but this appears to be true only in those parts where these are really rare.[14] Any other peculiarity of the eyes or sight may be equally suspect.

4. The stare of certain animals, in particular the snake, is thought to carry the evil eye.

5. Any form of admiration is feared as a potential vehicle for the evil eye.

The Defence-Selected Devices

Before the fact, as a regular ritual or habitual practice:

1. Fumigation, for which the wild rue in particular is almost universally used.

2. Use of charms, amulets, etc. Young children in particular are often covered with them. They may take many forms, from sheep's eyes to miniscule Korans. Cowry, agate, blue beads, onyx, horn, and mirrors are very widely used; and, as with the veil, the origin of the wearing of jewelry may be connected with fear of the evil eye. Tattooing is also cited. Brightly

coloured clothing is also used, and pieces of red rag are known as inimical to the evil eye (and witchcraft) from Donegal to Japan. Amulets may contain a leopard's claw or strands of wolf's hair, tokens of fierceness.

3. If bright colours distract, dirt disguises. Children are often left filthy and never washed, in order to protect them from the evil eye.

4. Avoidance of ambition and perfection (cf. Nemesis). It is usual to avoid round numbers, even in trade, and a shepherd will not count his sheep. (The "Thousand and One Nights" and other similar figures may derive from this, but see *Encyclopaedia of Islam,* second edition, the article, *"Alf Layla wa Layla"*).

5. The five fingers of the outstretched hand (which is never identifiable as either right or left). This appears to be restricted to North Africa, perhaps because it has acquired a religious symbolism among Shi'a Muslims further east, among whom it represents the hand of Abbas that was severed at the battle of Kerbala.[15]

After the (suspected) *fact* (for instance, in the case of sickness, or if someone has expressed undue admiration for one's child):

1. Fumigation (as above).

2. The burning of alum, which pops like an eye bursting.

3. Recitation of various formulae.

4. Salt is generally regarded as inimical to the evil eye, and there are a number of practices that involve its use.

5. The giving away of sweets at joyful events or after particular successes may be explained as an effort to prevent envy and the evil eye,[16] and a general symbolic opposition between sweet and salt has been suggested.[17]

6. Spitting.

Divining the culprit: generally, a number of small objects (e.g. eggs, stones) are taken, and each is designated to represent a particular suspect. A simple ritual then exposes the culprit. A common method is for someone to hold an egg lengthwise between his palms, and to press on it as the name of each suspect is spoken. At the name of the guilty person the egg will break. When the cause is thus established, a common measure is to obtain a piece of the guilty person's clothing and burn it, either separately, in the fumigation ritual, or with a piece of alum.

NOTES

1. In the preparation of this short survey I have greatly benefited from discussion with the following, who have recently conducted anthropological fieldwork in Islamic communities: Dr. Nadia Abu-Zahra, Mr. D. H. M. Brooks, Dr. and Mrs. R. Tapper. Dr. Rodney Needham also kindly drew my attention to some items of bibliography.
2. See, for example, Andrée, pp. 35–45.
3. Donaldson, pp. 15–16.   4. Jaussen, p. 377.   5. See Hocart.
6. Koran 113 in Arberry, vol. 2, p. 362.   7. See Murray, p. 72.
8. See, for example, Barth, p. 145.
9. Personal communication from Dr. William G. Irons.
10. See Evans-Pritchard, p. 15.
11. Barth (p. 145) states that "since it is the unconscious envy that harms, only friends, acquaintances and relations (khodeman—one's own people) cast the evil eye, while declared enemies are impotent to do so." In my own experience it is not only unconscious envy that harms. Further, "one's own people" in Persia is a concept that varies according to context, and, among peasants, would not normally include acquaintances or more distant relatives. It is, however, just these categories (again, in my own experience) that are most open to suspicion. Similarly, in the peasant society of southern Egypt, "which suffers greatly from the stresses and strains that obtain between relatives," it is especially necessary to guard against the effects of the evil eye from relatives (Ammar, p. 62). Presumably this must mean relatives outside the economic family unit.
12. Canaan, p. 181.   13. See Marçias.
14. According to Amin (p. 58), in Egypt the color green (akhḍar) is inauspicious and blue is auspicious, and he actually goes on to say that blue is confused with green.
15. See Donaldson, p. 208.   16. Barth, p. 145.
17. By Mr. D. H. M. Brooks in a personal communication.

BIBLIOGRAPHY

This is not a comprehensive bibliography of the evil eye, but includes all the references which have come to my notice concerning the Near East and which may be said to have some analytical value (Dr. Rodney Needham kindly drew my attention to some of them). Few even of these are rewarding. I have not so far been able to consult Einssler, Seligmann, or Koşay.

Of the more noteworthy items: Hasting's Encyclopaedia has a good general article, but is mostly concerned with Europe. Elworthy provides an impressively detailed catalogue of practices, devices, and gestures, mainly from southern Europe but with references to North Africa. The best brief general account for the Islamic world is Marçais. The most detailed account of Islamic practices is in Westermarck (chapter 8); most of the practices he catalogues were observed in Morocco, but are found throughout North Africa and the Near East. The first chapter of Donaldson is devoted to attitudes and practices observed in the northeast of Iran; and Doutté has ten pages (pp. 317–27) on the evil eye in the Maghreb. All these works also contain further bibliography.

Amin, Ahmad. *Qāmūs al-'Ādāt wa'l-Taqālid wa'l-Ta 'ābir al Miṣriyya* (in Arabic). Cariro, 1953.

Ammar, H. *Growing up in an Egyptian Village*. London: Routledge and Kegan Paul, 1954.

Andrée, Richard. *Ethnographische Parallelen und Vergleiche*. Stuttgart: Maier, 1878. Pp. 35–38 (includes further bibliography).

Arberry, A. J. *The Koran Interpreted*. 2 vols. London: Allen and Unwin, 1956.

Barth, F. *Nomads of South Persia*. London: Allen and Unwin, 1961. Pp. 144 ff.

Blackman, W. S. *The Fellahin of Upper Egypt*. London: Cass, 1968. Pp. 218 ff.

Canaan, T. "The Child in Palestinian Arab Superstition," *Journal of the Palestinian Oriental Society* 7 (1927).

Donaldson, B. A. *The Wild Rue*. London: Luzac, 1938.

Douglas, Mary. "Thirty Years After: Witchcraft Oracles and Magic among the Azande," in *Witchcraft Confessions and Accusations*, M. Douglas, ed. Association of Social Anthropologists Monograph no. 9. London: Tavistock, 1970.

Doutté, E. *Magie et Religion dans l'Afrique du Nord*. Algiers: A. Jourdan, 1908.

Einssler, Lydia. "Das Böse Auge," *Zeitschrift der Deutschen Palästinavereins*, 10 (1889), 200 ff.

Elworthy, F. T. *The Evil Eye*. London: Murray, 1895.

Evans-Pritchard, E. E. *Nuer Religion*. Oxford: Clarendon Press, 1956.

Foster, George. "The Anatomy of Envy: A Study of Symbolic Behavior," *Current Anthropology* 13 no. 2 (1972) pp. 165–202.

Granqvist, H. *Birth and Childhood among the Arabs*. Helsinki and Copenhagen: Helsingfors, Soderstrom, 1947.

—— *Child Problems among the Arabs*. Helsinki and Copenhagen: Helsingfors, Soderstrom, 1950.

—— *Marriage Conditions in a Palestinian Village*. 2 vols. Helsinki: Akademisches Buchhandlung, 1931 and 1935.

—— *Muslim Death and Burial*. Helsinki, 1965.

Hastings, J. *Encyclopaedia of Religion and Ethics*. Edinburgh: Clark, 1908.

Hedayat, S. "Čašme-e-zakhm," in *Neirangestan* (in Persian), 2d ed. Tehran, 1956.

Hocart, A. M. "The Mechanism of the Evil Eye," *Folklore* 49 (1938), 156–57.

Jaussen, A. *Coutumes arabes au pays de Moab*. Paris: Secaffre, 1908.

Kennedy, John. "Psychosocial Dynamics of Witchcraft Systems," *International Journal of Social Psychiatry* 15, no. 3 (1969), 165–78.

Koşay, Hamit. "Efnografya müzesindeki nazarlık, muska ve hamiller," *Türk Etografya Dergisi* 1 (1956), 86–90.

Kriss, R., and H. Kriss-Heinrich. *Volksglaube im Bereich des Islam*. 2 vols. Weisbaden: O. Harrassowitz, 1960–62.

Lane, E. W. *The Manners and Customs of Modern Egyptians*. 1836. Reprint, London: Dent, Everyman's Library, 1966. Pp. 58, 59, 148, 256 ff., 511, 513.

Marçais, P. H. " 'Ayn," in *Encyclopaedia of Islam*, 2nd ed.

Murray, G. W. *Sons of Ishmael*. London: Routledge and Kegan Paul, 1935.

Schlimmer, J. L. *Terminologie Medico-Pharmaceutique et Anthropologique*. . . . *Tehran (lithograph), 1874.*

Seligmann, Sigfried. *Der Böse Blick.* 2 vols. Berlin: Barsdorf, 1910.

—— *Die Zauberkraft des Auges und das Berufen.* Hamburg, 1922.

Szyliowicz, Joseph S. *Political Change in Rural Turkey: Erdemli.* Paris: Mouton, 1966. P. 105.

Thomas, Bertram. *Arabia Felix.* London: Cape, 1938. Pp. 80–81, 94, 144, and photo facing p. 14.

Thompson, R. C. *Semitic Magic.* London: Luzac, 1908.

Weber, Max. *The Theory of Social and Economic Organization.* New York: The Free Press, 1948.

Westermarck, E. *Ritual and Beliefs in Morocco.* London: Macmillan, 1926.

RONALD A. REMINICK

7. ETHIOPIA

The Evil Eye Belief among
the Amhara

VARIATIONS OF THE BELIEF in the evil eye are known throughout much of the world, yet surprisingly little attention has been given to explaining the dynamics of this aspect of culture.[1] The Amhara of Ethiopia hold to this belief. Data for this study were gathered among the Mänze Amhara of the central highlands of Shoa Province, Ethiopia.[2] Their habitat is a rolling plateau ranging in altitude from 9,500 to 13,000 feet. The seasons vary from temperate and dry to wet and cold. The Amhara are settled agriculturists, raising primarily barley, wheat, and a variety of beans and importing *teff* grain, cotton, and spices from the lower and warmer regions in the gorges and valleys nearby. Amhara technology is simple, involving the bull-drawn plow, crop rotation, soil furrowing for drainage, and some irrigation where streams are accessible. The soil is rich enough to maintain three harvests annually. Other important technological items include the sickle, the loom, and the walking and fighting stick for the men; the spindle, the large clay water jug, the grindstone, and cooking utensils for

RONALD REMINICK teaches in the Department of Anthropology at The Cleveland State University. He received his Ph.D. from the University of Chicago and specializes in psychological anthropology, social anthropological theory, and peoples of Africa; he has also done research in Jamaica.

The research on which this paper was based was conducted in Ethiopia, among the Mänza Amhara, in 1967–69.

This chapter has been reprinted with minor stylistic changes, from *Ethnology* 8, no. 3 (July 1974), pp. 279–91. The Editor is grateful to the editors of *Ethnology* for permission to publish it in this volume.

the women. The most highly prized item of technology is the rifle, which symbolizes the proud warrior traditions of the Amhara and a man's duty to defend his inherited land.

The homestead is the primary domain of authority within the larger political structure. The homestead varies in size from that of a nuclear family to a large hamlet consisting of several related families and their servants, tenants, and former slaves. The system of authority can be characterized in terms of Weber's patriarchalism, where a group is organized on the basis of kinship and economics with authority exercised by a particular person controlling the resources upon which the group depends.[3] Obedience and loyalty are owed to the person rather than to the role or the rule, and this person rules only by the consent of the group members who stand to gain a portion of their patriarch's wealth as a legacy upon his death. This institution of patriarchal authority is reinforced by a cultural emphasis on male qualities of aggressiveness oriented around the acquisition and defense of land. Land is the fundamental requirement of the patriarchal system, for without it a man cannot fulfill his basic role of supporting his dependents and providing a legacy for his children as a reward for their loyalty and service. But land is a scarce resource, and there are often more claims to land than can be supported. Thus, closest siblings may unite against a more distant relative to maintain land among themselves, or siblings may compete for scarce land among themselves, becoming bitter enemies and dividing the kinship or domestic group.

The Amhara peasant's supernatural world includes both Christian and pagan elements. Although Monophysite Christianity is the legitimate religion of the Amhara people, who in fact define their tribal identity largely in terms of their Christian God, the pagan or "nonlegitimate" systems of belief also play an important role in the everyday routine of the peasant's social and cultural life. There are essentially four separate realms of supernatural beliefs. First, there is the dominant Monophysite Christian religion involving the Almighty God, the Devil, and the saints and angels in Heaven. Second, there are the *zar* and the *adbar* spirits, "protectors" who exact tribute in return for physical and emotional security and who deal out punishments for failure to recognize them through the practice of the appropriate rituals. Third is the belief in the *buda,* a class of people who possess the evil eye, and who exert a deadly power over the descendents of God's "chosen children." The fourth category of beliefs includes the *čiraq* and *satan,* ghouls and devils that prowl the countryside, creating danger to unsuspecting persons who cross their path.

The Status of the Evil Eye People

In contrast to much of sub-Saharan Africa, among the Amhara evil power is not attributed to a person occupying a status at a point of social disjunction within the structure of social relations. Rather, those people who are believed to have a dangerous power are not a part of Amhara society. The *buda* or evil eye people are a completely separate category of population of different ethnic origin, with a rather minimum amount of interaction with the Amhara people. The *buda* own no land and therefore work in handicrafts, making pots from clay, fashioning tools from iron, and weaving cloth from hand-spun cotton and sheep's hair. They are known generally as *ṭayb*. The term is derived from the noun *ṭebib*, which means "craftsman." It is also associated with an idea that means "to be wise" or "to be very clever." The terms *ṭayb* and *buda* are synonymous. To be *buda* is to have the evil eye. The term "evil eye" is also known as *'ayn og* and sometimes *kifu 'ayn*. It designates the power to curse and destroy and reincarnate, harnessing the labor of the dead for one's own ends.

The beautiful craftsmanship of the *buda*'s work is one sign of his status. The finely made, well-proportioned water pots with their black finish are unmatched by any Amhara peasant who would deign to make one in the first place. Fashioning tools from iron takes considerably more skill and is not practiced by anyone but the *ṭayb* people. Although weaving is associated with the *ṭayb* people, many Mänze peasants have also taken up the skill, not as a trade but to accumulate needed cash. Yet the peasants say the *ṭayb* know a special form of weaving that the Amhara cannot learn. There is, though, a critical distinction made by the Amhara peasant that frees him from the stigma of the craft, *viz.*, that he did not inherit the trade from his father.

There are, then, two major social categories. The *rega* are those people whose ancestry are *niṣu atint*, of "clean bone," unblemished by social stigma or bodily catastrophe, such as leprosy. They are the "noble people." Most Amhara trace their lineages to a near relative or ancestor who had wealth and status and who was patron of many who worked the land of his estates. A *rega* person is known by his community; his relatives and ancestors are known, and hence he cannot be suspected of being "impure." The *buda* person, on the other hand, is one who has inherited through his line the lower status. One may inherit status through either the mother's or the father's line, or both. One cannot avoid the status of *buda*. It is the *buda*'s destiny to be born into the tradition.

Anyone whose ancestry or kin are unknown may be suspect. If one is suspected of being *buda,* he may be liable to accusation by a family that fears that he "attacked" or "ate" or "stabbed" one of their members. Accusation must be carried out on one's own without the sanction of the courts. If one marries a person whose family is unknown, and it is later learned that the relatives were of *buda* status, the *rega* spouse will be forced to effect a divorce and another spouse of "clean bone" will then be found as a substitute. Sometimes the spouse who is *buda* will be driven from the community, or more rarely killed, for attempting to taint a family's line.

There is no sure way to recognize *budas,* for their physical qualities may not differ discernibly from those of other people. They may be thinner than usual, because their blood is believed to be thinner than a normal Amhara person's blood. They may have an eye deformity or suffer discharge of tears or pus from their eyes. They may tend to look sidewise at people, or they may have very light skin, or they may be believed to have an ashen substance in their mouths and be unable to spit saliva. But these qualities are not, in themselves, sufficient to arouse suspicion. There are other more convincing characteristics, such as occupation. If a stranger comes to town and is overly friendly, suspicion may be aroused that he is too eager to befriend others, and hence, possibly overanxious about concealing his true identity. The relations of *buda* people with *rega* people are in *status quo,* being neither overly peaceful nor overly combative. They mix with each other easily, as in court, in the shops, and in market places, without repercussions, as long as their social relations are on a superficial basis.

The Attack of the Evil Eye

The real threat of the *buda* people to the *rega* people is the ever-present possibility of attack. Most people are fearful of even mentioning the *buda,* especially at night, because if they are overheard by a *buda* he will become angry and may "eat" one of the family, thereby causing sickness or death. A person is most vulnerable to being "eaten" when the *buda* sees fear, worry, or anxiety in his potential victim. Therefore, it helps to maintain one's composure when in the presence of a *buda,* acting naturally, as if the *buda* did not matter at all. The peasant who is especially good looking or whose child is considered beautiful, or someone who does something extraordinary, may fear the attack of the evil eye because of the envy believed to be kindled in the *buda.* The attack is not limited to human beings. The evil eye can attack any living object. When a person is "eaten" he may know immediately that he has been attacked, for the consequences may occur at the same time as the strike. But the symptoms can just as easily be delayed for a few hours, a day, or a week, rarely longer. If a *buda* has planned an attack on some victim, but this victim suddenly falls ill before the strike is to be made, then the *buda* may merely wait patiently to see the outcome of the patient's illness. If the person recovers, the *buda* may then attack. If he dies, the *buda* will then attend to the activity that involves *buda* people with the dead. It is believed that when one is feeling ill the body is more vulnerable than ever to an attack by the evil eye.

The process of attack may occur in one of several different manners. Because of the power of the evil eye, *buda* people can change into hyenas and roam the countryside at night. It is convenient for a *buda* to attack a victim in this form in order to conceal his human identity. The Amhara attach great salience to the hyena, partly because they believe in both the natural and the supernatural forms of this animal. If the *buda,* in seeking out a victim, assumes the form of the hyena, the transformation takes place by his first taking off the hair and then rolling in the ashes of the hearth. Once transformed into a hyena, he then searches for a victim, and on finding one, fixes the unfortunate person with an evil gaze, returns home, rolls in the ashes to turn back into human form, and waits for the victim to die. The second method of attack involves the evil eye person's finding a victim, twisting the root of a certain plant, and forming a loop with this root as if tying a knot. The loop is then drawn smaller very slowly, and while this is being done, the victim dies. After the victim is buried, the *buda* squats by the graveside and slowly loosens the knot while shouting to the corpse to arise. The body is exhumed and the grave is then closed up again by retightening the knot. The third method of attack involves giving the evil eye gaze to the victim and then waiting for his death. After burial the body is exhumed by carrying two round, thin, lentil-pancake breads to the grave, one lying flat and the other folded twice. Unfolding the one bread opens the grave and brings out the body. Folding up the other recloses the grave.

The people most liable to attack are those who have a bit more wealth than the average person, who are handsome, and who are proud of their beautiful children. Those who become especially liable to attack are those who become too familiar with the *buda* person, which heightens one's chances of succumbing to the gaze of the evil eye. One comes into physical proximity with *buda* people in daily affairs, but social distance is usually maintained. A likely danger to the *rega* people is the presence of a beautiful *buda* woman or handsome *buda* man. A *rega* who sleeps with a *buda* will grow thinner and thinner because the eye of the *buda* will suck the blood out of the victim, causing the victim to lose his or her appetite and to become weak and helpless. When a *rega* is attracted to a *buda* and the *buda* wishes to draw the *rega* nearer, the *buda* will wait for a moment of privacy and then will utter to the *rega* something about seeing the genitals revealed through the *rega*'s clothes. This will fill the *rega* with excitement and then the *rega* will "fall with" the *buda* lover. The warm, affectionate relationship can be maintained without serious danger; but when there is a quarrel, the *rega*, already weakened by the blood given up to the *buda*, will be "eaten" and become seriously ill.

However the attack is effectuated, and however the corpse is taken from the grave, the ultimate goal of the *buda* is to use the victim as a slave. After being exhumed, the corpse is taken to the house of the *buda*, where it is brought back to life in order to serve the *buda*. But the slave is mute, unable to utter a single sound. The *buda* owns two switches. One switch is used to turn the slave into a pot when visitors come; and then when the outsiders have left, a rap on the pot with the other switch transforms the pot into a slave again. In this way outside interference is prevented. When the slave is treated cruelly, it will shed silent tears, desperately trying to weep. (It is interesting to note that to be silent in the presence of one's superiors and to suffer indignities in silence are the obligation of children and the traits attributed to the despised dog.) The slave of the *buda* does not go on indefinitely in its risen state. After seven years the body begins to disintegrate, finally turning into ashes and leaving the *buda* without a "helper."

The *buda*'s distinctive activities are not fully intentional. The *buda* has within his body a quality or power known as *qalb*. *Qalb* is a subtle, internal, unconscious desire to perform those activities that make the *buda* so notorious. In the *buda*'s daily interactions with the *rega* people of the community, there is really little difference between the two groups, both sharing feelings of love and hate, envy and covetousness, anger and aggression. But the *buda* has this additional power gained from the association with the Devil that creates an illegitimate advantage over those of higher status and greater legitimate advantage. The *buda*, by his very nature, must "eat" others. He does this in order to better his chances for gaining opportunities and achieving success in his daily life among the *rega* people. He uses his power, then, to make himself equal with others who have more land, more "helpers" such as tenants, servants, and former slaves, and thus he attempts to acquire those objects, persons, and services that he covets among the *rega* people. There is a difference of opinion as to whether the *buda* himself can be the object and victim of evil eye attack. Some Amhara say that just as the *rega* fight among themselves for the wealth of the lineage, so the *buda* people fight and attack each other with the evil eye for more equal shares of wealth. But other Amhara say that this is not true; that the *buda* people have much more to gain from the *rega*, and furthermore, know how to protect themselves from each other's attack.

Precautions against Evil Eye Attack

Since amorous relations with *buda* are not condoned by the Amhara, especially by the clergy, the priests teach that one's only protection against a *buda* lover is to crawl to church on one's hands and knees for seven days, the priest's intent being to frustrate the beginnings of such a relationship. Parents who fear their child is weak and vulnerable to the influence of the evil eye may, on the advice of a *däbtärä* (lower-order clergyman), adopt the custom of addressing their child in the gender opposite to the child's actual sex. The custom of shaving the heads of children, leaving only a tuft of hair over the former fontanelle of the boys and a ring of hair around the heads of the girls, provides protection against minor attacks of lice, most often considered initiated by an envious *buda*. If an Amhara is worried about a child's imminent danger from an evil glance, a light, rapid spitting into the child's face provides a short-term protection. Compliments are always suspect if not accompanied with the invocation, "Let God protect you from the evil eye!" And at feasts all must be served equally lest someone deprived should become envious and curse the food, making the participants sick.

Another precaution taken by the Amhara peasant against the possibility of attack is to be silent and guarded. When one expresses his emotions too freely and becomes too outgoing with others, he places himself in a position of

Figure 7.2 A girl (*left*) and two boys wear little bundles of ground roots and herbs, concocted by a wizard, as safeguard against the evil eye. (The girl also wears a necklace of plastic rings, which is only decorative.) Children of both sexes have their hair shaved except for the top; this is also protection against the evil eye, for one children's malady the eye can inflict is head lice.

Figure 7.1 Girl wearing a *qitab*, believed potent against the evil eye and other sources of malady. The leather roll contains a strip of parchment, written in the ecclesiastical Giïz language, listing illness and misfortunes of peasants together with prayers and exhortations to saints and to God and magic designs in red and black ink. The local wizard can prepare one for Eth. $5 or $10.

vulnerability to the evil eye. This disposition is fairly generalized. When one is seen laughing and joking freely with others it is usually with close and trusted friends and relatives. At most other times the peasant presents a facade of stolidity and silence. In this way one does not attract the attention of an envious *buda*, who may resent persons enjoying themselves while he is not invited to share in the mirth. The custom of hiding one's face behind the large soft cloak, concealing especially the mouth and the nose, is one common way to avoid the penetration of the evil eye.

If a person succumbs to the attack of the evil eye, the family of the deceased may intercede and prevent the *buda* from wresting the corpse from its grave. A member of the family must watch the grave for forty days and forty nights (some say twelve days and twelve nights) after the body has been interred, allowing sufficient time to elapse so that the body will be adequately decomposed and thereby deprive the *buda* of a body to possess. If the grave is watched the *buda* will not come. In this way the family saves its relative from seven years of slavery.

Diagnosis and Cures for the Evil Eye Attack

Diagnosis of the symptoms and subsequent treatment may be carried out in one of four ways. In the first method, if the family members are poor and they know a *däbtärä* of the local church, they may take the patient to him. For a modest fee, he performs a rite over holy water, praying and pronouncing words in the ancient language of Gïïz used in the Christian religious ceremonies. The patient then drinks the holy water and breathes in the smoke of a burning root. The *däbtärä* may find the diagnostic answer in his magic star book, while the holy water and inhaled smoke may effect a cure.

A second alternative is to bring the patient to a wizard, one who has powers gained through agents of the Devil, to communicate with the *zar* spirits and to effect cures for many kinds of illness. First, a silver bracelet is placed on the patient's left wrist. The wizard then goes into a trance, seeking possession by a devil who may reveal the appropriate cure for the illness. To seek out the attacker, a very hot fire is made in the hearth and a piece of metal, a sickle or knife blade, is put into the flames and heated until glowing. The hot metal is applied to the patient's face, making a small pattern of burns. As the wounds heal, the scars will become transferred onto the face of the attacker in the same place and with the same pattern. The family must then seek out the guilty party.

A third method does not involve the use of specialists except an elder member of the family who knows the procedures and whose age gives him a bit better judgment. When a person begins biting his lip it is the first sign that he has been attacked by the evil eye, although this symptom does not always appear. If relatives are around they will first tie the victim's left thumb with string. Then the victim will be made to breathe the smoke from the dung fire. After taking in sufficient dung smoke, the victim gains the power to speak in the spirit and voice of his attacker. The victim begins recounting the chain of events of his attacker that led to the confrontation and the attack. Then the relatives ask the possessed victim what form of compensation should be given to counteract the attack. The victim, speaking in the voice of the attacker, demands some filthy matter such as beer dregs, ashes, a dead rat, or human or animal excrement. The victim eats this and soon cries, "I've left him! I've left my victim!" or something of this order. Then the family knows that the devil has left the body, and the stricken person may now recover. The cure involves active vocal participation. If the victim cannot speak, he will surely die.

The fourth method of diagnosis and counteraction involves the evil eye person in a more direct, mundane way. When the victim is attacked and he begins to bite his lip and to act strangely, he may appear to go into a daze and begin to jump and shout "in tongues." At this point, a relative must try to get the victim to utter the name of his attacker. If he does not, the family may tie a rope to the victim and then have the victim lead the relatives to the house of his attacker. If neither of these tactics is successful, there may be one other indication. If the victim begins crying suddenly, it is a sign that the attacker is in close proximity and that the relatives need only scout the area and seize the *buda* person they come across. If the suspect is found, he is brought to the bedside of the victim, by gunpoint if need be. The relatives take a lock of hair and a bit of clothing from the *buda,* preferably without his knowledge, and then the *buda* is made to spit on the victim and walk over him. A fire is built with the hair and cloth and the victim then breathes in the smoke. He continues inhaling the smoke until he cries, in the voice of the spirit, that the illness has left his body.

No matter what the method, if the *buda* gives up his victim there will be no reprisals by the victim's family. If the victim dies, the *buda* may be ejected from the community or killed.

The Mythology of the Origin of the Buda People

According to the Amhara, the beginnings of *buda* status go back to Creation. It is said that Eve had thirty children, and one day God asked her to show him her children. Eve became suspicious and apprehensive and hid fifteen of them from the sight of God. God knew her act of disobedience and declared the fifteen children she showed God as his chosen children and cursed the fifteen she hid, decreeing that they go henceforth into the world as devils and wretched creatures of the earth. Now some of the children complained and begged God's mercy. God heard them and, being merciful, made some of them foxes, jackals, rabbits, etc., so that they might exist as

Earth's creatures in a dignified manner. Some of the hidden children he left human, but sent them away with the curse of being agents of the Devil. These human counterparts of the Devil are the ancestors of the *buda* people. There occurs a pleat in time and the story takes up its theme again when Christ was baptized at the age of thirty. As told by an old Amhara peasant farmer:

The angry devils, envious of God's favoring Christ while they suffered God's curse, tried to kill Christ. But Christ ran and fled his enemies. He hid in the crevice of a great cliff, sharing it with the giant *gabalo* lizard. While he was hidden, many children were killed by the devils in their search for "God's child," but they were unsuccessful in finding Christ. All the animals were asked to betray the whereabouts of Christ, but they refused and they were beaten and tortured to no avail. But the lizard waved his head from side to side showing Christ's pursuers where he hid. Christ saw this and cursed the lizard so that to this day this lizard still sways his head so. No one could get Christ down out of the crevice in the cliff. They tried with ropes and ladders to no avail. Then, the clever *buda* people made giant tongs of wood and plucked Jesus Christ out of the crevice. The blacksmiths made the nails and the carpenters made the cross and while Christ hung on the cross he cursed those people whose skills made it possible to crucify him.

Some Amhara claim that the Devil is the sole source of *buda* qualities and power. Others say the origin of *buda* existence is different from the source of their power. Although their existence is associated with the Devil, their power comes from a different source only questionably related to the Devil. Although there are several versions of the myth, the following example narrated by an adolescent Amhara student is typical:

The source of *buda* power is an ancient man who has immortality. He has no arms and no legs. He is like a lump of flesh and just sits at a place called Yerimma that is a cave of extremely great depth. He is, indeed, endowed with supernatural powers. Each year the *buda* people make their annual visit to this lump of man with their small children who are just learning to walk and to talk. This ancient man can distinguish between the *rega* who may come and the *buda* themselves. He rejects the former and accepts the latter. The ancient man then teaches the *buda* children all the "arts" to the *buda* trade and then presents the child with the leaf from an *is* plant [also used by devils to make themselves invisible so as to avoid being eaten by the hyena]. And every year each *buda* must make a sacrifice to this ancient man of one human being. The sacrifice is like a tax, and if the *buda* cannot find a suitable victim by the time the sacrifice is due, he must sacrifice his own child.

Interpretation

There are essentially three analytically separable levels of behavior upon which to focus. First, there is the overt and manifest level of verbal behavior that expresses the configuration of ideas and feelings recognized as the evil eye belief system. This level of behavior is explicated through ethnographic description. Second, there is the analysis of values and psychological predispositions, areas of positive attraction, indifference, anger, and fear or dread. The symbols in the cultural configurations, as expressed through the narratives of the Amhara, point out these areas of emotional salience and foci of concern. Through a symbolic analysis particular kinds of themes become evident. Some of these themes are based in the manifest functions of the belief, while others point to covert symbolic and latent functions of the belief system. Third, there is the social context that the symbols express and the social context of the actual behavior that expresses the evil eye belief.

With this approach it is possible to examine "the relationship between explicit cultural forms (symbols) and underlying cultural orientations," [4] where these symbolic forms provide the vehicle for the analysis of the relationships between underlying cultural orientations and observable patterns of sociocultural behavior. Foster [5] offers a caveat that must be taken into consideration when analyzing the motivational significance of a particular belief or custom, which is, original motives often disappear with the institutionalization of the belief or custom, and in its place, habit becomes the primary source for the reinforcement of the pattern. Also Kennedy argues against the more familiar teleological functional interpretations offered by social anthropologists when he suggests that these institutionalized beliefs and customs may themselves be the source of fears, or may be pathological responses to situations that present no real threat and could conceivably be defined in more innocuous terms. In his discussion of witchcraft belief, Kennedy states: "witchcraft systems are forms of institutionalized patterns of psychopathology which tend to be pathogenic and which create built-in self-perpetuating stress systems . . . [and] tend to regularly generate the hate and aggression which they allegedly function to relieve." [6]

Including the evil eye belief within the purview of the problem of witchcraft is not without justification, for although there are quite noticeable differences, the similarities demand some scrutiny. Spooner notes how well known the evil eye belief is to us all, yet how little attention has been given to it by ethnographers: "the concept of the Evil Eye is reported throughout Europe, the Middle East, and North Africa, and in so many cultures elsewhere that it may be regarded as a universal phenomenon. Further, it is reported in circumstances which show it to be undoubtedly of the same order of phenomena as witchcraft." [7]

Douglas, in agreement with Spooner, identifies the evil eye belief as a special case of witchcraft belief that becomes expressed at critical social disjunctions between persons who hold structurally generated enmity toward each other. Her definition of a witch can be generalized to the Amhara's conception of the *buda:* "The witch is an attacker and deceiver. He uses what is impure and potent to harm what is pure and helpless. The symbols of what we recognize across the globe as witchcraft all build on the theme of vulnerable internal goodness attacked by external power." [8]

Douglas fits the evil eye belief into a typology she develops from the cases written up in the volume she edited. She proposes two general categories of witches: (a) the witch as outsider, and (b) the witch as internal enemy. Each of these categories has subtypes. The outsider type can be either (1) a witch not identified or punished, or (2) a witch expelled from the community. In this outsider type, the primary function of accusation is to redefine the boundaries of social solidarity. The witch as internal enemy appears in the more complexly organized societies, where two or more factions are involved within the community. The body of the victim is usually symbolized in the image of the betrayed community, where the internal strength is sapped or polluted by one in close contact with the other members of the community. Where the witch is conceived as an internal enemy, the witch can be identified (1) as a member of a rival faction, where the function of the accusation is to redefine faction boundaries or the faction hierarchy; (2) as a dangerous deviant, where the function of the accusation is to control the deviant in the name of community values; or (3) as an internal enemy with outside liaisons, where the function of accusation is to promote factional rivalry, split the community, and/or redefine the hierarchy. [9] Given this typology, Douglas then suggests an hypothesis for further testing: "when the source of witchcraft power is thought to come from inside the witch, particularly from an area beyond conscious control, the social situation will correspond to type 3 above where the witch is seen as an internal enemy, not as a member of a rival faction." [10]

In the Amhara case, we can recognize similar qualities in the witch defined by Douglas and the *buda* as conceived by the Amhara peasant. However, the correspondence that Douglas suggests is not borne out in the Amhara case. The *buda* is not conceived of as a person internal to the Amhara group. The Amhara conceive of the *buda* as an outsider who nevertheless lives, geographically but not integrally, within the social networks of the Amhara people. Thus, the *buda* does not quite fit into any of the categories that Douglas has proposed. This exception of her typology suggests that much wider comparison is still necessary.

The dominant theme expressed in the Amhara evil eye belief system is one that is shared by possibly all those societies that maintain a belief in the evil eye: the fear of being envied and the interpretation of certain misfortunes as the consequences of another's envy. In Spooner's discussion of the evil eye belief in the Middle East, this theme is especially salient: "the concept of the Evil Eye appears to be an institutionalized psychological idiom for the . . . personification of misfortune, . . . insofar as misfortune, or the fear of it, may relate to the fear of outsiders and their envy." [11]

In his careful analysis of the concept of envy Foster defines envy as the act of looking maliciously upon someone; looking askance at; casting an evil eye upon; feeling displeasure and/or ill will in relation to the superiority of another person. Foster states that envy, along with the closely associated feeling of jealousy, "involves a dyad . . . whose relationship is mediated, or structured, by an intervening property or object." [12] Thus, a jealous person is jealous of what he possesses and fears he might lose, while an envious person does not envy the thing but rather envies the person who has it. Foster considers the predisposition to envy to be most apparent in peasant societies, or in what he calls "deprivation societies" of scarce resources where people hold to the "image of limited good" and where social interaction and transaction is defined and perceived as a "zero-sum" game, and where one's advantage derives from the other's loss. Foster maintains that in those societies where the zero-sum game is the definition of the situation, it is the relative differences between two parties that trigger the omnipresently latent envy into overt expression. He further notes that in primitive and peasant societies, food, children, and health, those things most vital for the survival of the family, rank at the top as objects of envy. Cattle and crops have some but lesser salience.

Congruent with sub-Saharan witchcraft belief in the context of well-defined and enforced rules and norms, envy and its consequences are mitigated to a considerable degree, primarily because the structures both of the family and of the class/caste system involve cultural definitions stipulating that the relationships between status classes or between the generations are noncompetitive. Foster maintains that the function of this kind of definition is to eliminate or mitigate rivalry between persons in different categories of status or between persons in different social classes, thereby lubricating interclass and interpersonal transactions.[13] Among the Amhara, the principle of patriarchal domination maintains order in domestic and political groups. The absence of the patriarch or of a mediating superior authority generates, or is believed to generate, anarchy within a group having no mediating authority among equals. Although this principle holds among the Amhara, the *buda* people are of non-Amhara tribal identity, and hence can only pose a threat to the Amhara by virtue of their being different. This difference, I maintain, is symbolic of what the Amhara detest, fear, or dread.

The *buda* people are "strangers" to the land of the Amhara. Originating from a different region, they are landless and make a living with their manual skills of smithing, tanning, weaving, and pottery making. *Buda* status contrasts with *rega* or "nobility" status. Both are inherited consanguineally on a bilateral basis. The origin myth of the *buda* people expresses the basic themes found in the belief system in general and in certain actual social situations: envy and conflict between siblings who are treated differentially by a superior authority. In the myth, envy and conflict are generated by the curse of God for the sins of the mother Eve. Added to this is God's favoring of his child, Christ, the "chosen" son of God. The story of the envious siblings' hunting down of Christ in order to attain equality among siblings has a strong parallel in real-life situations where a father favors one child with the lion's share of land, creating sibling conflict over the equalization of their rights to their father's land.[14] The myth and the belief have it that the *buda* people inherit their *qalb,* a power gained from the Devil that gives them the uncontrollable drive to "eat" the *rega* people, who happen to be the Amhara, to cause their death, and to bring them back to life as slaves. It is a conception that expresses a dominant theme of envious status inferiors using illegitimate means to gain an advantage over status superiors who possess a legitimate means of domination.

The *buda* belief suggests that the *buda* are the symbolic expression of the latent consequences of unmediated equal-status relationships between men and between a man and a woman. Without pyramidal control mechanisms, this form of relationship generates the anxiety of unstable and unpredictable consequences between two dependent and self-oriented egos, the ultimate consequences of which are symbolized in the logically extended extreme of domination—the relationship of master and slave. The function of the evil eye belief in maintaining the social system can be teleologically interpreted as the displacement of a threat and its projection onto an outgroup. The threat of equal-status rivalry between kin and siblings outside of well-defined situations is projected onto the *buda* people, thereby preserving the internal solidarity (what there is of it) of the Amhara people. *Buda* belief appears to be a function of a power superiority among status equals based on the model of the eldest son as the object of envy by his less fortunate younger siblings, for it is the eldest son, in Mänz, who normally is the favored one and who inherits the lion's share of the father's land.

Belief in the evil eye among the Mänze Amhara, then, has a projective function that, through the transformation from personality trait to cultural configuration, becomes manifest as a form of domination anxiety expressed through culturally legitimated ideas of reference. This projective process is by no means complete, for it is known that the most serious concerns of the Amhara involve sibling and other kin conflicts over unequal usufructuary rights to land. The landless *buda*, who is dependent upon others for his livelihood, is the symbolic reflection of the threat of becoming landless and without authority, *ergo* without identity, because of the ambitions of a more powerful relative or the father's curse of disinheritance.

N O T E S

1. See, for example, Spooner, Foster, and Douglas.
2. The research upon which this paper is based was carried out in the central highlands of Shoa Province, Ethiopia, from July 1, 1967, to March 1, 1969. I wish to acknowledge the financial support of the National Institute of Mental Health. Partial supplementary funding was also made available to me by the Committee on African Studies, University of Chicago.
3. Weber, pp. 346 ff.   4. Ortner, p. 49.   5. Foster, p. 166.
6. Kennedy, p. 177.   7. Spooner, p. 311.   8. Douglas, p. xxx.
9. Ibid., p. xxvii.   10. Ibid., p. xxx.   11. Spooner, p. 314.
12. Foster, p. 168.   13. Ibid., p. 171.
14. Within the structure of this myth a Freudian oedipal theme is present that employs universal types of symbols. The favored son seeks refuge and security in a

crevice of a large cliff, which is the opening to a deep cave. The crevice and cave are classic symbols of female sexuality and maternal succorance. The lizard's phallic function is obvious here. Its presence in the cave and its defense of its abode have very sexual connotations. And the lizard's betrayal of Christ, because of its wish to rid itself of this interloper, is also quite significant in its oedipal function. But the role of the envious and hostile siblings, and Christ's death rather than the lizard's, complicates the problem. It may be that we must look at this theme with more generalized symbolic significance, where the cave represents patriarchal sanctuary and domestic security, and where the lizard could represent the male's jural and sexual rights of domain. Christ is then put in a less favorable light, for the message then becomes one of equal rights among siblings, where Christ has been given unfair advantage by the all-powerful patriarch. The custom of favoritism existing within the structure of patriarchal authority in this Amhara region is, in a subtle way, under criticism for its tendency to generate tension and conflict among the sib group, since it is the sib group that is vital for the protection of the extended family and domestic group.

BIBLIOGRAPHY

Douglas, M. "Thirty Years After: Witchcraft Oracles and Magic among the Azande," in *Witchcraft, Confessions and Accusations,* M. Douglas, ed. Association of Social Anthropologists Monograph no. 9. London: Tavistock, 1970.

Foster, G. M. "The Anatomy of Envy: A Study of Symbolic Behavior," *Current Anthropology* 13 (1972), 165–202.

Kennedy, J. "Psychosocial Dynamics of Witchcraft Systems," *International Journal of Social Psychiatry* 15, no. 3 (1969), pp. 165–78.

Ortner, S. "Sherpa Purity," *American Anthropologist* 75 (1973), 49–63.

Spooner, B. "The Evil Eye in the Middle East," in *Witchcraft Confessions and Accusations,* M. Douglas, ed. Association of Social Anthropologists Monograph no. 9. London: Tavistock, 1970.

Weber, M. *The Theory of Social and Economic Organization.* New York, 1948.

CLARENCE MALONEY

8. INDIA

Don't Say "Pretty Baby" Lest You Zap It with Your Eye—The Evil Eye in South Asia

I BECAME INTERESTED in studying the evil eye after I was suspected several times of having been an invidious influence because I had looked on, while doing anthropological fieldwork in villages in the state of Tamil Nadu in southern India. Here are two such instances.

I visited the house of two brothers of a potter caste daily for two weeks to photograph the complete potting process. Seeing many broken pots about the kiln one day, I inquired the reason for the breakage. The younger brother answered, "All was lost last time because people looked on. This is hand work, isn't it? So eyes shouldn't fall on it."

A few days later it drizzled in the morning, and I did not go to that village. But the potter brothers had fired their kiln on that day, and the following day as they were unloading it I appeared. Many pots were broken, and I again inquired as to the reason.

CLARENCE MALONEY has taught anthropology in several universities and colleges and is presently Visiting Professor in the University of Madras. He lived in South India for twenty years and has done rural development and educational work there. He has done anthropology fieldwork in all the South Asian countries, especially on culture history, village religion and world-view systems, and population and subsistence. He is author of the text *Peoples of South Asia* (1974) and *People of the Maldive Islands* (due 1977), and editor of *South Asia: Seven Community Profiles* (1974) and *Language and Civilization Dynamics in South Asia* (due 1977).

The research on which this article was based was conducted in several South Asian countries during the summers of 1970, 1973, 1974, and 1975.

"It was not hot enough," said the elder brother.

"But what about the drizzle yesterday?" I asked.

"Yes, they spoiled because of the drizzle, too."

But the potter's wife added, "It was because of the drizzle *and* the eye," and so saying, she became wrought up at a crowd of restless boys milling about the kiln and peering in, and proceeded to heave large flakes of dried cow dung at them: "Shoo, go on, get out."

The two men began loading the kiln again, and when it was nearly full the drizzle returned. I remarked that many of the pots had broken during the firing on the previous day.

"Yes, they broke because of the drizzle yesterday," the elder acknowledged, as he prepared to light the fire anyway.

"But your brother and your wife said it was because of the eye," I reminded him.

"One should not look on," he said curtly.

"Who should not? These children, or adults?"

"It's all the same."

"And if I look on?"

"Big people's eyes are not harmful," he said diplomatically.

Then the younger brother gave a fourth reason for the breakage: "Yesterday there was no sun; the pots should dry in the sun so they are hot to the touch before we put them in the kiln."

After all the pots were stacked in, with coconut husks interspersed, the fire was lit underneath, and as it began to take hold the whole family performed *pūjā* (worship rituals) at a little whitewashed mud pyramid shrine at the edge of the kiln. The elder brother, acting as priest, split a coconut and offered it, along with bananas, incense, crimson powder, areca nut and betel leaf, sesame seed with sugar, and a flower. He lit a lamp with fire from the kiln and waved it protectively over the little pyramid. Then he put a spot of sandal paste on the foreheads of his younger brother, his wife, and his children, and concluded the worship by drinking some of the consecrated water in a brass jug. His wife commented, for the benefit of the rich-appearing anthropologist, that it would require 100 rupees to make a respectable platform for the pyramid and that the family had spent all its savings on a recent funeral; they used to sacrifice goats to this patron deity of potters, but now that a goat cost 50 rupees they made do with a chicken three or four times a year, sprinkling the blood around. With the deity's assistance invoked by the completion of *pūjā*, the brothers covered the kiln with straw and black mud to prevent air from flowing down into it, and awaited the outcome.

The following day I arrived as they were unloading the kiln. Lo, half the pots were broken!

"It's all right if five or ten out of a hundred break," the elder brother moaned, "but this is over fifty out of a hundred. The lot is spoiled."

"What is the reason?" I asked again.

"It is the lack of sun to dry the pots. It is the drizzle. It is the eye. All these things caused the pots to split."

"Can you do something so they won't break next time?" I asked, this being the third successive batch to spoil.

"What am I able to do?" he shrugged.

They had indeed done all that could be expected by performing *pūjā*, and who could deny that the eye of a presumably powerful foreigner had as much effect as the drizzle or lack of sun, and in spite of their denial that "big people's" eyes were harmful, I understood by their demeanor that they suspected me.

On another occasion I visited a village to observe the annual festival for the most important deity there. A leaf arbor had been erected in front of the little temple, and it was decked out with fluorescent lights and a rented loudspeaker for the benefit of a hired musical troupe that narrated epic stories for the occasion. I took many pictures, including some of various supplicant rituals inside the little temple. These included a few quick shots of the deity, though not many because the priest objected; it is commonly believed that a camera pointed at a temple deity might affect it. Gods, too, are subject to malevolent eyes. As the night wore on I left, and in the morning started back toward the village to see the goat sacrifices. But many people were coming away from the village, walking in groups and strangely silent. Upon inquiry I was told that shortly after I had left, the electricity in the leaf arbor had gone off. The wire to light the festival had originally been strung by a villager from a utility pole in a field (without authorization, so they could steal the electricity), and that man had immediately gone out to the field to fix the connection. He had been electrocuted, and died on the spot. All the people going from the village in the morning were on their way to view the body. I was advised firmly that the balance of the festival, including the goat sacrifices, had been called off, and it seemed prudent to turn back. I sent word canceling appointments I had made with informants in the village, and was told by friends that my observation of the proceedings and pictures of the deity inside the sanctum were considered to be malevolent, perhaps angering the god. Two months later, however, I was able to resume work in that village without eliciting further comment on the incident.

It was clear from both episodes that people believed that what happened in their universe was not chaotic, but ordered, and that there were reasons for whatever happened, one such reason being the ability of an onlooker to project his psychic power through his eyes.

Who and What Are Susceptible?

Before investigating the cultural ramifications and theoretical possibilities of this phenomenon, I shall discuss how it is believed to operate, and what measures can be taken to counteract it. The most detailed data, including the linguistic evidence, are taken from the Tamil region of South India; but some data come from western India and other parts of the country, and also from Pakistan, Bangladesh, Nepal, Sri Lanka, and the Maldives, for the belief exists in all the major regions and religions of South Asia.

Babies and children are more susceptible to illness caused by the evil eye than are adults; they may even die from it. For example, in a family in the state of Kerala a boy of four suddenly died, though he had not previously been sick. The mother, searching for a reason, concluded that it was because two weeks earlier she had taken the boy on a trip to relatives, thus exposing him to the deleterious and envious glances of strangers. According to the folk diagnosis of disease causation, epidemic diseases affecting adults are often attributable to particular deities, such as the Goddess of Smallpox placated by Hindu villagers everywhere. But babies are more susceptible to the evil eye because they do not have the force of personality to deflect its influence. Also, bad *karma,* the accumulated effect of previous bad deeds, may be invoked in the case of adults, for there is a pervasive if often vague feeling that one's fate is the fruit of one's previous moral behavior; but this is an unsatisfactory explanation of sickness in children, and it is more convenient to blame a stranger's invidious intent.[1]

Pregnant women are susceptible, and may particularly be affected by envious looks of a barren woman. In one household, an old woman cautioned

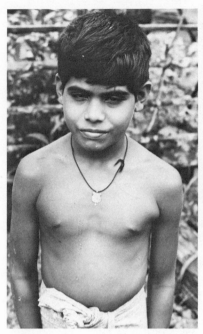

Figure 8.1 In Sri Lanka, a Sinhala Buddhist boy wearing an amulet tied with black cord, similar to those worn by children in all South Asian countries. The amulets and also the cords are prepared by a local healing specialist to avert specific diseases, or to afford protection in general.

Figure 8.2 Clay idols fashioned by the potters described at the beginning of this chapter, commissioned by local villagers for a particular festival. While the idols are drying in the air and awaiting firing, their faces are kept covered so that no evil eye can penetrate them.

the younger women that they should not go out when pregnant unless duly protected by charms, and then not too often.

Women in general are more susceptible than men, and this is more true in the parts of South Asia where the sex roles are strongly contrasted. Women may be affected either by an envious stranger or by a lover's attentive looks. Many, if not most, items of adornment are to some extent related to this belief.

Anyone in the process of eating is susceptible, as is the food in front of him. A hungry look at someone's food may make the eater sick or give him diarrhea. Therefore, a poor or hungry person should not see one eating, nor should one eat in the presence of others without giving them some of the food. This belief is to some extent tied in with the belief that food should retain ritual purity, and that cooked foods have the property of readily transmitting ritual pollution.

Anyone with something enviable is susceptible. A Tamil villager once expressed it thus: "If I come down the road wearing a suit and having money, and if another meets me and sees it, some harm will come to me."

One's animals are affected, especially cattle. If someone sees and favorably comments on a large ox, or a cow with a large udder, the animal might get sick. A stranger glancing at a good cow being milked might spoil the milk or ruin the udder; so milking should be done in a corner or behind a screen. A family in Kerala had a goat with a big udder. Someone came and commented on it, and the next day that goat gave bloody milk. Soon the milk decreased to the point where the goat had to be sold. Another example occurred in the household of an Indian family in Washington, D. C. That family had a special parrot that was trained to say the names of many people. One day friends dropped by and commented favorably on the parrot, and that very afternoon it dropped dead. The cause was thought to be the compliment—and this was in a Christian family.[2]

One's crops and plants are affected. People walking by a field of ripening grain or vegetables may see the abundance and cause the crop to become diseased, or prevent it from ripening; hence protective devices are set up in the fields. One family said that they had had a coconut tree exceptionally laden with coconuts. Someone came by and admired it, and soon the coconut bunches began to bend and droop.

Anything in process of preparation, especially food, may turn out badly. A glance may cause milk not to form curds, or pickles not to turn out properly flavored. A woman in the state of Maharashtra prepared an especially tasty dish for her new son-in-law, but it did not turn out with the proper taste. She thought and thought, and could not remember any error in her cooking. Finally she remembered that a neighbor woman had come into the kitchen while the dish was being prepared and had commented on it.[3]

One's valued inanimate objects are also affected. Gujarati Bhīls believe that if someone looks in a good well the well may go dry. In Kerala people think that if someone looks at a nice house while it is being constructed, lightening might strike it that very night.

Animals may be affected even if they have no owners. In one village people explained the illness of a street dog by saying that envious glances had been cast at its food. Diehl reports that a young elephant in the Mīnākshi Temple in Madurai, Tamil Nadu, had to have an amulet for protection while eating, but that the keeper had said adult elephants did not need such protection.

Even inanimate objects not owned by anyone may be affected; some people may have a look piercing enough to shatter a stone.

The gods may be affected by baleful glances of both humans and other gods, and this might cause idols to shatter. As we note below, much of the *pūjā* ceremony, the daily service to the deity, may be explained in terms of this belief.

Who Casts the Powerful Eye?

There are varying ideas about who and what kinds of people have powerful eyes. In one Tamil village, for instance, the following responses were given to questions about it. A village priest (not a Brāhman) said it is found among all castes and in either sex; about one in four people have it. A farmer said playing children do not have it. A landless laborer said old ladies have it, and it is feared by other old ladies. A Brāhman said not all eyes are bad, only those with too much envy in them, and thought that the power is found in men or women over twenty. Yet another man said that all eyes are indeed potentially cruel or harsh. It was agreed, however, that ghosts and goblins do not have this power.

A poor or hungry person is likely to cast an envious eye on the food of another whom he sees eating. This belief is widespread, and is frequently invoked to explain stomachache.

A barren woman is likely to envy the healthy children of other women, or pregnant women, causing harm.

An old woman, or anyone dissatisfied with his or her lot in life, is suspect.

A child whose mother had unfulfilled longings during pregancy, some aver, will grow up having this power.

A person of unusual appearance may have the power. William Crooke, who served long in the Bengal Civil Service, recounted that he had had a one-eyed clerk with whom colleagues refused to sit in the same office, saying that their accounts always went wrong when he looked at them.[4] A person with eyebrows meeting over the nose may be suspect. In Iran blue eyes are suspect, according to Barth.[5] They are rare, and also perhaps thought to have a piercing quality. I did not come across this belief in South India, and the phrase ''green-eyed envy'' is not found in South Asia because green eyes are scarcely to be seen. Generally red and blue are more benevolently powerful than other colors.

In North India people believe that babies who eat feces will grow up having evil eye power; so mothers are careful to not allow babies to get their faces smeared with feces, according to Minturn and Hitchcock.[6] People in Trinidad of North Indian extraction also retain this belief.[7]

Animals may also have this power, especially those with prominent eyes. Jackson cites an instance of a mother in Maharashtra whose child got sick, and she concluded that it was because the household cat looked on hungrily while the child ate. He also cites a ritual to offset the effect of the eye of a tiger on cattle. Gifford cites an account appearing in an English newspaper in 1858: a hawk flew too close to a cobra, which raised its head and hissed; the hawk shrieked and flapped its wings with all its might, trying to fly away, but the eye of the snake was stronger, and after the hawk had seemed suspended in the air for some time it came down and died.[8] The attribution of a mystical quality to snake eyes is not limited to India, of course.

Some eyelike objects may have the power. A single peacock's feather with an eye on it is malevolent. But eye-like semiprecious stones worn in rings or pendants in protohistoric times were regarded as helpful charms.

The gods may have the power. In Nepal a certain plague was thought to have been caused by the malevolent eye of Sani, that is, Saturn, and other planets that had come together in an unusual formation. Also in Nepal, however, the gods manifest their benevolent and protective power through large eyes painted on Buddhist temples.

Therefore, the implication is that what we term the evil eye might better be termed the *powerful eye,* and further support for this is given below. In this respect South Asia may differ somewhat from other parts of the world having the evil eye belief.

Finally, we may ask whether people who cast evil or powerful eyes are generally enemies and strangers, or kin and friends. Barth says of Iranian nomads that the eye is cast by kin and friends, not enemies.[9] Possibly this reflects something of the intensity of interpersonal relationships and rivalry in the tribelike societies of that region, but it cannot be said to be true for India. A good example of who may be suspect is provided by Rivers' account of the Toḍas, a hill tribe in Tamil Nadu. If a Toḍa suffers from indigestion and suspects a powerful eye as the cause, a specialist will be called who performs an incantation. The incantor says of the afflicted, "May his mother's eye perish, may it be destroyed." Then for the word "mother" he substitutes in turn elder brother, younger brother, mother's brother, father's sister, grandfather, and grandmother, then Tamils (in whose midst Toḍas form a tiny minority), Ceṭṭis (a caste of merchants), and Kurumbas, Iruḷas, and Pāṇiyas (the other tribal groups of those hills); finally the imprecation is extended to the women of all these peoples.[10]

Curatives

It would be possible to list hundreds of curative and preventative devices or rituals associated with ill effects of the powerful eye, of which only a good sample will be given here. Though listed according to the Indian state or ethnic group for which they were noted, some have currency throughout the subcontinent, and even beyond it to the Mediterranean. Others may have faded away because the evil eye belief is declining. Many of the practices listed below for the western Indian states of Maharashtra and Gujarat were recorded by A. T. M. Jackson, a British civil servant and recorder of folklore detail in the first decade of this century.

South Asia everywhere: For any sickness, and also as a charm to prevent sickness and evil eye influence, tie a black string around the waist or arm, perhaps with a particular number of knots, amulets, or a silver cylinder containing magic designs drawn on metal by a village healer. This is the most common curative and preventative, used by Hindus, Muslims, Buddhists, and occasionally Christians.

South India, with variants throughout South Asia: For stomach trouble or other illness caused by an evil eye, wave several chilies and salt three times around the head of the afflicted and throw them into the fire. If the pungent smoke permeates the room, the evil effect is controlled. If the afflicted coughs, it means the evil is coming out; also ask him to spit. If there are no pungent fumes, or if one of the chilies falls to the side of the fire, the bad influence is not being controlled.

Tamil Nadu: To cure a sick child take sticks from a new, unused broom, set them on fire, and wave them around his head. Mark the forehead with the ashes, then wave camphor, rice dyed black and red, chilies, salt, hair, nail parings, and earth from the pit of the door post, and throw these in the fire. If there is a thick odor the prognosis is good.[11] For stomachache, heat a piece of iron red hot and dip it in curry that is to be eaten. For muscle ache, headache, or fever, take one or two chilies, break them, wrap them in an old cloth along with black mustard seed and tamarind, cross the bundle over the afflicted's face three times and once over his head, have him spit three times, and throw it into the fire. Thus the evil eye is plucked out. Or wave salt around the afflicted's face three times, throw it in the fire, and smear ashes on his forehead. Or if there is smallpox in the house, hang up mango or *nim* (margosa) leaves on the doorway or gate. (This procedure may also avert other kinds of evil influences.) If you do not know whether a sickness was caused by an evil eye, call in a *mantiravāti,* an incantor, who will look at a flame and tell from it whether the disease is a result of black magic, the evil eye, or natural causes.

Sri Lanka: Employ a *bhikku* (Buddhist monk) to chant Pāli scriptures from the *Sutta Piṭaka* over a pot of water; have him pass a thread around all persons present and tie it on the arm or neck of the afflicted, and then sprinkle the charmed water on the subject's face. Or simply sprinkle the charmed water on the subject.

Maharashtra: Take three pebbles from a road junction, wave them over the face of the afflicted, and throw them away. Or take seven pebbles from a junction of three roads and heat them in the hearth; have the sick child sit in front of the fire and with tongs take out each stone, wave it around his face, and put it in a brass dish with turmeric water in front of the child; when the water gets red, the evil has come out. Or wave alum around the head of the afflicted and throw in the fire, or take it out to a junction of three roads. Or put chilies, mustard, salt, garlic, onion leaves, and road stones on the fire, wave them over the afflicted, and throw them away. Or charm black strings by heating them over burning incense and tie them on the patient. Or wave a left sandal over the afflicted and throw it away, or use a flower instead. Or wave a red-hot iron bar over the afflicted and cool it in tumeric water. Or wave twenty-one date leaves, each with a knot, over the afflicted and throw them in a pot with charcoal; keep the pot in a corner of the room overnight with a basket, broom, or old shoe on top, and in the morning throw the contents away. Or wave burning sticks of tamarind over the afflicted and extinguish them in a copper plate. Or wave two large stones over his head and strike them together; if one breaks, the malevolent effect is removed. Or wave boiled rice, curds, bread, and oil over his head and throw on the road. For an ill man, wave rice boiled with chicken over his head and throw away; if there is no success, maybe the effect of the malevolent eye has entered into his bones; so in the evening bring in an animal bone, smear it with oil and turmeric, dress it in a yellow cloth, put on yellow and black ointment (performing *pūjā* to the bone), wave it over the afflicted, and throw it away at a junction of three roads. For a crying baby that cannot be quieted, take seven chilies, salt, and mustard seed, wave them around its head, and throw them in the fire. If a domestic animal is sick because of the evil look of a tiger, burn an oil lamp in the eye socket of a dead tiger and have a Mahār (low caste) man wave the lamp around the afflicted animal; then give the Mahār some bread made of "the eight kinds" of grain.[12]

Gujarat: After sunset, fill a bowl with water and pass it around the afflicted; empty it over a jar overturned over a hot coal on a dinner plate; place a scythe over the bowl; if the water hisses when poured over the heated jar, it speaks. Or pass milk three times around the head of an afflicted child, pour it into a black earthen pot, and offer it to a bitch; do this on Sundays or Tuesdays. Or place in a bell-metal cup some mustard seeds, salt, chilies, and seven stones from the village gate, wave the cup over the head of the afflicted, put in some charcoal, overturn the cup, and place it on a bell-metal plate; pour cow-dung water over it; if the cup adheres to the plate, "the evil eye has stuck fast" and the patient is cured. Or get an exorcist to wave a bowl of water around the head of the afflicted and drink it, thereby drinking up the evil. Or bake a millet bread on one side and apply *ghī* (butter oil) on that side; pass a fine cotton thread around the bread, wave it over the afflicted, and put in the fire; if the thread is not burned the evil eye is the cause of the illness. Or instead offer the loaf to a dog. Or if a woman is known to have cast the evil eye at a sick child, have the woman come and put her hand over the child's head. Or put a certain herb and a certain twig, salt, a nail, and charcoal in an unused pot; take it with a pot of water to the village boundary without looking back, and pour the water over the pot of things seven times. Or if a baby is ill get dust from a road junction, or red lead that has been offered to Hanuman (the monkey-faced deity), a chili, and an iron nail, tie them in a cloth with black wool thread, and tie the package onto the cradle.[13]

Bihar: If crops are poor, a child ails, a cow is dry, or pots break while being fired in the kiln, it is likely that a witch has cast an evil eye; perform sympathetic magic to destroy her.

Toḍa tribe (Tamil Nadu): If one suffers from indigestion, or suffers in any other way from an "anxious look," bring in an incantor to rub the afflicted's belly, hold the corner of the cloak of the afflicted with the left hand, put salt on the cloak, stroke the salt with a thorn, and put the salt and thorn into the fire with the imprecation, "May his eye perish" recited for various people or neighboring ethnic groups who might have cast the evil eye; let the patient eat some of the salt. For a sick buffalo, perform the same ritual and let the buffalo eat the salt. If the malevolence was produced by someone who commented on the afflicted's being well dressed, squeeze the juice from a particular root into a vessel and pronounce similar imprecations. If the afflicted is absent, have the incantor put salt on the ground and stroke it with a thorn, repeating the imprecations; send the salt to the afflicted to eat.[14]

Bhīl tribe (Gujarat): Wave seven cow-dung cakes over the afflicted.

Santāl tribe (Bihar): For the ill effect of the evil eye cast by a woman, or of an evil shadow, tie mustard seeds in a cloth and hang the bundle around the neck of the afflicted. Or call the exorcist.[15]

Indians in Trinidad: Go to the exorcist, who can cure illness such as a sunburn caused by evil eyes; the exorcist will touch it to affect a cure.[16]

Bangladesh: For the evil eye cast on children by their stepmother, Hindus should visit a *sādhu* and Muslims a *pīr* (saint) and obtain an amulet or talisman.

Panjab, Pakistan: Collect dust from a crossroads, burn a large chili on the dust, and let the smoke pervade the room so as to envelope the children and the milk utensils.

Sindh, Pakistan: Find an old woman who knows how to "cut" the evil eye influence; have her take three mud cakes, tie each with a string into quarters, and cut them with a knife while pressing them against her eyes; then sacrifice the mud cakes over the patient and throw them into a pond or tank; have the old woman perform this for three days in succession.[17]

Maldive Islands: If one is afflicted, call an incantor who will sprinkle holy water on the patient thrice while reciting some Arabic-sounding phrases, for phrases from the Koran are the most potent force to counter evil eye power. Have the incantor make a magic diagram on a sheet of gold, silver, brass, or vellum (according to one's wealth) with Arabic-looking symbols around it, to be rolled up and inserted in a silver casket to be worn on a string around the waist. (A silver casket is prescribed because a gold one is to increase one's wealth or power and a brass one is to counteract *jinns*.)

Preventatives

Even more numerous than the cures are the devices and rituals employed to avert, deflect, or neutralize the power of the eyes. It should be understood that many of the following devices are used against evil spirits, ghosts, or

Figure 8.3 House under construction in Kerala state; straw-stuffed manikin diverts envious glances.

Figure 8.4 Hut of a Muslim farmer in Bangladesh, protected from the evil eye by a painted potsherd.

insidious deities, but all of them have been mentioned in at least some situations as being potent against the evil eye.

HOUSES

New houses erected throughout India, even multistoried concrete buildings in major cities, may be protected by a manikin, usually of old cloth stuffed with straw or of wood, set up on the scaffold. The manikin fascinates onlookers, who look curiously at it rather than enviously at the building. To make it even more irresistible, it may have sexual features, such as a very large penis painted bright red. Also, all over South Asia from Pakistan to Bangladesh to Tamil Nadu, one can see here and there newer houses with an upturned pot or potsherd somehwere on top, often black or with white spots or stripes.

Kerala: To protect a building under construction, tie branches of a particular tree to the four corners. In one family the mother was preparing to do this for their house under construction, but as it was a Catholic family, her son suggested that she tie on four pictures of Catholic saints instead, which she did.[18]

Tamil Nadu: Make white palm prints on the door of the house, or on the

Figure 8.5 Muslim scooter-ricksha driver in Peshawar, Pakistan, protects his bright new vehicle from the evil eye with a black ribbon attached to the windshield wiper.

doorway. Make a *kōlam* (an elaborate design of powdered chalk) on the ground in front of the main doorway; women should do this as part of their morning household ritual. One Tamil Brāhmaṇ told me he protected his house from evil eyes by (1) sweeping it, (2) having the floor and steps washed with cow-dung wash in the morning, (3) making a *kōlam* outside the front doorway, (4) making a miniature *kōlam* before the household idol, and (5) leaving a lamp to burn all night. All these protect from evil forces in general, however, and not just the evil eye.

Maharashtra: Before moving into a new house wave bread and rice in front, then throw them away.

Uttar Pradesh: Make black palm prints on each side of the doorway to ward off evil glances. Or make chalk designs on the compound wall facing the street.

Maldive Islands: Write Arabic magical phrases on four pieces of wood and bury them at the four corners of the house under the eaves.

VEHICLES

Protect a vehicle such as a truck or taxi with an idol on a little shelf near the driver, or at least a picture of the deity, and by regular *pūjā* and *mantras* (incantations or magic verses).

Figure 8.6 Rice field in Tamil Nadu state with straw manikin set up before the harvest; manikin, which has a bright red penis, distracts glances of potentially envious passersby.

Pakistan and Afghanistan: Write on the side of a truck a verse from the Koran followed by the phrase, "Dispel the evil eye." For any vehicle, especially a bright new one painted in attractive colors, tie a black ribbon on the windshield wiper or elsewhere in a prominent place.

Tamil Nadu: Paint the differential housing of a new truck with an outlandish and spooky face, so that people who see the truck from behind or those in a following vehicle will be fascinated by the outlandish head between the back wheels and not envy the whole truck.

Maldive Islands: Protect a fishing boat by hanging some green coconuts blessed by an incantor in the bow. Or erect a pole with a white rag, preferably bearing a phrase in Arabic.

CROPS

Overturn a pot on a stick in the field; it may be a black pot, or white, or black with painted white spots; or set up a scarecrow-like manikin of cloth or straw; this attracts the attention of passersby so they will not look at the crops. (While these are not seen in the majority of fields, they are set up in all parts of South Asia, especially by marginal farmers.)

Maharashtra: Tie a coconut shell or an old shoe on a choice fruit tree or vine.

Pakistan: Hang up a black rag in the field.

Orāon tribe (*Bihar*): Plant a stick in the field and split its top into three parts.

Tie cowrie shells to the neck or forehead of a good ox or cow. (This is practiced in most regions.)

Uttar Pradesh: Tie colored strings to the horns or legs of a good buffalo about to freshen.[19]

Tamil Nadu: Milk behind a palm-leaf screen or out of sight of passersby, for if someone notices that the milk is abundant the next day it will diminish.

Iran: Exclaim, "May the milk be plentiful" if you happen to pass by when someone is milking.[20]

FOODS

Foods should be prepared and eaten away from the public gaze. Probably this is more to avoid ritual pollution than to avoid the evil eye, but the two are not really separable. High-caste people are particularly fastidious about ritual purity of foods, and the subject consumes more space in Hindu lawbooks than any subject save marriage. Even among the modern urban elite, who may have no conscious belief in the evil eye, people prefer to eat in private. Hence restaurants have curtained stalls for their more prestigious customers. Generally mealtime is not the occasion for convivial conversation; that comes afterward. The widespread custom of offering sweets to guests on special occasions or on any occasion, and the giving of a guest areca nuts and betel leaf almost as a ritual, may be thought of as having some countervailing influence. Some people are reluctant to eat while others are present, as in a train compartment, without sharing the food. A sight often novel to foreign visitors is coolies having lunch; in some areas they each sit facing a wall, or somewhat apart from one another, and gulp the food without a word. All these practices may be devoid of conscious association with the evil eye belief in most cases, but such a belief was a factor in their origin.

Maharashtra: If food being eaten may be affected by an evil eye, raise three morsels to the mouth and throw them in the fire.

Gujarat: If you cannot avoid company while eating, at least throw a morsel of food behind you, or set some on the ground "as an offering to the evil

Figure 8.7 Old man in Gujarat state prefers to eat by himself so that no one can make him sick by casting an envious eye at his food.

eye." When making pickles, to prevent their acquiring an unwanted flavor put in a lime or an iron nail during preparation. While making a rice pudding with milk and sugar, put in a piece of charcoal.[21]

Panjab, Pakistan: When churning milk in the morning, especially if it is nice, creamy milk likely to be envied by passersby, attach a black ribbon to the churn handle and let it flutter with each revolution; an envious glance at the milk might otherwise make family members sick. Also, you may take food that is to be eaten into a separate room and consume it with the back turned to other family members; old women especially are wont to do this.

Karnataka: Boys eating sacrificed buffalo meat should do so under a large cloth.[22]

Higher-caste or orthodox Hindus may regularly invoke a blessing over food before eating, though most families do not observe this custom. Christians often protect the food by blessing it before the meal, fusing the missionary teachings about saying grace with the Indian idea of the sensitivity of food to evil influences.

THE BODY

Many items worn for adornment or as charms also have power to counteract evil eyes, or to deflect their rays. These include tiger nails or teeth worn around the neck, a lime in the turban, a black spot on the cheek of a child that looks like a blemish (common throughout India), or an iron ring on the finger. There is also a large variety of amulets: cylindrical ones worn by

Hindus have copper plates with magic drawings rolled up in them, while those worn by Muslims have slips of paper with verses from the Koran. Such are to be seen in practically every village. The black threads with which the amulets are tied are potent themselves; they may be made of five kinds of silk spun by a virgin, tied in seven knots, or tied onto the arm of the afflicted on the fourteenth day of the waning of the moon; they may have seven, fourteen, or twenty-one knots, with three folds, and seven twists. Such strings and amulets when worn by adults are curatives, but when worn by children are often preventatives, and many babies wear them as a matter of course.

While a specific magical function cannot be ascribed to most items of adornment, there is a diffuse feeling that many of them are auspicious. Blue beads, red beads, and conch-shell bangles were all popular in protohistoric and ancient times, and are still vaguely thought to be protective. Gems in general, especially sapphires and rubies and red coral, are protective. Gold is valued not only for its intrinsic value; it is the noblest of metals because it does not tarnish, and the goldsmith performs priestly functions in ceremonies, as when he prepares gold adornment for a bride. In some areas there is the belief, especially among merchant castes, that wearing a little gold somewhere on the body protects it. Though gold and gems attract attention to the wearer and afford prestige, they also have the ability to deflect the beams of a powerful eye. Fear of the evil eye, however, has been only a subsidiary reason for the popularity of such items of adornment in South Asia.

Glass, however, is definitely thought to reflect away the evil eye. The Tamil word for glass, and also for looking glass, is *kaṇṇāḍi*, "eye-strike."

The veil or sari-end used to partially conceal women's faces, as where women are in *pardā* (seclusion), protects the women from interested eyes. There is the feeling that the lusting eye or the loving eye may also be baleful. The various devices employed to partially conceal or to seclude women, especially in western parts of South Asia and among landowning Muslims in particular, are part of this social syndrome, for a man is largely esteemed according to the protection he is able to afford for his women.

Iran: Tie on the subject a string of blue beads, rags, broken potsherds, or other striking objects, or a *tavis* (amulet) given by the sayyid.

Tamil Nadu: When complimented on physical appearance, spit and say *chī* (a term of derision).

Figure 8.8 Family of Lambāḍis, a caste of gypsy-like migrant workers, in Andhra state. The woman wears glass pieces sewn in her dress to reflect away evil influences. Plastic bangles (formerly made of conch shells) are also vaguely thought to be auspicious.

Bengal: Women should not go out at dusk with long hair hanging down, for it causes envy and brings malevolence.

Gypsies in Andhra: Sew many little pieces of glass into the dresses of women and girls.

Panjab: Wear an iron bangle as protection. This is commonly done by men of the Sikh religion.

CHILDREN

Since babies and children are quite susceptible to insidious influences, the devices employed to protect them are numerous. A black string around a baby's waist encircles and generally protects the child (though Minturn and Hitchcock report that it also has the specific function of making the vein in the penis grow straight so that the child will not grow up impotent). Sometimes a red string is used, and gives explicit protection from the evil eye.

A baby that is very attractive invites evil eyes. This belief is in keeping with the common sentiment that something complete is inauspicious (hence

Hindus prefer to give 101 rupees rather than 100, etc.). Babies should not be dressed too beautifully when taken on a trip (in practice, however, most babies on trains and buses are well dressed, though older women may disapprove). Complimenting babies is not readily done, and if a foreigner inadvertently lavishes compliments on a child, the parents may become apprehensive or even remove the child. Among Hindus everywhere, a large spot of lampblack is applied to the middle of the forehead (discussed below), and if that is not enough to deflect the evil eye, a black smudge or spot elsewhere, commonly on the cheek or even on the foot, will make the baby look sufficiently imperfect.

Karnataka: Wave a lamp around a baby before taking it to another village.

Maharashtra: Before taking a child out, scatter rice at the village boundary, at bridges, rivers, and other dangerous places, wave coconuts over the baby and throw them beyond the village boundary, and apply black ointment to its eyes, cheeks, and forehead.

Bengal: If a child is seen by a woman suspected of having the evil eye, the mother should spit directly on the hand and face of the child, or at least pretend to spit. Before a mother takes a baby out for the first time the grandmother should spit on the child's hand.

Uttar Pradesh: During the day, when an infant is not in need of food and attention, place it on a cot with a quilt or sheet entirely covering it, to protect both from insects and envious glances. Keep the baby wrapped up and well hidden during the ceremony following birth; no visitor who comes to that ceremony should see it. Tie a black cord around its waist. Do not elaborately groom the child so as to attract attention, and reserve the use of eye makeup for festival occasions. No visitor should admire a baby openly, nor praise its healthfulness or good looks.[23]

Pāhāris of the Himalayan foothills: Protect a child by putting amulets on it, and also give extra to charity.

Orāon tribe (Bihar): At the boys' initiation ceremony, when they take jugs of water for ritual use they should keep them hidden in a corner till needed; if anyone sees the jugs, the boys should move them lest the water be affected.[24]

Toḍa tribe: Keep a baby's face covered most of the time until the fortieth day or the third month, and keep it in the house with its mother, then perform the face-uncovering ceremony. If the baby is a boy, the father takes him early in the morning to the dairy and both bow at its threshold, then the father takes him to the buffaloes and uncovers his face, making him look first at the sun. If the baby is a girl, the mother takes her to the place where the women get buttermilk from the dairy and there uncovers her face (the objects a baby sees first—dairy, buffaloes, and sun—are most sacred to the Toḍas). After the face-uncovering ceremony, the baby should be named, and a string tied around it with stones of a particular kind bought in the bazaar, which should alternate on the string with bird bones of a particular kind; this waistband is specifically for protection against "the eye." [25]

Tamil Nadu: When washing a new child bring ashes from the ash heap and smear them on it so it will not look so enviable. A mother should speak of her "ugly child" in the presence of a stranger.

Karnataka: Put a baby into a winnowing fan and drag it on the manure pit by the left foot; this will deceive fate into believing the child's parents are so indifferent that the child is not worth taking.[26]

Orissa: Give the child to a low-caste woman, who anoints and returns it, then give it the name of the caste of that woman so the child will not appear so enviable; hereby the sins of the mother may also be transferred to that low-caste woman.[27]

Panjab Hindus: Give a child to a sweeper woman to suckle (reported to have been common practice), or if the pollution caused thereby is too much to bear give it to a Muslim woman to suckle. Or sell it and buy it back for a few small coins so it appears of little worth.

Iran: Cover a baby's head with soot, preferably as soon as the head appears and before complete delivery.[28]

North India: Sell a baby to a low-caste or poor woman and buy it back for a few cowries; name that baby according to the price: Half-Cowrie, Three-Cowries, or Five-Cowries. Or throw it on a rubbish heap or dung heap and name it Rubbish, Dung Heap, Lord of Refuse, Broomstick, or Pot. Or dress the child in rags, or dress a boy as a girl.[29]

Western India: Name a boy as a girl. Put a new baby into a winnowing basket along with house sweepings and drag it into the yard; name that child Winnowing Basket, or Dragged. To avoid perfection in a child a mother may chop off a piece of the child's ear and eat it.[30]

Gujarat: Put a child on a dunghill, or roll it in dust, then take it back; name the child Useless, False, Refuse, Black, Mad, Stupid, Eccentric, Lame, Fool, Dunghill, Lord (ironical), Noise, Negro-like, Womanish, Bitter. Carry earthen figures of it through the streets at the time of the Holi festival.[31]

Sindh Muslims (Pakistan): Name a girl after a slave. Name a boy Stone, Beggar, Dunghill Inhabitant, Dust, Bone, Thorn, Simpleton, Madman, Cemetery, Jungle, Ghost, Rags, Fly, Rat, Cat, Dog, Pepper, Ash, or Black Monkey.[32]

Of course, these latter practices are much less common today than at the beginning of this century.

AT WEDDINGS

Wedding rituals are replete with efforts to avoid envious glances or void their power. Diehl notes the following, retained even among Christians in Tamil Nadu as late as the 1950s. To the forehead of the bride, and sometimes of the groom too, is tied a gold strap or frontlet, which is specifically said to attract glances of strangers and prevent such glances from falling on the person; this practice is found "among the poorer class of Christians," according to pastors' reports. After the groom ties the wedding pendant on the bride, which is called a *tāli* (the term certifies that it originated as a protective charm), the couple is bathed in turmeric water; this is the last ritual of the ceremony and is said to remove "eye destruction" or the "Seeing Eye" and abates the curse of the public gaze. This is called *ālatti* (Hindi: *ārtī*), the term generally used for the waving of fire in front of an idol during *pūjā* and worship. Before the bride and groom enter the house a tray with fruit and flowers and burning camphor is waved before them; Christians sometimes performed this Hindu rite until about 1952, and called it *ālatti*. Turmeric water may again be poured on the ground under the feet of the wedded couple, in a final effort to remove the effect of the public gaze, as they enter their house.[33]

The Gods

In a Tamil village at the annual festival of the local goddess Punnavanattamman, I enquired of the local priest (not a Brāhmaṇ) why several people became possessed and danced in trance, instead of only the chief devotee as is usual. In reply, the priest narrated a story in explanation:

Punnavanatamman had no children, but she had a younger sister, Muppaḍāti Amman, who had four. One day the elder sister came to see the younger sister's children, but the younger feared the eye of the elder, who was barren, and hid the children in a basket. When the elder came, the younger said the children were all

Figure 8.10 Image of Buddha in *vihāra* in Sri Lanka; curtains are pulled almost shut most of the time to protect the image from malevolent influence.

Figure 8.9 Brāhmaṇ priest in a Vaishnavite temple in Karnataka state waving the protective fire in front of the idol during *pūjā*.

out playing, so the elder left. When the younger opened the basket, behold, all four children were dead! So she ran to Punnavanatamman's house, crying, "I hid them when you came, and now they have all *fainted*. Come and get *your* children." The elder sister then came, sprinkled some water, and made the children get up; they left their mother and followed their aunt. So at festival time several people dance in trance because they are possessed by both sisters and also by the four children.

A barren goddess, then, can be envious enough of her sister's children to zap them to death with her eye, then revive them by sprinkling holy water on them. Human interpersonal relations are projected into the world of the gods.

The gods (as idols) can be assisted by humans who take pains to protect them from indivious eyes. Indeed, many items of the *pūjā* ceremony, the daily or periodic service to the deity, are associated with or can be partially explained by the evil eye belief. The waving of a torch or lamp around the deity, always part of *pūjā*, most certainly has this function. The entire *pūjā* ceremony treats the idol as if it were a person of high rank: washing, perfuming, dressing, garlanding, feeding it. People of high rank are susceptible to pollution or harm by people of very low rank. An Englishman in the service of the Shah of Iran in 1808 wrote that when the Shah made a public appearance no women were permitted among the spectators lest the Shah be struck by an eye.[34] The Abbé Dubois wrote that in Karnataka, about 1800, a torch was constantly waved (*ālatti* or *āratti*) before persons of high rank, such as *rājās* and generals, when they came out; princes employed dancing girls to do this. The waving of a lamp or torch in front of the idol is performed especially after the idol has been dressed and prepared and the curtain is opened so the public can gaze and worship. It is performed even more intensely when the idol is taken from the temple during its annual celebration and carried through the streets in a palanquin or a temple car, through crowds of devotees. The purifying fire of the *ālatti* protects the deity or high-ranking person from any unpleasant consequences or pollution arising from the public gaze.

Similarly, during the height of the *pūjā* ceremony bells are rung, and if the ceremony is important enough so that a troupe of musicians is in the temple, they make the greatest noise at this time. The bells and music are not to call the god but to distract the attention of any potentially malevolent onlookers; musicians make a great noise during the most crucial moment of the wedding ceremony for the same reason. Incense wafted during *pūjā* has a purifying effect (like burning chilies as a curative rite). Also the gems, gold, and rich dress with which the idol is often decked have the effect of distracting the attention of onlookers from the idol itself.

I suspect that the *lingam,* cylindrical symbol of male virility generally placed around the sanctum in Śaivite temples, had as one of its original functions the distraction of the gaze of onlookers (similar to the purpose of the red enlarged sexual organs sometimes embellishing manikins set up on new buildings or in fields). People of the Lingāyat sect in Karnataka state wear the *lingam* in a silver casket on their persons as a protective charm. Also, the guardian figures often protecting either side of the entrance to a temple may have noticeably erect sexual organs, which certainly do distract the passerby. Even on the temple of the Jain religion on Mount Abu one of the guardian figures, a human, has clearly sculpted sexual organs smeared with vermillion.

The curtain of the inner sanctuary in a temple, where it exists, screens out malevolent influences, for it is pulled shut when the idol is being dressed and is most vulnerable to bad influence. If there is no curtain sometimes the village priest will simply hold a cloth in front of the idol while it is being dressed and prepared for the public gaze. In Sri Lanka images of Buddha are often curtained off, perhaps with a slit between the curtains where the Buddha can peek out, and left that way all day. But when *pūjā* is completed and the devotees appear, the curtains are pulled back, for then the idol is protected by the fire, incense, and offerings.

The Forehead Dot (Tilak)

The red or black spot on the forehead, known in the North as *tilak* and in the South as *tilakam* or *poṭṭu,* is worn by the majority of Hindu women; they may have had it tatooed, or nowadays may wear it in any color to match their saris. Men may have a sandal-paste spot with a vermillion center applied after worshiping in temples. Babies generally have a large spot of lampblack on the forehead when they are taken out.

Whenever I have asked women the meaning of their forehead spot (it is not a caste mark, as some Americans think), the answer is almost always, "simply for decoration." For modern urban women this is true, and in Bangladesh even Muslim women wear it, simply as part of their makeup. However, when Hindu men wear such a spot, it generally indicates that they have recently worshiped in the temple or at least performed *pūjā* at home. Among traditional high-caste Hindus a respectable man who has not had the spot applied by noon is thought to be impure or perhaps to be undergoing a fast. As a village astrologer said to me, "When you do your duty, such as putting on the *poṭṭu,* then the heart is clean; after that the soul becomes clean, too."

Whenever I broached the suggestion that this mark might be related to the complex of beliefs about the powerful eye, the suggestion was generally denied. I think, however, that the connection is inescapable, at least as regards the origin of the forehead mark. At weddings the frontlet of gold with gems or with entwined flowers, worn on the forehead of the bride and sometimes of the groom in South India, is also called *poṭṭu,* and is specifically to distract envious glances that might otherwise fall on their faces or into their eyes; dancing girls also wear such frontlets. In mythology the cobra is represented as having a gem, generally a ruby, set in the center of its forehead, which deflects evil effects. The word *tilakam* in South India means both the forehead gem, and the applied spot. Red is a color deemed potent to divert the evil eye from the Mediterranean to India.

Not only does the ruby in the serpent's head divert the evil eye; it exudes wisdom or psychic power. In men too, the center of the forehead is the focus of special powers, which concentrate there as during yoga practice. The Tamil word *nutal* means (1) forehead, and (2) aim, design, or thought. Projection of psychic powers through the center of the forehead is exemplified in the deity Śiva, who has a third eye in the middle of his forehead. While the eye in the forehead is a feature of mythological figures, such as Cyclops of Greece and Balor of the Celts, Śiva's is vertical, and supplements his other two eyes; Śiva's consort has this third eye, too. According to a tale in Karnataka, a certain goddess wished to marry Vishṇu, who would not marry her but sent her to Brahmā, who in turn sent her to Śiva. She danced for Śiva and enticed him, disturbing his meditation (women are thought to drain psychic energy from men); nevertheless he agreed to marry her in return for the boon of a rug to sit on, betel leaves, and a third eye. The goddess granted this boon, and when Śiva opened his third eye the first thing he did with it was train it on that goddess and zap her to ashes! In effect, he destroyed all womankind, but later regretted his rash act, collected the ashes, and fashioned from them wives for himself, Vishṇu, and Brahmā.

On another occasion, according to the mythology, Śiva was deep in meditation in the Himalayas, when the god Indra sent Kāma, the Indian god of love, to arouse sexual desire in Śiva and make him marry the goddess Umā. Kāma went to Śiva's meditation place and there happened to spy Umā presenting an excellent profile to Śiva as she plucked flowers. Kāma shot his arrow laden with love at her, and the shaft by error struck Śiva. That lord interrupted his meditation only long enough to train his third eye on Kāma and expel a ray that zapped him as he was slinking away with his bow and arrow, reducing that cupid to ashes.

Probably the reason the *tilak* came to be worn as a matter of course by women is that they have been obliged to avert lustful gazes; even the eye of a lover can be potentially harmful. The Tamil phrase *kaṇ poḍa,* literally "to put the eye," means (1) to look with envy or desire, and (2) to fall in love. After all, Śiva's middle eye dealt with lust effectively. But long ago the forehead spot became an item of toilette, applied daily as a matter of course. Likewise, the large lampblack spot applied to babies' foreheads diverts envious looks so they do not penetrate the babies' eyes, whereas the smudge commonly applied to their cheeks or necks is to make the babies look blemished or imperfect.

The center of the forehead thus exudes psychic energy and exerts a countervailing power to any malevolent influence. The application of the forehead spot during *pūjā,* after purification and meditation, symbolizes the concentration of the devotee's psychic energies in that spot, and through that point one's thoughts and deeds have an effect permeating the whole universe.

The Mystique and Power of the Eyes

Many words referring to eyes and seeing in Indian languages also refer to mental processes or to insight. The Sanskrit word *dṛshṭi,* "sight," is elaborated as *kudṛshṭi* meaning "weak sight," "evil eye or sinister eye," as well as "heterodox opinion or doctrine." The word *pāpdṛshṭi* is literally "sin-sight" and means "evil eye." These words are also current in Hindi, and in some other languages *dṛshṭi* or its derivatives by themselves imply "evil eye," at least in colloquial speech. The related Tamil term *tirushṭi* commonly refers to the evil eye, but in more formal language it also means sight or knowledge. People often use the redundant term *tirushṭi kaṇ, kaṇ* in Tamil being the commonest term for eye, and also meaning wisdom; its verbal form *kaṇṇu* means to think or judge. The common Hindi and Urdu term *nazar lagnā* means to be under the influence of the evil eye; *nazar* means evil eye influence, but also has the broader meanings of sight, vision, countenance, or reference.

Another common Tamil word, *pār,* means both to see, and to intend. *Nōkkam* means sight, intention, or inclination of mind. *Nōkku vittai,* literally "looking science," means legerdemain and *kaṇ kaṭṭu vittai,* literally "blindfold science," means conjuring. The god Indra is pictorially represented as having a thousand eyes over his body, which imply his omniscience, and the same symbolism is applied to Vishṇu, as to two aspects of that god, Nārāyaṇa and Kṛshṇa. Therefore Vishṇu is referred to in Tamil literature as *Kaṇṇan,* "eyed one," for his power permeates the universe.

The eye is also precious, analagous to the sentiment expressed in English by the phrase "apple of my eye." In Tamil *kaṇṇē,* "O eye," is a term of endearment used for babies. A wife may call her husband *kaṇṇāḷan,* and a husband his wife *kaṇṇāṭṭi.*

Figure 8.11 Buddhist temple of Swayambhu Nāth outside Kathmandu, Nepal; protective eyes look in four directions out over the valley.

In all South Asian art, from the earliest terracottas to modern paintings, the eyes are portrayed relatively large; this tendency is perhaps traceable back to ancient Sumer. There may be some physiological basis for this in South Asia, for the eyes appear large and contrastive because the skin around the eye sockets tends to be darker than the rest of the face. It is also likely, however, that this tendency to depict the eyes large reflects a certain mystique about them characteristic of this part of the world now as well as in protohistoric times. Fishing boats occasionally have occuli painted on the prows, as may also be seen today in some Mediterranean regions. The function of the occuli is both to help the boat find its way and to protect the boat and its passengers.

Eyes may be thought of as protective as well as malevolent. The goddess of the great temple in Madurai, South India, is Mīnākshi, and she is a consort of Śiva. Her name means "fish-eye." W. Norman Brown has listed several possible reasons behind the local application of this name to the consort: she was perhaps originally venerated by fisher folk; her eyes are fish-shaped; her eyes are love-filled; they dart about like a fish; they are large like the eyes of fish (the answer people most commonly give). He concludes, however, that more important is the implication that her eyes never close, nor even wink; neither does she sleep. Even the gods of the *Ṛgveda* did not wink, and the Sanskrit word *animisha,* literally "non-winking," means both "god" and "fish." Among all the gods, only Brahmā ever sleeps, and when he does so the world enters a phase of dissolution that is a night of 4.3 billion years, followed by a new creation and a day as long as the night of Brahmā. The gods cannot sleep while the universe functions, according to Hindu cosmology.

The protective function of the eye is particularly emphasized in the zone of Tibetan Buddhism. In Nepal, at the great temple of Swayambhu Nāth, a Buddhist edifice, there are four huge pairs of eyes painted on the tower over the sanctum, looking out over the valley in four directions to protect the pious. The benevolent aspect of the eyes common to Tibet, Bhutan, and northern Nepal, is in complementary relationship with the belief that it is the mouth that transmits malevolence, for this area is outside the primary zone of diffusion of the evil eye belief. The concept of the benevolent eye in popular Hinduism, though having ancient roots, has become almost lost because of the evil eye belief, and both have been partially absorbed into the broader concepts of the third eye and the projection of one's psyche through the forehead.

Thus there is a long tradition in India of considering the eyes as more than holes to see out of; *they transmit various emotions and functions of the mind: envy, malice, love, wisdom, and protection.*

The concept of *karma,* one could hypothecize, could be invoked to explain the evil eye belief in India; the effects of one's past deeds, in this life or a previous one, accumulate within and determine one's fate. Villagers themselves have responded that there is an association between having the evil eye and bad *karma.* One who is poor, or hungry, or maimed, or barren, also suffers from bad *karma,* or was at least so fated by an unlucky star. One who is envious of another's property may be said to have been deprived of what he wants because of bad *karma* and bad fate. If bad *karma* causes the evil eye, then whether it is cast by relatives and kin or by strangers and enemies is irrelevant.

But the association between evil eye power and the bad *karma* breaks down in many situations. A mother will greet her son returning home after an absence of many months or years with the statement, "You have gotten too thin!" when in fact the son may be stouter than when he left home. The mother, as one respondent said, "will agree in her mind that her son is fatter, but she will not say so." This is common in South India. Friends and relatives do not generally comment on another's healthfulness, nor on nice dress. Any such compliment is unexpected in South Asian society and is therefore suspect. Envy plays little part in this patterning of behavior.

Moreover, envy plays little part in instances of the evil eye cast by a person of higher status upon one of lower status. When the potters whom I visited feared that my looking on had caused their pots to break, it was not thought that I coveted the pots. Nor did the potters think that I had bad *karma,* for as a person accorded relatively high status I must have had considerable good *karma.* Rather, I was perceived as a person having certain power and authority that they feared and that I could presumably project in several ways.

The Abbé Dubois, in his well-known observation of life in Karnataka about 1800, wrote that soon after he arrived, and before he knew the etiquette of the land, he happened upon some fishermen taking fish in a reservoir. They drew up a good quantity with every haul, and the Abbé congratulated them on their good luck. "But my civility," he wrote, "had a most unlooked-for result, for these worthy people gathered up their nets and their fish without a word, and looking at me very indignantly, promptly went off, grumbling to each other under their breath: 'What have we done to this Feringhi [Portuguese] *guru* that he comes here and is so jealous of us.' " [35] In fact, it was not so much his envy that they feared, but that he was a very unusual person, and a holy man, too.

Kings and warriors are described in the literature as "cruel-eyed." This is not because of their envy, but because they are powerful. Again, Śiva burned Kāma up with his third eye as a manifestation of his power to overcome a nuisance. It has been narrated that a certain Catholic priest in Kerala once got angry with someone, looked at him with piercing eyes, and made some mumbling statement; that person soon became paralyzed. Such powerful but not envious eyes are more commonly attributed to men than to women. We have to conclude that in such instances attribution of the evil eye is not so much a matter of envy, but that *the powerful eye is simply one means among many whereby a person of higher rank projects his authority over a person of lower rank.*

The Evil Mouth and Other Bodily Emanations

The concept of the evil mouth seems to have been largely assimilated into that of the evil eye in South Asia, though it is found as a distinct but parallel belief in the Himalayas, Kerala, Sri Lanka, and the Maldive Islands at least. There is not nearly as much common reference to it as to the evil eye, and the etymological suggestions are not nearly so rich. In Tamil *kaṇṇūṟu* means eye wound, hindrance, or murder, and parallel to this is the word *nāvūṟu* referring to the same for the tongue. In Kerala in particular there is a common belief that a *karinākkan*, a "black-tongued one," can effect evil by his words. A small percentage of people do indeed have dark spots on their tongues and gums, and such persons are pointed out as potentially malevolent. It is reported for the Orāons, a large Dravidian-speaking tribe in southern Bihar, that a third of those in a sample of 400 had blue or purple spots on the tongue, occasionally forming a dark rim around it; this feature increases with the age of the individual.[36]

In Sri Lanka the evil mouth seems to be as important as the evil eye. It seems to be vaguely connected with demon infestation but there is no countervailing action prescribed.

There is a strong tradition in Hinduism, and in all South Asian religions, that words in their own right are frought with power, as in the saying of *mantras* (incantations), recitation of the Vedas, repetition of sacred syllables, such as Om, or verses from the Koran. Village *mantiravātis* (incantors) can recite *mantras* for sundry critical situations, yet malevolent *mantras,* or the use of magic syllables to perform black magic, are not so common, and *mantiravātis* do not generally recite any, for that is the sorcerer's work. Powerful *mantras* that can influence the high gods should be repeated only by one who is in a ritually pure state appropriate to the power of the *mantra,* and it can then alleviate human suffering or bend the will of the gods. Hence Brāhmaṇs undergo continuous ablutions, and village *mantiravātis* maintain a state of devotion and can quickly generate psychic projections if called upon. By analogy, there is the vague feeling that malevolent words, such as those emanating from a "black-tongued" person, a witch, conjurer, or envious person, are imbued with the bad *karma* of that person; workers of black magic are generally of low caste.

In Bengal the concept of evil eye is expressed by *mukh-lāge,* "evil face," which includes the mouth and eyes. Again, this is not always associated with envy.

Spitting is one of the means employed to rid the body of the effects of a malevolent eye. Now in India, any bodily secretion is polluting (hence eating and drinking are done in such a way that saliva is not returned to the mouth). Spitting is particularly employed as a countervailing force in Bengal. In western South Asia, and to some extent in other parts too, shy women tend to cover the mouth with a corner of the sari upon meeting a man. There is an old custom of the inferior, upon greeting his superior, keeping his hand over his mouth. This prevents any possibility of saliva pollution. Thus there is a diffuse tradition that the mouth has a potentially malevolent influence.

The breath is polluting. An orthodox Hindu will not wish to blow on a fire, especially a sacred fire, for the fire is the god Agni. But the breath is not thought to transfer evil intent from one person to another.

The shadow, at least in the Santāl tribe of Bihar, is sometimes thought of as evil, and a few men are thought to possess an evil shadow.[37]

The touch is occasionally, but not commonly, used to cure the effects of the powerful eye, applied either by the person casting the evil or by a magical healer. More commonly among Hindus, however, the touch is thought to transmit pollution. Hence there are Untouchables, and people do not have the custom of shaking hands or backslapping. A malevolent touch is not generally thought of as willful projection of evil; it is the effect of bad *karma*. Along with the powerful eye, it is one more way a person transmits his inner qualities to those around him.

The Powerful Eye Belief, Caste, and Egalitarianism

It is curious that the traditional elite do not relegate the evil eye belief to "superstition" of the nonelite; the power of the eyes is acknowledged in the formal religious systems. Brāhmaṇs, who usually reject many rites and beliefs of village Hinduism, such as spirit-possessed dancing and fire-walking, do take precautions to protect themselves from the influence of baleful eyes and have lent the weight of Hindu orthodoxy to the perpetuation of this belief. In Pakistan the *mullās,* religious practitioners in the mosques, advise people to protect themselves from the evil eye by employing verses from the Koran. Obviously the belief is somehow socially functional.

One important function is that it affords an explanation for misfortune, discussed below in the context of villagers' world-view system. A person of means can blame any loss on the envious or malevolent influence of a lower order of person.

Envy is an essential part of social interaction in India, more so than in more egalitarian societies or in small-scale cultural systems. Such qualities as wealth, political power, or ritual purity mean little except in terms of social differentiation and hierarchy. Brāhmaṇs, Rājpūts, the Westernized elite, and other groups who feel their behavior and ideals should be emulated expect others to envy them, and without this the well-documented processes of caste mobility, Sanskritization, Rājpūtization, and the like would not operate. And the pure gods are so high that they are bound to be even more the objects of envy and to suffer from the pollution or bad *karma* of lower orders of beings. Thus it is that when villagers are questioned as to the meaning of the evil eye they generally respond that envy is at the base of it. But as we have shown, the whole complex of beliefs about the power of eyes cannot be subsumed under envy.

Paradoxically, the evil eye belief can also be construed as promoting egalitarianism, especially within a village where people know each other. It is one of the forms of pressure brought to bear on a prosperous person to distribute some of his wealth. Among peasants the most important signs of prosperity are a nice house and good crops, and in some areas, oxen and cows. It is not unexpected that these very possessions are thought to need the most protection from evil eye influence—aside from the body itself. Fear of envy puts some restraint on conspicuous consumption within a village.

The gradual decline of the evil eye belief among the urbane classes in South Asia has been accompanied by increased consumption of manufactured goods, and the envy aspect of the belief is less functional than in the economy of a village, where goods and services have been exchanged according to the traditional *jajmānī* system. It may be suggested, however, that the social pressures prevailing within a village to distribute the wealth within it, and the antipathy toward merchants, are to some extent projected nationally in the socialist ideology of the ruling Congress Party of India.

Now if it appears contradictory to the reader to say that the evil eye belief may function both to reinforce social hierarchy and to promote economic egalitarianism, so be it; we have shown that in some situations no economic considerations at all are involved, as when doting kin are believed to cause a child's illness, or when a foreigner is believed to have cast the evil eye simply because he is a different kind of person and presumably capable of exerting power. Thus it should be clear that *the evil eye belief is not a single belief, but a cluster whose only common factor is a conviction that a person's inner qualities and intentions can emanate from his eyes; this cluster of beliefs cannot be reduced to a single explanation, such as envy, nor contained within a single structural model.* The belief may have served a more specific social function in the Near East or wherever it originated, but as it

became integrated into South Asian civilization and ethos it became much
more diffuse.

Reluctance to Compliment

It is not just envy but any expression of appreciation that is suspect. A South
Asian generally does not greet his fellow in the morning by telling him how
fine he looks today, nor does he compliment a lady on her new sari; he may
express curiosity about some household item but does not gushingly admire
it as a way of praising its owner. This reluctance to compliment others is
common to most peasant societies, and is not particularly unpleasant, for
one's attitude toward others is judged by his face, demeanor, and what he
does. Indeed, many American visitors to South Asia find something deeply
satisfying about its pattern of interpersonal relations.

Complimenting a baby, of course, may be interpreted as envy, and as
designed ultimately to have an invidious effect on the parents. As Minturn
and Hitchcock point out, a village mother would no more show off her baby
to an admiring visitor than an American mother would deliberately expose
an infant to a contagious disease. A foreign visitor effusively commenting
on a baby's appearance in such a village might cause panic.

But reluctance of adults to praise older children cannot be explained in
terms of envy. Children are, as a matter of course, expected to do thus and
so; in observing parent-child relations in a village in Uttar Pradesh, Minturn
never saw children being given rewards or special privileges for being good,
and recorded only one instance of a mother praising her child; this was a
statement by the mother of a five-year-old, "Oh, you have washed the
dishes, good." [38] Parents in fact tended to belittle such hard work as their
children did. People believed that praising children to their faces would spoil
them, though they might speak well of children in their absence. Villagers
thought, "If we praise, the child will think we love him too much, and then
he will not be under our control." Some men thought children were not as
obedient to the women as to the men because their women loved the children too much. [39]

Similarly, a husband in South Asia seldom praises his wife's cooking, except in the eating. A household servant or a laborer does not expect praise
for work he is employed to perform—something Americans living in India
find difficulty in adjusting to.

This reluctance to praise is not, of course, entirely the result of fear of the

evil eye or evil mouth, but it fits into the pattern, so that praise is unexpected and therefore to some extent feared. The individual is socialized to
do his duty without expecting special recognition; a child brought up in this
way is amenable to performing his role in society in accord with the norms
for his caste, kin, and acquired social position, so that performance of his
duty is his *dharma*.

The Evil Eye, Witchcraft, and Social Tensions

Witchcraft is of relatively little importance in South Asia, owing to the nature of the society. People may have heresay knowledge of it, or of black
magic, but only a minority of villagers have personal experiences to recite.
The evil eye belief is regarded as distinct from witchcraft, and seems to perform some of the functions of expressing and releasing social tension that
witchcraft does in some other societies.

In traditional tribal African societies, where witchcraft is often practiced
among kin or affines, or in Oceania, where people of adjacent ethnic groups
perform bone-pointing and other black-magic rituals against each other,
social tensions are different from those in India. In India the family structure
and kinship network are so elaborately idealized that there is a limit to the
extent to which disruptive social tensions can be manifest within them.
Also, in South Asian peasant society there is little scope for tensions between geographically contiguous ethnic groups, because the ethnic sub-
groups are piled on top of each other as castes. It is caste that allows for
social differentiation, for politically dominant groups, for ritually pure or
pious groups, and for predominantly landowning groups. Challenges to
these partial monopolies turn out to be class conflicts more often than caste
conflicts. Foster and Kolenda have suggested that one of the functions of
caste is to reduce envy.[40]

When invidious qualities are attributed to an individual, the tendency is to
think of these as expressions of his social situation and his *karma* rather than
attack his personality, as in a witch-hunt. If one is poor, low-caste, ritually
polluting, crippled, barren, female, or otherwise in unfortunate circumstances, it is more or less presumed that there is a reason for the situation.
The lowest and most polluting castes were thought in the nineteenth century
to be able to pollute higher-caste men over a distance of a number of yards;
and the lowest of the Untouchables in South India, those who washed the

washermen's clothes, were regarded as Unseeables and polluting to the sight! Brāhmaṇs can recite the benevolently powerful Vedas, but workers of black magic and conjurers are generally of low caste. In the world of the gods, too, from the Brāhmaṇ viewpoint, the high gods are generally benign and are to be satiated with vegetarian *pūjā* by devotees in a pure state, but the low gods are sometimes malevolent and cause disease, and need to be appeased with bloody sacrifices. The tendency, therefore, is not to blame personally the one suspected of having cast an evil eye, but to attribute his malevolence to his *karma* or social state. This still allows one to invoke a scapegoat to explain how a prosperous person lost his health or wealth, and allows the upper classes to exaggerate (as they apprently do in all societies) the extent to which those not so fortunate are envious of them. But we should reiterate that the evil eye belief is too diffuse to be explained in all cases by the envy theory or by the bad *karma* of the one who casts it.

In most cases one suffering from the evil eye is not able to identify the caster, and even if suspicion does tend to focus on one person, action is seldom taken against him. In Tamil Nadu, when I asked what could be done to an evil eye suspect, the answer was usually "nothing." If a child becomes sick and the mother remembers that someone passed by who might have zapped the child, if the mother spies that person coming again she will simply take the child up onto the porch of the house, and not go on a witch-hunt. Witch-hunting seems in general to be contrary to the values of Indian society, for there is a mildness, especially in the southern and eastern parts of the subcontinent, that tempers the violence of revenge.

I could only find a few methods by which people could identify evil eye casters. One used in Maharashtra, according to Jackson, is to heat a potsherd in the hearth and spit on it repeatedly, uttering the names of various suspects; when it gets red the right name has been uttered. But the only action taken against a suspect so identified is verbal abuse. Jackson also recorded for Gujarat that a woman who is suspected of having cast the evil eye at a child will be called in and made to put her hands on the child to remove the evil. Also, one may wave alum around the head of an afflicted one and throw the alum in the fire; if the pieces come together in the shape of a male or female, the sex of the offender can be ascertained. I was told in Pakistan, in a Panjab village, that if someone is suspected of having cast the evil eye, one should put pins in a rag doll and throw it in the suspect's house, or else kill a chicken, put it in a bag, and throw it in that house. But in that village nobody could remember any direct action other than these rituals of sympathetic magic ever being taken against one suspected of having cast the evil eye.

Witches are not generally accused of having cast the evil eye, though on occasion they might be suspected (instances have been noted in Karnataka and in the Bhīl tribe). The only instance I have heard about of a witch-hunt against an evil eye suspect was recorded by O'Malley for Bihar. There an exorcist may be called to denounce the witch, who is assumed to be female. It is thought that witches make images of the person they wish to kill and put pins in them, or torture them, and that they assemble at night in the cremation ground, naked and chanting unholy incantations. It is said that in 1928 in Bihar nine witches were killed. But whereas witches hate and willfully attack, one who casts the evil eye in most cases does not even know that he has that power.

Black magic is known to most Tamil villagers but is thought of as distinct from the evil eye. When the art is performed it is by a man, not a woman, and the man is generally hired to do the job. It is thought that such a person can cause stones to rain down on an enemy's house, or cause his house to catch fire, or make him see visions of running dogs in the dark. This power is believed to operate by natural laws in response to the performance of the sorcerer. Personal animosity is much more likely to be expressed through litigation these days than through black magic.

The advantage of the evil eye belief in South Asian society is that it allows one to absolve himself of responsibility for misfortune, and find a scapegoat, without necessarily pointing his finger at someone or trying to destroy him. The evil eye belief performs some of the social functions of sorcery and witch-hunting, but at much less social cost because of the relative anonymity of the accused.

World View

Indian villagers do not perceive the universe as chaotic, but as operating according to natural forces and in reasonable patterns. Tamil villagers have told me, "If a snake bites, there is a reason." "If the crops dry up, there is a reason." The chief categories of reason invoked are: (1) birth stars or other astrological forces, (2) *karma*, deeds in this life or a past life that determine one's qualities and fate, (3) the action of a deity, (4) the action of another person, as through his powerful eye, pollution, or sorcery, and (5) natural causes, such as germs. As one magical healer told me, "Germs exist, but they only tell how one became ill, not why." It is also recognized that different kinds of people have different levels of susceptibility or resistance to these forces. As one villager said, "The evil eye is true, but not for all."

Thus it is not irrational to explain events through several levels of causes operating simultaneously. It certainly did not seem irrational to the potters who told me their pots split in the kiln because (1) I looked on, (2) it drizzled, (3) the kiln was not hot enough, (4) there was not enough sun to dry the pots. The elder potter concluded, "What am I able to do?" Other explanations for pots breaking in the kiln are offered elsewhere in India; in Kerala it is thought that demons cause the breakage, and in Bihar it may be attributed to witches.

Generally speaking, no more witch-hunting is directed toward the gods than toward people. Fear is not the chief reason people worship gods, for supplicants even of the low gods usually ask their assistance either in solving some present problem or in preventing future disabilities, and people seldom beseech the gods to restrain themselves from committing malicious deeds. People have power over the gods both through vows and through moral suasion, and men can help the gods by keeping malevolent forces and evil eyes away, as by *ālatti* or the waving of fire in front of the idol. The gods, in return, project their protective power through their eyes, symbolized in the fabulous gems often set in the eye-sockets of temple idols; Śiva and his consorts project their power through their third eye, and Vishṇu through his thousand eyes.

Thus the evil eye in South Asia is but a vague malaise; it is just one means among several of explaining events due to other people's presence without necessarily implicating them personally. Interpersonal relations are characterized by continual convivial conversation, a high level of oral artistry and bantering, and by a respect for other people's persons and interests. South Asian society does not seem to me to be characterized by the compulsive fear and suspicion reported for parts of the Near East, and is certainly not paranoid in the way that Kearney describes some Mexican Amerinds as being (chapter 11 in this book).

The Evil Eye Belief in Culture History

The distribution of the evil eye belief in South Asia suggests that it came into the subcontinent from the west, and/or it evolved along with the evolution of complex peasant-urban society. The belief is found from Iran to Sri Lanka in all peasant populations, and as far east as the eastern edge of the Bengal plain. Beyond Bengal, in the hills south and east of Assam, are people speaking Tibeto-Burmese languages, Mongoloid in appearance, who are really Southeast Asian hill people and not at all part of the Indic population of the plains of Bangladesh and India. Ethnographic reports of these tribal hill people, such as the various Nāga groups, Gāros, Lakhers, Padam-Minyong, and even the Maṇipuris, lack any substantial mention of the evil eye belief. Instead, these people have witches. Parry says of the Lakhers that they have the idea that the spirit of an envious person can give the envied a stomachache. The afflicted can spit out that spirit into a spoon containing food for it, and the food and the spirit can then be thrown outside. While this belief invokes envy to explain sickness, it is not the same as the evil eye belief. It is not surprising that the evil eye is not found among these hill people, for other Tibeto-Burmese peoples do not have any such clear-cut belief, nor do the Mongoloid and Southeast Asian peoples to the east of them.

The Himalayan regions do not have the belief, unless it is borrowed from India. Tibetans, Lepchas of Sikkim, and Bhotiyas have instead the idea that one can project harm through one's "working mouth." In Jansaur on the northern fringe of Uttar Pradesh the evil eye is associated with the evil mouth, and even in Bengal is partly subsumed under the "evil face." The Pahāris of the lower Himalayas, according to Berreman, do believe that the eye may cause one to get sick, a cow to go dry, or a thing to break, but unlike the plains Indic peoples, Pahāris do not hesitate to compliment children.

The evil eye belief seems to be only weakly developed in the plethora of tribal groups in the low hills of east-central India. It seems especially weak among the Muṇḍa-speaking peoples, whose languages and horticultural techniques are traceable to the hill regions east of Bengal and ultimately to Southeast Asia. The Hōs and Asuras, for instance, do not have this as a clearly defined belief, and in the large Santāl "tribe" women may possess the evil eye but men have the evil shadow.

Among the Dravidian-speaking tribal groups, it is interesting that the minuscule hill tribes of South India, having hunting-gathering traditions, such as the Kāḍar, do not have the evil eye belief, and neither do the Vāddās of Sri Lanka; among these groups sickness is thought to be accidental. In contrast with these hunting groups the tiny Toḍa tribe in the Nilgiri Hills, which has a dairy economy, strongly believes in the evil eye (as noted above). While the ethnic origin of the Toḍas is in dispute, there is no evidence that they were ever hunters; probably they were an offshoot of early intruders who were Dravidian-speaking cattle-herding or dairying people. Among the Central Indian Dravidian-speaking tribes, who are subsistence cultivators, the belief is not reported for the Kandh, Dhurwa, and some others, but a number of these tribes might have been originally Muṇḍa-speaking. The Orāons in southern Bihar do have the belief, and so do the Gōṇḍs, the largest Dravidian-speaking "tribe." These two groups were never Muṇḍa-speaking; historically they moved northeastward into the central Indian hill country to form a back eddy of the movement of Dravidian-speaking peoples, and so it is not surprising that they carried some traits of plains peasants.

Among the Indic-speaking tribal groups the evil eye belief is found most strongly in the large, peasant-like tribes toward the west of India, in Gujarat, western Madhya Pradesh, and Rajasthan. The Bhīls are the largest of these, and now speak a dialect of Gujarati, but they might once have been Dravidian-speaking. The evil eye belief occurs throughout tribal groups in the arid hills of western Pakistan and on into Afghanistan and Iran; some of these groups are nomadic and others are cultivators or urbanites.

We might inquire whether the evil eye belief could have taken shape with the diffusion into India of one of the linguistic stocks. The Tibeto-Burmese and Muṇḍa groups are eliminated from consideration because most speakers of those languages do not have the belief today, and because the belief clearly did not enter India from the east or northeast. As for Indo-European speech, the Dardic, Indic, and Persian linguistic families penetrated South Asia in that order. Speakers of languages of all three families have the belief today. And while the belief seems to be found across Eurasia among speakers of all linguistic families of the Indo-European phylum, the spread of that phylum could hardly have been responsible for diffusion of the belief in the Near East and the Mediterranean, nor, presumably, in India. The belief is not a particularly clearly defined one in the *Ṛgveda*. As for Dravid-

ian speech, we assume that it was current throughout western India and
Pakistan in protohistoric times, prior to the penetration of Indic speakers in
the mid-second millennium B.C., and that Dravidian languages, together
with the horse, iron technology, and plow cultivation, diffused into South
India soon after 1000 B.C.

Pursuing this question, I perused Tamil Śangam literature, written during
the first three centuries A.D., when there was minimal influence from
Sanskrit literature in the deep South. In this body of early Tamil literature
there are half a dozen references to the *tilakam,* the forehead spot, but
always in connection with women's adornment and toilette. Whatever original symbolism this mark might have had, even by that time it had come to
be subsumed under its cosmetic function, at least among the genteel folk of
ancient Tamil Nadu.[41] Dancers are said to have worn a frontlet, a pendant in
the center of the forehead.[42] Śiva is referred to several times as the Three-
Eyed,[43] and a consort of his, an early form of Mīnākshi, was a goddess
known as Kumāri who resided at Cape Comorin and who also had a third
eye. Roman soldiers who guarded the residence of the Pāṇḍiyan king were
called "harsh-eyed" and "cruel-eyed." [44] There are two references to tiger-
teeth charms, worn, it seems, by children,[45] and these are regarded today as
efficacious against the evil eye. The *tāli,* or wedding pendant, certainly had
a protective function then as now, and there are abundant references in this
literature to conch bangles, iron rings, bracelets, and gems in general. The
word *maṇi* refers to sapphires in particular, though also to rubies and pearls,
and *maṇi* has another meaning, the pupil of the eye. Blue and also red were
auspicious then as now. How much of this adornment was consciously to
protect against the evil eye we can never know. But there was a custom of
warriors' fastening mirrors onto the backs of their shields that would certainly seem to have had the function of averting the evil eye.[46]

Going back further, we inquire whether the belief might have prevailed in
the Indus civilization, which was at its peak about 2000 B.C. and was in all
probability Dravidian-speaking. Several points are suggestive, if not conclu-
sive. The name of the Tamil goddess Mīnākshi, Fish-Eye, may have had an
antecedent in the mythology associated with the fish in protohistoric western
South Asia. The fish symbol was by far the most common in the Indus
script, and occurred with the largest variety of modifying marks. Various
early tribes and lineages in western India had names like Mīna or Maccha,
meaning fish. The Dravidian word *mīn,* fish, is etymologically related to
mīn, meaning "brightness," "star," or "lightening," and also refers to

eyes with these qualities. The eyes of some figures in early art are indeed fish-shaped.

The stone figure sometimes called "the priest" excavated from Mohenjo-dāṛo has a frontlet held in place with a headband. And the excavations revealed a profusion of items known to have been used in historic times as charms: carnelian beads, conch bangles, little blue beads strung by the hundreds in necklaces. Also, the Indus civilization had the *lingam* as a sacred symbol. There was an insistence on privacy, so that featureless walls shielded the houses and the courtyards from the street, and no windows were available to curious passersby in these ancient cities. It is acknowledged even today that an important function of the long walls around compounds and houses, especially throughout western South Asia and among the elite everywhere, is to eliminate envious stares.[47] The women in the homes of the landed elite are to be particularly shielded from such stares; the seclusion of women is not an exclusively Islamic contribution to South Asia. The mystique of the eye must have been present in the Indus civilization, for pots excavated from the sites of Lothal and Kālibangān have rows of large eyes, with eyelashes, painted on. Also, there was a type of polyhedron bead with an eye-like dot on each facet. Old Babylonian records contemporary with the Indus civilization state that "fish-eyes" were among the things imported into Mesopotamia from lands probably identifiable with the coast of Pakistan and Gujarat.[48] Eyed beads are used even today in southern Europe and the Near East specifically as charms to avert the evil eye.

The evidence strongly suggests, therefore, that the evil eye as a definable belief evolved with the protohistoric pre-Āryan peasant-urban cultures of the Indus civilization and spread into the rest of South Asia from the west. It is probable that the belief was but one of a large number of religious beliefs and rituals that in protohistoric times stretched from the Mediterranean through the Near East to South Asia (a few of which are: smearing ashes on the forehead; ritual purity and water ablutions; beliefs about snakes, the fig tree, vines, etc., temple planning and temple functions, the office of priesthood; motifs in mythology, such as those of Gilgamesh and Noah; theory of the atomic nature of the universe; belief in rebirth; ideas associated with human hair and fingernails; similar charms and imprecations). Moreover, many remedies for ailments caused by the evil eye, and other specifics associated with the belief, range all the way from Scotland to Sri Lanka, as pointed out in the Introduction to this book.

If, then, the belief was current in the Indus civilization, it must have been introduced into the subcontinent by proto-Dravidian speakers (and evidence is accumulating of a linguistic relationship between Dravidian and proto-Elamite of southwestern Iran). This was the first fully developed peasant-urban civilization in South Asia. It may be significant that the evil eye belief is not very distinct in the *Ṛgveda*, which portrays an antique nomadic tribal ethos of the early Indo-Āryans. But the belief is found in the *Mahābhārata* and other epics, by which time the earlier and presumably Dravidian-speaking civilization had been rejuvenated under the catalyst of the Āryans and provided the basis of most of what we now call Hinduism.

The evil eye belief has a structural place in the societies of peasant-urban peoples in South Asia as elsewhere, but seems to be not needed in the simpler societies of hunters or shifting cultivators. The belief grew along with the development of complex cultures. We do not know whether it was a feature of the neolothic settlements of Afghanistan and western Pakistan prior to the Indus civilization, but it must have developed along with social hierarchy in that civilization. In its aftermath Dravidian-speaking cattle-keepers, farmers, and warriors moved down the peninsula to Sri Lanka (which explains why the belief is found in tribes that broke away from these early migrations, such as Toḍas and Orāons). It is absent among Dravidian-speaking hunting groups of the peninsula and among the Väddās, but the latter undoubtedly spoke languages eliminated by the impact of neolithic and farming cultures. Similarly, the belief was doubtless carried down the Gaṅgā plains by the Indic-speaking peoples who began to farm the plains as far east as Bengal by about 700 B.C. and overwhelmed the earlier Muṇḍa-speaking horticulturalists who probably did not have the evil eye belief. The complex of beliefs about the eye was perhaps reinforced by the intrusive Indo-European speakers. Certainly when Islam came to South Asia it further strengthened the belief, which had been picked up and throughly validated by that religion in the Arab and Persian lands before Muslims penetrated South Asia.

The increasingly complex urban society began to require mechanisms to institutionalize envy and measures to counteract its effect, in contrast with earlier hunting and shifting-cultivation societies, which lacked the hierarchy and role specialization of peasant-urban peoples. Also, as society became more complex and socially differentiated a larger variety of causative agents came to be invoked to explain unexpected events or misfortune, and among these was the power of the eye—not always linked with envy. And the use of various devices to ward off the evil eye gave people some feeling of control over their own fortune. At the same time, it allowed people to absolve themselves of responsibility for their misfortune by attributing ill events to other people's sinister intent—without going on witch-hunts, which would have been contrary to the respectful way people in India generally treat each other. And the reluctance to compliment was supportive of the specific role expectations of a caste society and of the child socialization necessary to maintain such a society. It was all part of the South Asian, essentially Hindu, way of life.

The South Asian data support John Roberts' conclusions (chapter 13) that the evil eye belief tends to be stronger where society is more hierarchical, sex roles more differentiated, patrilineal descent more pronounced, child socialization more strict, urbanization greater, and belief in a high god supportive of morality more definite. All these features are more pronounced in the western part of South Asia than in Bengal or South India or the Himalayan regions. I suspect, though, that these features are associated primarily with the evil eye belief as it relates to envy, while belief in the powerful eye, the protective eye, or symbolism highlighting the mystique of the eye, may not be stronger in Pakistan and western India than in other parts of the subcontinent.

The Evil Eye Belief in the 1970s

Even now, practically all villagers throughout peasant areas of South Asia are familiar with the evil eye belief. Some are conscious of it as an ever-present phenomenon or threat, and may quote the proverbial (Tamil) saying: "Even if you escape a thrown stone you still must escape the eye." More commonly, people might say, "I cannot believe it entirely, but there is a little truth in it."

Many of the preventatives and curatives listed above, such as throwing children on dung heaps or calling them by opprobrious names, have almost faded away. Such remedies as burning chilies and throwing salt are known everywhere, though mostly practiced now by old women. On the other hand, setting up pots in fields or on houses is fairly common in all South Asian countries, and most Hindus put up manikins on large buildings being erected. Tying on of amulets and charmed strings is common in almost all villages, Hindu, Muslim, and Buddhist.

Even if the "religious" aspects of the evil eye belief should fade away, there are behavior patterns that have evolved with it in South Asia that will presumably last indefinitely: the desire by those who can afford it to eat in private, as in booths in restaurants; the application of the forehead spot (even by Muslim women in Bangladesh); the use of colors and objects originally thought to avert the evil eye; maintenance of rituals involving fire, water, sweeping, incense, and the like, which may now be rationalized as cleanliness or purity; reluctance to compliment others; making the eyes large in paintings, and so on.

Some people among the modern urban elite have no conscious fear of the evil eye, and may be reluctant to discuss the "superstition." But many will admit to some degree of belief. One official in Pakistan, a Muslim who holds a top position in a government agency and had studied social science for six years in a major American university, confided to me that he still retains some vague feeling of uneasiness and suspicion when certain people look at him, and he cannot shake off the feeling by trying to be "rational."

Indeed, for many Hindus the whole matter is not irrational, and whether the evil eye is "true" is a bad question to ask. Fundamental presuppositions of life are that everyone's behavior and intentions affect the surrounding universe and have long-range implications, that the qualities of one's person are projected from his mind, and that one's psychic energy can be enhanced (as in yoga) and focused through the forehead. When educated Indians admit to some belief in the powerful eye, it is these presumed qualities of the human mind that they refer to. And who is to deny that research in parapsychology is veering toward the same opinion?

NOTES

1. Minturn and Hitchcock, p. 73, point out this difference in beliefs about causation of diseases in adults and those in children, based on their child socialization research in an Uttar Pradesh village.
2. Personal communication from Emmanuel Thomas, a sociologist from Kerala.
3. Jackson, pp. 61–62.   4. Narrated by Gifford, p. 20.
5. Barth, p. 145.   6. Minturn and Hitchcock, p. 76.
7. Klass, p. 182.   8. Narrated in Gifford, p. 44.
9. Barth, pp. 144–46.   10. Rivers, pp. 263–65.   11. Gifford, pp. 42–43.
12. Many of these examples from Maharashtra are from Jackson, and some are from Kale.
13. Many of these examples from Gujarat are from Jackson.

14. Rivers, pp. 263–65.   15. Mukherjea, pp. 289–90.
16. Klass, p. 182. In this case it was the anthropologist who suffered from sunburn, an ailment never seen by his landlord friends, who concluded it must be caused by *"maljeu."*
17. Thakur, p. 187.   18. Emmanuel Thomas, personal communication.
19. Minturn and Hitchcock, p. 76.   20. Barth, p. 145.
21. Jackson, p. 120.   22. Whitehead, p. 53.
23. Minturn and Hitchcock, p. 112.   24. Roy, p. 224.
25. Rivers, pp. 263–65.
26. From M. N. Srinivas, narrated in Foster, p. 176.
27. O'Malley, p. 138.   28. Gifford, p. 40.   29. O'Mally, p. 138.
30. Masani, pp. 73–75.   31. Ibid., p. 75.   32. Ibid., p. 72.
33. Diehl, *Church and Shrine,* pp. 111–13.   34. Gifford, p. 47.
35. Dubois, pp. 328–29.   36. Roy, pp. 86–88.
37. Mukherjea, pp. 289–90.
38. Minturn and Hitchcock, pp. 119–21. What was observed in this village probably holds true throughout most of western South Asia at least. That praising children would spoil them is an idea held most strongly by the middle-aged men, who are obliged to maintain a certain aloofness, and women in fact do praise their children sometimes. Old men, however, are accorded the privilege of doting on small children.
39. Minturn and Hitchcock, p. 119.
40. Pauline Kolenda, in her comments following the Foster article, states that Foster makes it respectable to think of caste as an envy-reducing mechanism.
41. References 39 through 44 pertain to texts in Old Tamil, published by the Saiva Siddhanta Book Publishing Society, Tirunelveli. *Kalittokai* 92.35; 97.11; 143.3; *Cilappatikāram* 4–54.
42. *Kalittokai* 92.35; 143.3.   43. *Puranānūru* 55.5; *Cilappatikāram* 12–78.
44. *Mullaipāṭṭu* 61.
45. *Akanānūru* 7.18; *Cilappatikāram* 12–28; see also Subrahmanian, p. 313.
46. *Kalavali* 28; also Subrahmanian, p. 150.
47. Hence the name of the Wisers' book, *Behind Mud Walls.*
48. Kramer, p. 111. Kramer suggests that "fish-eyes" might be pearls, but in view of the symbolism of fish eyes in South Asia they could as well be identified as eyed beads or eyed rings.

BIBLIOGRAPHY

Barth, Fredrik. *Nomads of South Persia.* London: Allen and Unwin, 1961.
Berreman, Gerald. *Hindus of the Himalayas.* Berkeley: University of California Press, 1963.
Brown, W. Norman. "The Name of the Goddess Mīnākṣi, 'Fish-eye.' " *Journal of the American Oriental Society* 67 (1947), 209–14.
Diehl, Carl G. *Church and Shrine.* Uppsala, 1965.
—— *Instrument and Purpose.* Lund, 1956.

Dubois, Abbé J. A. *Hindu Manners, Customs, and Ceremonies*. Henry Beauchamp, trans. 3d ed. Oxford: Oxford University Press, 1906.

Doshi, Shambhu Lal. *Bhils: Between Societal Self-Awareness and Cultural Synthesis*. New Delhi, 1971.

Foster, George M. "The Anatomy of Envy: A Study in Symbolic Behavior," *Current Anthropology* 13 (1972), 165–202.

Gifford, Edward. *The Evil Eye: Studies in the Folklore of Vision*. New York: Macmillan, 1958.

Jackson, A. T. M. *Folk Lore Notes,* R. E. Enthoven, ed. Vol. I, *Gujarat*. Vol. II, *Konkan*. Bombay, 1914.

Kale, D. N. *Agris: A Socio-Economic Survey*. Bombay, 1952.

Klass, Morton. *East Indians in Trinidad*. New York: Columbia University Press, 1961.

Kramer, S. N. "Dilmun: Quest for Paradise," *Antiquity* 37 (1963).

Krishna Iyer, L. A. *Social History of Kerala*. Vol. 2, *The Dravidians*. Madras, 1970.

Masani, R. P. *Folk Culture Reflected in Names*. Bombay, 1966.

Minturn, Leigh, and John Hitchcock. *The Rājpūts of Khalapur, India*. New York: Wiley, 1966.

Mukherjea, Charulal. *The Santals*. Calcutta, 1962.

O'Malley, L. S. S. *Popular Hinduism*. Cambridge: Cambridge University Press, 1935.

Parrey, N. E. *The Lakhers*. London: Macmillan, 1932.

Rivers, W. H. R. *The Todas*. 1906. Reprint, Oosterhout, Netherlands, 1967.

Roy, Sarat Chandra. *The Orāons of Chōṭā Nāgpūr*. Ranchi, 1915.

Subrahmanian, N. *Śangam Polity*. Bombay, 1966.

Thakur, V. T. *Sindhi Culture*. Bombay, n.d.

Whitehead, Henry. *The Village Gods of South India*. 2d ed. Calcutta, 1921.

Wijesekera, Nandadeva. *Veddas in Transition*. Colombo, 1964.

ENYA FLORES-MEISER

9. PHILIPPINES

The Hot Mouth and Evil Eye

IT SEEMS TO ME appropriate to warn the reader at the outset that this paper has little to say about the evil eye. The Filipinos about whom I am writing have no term for it—a literal or close translation of it—in their native languages.[1] Neither have they borrowed the Spanish term *mal ojo* to fill the void. What seems to approximate the evil eye best among Tagalog groups is the concept of the hot mouth (*mainit na bibig*). At the least, the parallel can be easily drawn between them: both the evil eye and the hot mouth are personal attributes believed to cast ills. On this basis, I accepted Dr. Maloney's invitation to participate in the symposium that gave rise to this book, in preparation for which I set out, during the summer of 1972, to interview some Filipino immigrants living in the Chicago area and in Indiana. This paper will attempt (1) to describe within the limits of available data the hot mouth phenomenon or complex; (2) to demonstrate its similarities to the evil eye belief; and (3) to identify its probable place and articulation among systems of folk belief in the Philippine cultures.

It might be worthwhile to note also that during the interviews I did not witness actual behaviors that would serve as empirical referents for the hot mouth phenomenon, as one might under the conditions permitted by direct participant observation. Since the hot mouth is associated with children's illness, as will be seen shortly, I covered in the main the ethnographies on Fil-

ENYA FLORES-MEISER is Associate Professor of Anthropology at Ball State University, Muncie, Indiana. She received her anthropological training at the University of the Philippines, the University of Iowa, and The Catholic University of America. She was raised in the Philippines, and has conducted research in that country among the Samal Muslims and also the Tagalogs of southern Luzon.

She is now conducting research among Philippinos in Chicago and Indiana, of which this paper is a partial result.

ipino child-rearing practices for empirical data.[2] Only Jocano's accounts from Panay have been very helpful. Where relevant, I will use some of his observations for illustration.

Childhood memories constituted the bulk of the data obtained from informants: what was said and heard when one was very young, or before going to college in Manila, or before one's grandparents died. A few gave accounts of actual experiences. In addition, I have tried to incorporate my own recollections for this presentation. Except for 3 female informants, none of the 43 individuals interviewed claimed belief in the concept at all. The interviewing required a great deal of patience, for too often an informant claimed ignorance right from the start. Even when the interview was finally given, the information was sketchy. Conceivably, the socioeconomic position of the informants could offer some explanation for this. Most of them were medical and paramedical professionals, dedicated to modern views long before emigration. Perhaps the fund of information lies elsewhere, among the native specialists who have been slowly outnumbered in their own communities and are not here. Still, perhaps the hot mouth might have been a vague idea to begin with, if not altogether rudimentary, thus assuming a position subsidiary to that of other existing beliefs.

Of the informants in the sample used in this research, 33 (15 males and 18 females) are originally from the Tagalog provinces and Manila; the rest are native Ilocano, Bicolano, Cebuano, and Ilongo speakers. They range in age from 25 to 65 years. All belong culturally to the dominant Christian groups. Non-Tagalogs were included in the sample for comparison, but unless otherwise noted, the data at hand pertain to the Tagalog sample. Interviews were unstructured and conducted both in English and in Tagalog languages. Although the informants may know others in the sample, they do not compose a community as such. At best, they maintain secondary relationships by acquiring memberships in and supporting regional medical associations and their auxiliaries and alumni clubs.

At the initiation of each interview, the informant was asked, "Do you know anything about the evil eye or the Spanish *mal ojo?*" None claimed he did, much less understood the term when translated literally into Tagalog. However, when the effects of the evil eye as reported in the literature were described to them, the informants identified the same as *bati.*

Bati *and Hot Mouth*

Bati means literally "to say something." More than this, it means "to cast ill through speech." Other Tagalog terms of more local usage are synonyms; southern Tagalogs use *balis* or *gaway,* while Manilans and northern Tagalogs prefer *bati* or *usog.* The latter terms are used extensively even among non-Tagalog speakers who had lived and had been schooled in Manila. An Ilongo informant referred to *bati* as *nababaan.* (*Baba* is the Ilongo word for mouth.) An Ilocano speaker described the same phenomenon using the term *baros.*

Bati is supposedly brought about by a hot mouth. According to this belief, children during their first few years of life are vulnerable objects, particularly if they are regarded as beautiful and healthy. Outstanding features of the Caucasoid type and cast, such as fair skin, deep-set eyes, natural waves and curls in the hair, and chubbiness (admired exclusively in children) are considered at once assets and liabilities. A child bearing any of them is constantly noticed, admired, and placed in imminent danger. I remember an incident to this effect when I was seven years old. My brother was already over two years old and had not had his first hair cut. Normally, a boy's first haircut is scheduled shortly after his first birthday. Because he had beautiful, curly hair the females in the household, including my mother, took great pleasure in combing and tying a ribbon around it. It seemed they were sufficiently persuasive to postpone the haircut another year. Then one day as he was being tended, my mother's maternal uncle told one of my aunts to get a pair of scissors. He said angrily: "Do you want this child to be noticed everywhere and get sick? You must all be crazy to keep him this way!" That very moment he grabbed the scissors and cut my brother's hair.

Admiration becomes *bati* when the child subsequently undergoes sudden change in physical condition for no apparent reason (i.e., when he does not have a fever). He becomes restless, cries incessantly, and refuses to eat or sleep. A commonly recognized specific symptom of *bati* is a distended stomach known as *kabag,* or in Spanish, *empacho.* When illness strikes, rational explanation is immediately sought within the strictures of modern medicine in the person of the medical doctor. If his diagnosis fails and he is unable to provide a fast cure, the child is pronounced *nabati* (i.e., victimized by *bati*) by the others around him. If no doctor is available, it is readily presumed that he might have been *nabati,* considering the child's attractive qualities and the precipitous manner in which illness visits him. The causative agent of *bati* is a person who has a hot mouth.

It is not clear when or why a person has a hot mouth. Explanations are generally ambiguous and expressed over a wide spectrum. One male informant claimed that "people who have hot mouths and can cause *bati* have certain powers in them in the same way that witches have powers," as opposed to normal individuals who are not so endowed. However, this informant was not equating the hot mouth with witchcraft. Rather, his parallel between them implies that both are due to highly personal power qualities and bear no relationship to each other. In the case of the Ilongo informant mentioned earlier, he believed that the hot mouth "ensues from one being in intense emotional state, particularly extreme anger." (He made no reference to envy or jealousy in similar context.) "In the height of anger," the informant continued, "a person may effectively cast *bati* as he would similarly a curse." Thus according to him an angry person is dangerous because he can cause another either *bati* or a curse. The distinction between *bati* and curse was suggested by the informant and from an analytical standpoint seems to lie in the degree of intentionality.[3] An angry person is not likely to admire anybody, even a child, unless he willfully desires to cause harm. This, of course, contradicts the majority's view that *bati* is an unintentional act on the part of the person believed to possess the hot mouth. At the other end of the spectrum, two individuals, while admitting knowledge of *bati,* and in one case claiming witness to an actual happening, have not heard of the hot mouth as the cause of *bati*. Extra-personal sources (e.g., spirits, saints, the Devil, God, etc.) were not delineated. Neither was it suggested that the possession of the hot mouth is acquired through biological inheritance or magic. The rest of the informants believed that having a hot mouth, and therefore the ability to cause *bati,* is potentially characteristic of everyone. Yet nobody in particular goes through life with the reputation for having a hot mouth. It is indeed conceivable for a person to have it in one instance, but not in the next. No person or group is in any way so marked permanently. The negative act of the hot mouth bearer in subtle ways is like that in the evil eye [4] and witchcraft. As with the witch and the person with the evil eye, knowledge of his offense and power invariably surprises the hot mouth bearer.

The Tagalog conception of the hot mouth comes very close to what Jocano had written about the people of Malitbog, Panay:

The people of Malitbog believe that everyone possesses an illness inducing breath. This comes from inside of the body (some say from the liver, others say from the stomach) and comes out through the pulse, the eyes, and the mouth (by the first word spoken). Should the pulse of two individuals beat at the same time their eyes meet, the one who utters the first word casts an ?usog power over the other. . . .

Aside from ?usog there is another illness inducing force inherent in spoken words and human breath. This is ?abay. . . . It is very close to "inner or psychic predisposition to illness or ill luck." [5]

The Tagalogs, however, do not draw a strict distinction; rather, they blend the above categories.

Suspicions of hot mouth are directed in general toward strangers and nonrelatives. Unlike the evil eye in some places,[6] the hot mouth is not attributed to relatives. But guests, casual acquaintances, newly acquired friends, and sometimes neighbors are not exempted from suspicion. Here emerges a class of persons, occupying a social space somewhere between kin and strangers, toward whom one is ambivalent. One male informant indicated that in his native town in Nueva Ecija Province, "women tend to be suspected, since they are likely to notice children more." Three women in the sample claimed that their children were supposedly victimized by females; this had been revealed to them by diviners. Older children are regarded as equally dangerous.

Precautions and Remedies

To ward off possible inflictions a person upon encountering a certain baby for the first time is expected to take some precautions: (1) apply a touch of saliva anywhere on the baby's body; (2) blow softly over its head; or (3) say to it *Puera usog* or *Puera bati*—literally, "Let no *usog* (or *bati*) be cast upon you." The last is a favorite among mothers because it is sanitary. The above measures, which are also curatives, bring to mind comparable acts related to the evil eye; among some Mexican groups, a slap on the baby's buttocks, a pat on its head, or a simple touch is believed effective.[7] Contrary to the situation in societies with developed evil eye beliefs, such as India or Mexico, in the Philippines children are not deliberately kept dirty or inconspicuously dressed to escape *bati*.[8] Their natural characteristics, not their dress and grooming, make them subject to it.

The first meeting with a person is critical because this is supposed to be the most opportune time for *bati*. The risk is lessened with increasing exposure to the same person. Sometimes unnecessary exhibition of children's photographs is also deemed unsafe. In a letter to me my brother wrote about a snapshot of my daughter taken when she was nine months old:

> I showed Cristina's picture to everyone at work. They were all taken by her. One of my women friends asked if she might keep it for a while because she is conceiving. She said she would like to have a child as healthy as Cristina. I, of course, loaned it to her only after she applied her saliva to it. I told her to do so or else Cristina might grow thin.[9]

When *bati* is thought to have been cast, the suspected individuals are summoned. Beginning with the last person to have seen the child, and going backward in time, the search continues until the owner of the hot mouth is established. Quite simply, the saliva of the person responsible when applied to the child should supposedly restore him to health. The following observation describes the procedure:

> Bilin went home one afternoon after a short visit at the neighbor's house. She hardly reached home when the neighbor's son came running after her. When asked what he wanted, the boy said he was sent by his mother to call for Bilin because his younger sister (a seven-month-old baby) was crying hard after she left. At first Bilin refused to return: "Why, am I a witch? Or a sorcerer? I have nothing to do with the crying of a child." However, the boy insisted saying that "you might have cast an ?usog on my little sister." Bilin's mother also prevailed upon her to help the child. "Pity the child," the mother said. So Bilin went back. The baby was crying hard when they arrived. Bilin drenched her index and middle fingers with saliva and applied these on the stomach of the infant. Momentarily, the baby stopped crying and went to sleep.[10]

A similar account was given by an informant, a nurse, according to whom,

> *bati* happens also to adults on rare occasions. I know a lady back home who is very pretty. She stands out more so because she married an ordinary looking man. Everywhere they went, she was quite noticeable. One day she was suddenly seized by severe pains. For three days she suffered from stomachaches until everyone she remembered meeting or visiting her prior to the pains was summoned to the house to touch her. Presumably, the person who caused her condition was found because she recovered soon afterward.

To take notice does not necessarily constitute *bati*. Rather, it is what one might have said or thought privately that counts and poses the danger. Perhaps it is here that a significant connection between the eye and the mouth may be sought: both act as media for something else that is viewed as intrinsically negative. Two other informants from the sample thought that a mere stare (*pansin*) might equally cast *bati*. The first, a 27-year-old medical technician, told of the following incident:

> My girl friend and I were interns at a hospital in Baguio City. One day we went to the market place to shop. There were a number of Igorots in the area and the place was crowded. My girl friend has an attractive face. Its skin is very smooth. That night when we returned to the dormitory, I noticed that her face was all blown up. Its texture had grown very coarse. Immediately, she went to the resident doctor in the hospital for help. Two days passed and there appeared to have been no improvements at all. So she asked permission to go to Manila to consult with a leading dermatologist. I offered to accompany her. A few weeks later, her face seemed to have grown much worse. Just then she started asking around for the ablest curer. A friend of hers led us to a diviner-curer practicing in Manila. Supposedly, he had been to the United States. The consultation was private so I was unable to see everything. He asked us to give him all the details of that day at the market place—what we did, whom we saw and what was said.
>
> He told her that an Igorot took notice of her and might have admired her face. He applied some type of cream to her face and told her to come back the following week. After the second visit, my friend was cured! It was possible that the cream was chemically powerful. After all, he had been to the States and he might have brought it back with him. But going through it all with her, I cannot but believe the whole thing!

The second informant, a medical doctor, noted "that while some people might have hot mouths, some may have hot eyes. In either case they can cause *bati*," he said. When asked if only hot-mouthed individuals can cause *bati*, a female informant noted: "A person with hot hands can also cause a child to become sick by inadvertently touching it. This is also *usog*."

The sudden appearance of *bati* symptoms is accompanied by the expectation of instant cure. Within 48 hours it is anticipated that the causative agent will be discovered. If, afterwards, the medical doctor could not provide a cure and the causative agent could not be found, then the case is brought to a diviner-curer. The divining process to detect *bati* and other phenomena causing ill is called *suob*. A female informant narrates the following story:

> It was during the Japanese occupation, and we were living in Manila when this incident happened. My eldest daughter, then nine months old, was crying continuously and would not eat. We took her to our family doctor but he found nothing wrong with her. She had no fever. Several days passed and she seemed to have become worse. She began to lose weight, which really scared us. So my mother,

despite my husband's objections, decided to send for a woman from Bulacan to examine my daughter's condition.

She held the child naked over smoking charcoal several times. Then she covered her body with wide leaves. The leaves were then viewed against the light for impressions. Believe it or not, there were impressions, all right. What stood out most is the image of a head with pigtails hanging. According to this woman, the diviner, my daughter was a victim of *usog* caused by a woman in pigtails. There were also some leaves bearing dog-like impressions. She said: "Your daughter's eyes were noticed by this woman. Also, a big dog scared her."

No one seemed to know who this woman could be. There was no way to find her. So, for three days, the diviner repeated the smoking process until no more impressions appeared on the leaves. She rubbed my daughter's body with some herbal mixture in oil medium, and periodically uttered some spells over her head. In no time my child was back to normal.

A variation of the above cure, cited by another informant, involved melting of some rock composite, which when cooled off would form certain figures. "They will indicate whether a person is the cause of the illness. If so, the sex may also be identified," she said.

No informant knew of any case in which a child's death was attributed to *bati*. As most of them rationalized, the steady medication prescribed by the doctor will sooner or later lead to recovery. Most informants maintained that *bati,* if not in direct association with sorcery, is very much like it. The parallel was put succintly by a male informant when he said: "*Bati* is to children as *kulam* [sorcery] is to adults." However, this analogy breaks down when one considers that *kulam* is voluntary, whereas *bati* is not.

As with the evil eye, *bati* is extended to plants and fruits. Seasonal fruits are believed especially susceptible. To admire a ripening fruit in another's orchard (e.g., a jackfruit, pineapple, santol) is to endanger its future. It might fall off, turn sour, rot, be attacked by animals. In any case keeping it after a compliment guarantees no gainful prospect for the owner. So he gives it to the admirer. If it is not ready to be plucked, he is asked to return for it at the proper time. The customary wrapping of fruits has a dual purpose: to shield it from animals and from *bati*. One informant thought that "pregnant women are especially detrimental to fruits. They can turn them sour and tasteless. However, pregnant women are no more *bati* agents than anybody else." Nobody in the sample knew for sure if *bati* might inflict domesticated animals and livestock. But as one informant surmised, "the carabao, especially, may be an object of sorcery. Maybe *bati* can also inflict it as well as pregnant animals and cause them to abort."

One last point must be mentioned here. A few informants, in describing what they believe *usog* to mean, would include not only the effects of human acts but also those of barking dogs. Diviners have been known to single out the dog as an *usog*-causing agent equal to the human being. Why only the dog, and not also other domesticated animals, is certainly curious. These same informants did not make clear whether the *usog*-causing dogs also have hot mouths like human agents.

The Hot Mouth–Bati Complex in Relation to Other Folk Beliefs

The hot mouth–*bati* complex is not at all easy to delineate. It is either quite particularized or too generalized. No doubt local origins as well as personal interpretations could account for the various associations informants have established. Nonetheless, the following characteristics can be specified:

1. As an event, the hot mouth–*bati* is generally seen to be brought about by a confluence of elements vague in the main, unique in every case, and bearing little predictability. It results in essence from the combination of persons, their predispositions, and timing. It simply happens. Unlike in magic, the compounding of the necessary elements is not the result of deliberate acts.

2. The hot mouth–*bati* is an expression of personal power generally obscure in origin, if not suspected to inhere in speech itself or in the spoken word. It is almost mana-like,[11] except for its negative value.[12] Neither the person endowed with the power nor, certainly, its victim derive any benefits from having it.

3. As part of a general theory of disease causation, the hot mouth–*bati* complex lies outside the scope of modern medicine and largely pertains to children. It is in a sense a major part of the "pediatrics" of native medicine, but remains subordinate to the more pervasive animistic explanations of disease in general. Animistic beliefs for Philippine Christian and non-Christian groups alike, are too well known to require specific documentation.

4. Perhaps the origin of the hot mouth–*bati* complex is rooted, remotely, in the hot-cold theory of pathology. Foster has traced this theory from the Greeks to the Arabs, to the Spaniards, to Latin America,[13] and presumably, to other societies influenced by Spain, of which the Philippines is one. The survival from this long process of diffusion may be found in the distinction between hot and cold foods. To my knowledge, a general inventory of these

categories has not been compiled for the Christian Philippines, as was done for Latin America. However, occasional reference to hot and cold foods is continually made:

> The two categories of food in Malitbog are the "cold" the "hot" foods. Hot foods are bad for the nursing mother. These include jackfruits, breadfruits, mangoes, and starchy tubers of plants known as gabi. . . . Vegetables, white rice, and seafood are considered cold foods and are good for the nursing mother.[14]

Some of the informants in the sample claimed that fruits in general are classified as cold and are not to be eaten in the morning before the intake of warm beverages lest one suffer from stomachaches. Another concept that may be related to the hot-cold taxonomy is the concept of the cool or cold hands (*malamig na kamay*), as opposed to hot hands (*mainit na kamay*). The former make plants grow well and are therefore most suited to agriculture; the latter have the reverse effect. There is also the person whose "blood is hot," an admission one makes to denote antipathy or dislike toward another. On the other hand, one has cool or cold blood toward a person of whom one is fond for unexplained reasons. The hot or cold quality of one's blood is, therefore, relative to his feelings toward someone. In examining the hot categories—hot mouth, hot eyes, hot hands, hot blood, or even hot foods—one cannot but be inclined to conclude that the hot quality by and large is given a negative value.

5. In more ways than one, the hot mouth–*bati* phenomenon, if not altogether separate from it, appears to be a variant of the evil eye. In the course of this paper, I have tried to establish their resemblances, which I will now summarize in the following section.

Parallels between the Hot Mouth–Bati and the Evil Eye

1. Both the hot mouth and the evil eye are thought to inflict ill unintentionally. Almost without exception, the knowledge of his power flabbergasts the owner. In this regard both the evil eye and the hot mouth are mildly reminiscent of witchcraft. However, the person who bears the evil eye or hot mouth is not, ipso facto, evil or bad. Both evil eye and hot mouth serve as an immediate explanation for a "bad" experience.

2. Babies and young children are almost always the victims. The ills that visit them, as described (especially for the Indian and Mexican societies),

are identical, as might be expected. After all, children's behaviors at a young age are circumscribed.

3. Therapy and prevention in both cases demand some slight physical contact (touch, slap, etc.) between the probable or potential offender and the victim. To restore or maintain health the offender must give to the victim a little of himself. While in more elaborated evil eye beliefs wearing of charms, jewelry, and the like is a deflecting device, among Filipinos such trappings on children are intended to protect them from animistic spirits.

4. Plants are believed to be subject to both phenomena. The power of the evil eye may affect animals and inanimate objects as well,[15] whereas, in the hot mouth–*bati,* effects on animals have not been fully established, and on things are unknown. But in the Tagalog *usog,* a synonym for *bati,* a human may be victimized not only by another human but also by a dog. This reverse effect was nowhere mentioned in the Mexican or Indian data.

5. In both cases any person is viewed potentially as an agent, although there is a tendency to blame women.[16]

6. Finally, both phenomena transpire while admiring or paying compliments to an object for its beauty and extraordinary characteristics.

To my mind, this last similarity brings the hot mouth into the same class as the evil eye. The intrinsic connection between them, of course, is the ultimate question. But a more immediate one is why in both cases the positive act of admiring or paying compliment to someone or something possessed by another should produce negative consequences in the object esteemed. I will not debate Foster's thesis on envy as the probable underlying psychological foundation for the symbolic or projective meaning of some folk beliefs, of which the evil eye is one. Nor am I to deny or affirm, based on the nature of my data, his theory of the limited good.

Instead, an explanation on a more immediate plane for the hot mouth–*bati* and evil eye behaviors may be sought in the principles of child-rearing practices. It is common knowledge that in many societies of the world there is skewed emphasis on direct application of negative sanctions as opposed to positive ones to achieve social conformity. The reverse is often noted for the United States. Accordingly, the direct praising of another, which is a recognized form of positive sanction, is done rarely in the former instance but generously in the latter. My own experience as a Tagalog and among a Samal group, supported by ethnographies on other Philippine groups,[17] bears this out. In the world of the adults direct praising or compliment is

hardly employed lest one embarrasses another. Toward older children similar acts are conducted in a teasing manner, as if to mute the aura of a serious
compliment. And finally, to babies, direct praise is tabooed behavior. This
is not to suggest that admiring or praising something or someone worthy of
such sanction is absent. Far from it. Rather it is communicated indirectly
through a middle person. It is largely in this social arrangement that the act
of approbation is interpreted to be well meant and satisfying for the intended
recipient.

If I may digress momentarily, I would like also to note that admiration,
compliment, etc., by indirect manner is the positive counterpart of transmitting gossip. In both instances, the individual, whether rewarded or rebuked,
learns of it through a circuitous process. Relative to this line of argument,
the belief in the evil eye, hot mouth, or any other variant thereof may be
viewed as a mechanism by which simple direct rewarding may be minimized
and made to support the enculturation process.

Under the conditions in which this research was conducted, it was most
difficult to determine or even speculate about the levels of sociocultural organization into which the hot mouth–*bati* complex is institutionalized.
Equally problematic is indicating precisely its functional significance in
those levels. The informants from whom the above data were taken compose
a marginal group, both professionally and culturally. They have experienced
in their lifetime transition from rural to urban living, from peasant to industrial existence, which probably accounts for their minimal knowledge of the
hot mouth–*bati* folk belief.

Conclusion

The degree to which the Tagalog hot mouth–*bati* belief is developed makes
it subordinate to the more predominant animistic beliefs, and marginal relative to other folk beliefs. Of the latter, two are probably most significant: the
hot-cold theory of pathology and the evil eye. Both have been fairly well
documented by Foster for Mexico and other Latin American societies, and
historically established to have originated from the Mediterranean area and
entered Latin America by a long process of cultural transmission. Presuming
a similar diffusion to the Philippines via the Iberian cultures, it is conceivable that the hot mouth–*bati* is a syncretic rearrangement of selected elements from these two folk beliefs. On the other hand, India, with elaborate

evil eye and evil mouth beliefs, is geographically closer and much older in its influence. There appears to be no sufficient evidence, however, for the existence of a comparable phenomenon among non-Christian groups. Yet we cannot be too quick to rule out the Indian connection, for it is a truism that ethnographies are not complete.[18] Similarly, the role of the itinerant Arabs in the diffusion cannot be dismissed. However, proof along this line will entail a closer examination also of Indonesian and Malayan societies.

Assuming that the evil eye is a foreign trait, I have not established any specific level of syncretism between it and the traditional animism from which the hot mouth–*bati* concept may have directly emerged. To clarify, the nature of the personal power involved in this belief has not been logically linked to the spirits. By and large, this power has remained ambiguous.

NOTES

1. There are some 80 languages in the Philippines, of which the major ones are Tagalog, Ilocano, Bicolano, Pampango, Cebuano, Ilongo, and Waray.
2. Guthrie and Jacobs, Jocano, Nurge, Nydegger and Nydegger.
3. I was not able to pursue any further the distinction between curse and *bati*.
4. Madsen, Levine and Levine, Romney and Romney, Minturn and Hitchcock.
5. Jocano, p. 29.   6. Madsen, p. 76.
7. See Clark; Foster, *Tzintzuntzan*; Madsen.
8. Minturn and Hitchcock, p. 312.
9. Personal communication.   10. Jocano, p. 290.
11. Codrington, pp. 119, 120.   12. Firth, pp. 483–89.
13. Foster, *Tzintzuntzan,* p. 185; Foster and Rowe.
14. Jocano, p. 27.   15. Madsen, p. 75.
16. Le Vine, pp. 137–38; Pitt-Rivers, p. 198.
17. Nurge, pp. 81–82; Nydegger.
18. Although I have not exhausted the literature on the non-Christian groups, I found no reference to the hot mouth in the ethnographies I read. I suspect that the hot mouth may be true only for the Philippine Christian groups. There is no similar evidence of the belief among Muslim Samals of whom I have firsthand knowledge.

BIBLIOGRAPHY

Clark, Margaret. *Health in the Mexican-American Culture*. Berkeley: University of California Press, 1970.
Codrington, R. H. *The Melanesians*. New York: Dover, 1971.

Firth, Raymond. "The Analysis of Mana: An Empirical Approach," *The Journal of Polynesian Society* 49 (1940), 483–510.

Foster, George M. "The Anatomy of Envy: A Study in Symbolic Behavior," *Current Anthropology* 13 (1972), 165–202.

—— "Cultural Responses to Expressions of Envy in Tzintzuntzan," *Southwestern Journal of Anthropology* 21 (1965), 24–35.

—— "Relationships between Spanish and Spanish American Folk Medicine," *Journal of American Folklore* 66 (1953), 201–17.

—— *Tzintzuntzan*. Boston: Little, Brown, 1967.

—— and John H. Rowe. "Suggestions for Field Recording of Information on the Hippocratic Classification of Diseases and Remedies," *Kroeber Anthropological Papers* 5 (1931), 1–3.

Guthrie, George M., and Pepita Jimenez Jacobs. *Child Rearing and Personality Development in the Philippines*. University Park: Pennsylvania State University Press, 1966.

Jocano, F. Landa. *Growing Up in a Philippine Barrio*. New York: Holt, Rinehart and Winston, 1969.

LeVine, Robert, and Barbara B. LeVine. "Nyansongo: A Gusii Community in Kenya," in *Six Cultures (Studies of Child Rearing)*, Beatrice Whiting, ed. New York: Wiley, 1963.

Lieban, Richard W. *Cebuano Sorcery*. Berkeley and Los Angeles: University of California Press, 1967.

Madsen, William. *The Mexican-Americans of South Texas*. New York: Holt, Rinehart and Winston, 1964.

Minturn, Leigh, and John T. Hitchcock. "The Rajputs of Khalapur, India," in *Six Cultures (Studies of Child Rearing)*, Beatrice Whiting, ed. New York: Wiley, 1963.

Nurge, Ethel. *Life in a Leyte Village*. Seattle: University of Washington Press, 1965.

Nydegger, William, and Corinne Nydegger. "Tarong: An Ilocano Barrio in the Philippines," in *Six Cultures (Studies of Child Rearing)*, Beatrice Whiting, ed. New York: Wiley, 1963.

Pitt-Rivers, Julian. *The People of the Sierra*. Chicago: University of Chicago Press, 1961.

Romney, Kimball, and Romaine Romney. "The Mixtecans of Juxtlahaca, Mexico," in *Six Cultures (Studies of Child Rearing)*, Beatrice Whiting, ed. New York: Wiley, 1963.

SHEILA COSMINSKY

10. GUATEMALA

The Evil Eye in a
Quiché Community

A TWO-MONTH-OLD female infant was sick with such symptoms as diarrhea, vomiting, listlessness, crying, anorexia, and one eye larger than the other. The godmother of the child performed a diagnostic test: two eggs from a black chicken were put in a basin of water and placed for an hour beneath the bed where the child slept. Then the eggs were broken and the pattern of the eggs in the water determined that the child had the illness known as the evil eye. Since the eggs draw the evil eye from the baby, this procedure also served as a treatment. The godmother had a reputation for being able to perform this diagnosis, but was not considered a specialist.

This diagnosis was supported by a retrospective analysis of the recent activities of the mother, a 24-year-old woman with three other children. The mother had taken the baby with her to a celebration of the anniversary of the local agricultural cooperative, where many people were present. Surely, someone there had given the baby the evil eye. The mother was scolded for going out in a crowd with such a young infant.

In addition to the egg test/cure, the baby was given a half a glass of a mixture of an egg of a black chicken with an infusion made from ten tips (top leaves) of the herb *ruda* or rue (*Ruta graveolens*), garlic, tobacco, and *sal de nitro* (from the pharmacy). The baby grew worse, however, and the

SHEILA COSMINSKY is Assistant Professor of Anthropology at Rutgers University, Camden, New Jersey. She received her Ph.D. from Brandeis University. She has worked on interethnic relations in Belize and on medical anthropology in Guatemalan Indian communities, on which she has published several articles.

She has made several research trips to Guatemala, the latest in the winter of 1975.

mother took her to a local midwife who was known for her ability to cure children's diseases. The midwife told her that the baby did not have the evil eye; rather the mother was not well because her milk was too "cold." This was the reason the baby was not nursing and was sick. She said the mother should not eat "cold" foods and drinks, especially soft drinks, but should eat "hot" foods and chicken soup. She should also take a purgative, then come back, and the midwife would give her some other medicine. The mother followed this advice but did not return because the baby began to recover.

From the parents' point of view, this recovery was not contradictory nor did it mean that the evil eye had necessarily been misdiagnosed. The child had had different illnesses with different causes. They were sure she had had the evil eye, especially since one eye was bigger than the other, and that the egg treatment had helped cure that. But she was also sick with *empacho* (indigestion), colic, and other symptoms of stomach ailments, which is what the midwife had diagnosed, and which were caused by the cold milk.

The Community

The above case occurred in the Indian community of Santa Lucia Utatlán, a town of around 6,000 people located at an altitude of approximately 8,500 feet in the highlands of Guatemala. My information on the evil eye was collected in the course of a study of medical beliefs and practices in Chuchexic, a rural settlement, or *aldea,* of this town.[1] The population of the *aldea* Chuchexic is about 1,600, of whom 96 percent are Quiché-speaking Mayan Indians and 4 percent Ladinos or non-Indians.[2] Over 60 percent of the males are bilingual in Quiché and Spanish, but only some 15 percent of the women can speak any Spanish.

The concept of the evil eye appears to have diffused to the New World from Spain and today is one of the most widespread folk beliefs concerning illness found in Spanish America. This paper is concerned with the causes, symptoms, diagnosis, and treatment of the evil eye "illness" as reported in that community. The data will be compared with data from other parts of Guatemala, and then will be discussed in terms of their ethnomedical and sociocultural context.

Causation

The Quiché term for the evil eye illness is *uwawinaq*.[3] The Spanish term *mal de ojo* is also frequently used. Adams has defined the evil eye as an invisible force that emanates from certain persons who are particularly strong. It should be noted, however, that the term "evil eye," at least in Santa Lucia, is used to refer to the condition or illness of the victim rather than the power of its owner.

The strength or force is often associated with or believed to derive from people who have "strong" blood or "hot" blood. This condition may be permanent, as determined by one's birth or destiny, or it may be temporary, as in the "hot" states of pregnancy, menstruation, or drunkenness. It is only in a "hot" state that one can cause harm. This force is sometimes attributed to strangers, since one is unfamiliar with their state. In Santa Lucia, the force can also come from certain animals, especially a female dog in heat. (Redfield and Villa Rojas remark on a similar type of evil eye in Chan Kom called dog-evil.) Sickness attributed to this source is considered more serious and stronger and is more common among two- to four-year-old children, whereas evil eye from a person usually occurs among infants under two years of age. In nearby Santa Catarina Ixtahuacan, reports Mary Marshall, an adolescent boy or girl, a recently married couple, dogs copulating, a pregnant woman, or a drunk person, may have power to give the evil eye. The first three have sexual implications.

Hurtado reports that in several parts of Guatemala people with eye defects such as lesions, corneal scars, and strabismus are also regarded as having this power in their gaze. He also mentions that in some parts of Guatemala evil eye effects can be caused by the sun or the moon.

The power to give the evil eye is usually unintentional or unpremeditated. The person may be unaware that he or she possesses this power, and thus is not to blame for it. Nevertheless, the evil eye is sometimes associated with envy, both in people's minds and in the minds of anthropologists.[4] A pregnant woman may give the evil eye because she may be envious of someone else's child. If she holds a baby, she should make the sign of the cross on its forehead so that nothing will happen to it. This same action, reported by Paul for San Pedro, however, is interpreted as offsetting the ill effects of her dangerous "hot" gaze on another's infant rather than envy. An admiring glance or compliment may imply envy, and counterenvy or counter-evil-eye acts are performed. But despite the widespread interpretation linking the evil eye with envy, several aspects of the complex of beliefs do not seem to be associated with any connotation of envy. That the evil eye can be caused by the sun or the moon or by an animal does not seem to have any relationship to envy. Also, the belief that a person usually does not know of his power, or even if he does, that the giving of the evil eye is unintentional, seems to show that the evil eye is unrelated to envy in many instances.

Vulnerability and Symptoms

The usual object of the evil eye is a young child—the younger, the more vulnerable. Children are considered innately weak and therefore highly susceptible to outside forces, such as the power of the evil eye. Although no mention was made of this during my stay, a report by the Instituto Indigenista Nacional stated that Lucianos believe that small animals, especially colts, and certain plants such as the *guicoy* and *chilcecayote* (two types of squash) can suffer from the evil eye. The vulnerability of small birds and animals to the evil eye has been reported by Hurtado and by Gillin for other parts of Guatemala. Reina reports that in Chinautla the evil eye can also cause new pottery to be poorly fired and to turn black.[5]

Many of the symptoms are ones that are general and common to many illnesses, such as diarrhea, vomiting, anorexia, crying, and listlessness. Fever is also sometimes mentioned. The folk illness *ajita* (Sp. *empacho;* Eng. indigestion), which is characterized by loss of appetite, stomach pains, and swollen stomach, is frequently mentioned as associated with evil eye cases. Characteristics that are emphasized as being specifically indicative of evil eye are screaming in one's sleep, being frightened easily, throwing the shoulders and head back and tossing them from side to side, a foul odor in the mouth (Quiché *shesh*) and having one eye smaller or larger than the other (this last trait was also reported by Redfield and Rojas for the Chan Kom Maya in Yucatan). Several of the symptoms associated with the evil eye are similar to those caused by malnutrition and intestinal parasites and probably represent such ailments to varying degrees.

Prevention

Prevention and protective measures are closely related to the potential sources of the evil eye. Danger is heightened when many people are present,

Figure 10.1 Baby wearing bright red bag of herbs on its chest and bracelet of red seeds (not visible) as evil eye protection. Baby is held by its great-aunt, in the village of Santa Lucia Utatlán.

such as during the twenty-day postpartum period when visitors come to the house, or at a fiesta or market when strangers are present. A baby is kept isolated or in the house for the first few weeks, when it is most susceptible. The baby is usually kept completely covered. A cap is put over its head, often covering the eyes, and it is wrapped in a blanket or shawl: it is not shown to strangers and is kept out of crowds. If the child becomes sick, the mother may be blamed for carelessness and improper protection of the child. Amulets are sometimes worn, such as little red bags of herbs made in the town of Totonicapan.[6] A small red bag containing the herbs rue and artemis is also put on the neck of a colt to prevent the evil eye.[7] Hurtado reports the use of various amulets, including different types of seeds and beans—especially the red *pito* seeds (*Erythrina corallodendrum*)—items of red plastic, and a tiger's canine tooth, for different parts of Guatemala. One day I was wearing a necklace made of seeds, including one called deer's eye (*ojo de venado*), and several people mentioned that it is used in other areas of Guatemala against the evil eye (it does not grow locally).

Diagnosis and Treatment

Certain diagnostic tests, such as the egg test mentioned earlier, are used for evil eye. Numerous variations of the egg test, for both diagnosis and treatment, have been mentioned in connection with other areas in Guatemala.[8] In one variation, one passes the egg over the body of the child in the sign of a cross, while reciting prayers; then the egg is broken in a basin of water and deposited under the bed for the night. If a change of color has occurred when the egg is examined the following day, the child has the evil eye. As Hurtado points out, this change always occurs because of the action of water on the albumen of the egg.[9] Reina gives another variation of an egg test/cure in Chinautla. An egg is rubbed on the child's body at noon. The egg becomes "cooked" by absorbing the heat of the body. Afterwards the egg is broken and placed in a receptacle where the child sleeps. At 8:00 P.M. the mother throws the contents over her shoulder behind the house. If there is no improvement, it is believed that the child's illness is due to a cause other than the evil eye. Simeon reports other variations for the egg treatment in Chinautla, but says that the contents must be thrown in the river, because its water flows and will carry the evil force away.

Chilies are also used in diagnostic tests in various parts of Guatemala,[10] although such tests were not mentioned in Santa Lucia. A number of chilies, usually nine, are passed over the body of the child in the form of a cross. Then the chilies are thrown on the hearth. If they explode or burst, the child has the evil eye.

In addition to such tests, a retrospective analysis is made of the people and situations to which the child has recently been exposed. Emphasis is placed on whether the child has been in a crowd or was near someone in a "hot" state, such as a pregnant or menstruating woman.

Eggs are often mixed with herbs and patent medicines. In the case illustrated at the beginning of this paper, eggs of a black chicken are mixed with ten tips of the herb rue, garlic, tobacco, and *sal de nitro*. Half a glass of this is given to the child three times during the week. If the evil eye is very strong, then the child is also given a purgative of three tablespoons of *aceite comer* (cooking vegetal oil).

Several variations of remedies using rue are used for treatment: (1) an infusion is made by adding rue and sugar to boiled water; (2) the rue is mashed first, then put in a bowl with hot water and rubbed on the body of the child, a cross being made on the forehead and on the heart; and (3) two sprigs of rue are cooked and the water is drunk. Simeon reports that rue is one of seven herbs that are used in a bath for the afflicted child.

Other remedies are patent medicines bought in the pharmacy, such as *pil-*

doras rosadas, bebida colorada, and *manā.* These are also used as purgatives and as remedies for children's stomach ailments, such as *empacho,* and are all classified as "hot." These medicines are often mixed with cinnamon, *hierba buena* (mint), and rue. Similar treatments for other parts of Guatemala are mentioned by Rodriguez and by Hurtado.

Discussion

Two principles of Luciano ethnomedicine, found as well in most other Mesoamerican societies, are of particular importance for an understanding of the above characteristics of the evil eye: the weak-strong and hot-cold principles.

As I pointed out earlier, an infant is regarded as innately weak, and this weakness makes him susceptible to illnesses and external forces. The younger the child, the weaker, and thus the more vulnerable. The two-month-old child in the case presented above was thus highly susceptible. This weakness contrasts with the strength of the person possessing the evil eye, which is a force acting upon this susceptibility. Adams and Hurtado have viewed this belief as an example of the general theory that illness is caused by a combination of an internal and an external condition. Thus, in the case of the evil eye, the weak state of the infant is the internal condition and the force of the evil eye is the external factor. Since nothing can be done to prevent the child's state, prevention is based on protection from the external force, primarily in the form of covering the child, not showing it to strangers, and using various amulets.

The force of the evil eye is closely related to beliefs about the condition of the blood. Hot blood gives one strength and power. The hot-cold classification is one of the basic cognitive principles of the Luciano belief system. In Santa Lucia, as in most of Spanish America,[11] foods, plants, medicines, illnesses, and bodily states are classified as either hot or cold. Hotness and coldness are considered innate qualities possessed by the substance in question and are not usually determined by observable characteristics or physical temperature. In a healthy body these qualities are in a state of equilibrium or balance, and illness results from an excess of hot or cold within the body. Treatment is based ideally on the application of opposites to restore the original balance; substances are administered that belong to the qualitative class opposite that of the illness, and items of the same class are avoided.

The force that causes the illness of evil eye is regarded as hot. Strong and hot blood, pregnancy, menstruation, or drunkenness are all states involving excess heat in the body, which may emanate as evil eye power. Marshall suggests that in Santa Catarina Ixtahuacan, the "heat from the eyes" of a person causes the illness in a child, and makes the child usually run a temperature and vomit. This hot force then upsets the balance of the victim's body. The illness, therefore, is usually reported in the literature, as by Kearney (in this volume) and by Logan, as being hot. However, in Santa Lucia, the disease itself is not classified; rather the symptoms associated with it are. Most of the symptoms, such as loss of appetite, diarrhea, and vomiting, are usually classified as cold; and most of the medicines used in treatment both herbal and patent, are classified as hot (e.g., garlic, tobacco, *bebida colorado, sal de nitro, pildoras rosadas*). One informant, however, emphasized that the child sweats from the heat from the evil eye, which sometimes produces fever, and is treated with things classified as fresh or cool (*fresco*), such as rue and *aceite comer*. It should be noted that most people (80 percent of informants asked) classified *aceite comer* as hot. There was considerable variation in the classification of rue, about half regarding it as hot and half as "fresh," or in between. Red is considered a hot color and is thus used in amulets. Eggs used are specifically from a black chicken, since black is a very hot color whereas normal eggs are classified as cold or as fresh.

The child in the above case study had symptoms that are common to evil eye and a cold source, the mother's milk being too cold. In order to restore her bodily balance, she had to take "hot" items and avoid cold ones. With milk of the right quality, the child as well as the mother would be in a healthy state.

One may raise the question, how does a hot force, such as the evil eye, generate symptoms or manifestations that are cold, and thus require hot remedies? Or, if the evil eye illness is classified as hot, as it seems to be in some places in Guatemala and Mexico, why is it treated with hot remedies? Ingham offers an explanation of displacement theory for such anomalies or inconsistencies that may be applicable here. In Tlayacapan, Mexico, where Ingham worked, the Devil and ants, both of which are hot, generate cold airs. He suggests that the Devil displaces the air in the caves that he inhabits and thus generates airs that are cold, and ants perhaps drive cold air from their underground networks.[12] A case of *enlechado*, or cold milk, may be caused by too much sun on the mother's back, displacing the cold in her body from her lungs into the breasts, compressing in them the cold and rendering her milk too cold. Displacement is not an emic explanation; it is not verbalized by the Tlayacapenses nor by Lucianos. It is the anthropologists' explanation consistent with the humoral theory for what otherwise may seem inconsistent. It should be kept in mind that the humoral theory might just be inconsistent in such cases, despite the anthropologists' drive for consistency. It may also represent an incomplete syncretism or nonsyncretism of Indian and Spanish beliefs. Another possibility may be that Lucianos are more concerned with the classification and corresponding treatment of the specific manifestations of an illness than with the source, at least on an immediate level. Or it may be that many of the remedies are used for treating the symptoms, whereas other aspects of the treatment, particularly the herb rue, which was the herb of grace in medieval times, the sign of the cross, and the egg (symbolic of the eye), are more specifically related to the etiology of the evil eye and thus are used to counteract the harmful force and remove it from the patient.

Belief in the etiology of the evil eye also serves as a means of social control and influences social interaction. Although this is true for several other illnesses in Santa Lucia (e.g., fright, illnesses caused by witchcraft), certain aspects of the evil eye complex reinforce the role expectations and relationships of women in particular. In the above case study, the mother was blamed for inadequately protecting the child and exposing her to a crowd and to strangers. The mother has the primary responsibility for taking care of her child. She should therefore stay in or near the house with her infant. The general restrictive pattern of women's role expectations, which tend to keep them at home, is thus reinforced. The belief that pregnant and menstruating women can give the evil eye because of their hot condition supports this belief that they should stay at home. This is consistent with beliefs about the modesty of women; such conditions should not be revealed openly, and if they are, there is a cause for shame. Social interaction with strangers and drunkards is limited, since they may possess the evil eye force. However, even though blame may be put on a stranger, there is still implied blame of the mother for exposing the child to the stranger.

On another level, the evil eye offers an explanation of why children, who are guiltless, become sick. They are in a weak state and highly vulnerable. This, in turn, puts more of a burden of responsibility on the mother to protect the child.

Conclusion

The Spanish and Mediterranean concept of the evil eye refers primarily to the eye of the person with the power and is sometimes associated with willful or intentional harm, particularly stemming from envy and jealousy (see Moss and Cappannari this volume). In Santa Lucia and elsewhere in Guatemala, however, the term is used mainly to designate an illness—the state of the receiver of the force of the evil eye—rather than the eye or force of the giver, and it is usually, though not always, unintentional. The belief that the possessor of the force may not know of his power, so that giving the evil eye is nonwillful, has been reported for several areas of Guatemala.[13] Although the concept of the evil eye diffused from Spain to the New World, today it is not exactly the same concept. One can question to what extent we are actually talking about the same phenomenon. There seems to be only a partial fit of native categories to Spanish ones. The reason for this difference may lie in the sociocultural matrix of Indian versus Spanish society and in historical factors, and is an interesting problem for future investigation.

Simeon suggests that one should keep analytically distinct the evil eye as an agent of misfortune (such as poverty and bad luck) and as one of illness. The latter is much more dominant in Guatemala. I propose that an analytic distinction should also be made between intentional and unintentional causation, the latter being more important in cases of the evil eye in Guatemala. Intentional harm, whether of illness or general misfortune, is often motivated by envy or jealousy and is usually associated with witchcraft or sorcery. The evil eye, on the other hand, is considered a "nonmerited" illness given by an agent with no deliberate intention of doing so, as Marshall suggests. Few categories exist to explain illness in children, so this one is often used. The evil eye, therefore, fills a lacuna in the belief system, offering an explanation of the occurrence of unwillful harm, especially to young children.

NOTES

1. See Cosminsky, "Decision Making." This study was supported by a fellowship from the Institute of Nutrition of Central America and Panama, and a National Institutes of Mental Health grant. The author wishes to thank Mary Marshall, Karen Kerner, and David Feingold for their helpful comments and suggestions.

2. The term "Ladino" refers to both descendants of former Spanish or mixed Spanish-Indian ancestors and to people of Spanish or Western culture, in contrast with people of Indian culture.
3. The Quiché term *uwawinaq* is probably derived from *u/wach/winaq,* which is, possessive pronoun/eye/person (Marshall, unpublished data).
4. See Foster, "The Anatomy of Envy," and Kearney in this volume.
5. Reina, p. 272.   6. Personal communication from Mary Marshall.
7. See the Guatemalan Instituto Indigenista Nacional report.
8. This has been reported by Hurtado, Rodriguez, Reina, and Simeon.
9. Hurtado, p. 22.
10. Reported by Hurtado and Rodriguez, among others.
11. See Adams and Rubel, and also Foster, "Relationships."
12. Ingham, p. 81.
13. By Adams, Marshall, Wisdom, Reina, Gillin, Wagley, and Simeon.

BIBLIOGRAPHY

Adams, Richard N. *Un Analisis de las Creencias y Practicas Medicas en un Pueblo Indigena de Guatemala.* Instituto Indigenista Nacional. Publ. Especiales no. 17. Guatemala City, 1952.
—— and Arthur J. Rubel. "Sickness and Social Relations," in *Handbook of Middle American Indians,* vol. 6. Robert Wauchope, general ed. Austin: University of Texas Press, 1967.
Cosminsky, Sheila. "Decision Making and Medical Care in a Guatemalan Indian Community." Unpublished Ph.D. dissertation, Brandeis University, 1972.
Foster, George M. "The Anatomy of Envy: A Study in Symbolic Behavior," *Current Anthropology* 13 (1972), 165–202.
—— "Relationships between Spanish and Spanish-American Folk Medicine," *Journal of American Folklore* 66 (1953), 201–17.
Gillin, J. *The Culture of Security in San Carlos.* Middle American Research Institute Publication no. 16. New Orleans: Tulane University, 1951.
Guatemala. Instituto Indigenista Nacional. "Santa Lucia Utatlan." Unpublished report, 1950.
Hurtado, J. "El 'Ojo,' " in Tradiciones de Guatemala, vol. 1. Guatemala City: El Centro de Estudias Folkloricos, University of San Carlos, 1968.
Ingham, J. "On Mexican Folk Medicine," *American Anthropologist* 72 (1970), 76–87.
Logan, M. "Humoral Medicine in Guatemala and Peasant Acceptance of Modern Medicine," *Human Organization* 32 (1973), 385–96.
Paul, Lois. "The Changing Role of the Midwife in San Pedro la Laguna, a Guatemalan Indian Community on Lake Atitlan." Unpublished MS, n.d.
Redfield, R., and A. Villa Rojas. *Chan Kom: A Maya Village.* Chicago: University of Chicago Press, 1934.
Reina, R. *Law of the Saints.* New York: Bobbs-Merrill, 1966.
Rodriguez Rouanet, F. "Practicas Medicas Tradicionales de los Indigenas de Guatemala, *Guatemala Indigena* 2 (1970), 52–86.

Simeon, G. "The Evil Eye in a Guatemalan Village," *Ethnomedizin* 2, no. 3 (1973), 437–41.

Wagley, Charles. *The Social and Religious Life of a Guatemalan Village*. Memoirs, no. 71. Washington, D.C.: American Anthropological Association, 1949.

Wisdom, C. *The Chorti Indians of Guatemala*. Chicago: University of Chicago Press, 1940.

MICHAEL KEARNEY

11. MEXICO

A World-View Explanation
of the Evil Eye

BELIEF IN THE EVIL EYE is widespread in Mexico. In Spanish
it is usually referred to as *mal de ojo, mal ojo,* or simply *ojo*. Children are
the main victims of evil eye attacks. The cause is most often said to be the
unintentional covetous look of an adult, often a stranger, although symptoms
may also be caused by someone who does not covet the child. Some people
are assumed just to have "strong vision." This paper presents an explanation of the symbolic function of evil eye beliefs; additional ethnographic details are given below in the course of the explanation.

Evil Eye Envy and Paranoia

The most common anthropological explanation of the presence and dynamics of the evil eye is in terms of envy. The envy theory is also the cross-
culturally most common folk explanation of the evil eye, and there is undoubtedly a dynamic interrelationship between envy and the evil eye in
some, perhaps all, of the societies where evil eye occurs.[1] There is, however, a weakness in the envy theory. Recently, in major theoretical works,
two scholars, Foster and Schoeck, have independently proposed that envy is

MICHAEL KEARNEY teaches in the Department of Anthropology, University of California, River-
side. He received his Ph.D. from the University of California, Berkeley. He specializes in comparative religion and world views and psychological anthropology. For the past seven years he
has been studying psychiatric aspects of spiritualistic healing in Baja California.
  This chapter derives from his fieldwork among the Zapotec of southern Mexico, about whom
he has written *The Winds of Ixtepeji: World View and Society in a Zapotec Town* (1972) as well
as several articles.

universally present in human societies, and that it is one of the basic motivating forces in human interaction. While uncertain as to the ultimate nature of envy's source, that is, whether it is primarily genetically or culturally determined, I do agree with Foster's and Schoeck's conclusions regarding its universality. Thus, granted that envy is universal, varying only in degree, it alone cannot be a good predictor of a nonuniversal trait or complex such as the evil eye.

If the universe of concern is limited to circum-Mediterranean societies, the correlation between envy and the evil eye is quite good. But the correlation presumably diminishes beyond this culture area. In other words, the evil eye is a good predictor of strong envy, but the reverse is not true. It appears that the belief originated once, most likely in the Mediterranean, and diffused to other psychosocially receptive areas, such as Latin America. Starting from this assumption, the primary objective in analyzing evil eye structure and symbolism is to lay bare the interrelations between them and other psychological, cultural, or social traits that maintain them.

In attempting this, I do not deny that there are dynamic interrelations between incidences of high envy and the evil eye where they occur together, as they do, for example, in Mexico. However, I argue that the belief is better explained in more general social-psychiatric terms by the concept of paranoia. Evil eye psychology, folk logic, and symbolism are consistent with a paranoid view of the world, a view in which a high concern with envy is also present. It is my contention that in explaining the evil eye in terms of the envy theory, anthropologists have stopped at the level of folk explanation. Presumably, if the paranoid theory is of greater value than the envy theory, it should also shed light on the folk explanation. In other words, rather than using envy to explain the evil eye, it is more accurate to speak of an evil eye–envy complex of symbols, beliefs, attitudes, and practices. Thus, according to the paranoid theory that I am proposing, the dynamics and symbolism of the evil eye and of envy, when they occur together, should both be encompassed as subsets within a more primary frame of reference that I refer to as a paranoid world view.

My interest in paranoid world views stems mainly from work in a society that I characterize as having such an outlook on life. Mexico is marked by tremendous ethnographic diversity, and yet one is struck by certain uniformities in such things as family structure, religion, and general folk beliefs and attitudes. Although the arguments about evil eye advanced in this paper pertain most directly to Ixtepeji, a Zapotec farming community in the state of Oaxaca,[2] I would maintain that they may be safely generalized to most of *mestizo* peasant Mexico, as well as to many, more Indian communities in Mexico.

"Paranoid" Societies

When Ruth Benedict attributed paranoid qualities to Dobuan and Kwakiutl cultures, she was roundly criticized for inappropriately applying concepts of individual psychology to total societies. But with the passage of time she seems to have been vindicated by a number of recent similar attempts. Benedict's ground-breaking work in culture and personality theory was, as is characteristic of the early phases of a new science or discipline, primarily descriptive. Whereas Benedict borrowed psychiatric concepts, such as paranoia or megalomania, for essentially typological purposes, recent studies have focused on the dynamics of paranoid societies. Hitson and Funkenstein, for example, argue that Burmese family structure and socialization promote a "strong paranoidal cast to Burmese personality [and] that the psychodynamic processes in operation situationally in many areas of Burmese life are similar to psychodynamic processes in operation generally, in paranoid patients." [3] These authors also indicate that Burmese mental illness "reveals a patterning that appears to be premised on what might be called a 'paranoidal' perception of environment." [4] Spiro similarly argues that the Burmese have a perceptual set characterized by the belief that "everybody hates me," and on the basis of this and other data he characterizes this orientation to the world as "paranoid-like."

Kennedy in a discussion of the psychosocial dynamics of witchcraft systems says of them, "In addition to its pathological *content,* the main structure of the witchcraft idea-system is almost identical to a paranoid delusion. . . . It is in this sense, I think that we could consider that the almost identical form of witchcraft systems to such a style makes it legitimate and even incumbent to speak of a paranoid world view." [5] Although not primarily concerned with paranoia, Landes, Barnouw points out, "discusses the megalomania of Chippewa medicine men and the resulting fear in which they are held. She points out that ordinary people, as well as shamans, may develop delusions of grandeur, and even whole villages may become affected with paranoid hysteria." [6] Barnouw maintains that this picture of

Chippewa society is also supported by his own work, and by that of Jenness and Hallowell. Hallowell himself has said that "the ground is well prepared in this society for the development of paranoid or pseudo-paranoid trends in individuals." [7] Recently, Schwartz has described "an area-wide paranoid ethos that underlies Melanesian cultures." [8] And speaking in general terms, Shapiro has described a "paranoid style" of functioning and Schwartz speaks of a "paranoid outlook on life." And in a similar vein, Anne Parsons discusses differences in American and Italian paranoid delusions (abstract versus concrete), and raises the question of the role of instinct versus culture as determinants. [9]

Paranoid Personality

The clinical picture of true paranoia is a rather clear-cut syndrome. There are, however, a number of other psychiatric diagnostic categories that have paranoid components; these categories range from paranoid schizophrenia to mildly neurotic or "normal" behavior.

> Thus, in addition to appearing in more or less pure form, paranoid behavior may be found associated with virtually every other clinical entity in the field of psychiatry as well as with many disturbances not generally considered psychiatric. It is also found widely spread in other dimensions, as, for instance, in both sexes, through all the years of adult life, and in many different sociocultural contexts from extreme physical danger to various positions of marginality (as in migrants and individuals in the process of acculturation). It may be temporary, intermittent, or lifelong. Finally, it occurs not only in the individual as distinct from his group but is found at times in whole groups which may range from small clusters, such as families or gangs, to tribes and even to nations. Indeed, it seems that paranoid behavior is, like weeping or laughter, a universal human reaction which may at times be normal and at others so severe, prolonged, inflexible, and inappropriate as to constitute a disorder. [10]

Meyer has postulated a "paranoic constitution":

> The paranoic character is one in which there is essentially a tone of suspicion [and] the perceptions of reality are colored by this predominating affect. The paranoic constitution is characterized by sensitiveness, suspicion, mistrust, and want of confidence in others, probably arising from feelings of inferiority or guilt. [11]

Rather than attempting to locate something such as Ixtepeji basic personality along a continuum of paranoia, I shall just say that this formulation of Meyer roughly describes dominant dimensions of Ixtepeji personality and related patterns of interpersonal relations that are the psychosocial substrate of the evil eye belief as it occurs there. The above definition is particularly applicable in that it emphasizes "suspicion, mistrust, and want of confidence in others." In my work in Ixtepeji prior to the formulation of this paper, I have underscored the importance of these dimensions of world view and interpersonal relations in Ixtepeji.[12] Another of Meyer's paranoic traits is sensitivity to nuances of the emotions and motivations of those with whom one is interacting. Such sensitivity is extremely well developed among Ixtepejanos, and serves to detect often equally subtly concealed hostility in others.[13]

To be more fully applicable to Ixtepeji the above definition should also emphasize a tendency to perceive forces and entities in the environment as hostile and powerful, for in labeling Ixtepeji culture as paranoid these traits are also diagnostic. For the most part these perceptions are realistic, but full-blown delusions and hallucinations are not uncommon. When they do occur, it appears that their content and structure are predisposed by the underlying paranoid orientation.[14] But what is of most interest to us here is the tendency to generalize this basic perception to inappropriate objects and situations, and to collectively generate projective systems and secondary institutions that are colored by this basic paranoid tendency.

Other dimensions of the paranoid personality are emphasized by the *Diagnostic and Statistical Manual* of the American Psychiatric Association:

> This behavioral pattern is characterized by hypersensitivity, rigidity, unwarranted suspicion, jealousy, envy, excessive self-importance, and a tendency to blame others and ascribe evil motives to them.[15]

This definition overlaps with Meyer's on the dimensions of sensitivity and suspicion/mistrust/lack of confidence in others. However, it adds another that is important for my characterization of Ixtepeji culture as paranoid—that is, envy/jealousy. "Institutionalized envy," to use Wolf's term, is well developed in Ixtepeji, and in a later part of this paper I shall indicate its role as a component of folk belief in the evil eye.[16]

Paranoid World View

In describing and analyzing the Ixtepeji world view, I derived several propositions that I believe to lie covertly at the base of it, and that explain behavior predicated on them. One of these propositions, the one that I consider to have the most power to explain a variety of folk beliefs, practices, and social-structural features, is the following: "The world (local, social, and geographic environment) is filled with omnipresent, unknown, and unknowable dangerous beings and entities (natural and supernatural) that constantly threaten the individual." [17]

This proposition depicts a negative and anxiety-ridden view of life. It describes a world permeated with mysterious dangers, a world in which one is never able to attain lasting security. Friends, relatives, strangers, spirits, and natural phenomena are seen as actually or potentially dangerous, and not to be relied on in time of need. The individual is essentially alone in a hostile world in which nothing is secure. Intimates, such as friends and relatives, and strangers are potentially the most dangerous.

Although I have not until now referred to Ixtepeji world view as "paranoid," such a designation is consistent with the above proposition. I was originally led to this proposition while attempting to understand the possible symbolic or projective meaning of several folk beliefs, and mainly the strongly held belief Ixtepejanos have about the power of the air of the atmosphere and other mysterious *aires* to harm and even to kill humans and other living creatures. I argued that the "air system" well symbolized the covert proposition, in that it is: (1) *Ubiquitous.* Air is everywhere, and as such is an apt phenomenon to symbolize the felt omnipresence of dangerous forces and entities in the environment. (2) *Unknown and unknowable.* "On a par with the ubiquity of air is the quality of invisibility. Air is everywhere, but it is never seen; one cannot tangibly grasp and comprehend it. Its ultimate nature must remain a mystery to man equipped with only his five senses." [18] (3) *Dangerous.* This is not so much an objective quality of air as one ascribed to it by folk belief. Ixtepejanos consider air to be the main cause of death and disease, which are two of their most serious concerns.

Now, what does *aire* have to do with the evil eye? I also argued that there are several *"aire-*like" folk concepts to which folk belief attributes similar insidious and malevolent qualities. One of these is the evil eye, for like *aire,* it is almost as ubiquitous and as hard to escape as the glance of a neighbor, and it, too, enters the body to harm it. [19]

There are also other symbolic and structural features that allow us to equate *mal ojo* with *aire.*

1. *Power Relationship.* Just as people who are in a vulnerable or weak-

Figure 11.1 Amulet commonly put on children in Mexico to protect them from the evil eye. This particular one, collected in Colton, California, consists of (*top to bottom*) coral, a piece of an herb, imitation jet, imitation amber, a seed called *ojo de venado* ("deer's eye," *Thevetia nitida*); on the seed is pasted a picture of Our Lady of San Juan de Los Lagos; attached to the bottom of the seed is a piece of red yarn.

ened state are more prone to an attack by *aire,* so are "weak" individuals more susceptible to *mal ojo.* This means that primarily children, but also women, are the main victims. Those most responsible for harming others are, accordingly, adults, who by virtue of being mature individuals are stronger than children, who because of their size and greater proneness to sickness are considered to be weaker. Similarly, women are more susceptible to harm by *ojo* than are men, but children are by far the most common victims. There is thus a conceptual power differential between victim and (for lack of a better word) aggressor, such that the malignant force of the aggressor flows from his eyes into the victim.

Principles of preventative and curative treatment are at least partially consistent with this notion. Thus amulets of salt or other objects are tied around the necks or wrists of infants and children to reflect this force away from them. Should they be diagnosed as having suffered an attack, and the aggressor is identified, he may neutralize the damage by touching the child on the head, or making a cross on its forehead with a finger moistened with his (the aggressor's) saliva. Touching the child in this manner might be thought of as "grounding" the child, so to speak, allowing the harmful force to return to the person it has come from. This procedure may also be done to prevent symptoms from appearing should there be reason to assume an aggressor has unwittingly given the child *mal ojo*. Should the aggressor be unidentifiable or unavailable, a different treatment is used. It consists essentially of rubbing the child with a fresh hen's egg, which, if done with proper ritual, will draw the harmful influence from the victim's body, so that it may be observed when the egg is later broken open.

Thus, as with *aire, ojo* victims are prone to sudden, largely unforeseeable attacks by forces in the environment that are more powerful than the victim. In the case of *aire* I argued that it symbolized dangerous aspects of virtually the total environment. *Mal ojo* is, however, specific to human threats. In other words, it is a symbolic subset of the general attitudes expressed by the proposition and generally symbolized by the *aire* system. But of all humans, potentially the most dangerous are strangers or other anonymous people who are likely to be unidentifiable or absent when symptoms develop. Thus they cannot be called on to effect the relatively simple and effective touching cure.[20] This is also consistent with general fears and attitudes regarding strangers in Ixtepeji.

2. *Penetration. Ojo* is further similar to *aire* in that both operate according to the principle of object intrusion, in that both enter the body to effect their harm.

3. *Contagion.* As elsewhere in Mexico, there are numerous similar beliefs in the contagious power of different objects that can infect humans and other creatures. This principle is roughly similar to the "power differential" mentioned above, but folk belief usually refers, for example, to the contagious, corrupting power of cadavers. Thus, special countermeasures, such as burning incense or sprinkling napthalene, are taken at funerals to drive these powers away. The symbols used to represent this concept have a looseness and fluidity in that, for example, within the course of a conversation on the malignant influence of a cadaver, a person may refer to the contagious force variously as *aire, gangrena, el diablo,* or *espíritus malignos.*[21]

Additional ethnographic evidence for the equation of *ojo* with *aire* comes from the Mayan area of eastern Mexico. In Chan Kom there is an even more elaborate folk taxonomy of *aires* than in Ixtepeji, with some informants listing up to seven or eight different kinds. They appear to have the same symbolic and affective meaning as in Ixtepeji.

However definitely each separate wind be thought of, and however much they are imagined as like men or like ordinary winds, generally and collectively they constitute an ever-present and pervasive danger. It is chiefly against the evil winds that a man must protect his child, his horse and himself.[22]

Whereas in Ixtepeji, *aire* seems to be the master symbol for a paranoid outlook, and *ojo* a sort of variant of it, they both appear to be of equal import and meaning in Chan Kom folk belief. Whereas in Ixtepeji most ailments are attributed to some variety of *aire* attack, in Chan Kom, "the term *ojo* is more widely used to refer to any communicable malignity. Thus the evil brought by the winds is one kind of *ojo* (*ojo*-ik), although a baleful glance has no part of it." [23]

In Ixtepeji, the main psychological function of *aire* and *ojo* seems to be to express covert, largely realistic attitudes regarding the existence of threatening, powerful agents in the local environment. In the sense that these perceptions of reality are "objective," it would be inappropriate to label the world view as "paranoid." But such a characterization is appropriate when such attitudes are widely generalized, or, if you like, projected, to nonobjective realities, such as witchcraft, *aire,* and the evil eye.

Evil Eye Envy and Paranoia

As discussed in the first part of this paper, the most common etic and folk explanation of Mexican evil eye is in terms of envy. The paranoid theory that I propose holds that envy itself is one permutation of an underlying paranoid world view, as I have described it. In Ixtepeji, this perception of the general nonhuman world is symbolized by the folk concept of *aire. Aire,* as a natural symbol, is envy free; envy is not in any way directly connected with beliefs about *aire.* The main affective dimension of the *aire* belief is a generalized anxiety, or fear, about rather insidious, threatening, nonhuman forces in the environment. But insofar as this world view encompasses the human world, the world of social relations, envy becomes a large part of it. But here again, as we saw above, envy is but another dimension of paranoia. Schoeck has shown that envy is itself a form of fear: "Envy is more comparable with 'being afraid'; we envy something or someone in the same way that we are afraid of something or someone. Envy is a directed emotion: without a target, without a victim, it cannot occur." [24]

Mal ojo often occurs without the dimension of envy, but insofar as envy is a part of *ojo,* it is a variant of this underlying sense of insecurity and relative vulnerability to powerful, hostile forces in the environment.[25]

In her study of medical attitudes in the Santa Clara Valley of California, Margaret Clark arrives at essentially the same conclusion:

> Among the Spanish-speaking folk of Sal si Puedes, the patient is regarded as a passive and innocent victim of malevolent forces in his environment. These forces may be witches, evil spirits, the consequences of poverty, or virulent bacteria which invade his body. The scapegoat may be a visiting social worker who unwittingly "cast the evil eye." . . . Mexican folk concepts of disease are based in part on the notion that people can be victimized by the careless or malicious behavior of others.[26]

Another aspect of the *mal ojo* syndrome in Ixtepeji is a disturbance of the hot-cold equilibrium in the victim. According to folk belief, the bad effects of an attack result from the "hot" force of the aggressor entering the child's body and throwing it out of balance.[27] Currier has shown how the Mexican hot-cold system is an unconscious folk model of social relations upon which social anxieties are projected. According to Currier,

> the nature of Mexican peasant society is such that each individual must continuously attempt to achieve a balance between two opposing social forces: the tendency toward intimacy and that toward withdrawal. [It is therefore proposed] that the individual's continuous preoccupation with achieving a balance between "heat" and "cold" is a way of reenacting, in symbolic terms, a fundamental activity in social relations.[28]

Insofar as the damaging force of *mal ojo* disrupts this symbolic equilibrium, it can be seen as expressing anxiety about interpersonal equilibria, so that, in this sense, too, fear is a dominant dimension of *mal ojo*. Envy arises when there is disequilibrium, that is, when one is perceived as having more of what is desired than another. In a society such as Ixtepeji, where almost all valued resources are perceived as existing in limited or diminishing quantities,[29] such disequilibria have grave implications for the economic survival of individuals and families, so that in this sense envy resulting from disequilibrium can be seen as virtually synonymous with fear. It is understandable that the folk system should emphasize envy, since it is one of the most immediately and consciously experienced emotions generated by the underlying paranoid aspects of the world view.[30]

Another structural symmetry is that *mal ojo* is a hot disease resulting from a person being in a "hot" condition, most commonly due to possession of "hot" emotions. Individuals who are possessed of hot emotions are dangerous to themselves and to others in this regard alone. *Mal ojo* is thus not only

Figure 11.2 The woman is "cleansing" the child by rubbing a raw hen's egg over his body, a combination diagnostic and treatment procedure in which the egg absorbs the "heat" of the evil eye. The photo was taken on the Isthmus of Tehuantepec, Mexico. Photo by Judith Brueske.

Figure 11.3 See figure 11.2. The egg has now been broken into a gourd and is being inspected to confirm the diagnosis of evil eye attack. Photo by Judith Brueske.

symbolic of fear of "strong," potentially threatening persons, but of individuals who are doubly threatening because they are both strong *and* hot.

Further suggestion of the paranoid nature of evil eye envy comes from the etymology of "envy."

> English "envy" stems from Latin *invidia* (which survives unchanged in modern Italian, and almost unchanged in Spanish *envidia*). Latin *invidia* is related to *invidēre,* a verbal form compounded from *in-* ("upon") plus *vidēre* ("to see"), i.e., to look maliciously upon, to look askance at, to cast an evil eye upon.[31]

This meaning suggests attack by object intrusion, in the sense that the glance is not so much onto the victim as *into* him, in the same way that *aire* and agents of witchcraft penetrate the victim's body to harm it.

One structural feature of the belief system remains to be explained, and that is, why are children considered to be the main victims? It is adults and not children who are primarily concerned with the evil eye, and if the belief is in fact a paranoid projection of adults, then one would expect that they, not children, would be the victims. The answer to this apparent inconsistency is suggested by folk beliefs about witchcraft. We have already indicated that children are more susceptible to the evil eye because of their inherent relative weakness; by the same token they are also considered to be more vulnerable to attack by witchcraft.

To the question, "Why should someone wish to so harm a child?" the inevitable reply is, in so many words, "What better way to make a mother or father suffer?" Within the belief system, then, a child is the Achilles' heel of an adult who is otherwise relatively invulnerable to witchcraft attack. There are in Mexico numerous practices that serve to protect children from attacks by black magic. Such attacks are usually assumed to be provoked by envy of someone's child, but they may also be provoked by desire to attack the parent for whatever reason. There is thus a perceptual set whereby one of the numerous ways in which harm can come to one is through harm to one's child. Kiev has also suggested that concern with evil eye attack on one's child is a projection of the parent's repressed hostility toward the child.[32] This may well be true, and does not negate the paranoid symbolic function of the belief. Indeed we might suspect that such widespread and institutionalized beliefs are so well developed precisely because they do serve multiple symbolic functions.

Elsewhere Kiev also likens the evil eye to a phobic state.[33] He also distinguishes between phobic and paranoid-obsessional symptoms, associating the former with the evil eye and the latter with witchcraft. Referring to Mexican-Americans in southern Texas, he concludes that socialization there promotes projective and phobic mechanisms by encouraging the child to think of himself as omnipotent, while at the same time fearing his own impulses.

> This kind of experience leads in varying degrees to a favoring of phobic and paranoid defensive or adaptive mechanisms and to both the explanations of illness and the content of illness found in this group. This experience also relates to the curandero's treatment approach, which appears to be of particular benefit for patients with phobic obsessional paranoid symptoms such as are found in *mal ojo* and *susto* (phobic), and in *embrujada* (paranoid-obsessional).[34]

Kiev's equation of *ojo* with a phobic state seems to contradict my paranoid argument. But Kiev also apparently contradicts himself when he also argues (as discussed above) that *ojo* can be seen as a projection of hostility. In psychoanalytic theory these are two rather incompatible ego defenses. Actually Kiev is more consistent than he appears to be, for part of the confusion stems from his oversight in clearly distinguishing two basic structural differences in evil eye patterns. It appears that in most of the Mediterranean, adults are the main victims, while in Mexico, evil eye concern is chiefly for the children of adults. When he speaks of the phobic dimension of evil eye he appears to be referring to the first pattern, viz., adult-as-victim. In his later discussion in *Transcultural Psychiatry,* where he develops this idea, most of his data are taken from the Mediterranean, where this is the primary pattern. However, when he speaks specifically of Mexico (in *Curandismo*), where the child-as-victim pattern is most common, it is interesting that in addition to classing *ojo* as a projection of hostility (which in psychoanalytic theory is compatible with paranoia) he also categorizes witchcraft as paranoid-obsessional. Just above I have demonstrated structural and psychological parallels between the child-as-victim patterns of *ojo* and witchcraft. Thus, insofar as witchcraft is similar to this pattern of *ojo,* Kiev's labeling of Mexican witchcraft as paranoid supports my paranoid theory of Mexican evil eye.

Although Kiev says that fear of the evil eye is universal,[35] to my knowledge its occurrence in Latin America dates from the Spanish Conquest. Assuming that it did diffuse from Europe, the immediate question that arises is, what psychological and social conditions favored its reception in Mesoamerica? Without attempting to definitively support it, I would offer the following explanation. The social, economic, cultural, and general chaos that occurred during the first centuries of the Spanish Conquest are well enough known generally not to need documentation here. The gross disruption of the fabric of native life due to Spanish colonial policies and practices could not have but profoundly altered the life-styles and world views of even the most aboriginally downtrodden native societies. The onslaught of widespread death, disease, slavery, and servitude that the Spanish overlords provoked maintained the native populations in grossly inferior power relationships to their masters and in generally miserable life conditions. It is easy to imagine that this situation would generate a paranoid sense of reality in the sense that I have described in this paper. One would suspect that such an orientation would provoke the paranoid personality characteristics that have been reported for refugees and migrants.[36] Such an orientation would thus provide fertile soil for the diffusion of the evil eye concept, which, as I have attempted to show, well serves as a symbol for the projection of paranoid attitudes.

The evil eye today is still a viable folk concept, and there is evidence that it is adapting to modern times. A presumably recent variation in the *mal ojo* complex in Mexico is the folk concept of *electricidad* (electricity), which appears to be a pseudoscientific notion to explain the way in which *mal ojo* is transmitted. A student of mine included the following quote from an elderly lady from Zacatecas, Mexico, in a term paper on Mexican folk medicine; it is also a good description of *electricidad* as thought of in Ixtepeji and elsewhere in Mexico:

Mal de ojo is a condition that is inherent in a person. It is when an individual has electricity in the eyes of such great intensity that it causes plants to dry up and children to become ill when this person looks at them. In order to keep the plants alive, the person must touch the plant after looking at it for any length of time.[37]

In another term paper on Chicano folk medical beliefs, two of my students wrote:

Ojo is due to a person that is carrying a lot of electricity in his body, [and] we suppose that a person having this attribute is born with it; he may not even know he has it. Having this electricity within one's body and giving it to someone else are different. They have said that if this electricity is transmitted it will make the other person or child very sick and it has been known to kill its victims.[38]

As a symbol, electricity has some of the same qualities (both natural and ascribed) as *aire*. It is invisible, rather pervasive, and dangerous. Electricity symbolism thus fits into the general paranoid picture of *mal ojo* and *aire*. As an informant of Rubel said, *mal ojo* "is like electricity." And from a clinical perspective, Parsons notes that the electricity image is frequently found in the delusions of paranoids.[39] I have discovered one such example in the case history of a man who believed himself to be the victim of an influencing machine that, among other things, "creates sensations that in part cannot be described because they are strange to the patient himself, and that in part are sensed as electrical, magnetic, or due to air-currents." [40]

Conclusion

The methodological approach to Mexican evil eye symbolism offered here has been to examine its fit within Ixtepeji world view. Presumably, once valid world-view propositions have been deductively derived from empirical data, they should be of value in explaining other symbolic and behavioral spheres within the same culture by predicting functional and structural similarities or other relationships between them. Thus, following this strategy I have attempted to point out parallels between the symbolism of *aire* (previously worked out according to the cited proposition) and that of *mal ojo*. The theoretical assumption here is that the attitude formally represented by the proposition is deeply embedded in cognitive structures, and, as such, colors perception of reality and generally shapes behavior and symbolic processes such as projection.[41]

NOTES

1. The following quotations are representative of the envy theory of the evil eye: "Almost everywhere it is felt that universal values, such as personal health, youthfulness, children, have to be protected from the evil eye, the active expression of envy, and this is evident in the proverbs and the behaviour patterns that are employed by so many peoples to ward it off" (Schoeck, p. 6). Summing up Lewis's discussion of envy in Tepoztlán, Schoeck says, "Here, clearly apparent is the fear of envy, the 'evil eye' of the other, which threatens all our prospects, all the assets to which we aspire" (ibid., p. 50). And referring to the Reichel-Dolmatoffs' description of life in Aritama, Colombia, Schoeck says, "In Aritama, as almost everywhere else, the evil eye (*mal ojo*) is an important and special form of malevolent magic. It can cause sickness, drought and decay. Significantly, 'economic assets such as houses, crops, domestic animals, or fruit trees are said to be much more exposed to the Evil Eye than people themselves. The reason: envy' " (ibid., p. 53). Similarly Foster says, "Belief in the evil eye is, of course, widespread in Latin America and in the Mediterranean, and it is generally recognized as an institutionalized expression of envy" (Foster, "Cultural Responses," p. 33). Speaking of south Texas, Madsen writes, "One of the most frequent manifestations of envy is *mal ojo* or evil eye. It is believed that some people are born with 'strong vision,' which can harmfully project their admiration or desire of possession into a person or thing. Children are especially susceptible to this misfortune for they lack the spiritual strength and defenses of the adult" (Madsen, p. 426).
2. See, Kearney, *Winds of Ixtepeji,* for data on which most of the arguments here will be based.
3. Hitson and Funkenstein, p. 190.
4. Ibid., p. 189; also Weidman, "Cultural Values."
5. Kennedy, pp. 168–69.   6. Barnouw, p. 146.   7. Hallowell, p. 424.
8. Theodore Schwartz, p. 154.   9. Parsons, pp. 204–11.
10. Leighton, et al., p. 67.   11. Sadler, p. 425.
12. Kearney, *Winds of Ixtepeji,* pp. 59–69, 72.
13. Ibid., pp. 77–80.   14. Ibid., pp. 108–10.
15. American Psychiatric Association, p. 42.
16. For discussions and descriptions of culturally patterned forms of the expression of envy in Mexican peasant society, see Foster, "Cultural Responses," and Wolf, "Types."

17. Kearney, *Winds of Ixtepeji*, p. 44.

18. Ibid., p. 47.   19. Ibid., p. 54.

20. "The importance of this common belief is that the *ojo* is apparently a pan-Mesoamerican illness usually derived from a stranger (Rubel, "Concepts of Disease"). It thus places the mother in the position of protecting her child against the world of outside dangers, for when caused by an outsider, the illness will not be cured by him" (Adams and Rubel, p. 345).

21. In describing Burmese paranoid perception of the environment, Hitson and Funkenstein give an example that is similar to Ixtepeji beliefs about *aire* and cadavers: "Strong odors, such as burning paper, burning rubber, the smell of a corpse and even exhaust fumes from vehicles, are greatly feared and are believed to have very harmful effects. The smell of frying oil and frying chilies, for example, is believed to spread through the body and make worse any sore or blemish" (p. 188).

Perhaps the first written expression of this attitude as it pertains to the evil eye is by Saint Thomas: "Santo Tomás de Aquino tenía la convicción, firmemente arraigada, de que el ojo humano estaba dotado, a veces, de tal potestad por una fuerte imaginación del alma y en este caso corrompe y envenena la atmósfera, en tal forma que los cuerpos débiles que caen dentro de su radio de acción pueden quedar dañosamente afectados. Es así como la vieja maléfica daña a los niños. El *mal de ojo* tuvo en Santo Tomás su más insigne intérprete. Es también llamado *herida de ojo* y *ojo de envidia,* denominaciones que permiten descubrir el mecanismo mental, proyección de los deseos hostiles, que le dio vida" (Aguirre Beltrán, p. 26).

22. Redfield and Villa Rojas, p. 167.

23. Ibid., p. 168.   24. Schoeck, p. 7.

25. Regarding the existence of envy-free evil eye in Texas, Rubel notes that, "although a relationship which contains elements of covetousness is the classic cause of *mal de ojo* in Mexiquito, this is generalized to include any kind of special attention paid one individual by another—El ojo es de bello y de feo (Evil eye affects the beautiful and the ugly in equal measure)" (Rubel, *Across the Tracks,* p. 160).

26. Clark, p. 197.

27. The "hot-cold" concepts referred to here derive from classical Greek humoral theory, which in altered form is the prevalent frame of reference for folk medical beliefs and practices in Ixtepeji, as in most of rural Mexico. Evil eye thinking is also structured to a great extent according to this symbolic system. The main principle is that of equilibrium; disease results from an excess of either hot or cold qualities. Accordingly, the mysterious force that is transmitted to an evil eye victim is classified as hot. Although "hot" generally refers to an abstract, non-thermal quality, in fact, when a diagnosis of *ojo* is made the sick person generally has a fever. The most common treatment thus consists of rubbing the body with a raw hen's egg, which is cold. The egg is said to draw the force from the body, as is sometimes demonstrated upon breaking the egg open and finding that the "heat" of the ojo has "cooked" the yolk.

28. Currier, p. 252.   29. Kearney, "An Exception."

30. I previously derived the following basic world-view proposition about folk attitudes regarding the role of envy in human psychology: "Human beings are very susceptible to frustration and are envious of others; both frustration and envy make one wish to harm others" (*Winds of Ixtepeji,* p. 44; cf. also pp. 70–80). When deriving this and the other basic propositions that define Ixtepeji world-view (ibid., pp.

43–45), I did not consider possible hierarchical relationships that might pertain among them. Now, however, after having worked through the analysis in this paper, I am inclined to argue that the *aire* proposition is a deeper, i.e., more general, proposition than the envy proposition.

31. Foster, "Anatomy of Envy," p. 167.
32. Kiev, *Curanderismo,* pp. 172–73.
33. Ibid., p. 171; Kiev, *Transcultural Psychiatry, pp. 75–79.*
34. Kiev, *Curanderismo,* p. 171. *Susto* (fright) refers to a folk medical syndrome triggered by any abrupt traumatic experience; *embrujada* refers to bewitchment.
35. Ibid., p. 102.
36. See Pedersen, "Psychopathological Reactions"; L. Tyhurst, "Displacement and Migration"; J. S. Tyhurst, "Paranoid Patterns," pp. 60–64.
37. Cardoza, p. 6.   38. Avila and Soliz, p. 3.
39. Parsons, p. 184   40. Tausk, p. 34.
41. For a fuller discussion of this theory of world view see Kearney, *Winds of Ixtepeji,* pp. 43–44.

BIBLIOGRAPHY

Adams, Richard N., and Arthur J. Rubel. "Sickness and Social Relations," in *Handbook of Middle American Indians,* vol. 6. Robert Wauchope, general ed. Austin: University of Texas Press, 1967.

Aguirre Beltrán, Gonzalo. *Medicina y Magía.* Mexico: Instituto Nacional Indigenista, 1963.

American Psychiatric Association. *Diagnostic and Statistical Manual of Mental Disorders.* Washington D.C.: The Committee on Nomenclature and Statistics of the American Psychiatric Association, 1968.

Avila, Justo, and Jesús Soliz. "Mexican Folk Medicine." Unpublished MS, n.d.

Barnouw, Victor. *Culture and Personality.* Homewood, Ill.: Dorsey Press, 1963.

Benedict, Ruth. "Anthropology and the Abnormal," *Journal of General Psychology* 10 (1934), 59–82.

Cardoza, Rafael. "Mexican Folk Medicine Today." Unpublished MS, n.d.

Clark, Margaret. *Health in the Mexican-American Culture.* Berkeley: University of California Press, 1959.

Currier, Richard L. "The Hot-Cold Syndrome and Symbolic Balance in Mexican and Spanish-American Folk Medicine," *Ethnology* 5 (1966), 251–63.

Foster, George M. "The Anatomy of Envy: A Study in Symbolic Behavior," *Current Anthropology* 13 (1972), 165–202

—— "Cultural Responses to Expressions of Envy in Tzintzuntzan," *Southwestern Journal of Anthropology* 21 (1965), 24–35.

Hallowell, A. Irving. *Culture and Experience.* Philadelphia: University of Pennsylvania Press, 1955.

Hitson (Weidman), Hazel M., and Daniel H. Funkenstein. "Family Patterns and Paranoidal Personality Structure in Boston and Burma," *International Journal of Social Psychiatry* 5 (1959), 182–90.

Kearney, Michael. "An Exception to the 'Image of Limited Good,' " *American Anthropologist* 71 (1969), 888–90.
—— *The Winds of Ixtepeji: World View and Society in a Zapotec Town.* New York: Holt, Rinehart, and Winston, 1972.
Kennedy John G. "Psychosocial Dynamics of Witchcraft Systems," *International Journal of Social Psychiatry* 15 (1969), 165–78.
Kiev, Ari. *Curanderismo: Mexican-American Folk Psychiatry.* New York: The Free Press, 1968.
—— *Transcultural Psychiatry.* New York: The Free Press, 1972.
Leighton, Alexander H., John A. Clausen, and Robert N. Wilson, eds. *Explorations in Social Psychiatry.* New York: Basic Books, 1957.
Madsen, William. "Value Conflicts and Folk Psychotherapy in South Texas," in *Magic, Faith, and Healing,* Ari Kiev, ed. New York: The Free Press, 1964.
Parsons, Anne. *Belief, Magic, and Anomie.* New York: The Free Press, 1969.
Pedersen, Stefi. "Psychopathological Reactions to Extreme Social Displacements (Refugee Neuroses)," *Psychoanalytic Review* 36 (1949), 344–54.
Redfield, Robert, and Alfonso Villa Rojas. *Chan Kom: A Maya Village.* Chicago: University of Chicago Press, 1934.
Rubel, Arthur J. *Across the Tracks: Mexican-Americans in a Texas City.* Austin: University of Texas Press, 1966.
—— "Concepts of Disease in Mexican-American Culture," *American Anthropologist* 62 (1960), 795–814.
Sadler, William S. *Practice of Psychiatry.* St. Louis: Mosby, 1953.
Shoeck, Helmut. *Envy: A Theory of Social Behavior.* Michael Glenny and Betty Ross, trans. New York: Harcourt, Brace, 1966.
Shapiro, David. *Neurotic Styles.* New York: Basic Books, 1965.
Spiro, Melford E. "The Psychological function of Witchcraft belief: The Burmese Case," in *Mental Research in Asia and the Pacific,* W. Caudill and Tsung-Yi Lin, eds. Honolulu: East-West Center Press, 1969. Pp. 245–58.
Schwartz, D. A. "A Review of the 'Paranoid' Concept," *Archives of General Psychiatry* 8 (1963), 349–61.
Schwartz, Theodore. "Cult and Context: The Paranoid Ethos in Melanesia," *Ethos* 1 (1973), 153–74.
Tausk, V. "On the Origin of the Influencing Machine in Schizophrenia," in *The Psychoanalytic Reader,* vol. 1. R. Fliess, ed. New York: International University Press, 1948.
Tyhurst, James S. "Paranoid Patterns," in *Explorations in Social Psychiatry,* Alexander H. Leighton, et al., eds. New York: Basic Books, 1957.
Tyhurst, L. "Displacement and Migration: A Study in Social Psychiatry," *American Journal of Psychiatry* 107 (1951), 561–68.
Weidman, Hazel Hitson. "Cultural Values, Concept of Self, and Projection: The Burmese Case," in *Mental Health Research in Asia and the Pacific,* W. Caudill and Tsung-Yi Lin, eds. Honolulu: East-West Center Press, 1969, pp. 259–85.
Wolf, Eric R. "Types of Latin American Peasantry: A Preliminary Discussion," *American Anthropologist* 57 (1955), 452–71.

HOWARD F. STEIN

12. SLOVAK-AMERICANS

Envy and the Evil Eye: An Essay in the Psychological Ontogeny of Belief and Ritual

IN THE ANTHROPOLOGICAL scheme of things, the widespread evil eye phenomenon is a subject of the inclusive set "witchcraft." Although there exists a gargantuan literature on witchcraft, little attention has been given to the *ontogeny* of belief in the evil eye and its significance for later witchcraft phenomena. My analysis of the evil eye among Slovak-American peasant immigrants and their descendants focuses on the interpersonal and intrapsychic dynamics of the "acquisition" of the belief and its overdetermined and manifest functional implications for social relations in adulthood. Through an analysis of the Slovak and Slovak-American folk system in continuity and change, I hope to illumine what the evil eye *does, means* and how it *comes into meaning*. One can state what the evil eye *is* only in terms of a precipitate whose dynamics are known. The analysis is based on ethnographic research conducted between January 1970 and December 1971 in several mill town communities in western Pennsylvania.[1]

HOWARD F. STEIN is Associate Professor of Anthropology in the Department of Psychiatry, Meharry Medical College, Nashville, Tennessee. He took his training in the University of Pittsburgh. His research and writing interests include psychoanalytic anthropology, contemporary American culture, revitalization movements, and ethnic-American personality development and family dynamics.

He was a recipient of a Maurice Falk Medical Fund Fellowship in Ethnicity, Racism, and Mental Health from 1967–72, which enabled him to live among Slovak-Americans in western Pennsylvania and led to the writing of this paper.

The chapter has been reprinted, with minor stylistic changes, from *Ethos* 2, no. 1 (1974), by permission of the University of California Press.

While I focus on the minute particulars of the evil eye among Slovak-Americans, I equally attempt to integrate this analysis with the wider phenomenon of the evil eye and its secure position in the cosmogony of witchcraft.

Compendia ranging from F. T. Elworthy's early work on the evil eye to Lucy Mair's recent volume on witchcraft are rich in case material, witchcraft "dogma," and the "micropolitics" of accusation. Yet without the human developmental perspective, the "deep structure" of *why* the evil eye works will elude us. Parenthetically I might add that although the evil eye is frequently distinguished from destructive envy or covetousness (see Evans-Pritchard and Middleton), an exploration of this "deep structure" reveals an intimate connection between them.

George Foster's recent essay on the "Anatomy of Envy" goes far to bridge the often vigilantly maintained abyss between "cultural" and "psychological" explanation by exploring culturally constituted psychological dynamics. Foster writes: "psychological interpretation of symbolic behavior tells a great deal about society and culture without in any way negating the importance of sociological analysis." [2] In this essay I explore the relation between the jealousy-envy syndrome and the evil eye within an *epigenetic* framework,[3] hopefully to illumine and be illumined by the psychocultural "anatomy" that Foster has dissected. Commenting on Foster's paper, Judith Brown writes: "Foster suggests that envy is pan-human because 'the good things' are everywhere scarce and unevenly distributed. I would like to add that the uneven distribution of 'good things' first becomes obvious in earliest childhood, a time when the individual is particularly impotent and vulnerable." [4]

Alfred Kroeber once wrote of culture: "perhaps *how it comes to be* is really more distinctive of culture than what is *is.*" [5] What is true of "culture" should be equally true for "culture carriers." More broadly, the present approach assumes a systematic "relationship between the organized values and institutional efforts of societies, on the one hand, and the nature of ego synthesis, on the other." [6] Through an exploration of a specific sequence of what Erikson called "the ontogeny of ritualization" in man this essay attempts to relate culture to those myriad official and unofficial ritualizations (and their underlying anxieties) pervading early childhood that communicate to the infant what life is all about.

In his analysis of Ifaluk ghosts, Melford Spiro suggests that a common experiential frame of reference is necessary for the perpetuation of culturally patterned beliefs. George Devereux has argued similarly in terms of an "ethnic unconscious." Ego mechanisms mediate to cathect, to invest in, cultural beliefs (values, etc.) that constitute "cognitive affirmation of experience," [7] and that are later confirmed and reaffirmed by experience. Heinz Hartmann pointed out that through a "change of function," these beliefs themselves become the referents and building blocks of cultural elaboration and manipulation, rather than their psychogenetic precursors. The adaptive, synthesizing ego mediates to symbolize and ritualize early conflicts and traumata without the early experiences themselves becoming *conscious* referents: for example, identification, repression, projection, displacement, rationalization, symbolization, condensation, isolation, and regression selectively operate to create and maintain new referents for the inchoate anxiety (see Homans), reciprocally affirming the agents of socialization as they establish, confirm, and channel these anxieties in those being enculturated. Devereux and Erikson have both emphasized the complementarity of the socializer and the socialized with respect to unconscious conflict.

However, behavior, affect, and cognitive patterning are not only (unconsciously) overdetermined, but multiply determined. Hence we cannot automatically infer unconscious dynamics from an item of behavior. We should keep in mind an ancient distinction made by Hartmann, Kris, and Loewenstein between "institutionalized" aspects of behavior (e.g., child-care practices, witchcraft accusation) and the "noninstitutionalized" aspects of behavior (e.g., maternal affect in relation to her infant, projection), and the care that must be taken when attempting directly to link them.

Let me add a word of caution. We must avoid letting the poverty of language impoverish our empirical studies and our theoretical constructions, lest we allow our ethnocentric semantic "black box" to prestructure our observations and our interpretations. Thus I do not know a priori what "envy" or the "evil eye" are. Foster began retroductively with the concept of envy, and attempted to confirm his hypothesis by induction from ethnographic data, in the process discovering envy everywhere. If Foster has already provided a universal "deep structure," then it is pointless to look "deeper," and needless to formulate a problem—because there already exists a solution. Rather than start with envy and the evil eye as "given," I wish to explore the dynamics of its "givenness." My starting point is a pattern of culture and its enculturation, and my end point is the elucidation of envy and the evil eye. This inquiry focuses on the clustering of words and meanings around the Slovak-American evil eye. What this evil eye *is,* its significance within the social structure and personality, will differentiate out of this context. I take the question of its "origins"—whether by diffusion, independent invention, or syncretism—to be a matter of indifference for the present analysis, since its psychodynamic and social-structural functions act as "selective forces" for its pervasive presence and persistence. Finally, this study of the "epigenesis" and "physiology" of envy among one group might be seen as complementary to Foster's universal "anatomical" formulation, exploring how the universal and the particular, the "theme" and the "variation," might reciprocally illumine—*and test*—one another.

If there are universal common denominators, then I suggest that we look for them in a common ontogenetic experience coupled with common functional prerequisites and implications. Thus I would suggest a basis in (1) the underlying experience of maternal hostility and ambivalence, precipitating deep frustration and rage in infancy; (2) its linkage with the psychodynamic and cultural elaborations of the jealousy-envy complex; (3) its proliferation in the sociocultural domain into witchcraft, counterwitchcraft, and curing; and (4) their relationship to the socioeconomic realities of scarcity and deprivation. Despite my difference with Foster over the "identity" of envy (which I hope to clarify), the fact that the "identical custom" of the evil eye is widespread and is closely affiliated with a common clustering of psychological traits ascribed to envy, suggests that an analysis of the ontogenetic transformations of envy into the evil eye in a single case *may* help illumine the dynamics of the universal. My insistence on configurationist integrity does not vitiate the need for functionalist comparison (see Goldschmidt), but, it seems to me, makes it possible without tearing down a cultural ethos into artificial "shreds and patches."

Weaning and the Ontogeny of the Slovak-American Evil Eye

In Slovak, several words relate to the evil eye. *"Oči"* literally means "eyes"; *"počarič"* translates "to cast a spell." The two words are used interchangeably to designate the English-language gloss "evil eye," which gloss was specifically used by Slovak-Americans with whom I worked. Furthermore, the Slovak word for "witch" is *"čaravnica"* (literally, "one who casts a spell" / "one who casts the evil eye" / "witch"). Although both male and female can intentionally or by accident cast the evil eye, none of my informants ever heard of a male "witch." Restated in anthropological terms: anyone can be a "witch," but only a female can be a "sorcerer." In addition, the proclivity to sorcery runs in families, from mother to daughter.

From lengthy discussions and long-term relationships I have established with Slovak- and Ruthenian-born mothers now in their sixties and seventies, I can with certainty extrapolate a folk account or "dogma" of the etiology of the evil eye: there exists a direct causal link between the capacity for having (casting) the evil eye and having been allowed to return to the mother's breast after weaning. In the *folk model,* it is a simple matter of cause and effect; and, by extension, of prevention.

I would like to explore this relation from two perspectives: first, from within Slovak-American culture, and second, from a psychoanalytic-ethnographic frame of reference. For heuristic purposes, I shall focus on the evil eye within the wider *field* of enculturation (though *not* as an isolate), exploring and delimiting its specific dynamics.[8]

With the beginning of the infant's second year of life (approximately), the absoluteness of the mother's will, heretofore experienced more through the rhythm of time and relation than the mere fact of feeding, is precipitously brought home to the infant through the relative coincidence of sudden weaning (exacerbated by its coincidence with teething) and the onset of severe toilet training (as one second-generation Lutheran Slovak-American male summarized it: "Shit or die!"). The infant "gets it" at both ends, and with a vengeance. The one-sidedness of mutual regulation that is based on modalities of giving and receiving, bestowing and accepting, incorporating and expelling, activity and passivity, etc., now expands zonally to encompass newly relevant body zones and psychomotor modalities, and exacerbates the relational vicissitudes of earlier ones, generating new variations on old, and solidly established, themes.[9]

The cultural ethos pervades and permeates each new psychosexual and separation-individuative stage [10] and infuses the infant's cumulative "hypothesis" about the nature of the world.[11] Intrapsychic structuring emerges to assure self-esteem and ward off anxiety; through introjection and identification, a personal and interpersonal (transactional) style consolidates to link individual personality with the cultural community of egos.[12] I would stress here that severe weaning does not independently "cause" the evil eye; rather, the weaning experience is *prototypic* or *archetypal* of the mother-child relationship, for it weaves into a "condensation" the strands of the

Slovak ethos, which together, as a gestalt, create the readiness to accept a cultural belief that resolves conflicts created by the quality of mother-infant relations. The folk explanation, here, as elsewhere, functions as a post hoc rationalization and explanation for beliefs and behaviors that are intuitively accepted as "natural." Nevertheless, the folk explanation, as a cultural memory screen, suggests the deeper issues by virtue of its partial translucence and partial opacity. It "leads" *as* it "misleads."

Among the Slovaks, weaning is sudden and uncompromising. There is absolutely no going back once the decision is made, and the mother refuses the breast or (in America) the bottle once and for all. The following interview excerpts will clarify the issue. The first example is Mrs. B, a Ruthenian Byzantine Catholic woman in her late seventies, married to a Slovak Latin Rite Catholic from a nearby *župa* (county). In the earlier part of the interview, I had first begun to suspect that weaning and the evil eye were somehow related, and asked her to tell me about the evil eye.

> I don't know what's truth. Those kind of people—get jealous of you—that you have something. They say baby get evil eye if mother go back nurse the child after she take him off the breast. When mother weans baby nine to twelve months. When baby cry—went back and nursed it further. Then that child has bad eyes. You never say: 'That's nice' [about the baby], because it will turn bad. A fellow had beautiful oxes—he was taking them to sell at market. Another fellow came up the road and say to him: 'That's nice oxes you have.' The yoke broke the oxes in two! He don't mean it—don't mean to do it. It's his eyes. Spit first and then say what you want. When you wean your baby, *don't ever go back! Finished! Done!* No matter how much it cries!

The second example is from Mrs. I, a Slovak Lutheran in her late seventies. We were talking about child rearing, and I asked her how she handled weaning.

> *Finished! Stop!* Then right to the table. No more breast. Quite final. Nine months, one year, 14–15 months breast feed. Once you stopped, you never go back. Evil eye: *počarič* . . . I never thought it about the children.

In a later interview with Mrs. I and her daughter, Mrs. D, Mrs. I continued talking about weaning:

> Weaning—one year. I give other foods before weaning—strained or mashed . . . vegetable soup . . . Milk dried up after I stopped feeding them. I feed them one year. They start bite and I take them off! [*wince, laugh*] One year, that's enough feeding baby breast. Beside them I feed them by table.

The third example is from a discussion with Mrs. G, a Slovak Byzantine Catholic in her mid-seventies.

I never gave my children the bottle. I feed them—just breast. About five months start giving soup, mashed potatoes, carrots. . . . Give breast all the time until year, year-and-a-half. When I stop giving breast—I never go back [*strong*]. Never, no more. Even if they cry—cry two days and two nights, but have to get used to it. I took Mike [eldest son] nine months off the breast. He cried three nights and three days. When Paul [second son] came around, I took him off one and a half years. I told him I was sick—he understood [Mike is 18 months older than Paul]. I nursed Steve [the youngest] twenty-two months. I born Paul when I'm 40. I let him have one and a half years because I love him like baby. He comes here every Sunday with wife and children the the *čeregy* [Slovak pastry]. . . . Go back to breast—baby later see something, destroy it. Superstitious. I never heard of anyone taking baby back where I come from [the village of Zubńe, in Zemplín *župa*]—let them cry. I don't believe the superstitions.

The fourth example is from Mrs. Ma, a Slovak Latin Rite Catholic in her late fifties, and her eldest daughter, Mrs. Hr. Mrs. Ma remarked on weaning:

Weaning ten months to a year. Start giving food after a couple of months. Then stopped with breast. Drinking milk from a cup. Never go back to feeding after that.

In a later interview, Mrs. Ma elaborated on weaning:

If she puts the baby back [i.e., gives the breast after she has weaned the baby]—something about the eyes. *Oči*—strangers shouldn't stare at babies. Stop once feeding baby breast—giving back causes *oči*. Baby gets sore eyes from staring. Baby could even die from it. I took her [eldest daughter, Mrs. Hr., with whom she lives] when she was a baby—a couple of months old. She was crying. Took hot pieces of coal from the stove and put them in [a container of] water. If they sink, you know they've been stared at. Dip your hand in the water [*motions, backhand movement*]. Rub baby's head with your hand. Throw the water over your shoulder . . . She doesn't sleep—cries. My husband lit three matches. Drop them in water. They sink—somebody must have stared. My [MoSiDa] died from that. If matches or coal stays on top, it's OK. If they go down, that happened.

The final example is from a discussion with Mrs. Z, a Slovak Independent Catholic in her late sixties, and her second eldest daughter, Mrs. T:

MRS. Z: Once you take the child off the bottle, never give it back. Weaning—as late as 14 months. Some weaned off themselves early. They wanted to eat [*shrug shoulders, smiling*]! This was the first. I never gave special baby foods.

Mashed potatoes, mashed carrots, noodles, mother's oats. Let them suck on pork chop bone. When you wean them, they cry for awhile. Give them an excuse [*laughs it off*]. The bogeyman took it. It broke. Give him a story.

MRS. T: When you're weaning at breast feeding—stop at teething.

In a later interview with Mrs. T (American born, in her early forties), she elaborated on the above:

Most of the babies were nursed by the mother. With one of them, I remember hearing the mother screamed: 'Oeee!' The baby must have taken a good bite out of her. The mother said: 'It's time—*uš čas!*' The baby was around a year old. The baby sometimes had walking shoes on. My mother was nursing the baby. I don't remember which one it was.

Teething and abrupt weaning coincide. The mother withdraws herself from intimate contact with the infant. Playing with the infant, although present even before, is at a minimum. From here on, giving is mediated through a deluge of things, food, and engulfing protection—substitutes for an omnipresent self whose very approaches are "avoidant." Giving never ceases to be a major theme, but becomes indirect—which does not diminish the intensity of mutual dependency. The mother never ceases lavishly to interpose and impose herself on the infant's oral intake (or, for that matter, throughout the life of her "children"). The temporal and affective quality of this pervasive theme is that the mother's will be *absolutely* done, for example, in her choice to respond or not respond to "demands" for feeding, evocations of crying, calls for "attention," and the like.

To summarize the general response to my questions about weaning: the infant cries and whines for a few days, but then it's all over with. Since in traditional Slovak life, however, the evil eye is of such importance as an explanation for the experience of misfortune and the divination of malevolence, and functions effectively as a means of social control, the fact that it is (allegedly) intimately connected with weaning suggests a far deeper importance to *the meaning of* weaning than the mothers give in their matter-of-fact accounts of how quickly the weaning experience is out of sight and out of mind. Their other associations with weaning attest to their deep concern that their child not develop the evil eye. In a sense, the evil eye is a "communicable disease," since giving the infant the breast after it has been weaned is likely to "give" the infant the dread "eye disease." All of this communicated to the child, and this communication summated into a "formula." Weaning is decisive, final—the mother must not go back, "no matter how much it cries." Then comes the explanation, the opposite side of the "equation," that the capacity to cast the evil eye is directly traceable to the fact that a mother gave in, went back, which somehow *caused* the child's eyes to go bad. As a consequence, anything this person says admiringly (without spitting first, thereby breaking the spell) will cause immediate destruction to what is admired. It can kill oxen. An inadvertent compliment or stare will kill an infant.

"Jealousy" and the Evil Eye in the American Experience

The evil eye is not talked about much in America—even among the older people of the immigrant generation. It is denied even as it is vividly attested to. Many laughingly dismiss it as superstition, ideologically disowning it, though living as though it were devastatingly true. These same people continuously speak of the Slovaks as "the most jealous people in the world." *Jealousy* is a term that I have heard in virtually every Slovak household I visited. It is always used with reference to "the others." Numerous first-generation (immigrant) and second-generation Slovak-American businessmen (e.g., grocers, barbers, tavern owners, morticians) and steel mill workers achieving advancement (e.g., foremen, machinists, and other skilled and/or supervisory positions) are berated both by family and Slovak "constituency" alike for trying to get ahead at everyone else's expense, for regarding themselves as somehow superior to others. Without exception, every Slovak businessman with whom I spoke complained bitterly that his own people would rather frequent the business establishments of those of other ethnic origins than support their own—even in such instances of convenience where the Slovak market would be closer.

Another form taken by this "jealousy" is the frequent refusal of the father even into the third and fourth generations to allow his children to advance. A typical expression would be: "I've taken care of you long enough. You're old enough to start bringing in something yourself." One father, a very successful businessman in an East/Central European ethnic-American enclave, moved his family into a stone home in the most wealthy part of the city. Yet when his oldest son, now 22, expressed his wish to go to college, the father snapped: "What do you need to go to college for? When I was your age, I already had a job. I wasn't even able to complete high school. The education I had was good enough for me. I did it—you can do it.'' At the core of the value of being ''the provider'' was a deep resentment against it which was inverted through reaction formation into a fundamental source of self-esteem, but which resentment nevertheless could not be hidden. The father had worked hard for what he had, and spent his life providing for his ungrateful children; now it was their turn to bring in some money. Why should they have it better than he—even though he himself had desperately sought to have it, and succeeded in having it, better than his parents? [13] In Slovakia, the worker/provider ethic was predominantly male, but in America, with the possibility of female employment (e.g., as domestics, secretaries, bank tellers, waitresses), the female offspring frequently were inducted into the exploitable family labor force.

Yet a converse and contradictory ''value orientation'' and motivation existed (and exists) in the United States, and even underlay the motive for migration: the image of the American Dream, in which America was imagined as a utopia with streets paved with gold, where one could be free of the constricting bonds of dependency and authority. One wanted and sought more and more of ''the pie'' (and more pies) for oneself. Nevertheless, the vicious ''jealousy'' persisted and infused the experience of an emerging (and imagined) plenty. In one largely multigeneration Slovak/Ruthenian/Hungarian-American neighborhood in a western Pennsylvania mill town, I witnessed the not infrequent phenomenon (and was reminded that the pattern had been present since the turn of the century) that when one household bought a new radio or remodeled its kitchen, a neighboring or kin-related household would immediately embark on ''doing one better,'' with a long-term status/prestige war of conspicuous consumption being waged. The *centrifugality* that was kept within limits in the peasant village through gossip, accusations of ''jealousy,'' and the reality of ''limited goods'' in America erupted and ran rife. One accuses another of ''jealousy,'' yet makes a counterresponse that guarantees the irruption and accusation of ''jealousy'' by the one originally accused . . . and so the circle goes.

Similarly, just as a father or mother is deeply ''jealous'' of the possible success of his or her children (especially those of the same sex as the parent), the parents' own impetus for the American ethos of success, achievement, mobility, and independence induces a narcissistic identifica-

tion with the potential success of their offspring, this enabling them vi-
cariously to succeed through their children, even as they envy and resent
that very success they were unable or unwilling to try for.[14] Thus the father
discussed two parapraphs above finally relented and sent his son to college,
but only after the son had convinced him that higher education was the only
way to get a decent job today. When I visited with the family (the son had
already been in college for three years), the father proudly told me that he
was putting his son through college; that he strongly admired anyone who
sought to advance himself through education; and that, as part of his contribution to his son's education, he had given up drinking liquor, giving the
money that would have been spent on it to his son as an allowance.

The vicissitudes of ''jealousy'' are inevitably built into the dynamics of
sibling rivalry that run rife within the family and between families. Behind
the severely strong ethic of cooperation and sharing is the constant *competition* for what seems to be demonstrations of love (that are rarely forthcoming), by *outdoing others* in demonstrations of love. Paradoxically, this ethic
creates its opposite: hostility, resentment, and more intense competitiveness.
Mrs. D (quoted above), a woman in her forties, said to me:

> Whatever we did it was to try to please our parents. We got so very little praise
> for it. We were so hungry for the praise we never got [*imploringly*]. It was ex-
> pected of us—to do our jobs. We tried all the harder to do right—to get their
> praise. . . . When we learned to scrub the floor, we were told how to do it. We
> didn't dare to do it it any other way. Always more criticism than praise.

This competition for rare pittances of approval and confirmation has the reciprocal effect of ''playing into'' the mother's needs, since the children are
contending all the harder for demonstrations or signs of her love, each outdoing the other. In adulthood, one continues to preach and practice the ethic
of cooperation, giving, and sharing—while simultaneously protesting
against it (e.g., through constant complaint, ''suffering,'' and occasional
negativistic ''undoing'').

As ''giving'' took on an overcompensatory quality, so does ''sharing,''
being a subset of ''giving.'' One must renounce wanting, and the transformation is made from: ''What I want I cannot have,'' to ''What I cannot
have I do not want.'' Here, as a consequence of the repression of the desire
of ''wanting,'' the desire later emerges as a ''symptom.'' The following episode was related by Mrs. D; she was speaking of the different kinds of work

she did after coming of age—that is, when she was sent to work, around age 10.

> I was baby-sitting and scrubbing floors when I was 12 or 13. I was 10 years old when [my eldest sister's] first baby was born. And I took care of her. Just like my own baby. I bathed her, fed her. . . . I had to scrub floors for other people. I *hated* it [referring to one woman's floor]: It was a beautifully scrubbed floor. It was so clean that they could eat off it. They probably did. But . . . they were careless with their things. She told me her necklace was missing. I didn't take it. I felt very guilty about it. Very guilty. We, too, had guilt complexes. I felt guilty about it a long time after. I still feel guilty about it. I wanted to tell her it wouldn't have gotten lost if they had taken care of her things. We weren't allowed to tell what we thought . . . why we were so suppressed in our communication. Everyone else was right—no matter what they said. You didn't dare answer back. The respect for our parents was the most important thing. They were our authority at the time.

The authoritarian atmosphere of the home conspired to make this young domestic's guilt unbearable, for there was no option for her to express herself, save to deny that she had stolen the necklace—and silence. Her tenuous self-esteem contingent on being a superdomestic was shattered because a single item was missing (out of place). What she hated she performed dutifully, religiously. Part of her guilt reflects her inner rebellion against a compulsive perfectionism. Another aspect of the guilt is her need for punishment for secretly coveting (casting the evil eye upon?) what belonged to another, which guilt she attempted to deny by focusing on her employer's carelessness. Her insistent innocence is counterpointed by a gnawing and enduring guilt, which suggests a wish that is equally enduring, but whose referent extends far beyond the necklace. Furthermore, her recollection of this episode immediately follows her expression of resentment for having to do so much for, give so much to, others. She contrasts this orientation toward others with a secret craving to meet her own needs, and renounces the latter while protesting the former—which constitutes a major strand in the ontogeny of "jealousy." The "jealousy" now extends to her own children, to whom she gives nothing that they want, unless they first work for it, earn it. As she suffered for the little she has (although she and her family live a "middle class" life), so must they for their wants. Because she denies what she craves, she cannot minister to her own children except as mediated through her own repressed needs: consequently, what she repressed in herself, she "represses" in her children.

During an interview with this woman's elder sister (the eldest in the family, in her fifties), I asked about the statement that I had often heard that the Slovaks are a very jealous people. She leaped on it in assent:

> That's so true. There's a proverb what says: "A Slovak wouldn't help another one out of a ditch." A mother and brothers do stick together. The Slovak people stick together. In the family sticks together. . . . Your neighbor will be jealous if we have something more. They were jealous also in Europe.

The Slovaks are "jealous," but they "stick together." Within one's own family "jealousy" is denied. One is not "jealous" of others—including family members. It is the others who are "jealous" of what one has. One is constantly giving to others, sharing with others, and doing for others—all compulsively, resentfully. Manifestly, one affirms the solidarity of the group; latently, one defends against the possibility that one's "jealousy" may be found out. One loves, one gives, but hates it. One seeks love desperately, and never receives it. Yet one must love, because those who had parented them domonstratively insisted on their love for their progeny, even as they communicated the opposite (that they were unwanted, burdensome) along other bands of the communication spectrum. One cannot openly dislike, hate, or envy anyone with whom one is closely bound up. The adaptive solution is through denial, repression, and reaction formation. As one brother said of his envied elder brother who was the favorite in the household: "What the hell. What can you say? He's egocentric and that's it. All you can do is love him to death." Killing with love is the only viable solution where vapid envy ("jealousy") consumes but must be denied, or, using the metaphor of the evil eye, *spat out*.

The following quotation from a second generation Slovak-American Latin Rite Catholic in his 50s nicely incorporates many of the issues discussed thus far, and adumbrates the ensuing discussion of the psychocultural dynamics of "jealousy," including such foci as the separation-individuation process; the relationship between the American Dream and the traditional ethic of "limited good"; [15] the relationship between hostility, guilt, and the "susceptibility" to the evil eye; and the relationship between the "bewitcher" and the "bewitched," both in terms of current reality and early experiences that influence the response to this "reality." I asked him to tell me what he remembered about the evil eye. He began:

> I don't know nothing about the evil eye. My mother and dad—they never talked about the evil eye. I never heard them mention it. But I know there are these women—*čaravnica*—who can put the whammy on you if they don't like you.

Maybe it's only women—I never heard of a man being a witch. Somebody who can put the whammy on you, like a curse. I never believed in it until it happened to my father. I was just little then—but even my older brothers talk about it and remember it. My dad was in his twenties—around 28. He came to this country when he was 14. He went to the South Side [Pittsburgh] and got a job in the mill. In them days you just went to the mill and went right to work—not like today when you first got to apply. . . . He was a hard worker. You work for what you get. You work hard so you can make it yourself, so you can go out on your own. You want to better yourself, not stay there in the slum. Work your way out of the slum. . . . When my father came here [before World War I], he took a room in a boarding house run by a woman from his village. That's how they all did it. They came over here and find out who's from where they come from. She helped lots of people get started. She was here maybe 10–15 years before my dad came. She boarded 8–10 men. When my dad got married, after they started having 3–4 children, it was impossible for all of them to live in just these two rooms. The family just got too big, and we had to move out. So he bought himself a frame house on Josephine Street, near the mill [but up on the hill, rather than on the floodplain where he had originally rented]. It was an old, run-down house, but he'd work on it to put it in shape. This woman, she didn't like the idea of losing the money for rent. She was mad at him for leaving, and put the whammy on him. They couldn't think of anybody else that had hard feelings for him, and she was known for witchcraft in Europe, so that they thought it was her. She know he was a hard worker, and that's how she'd get back at him. She was jealous that he'd gone off and left her. I wouldn't have believed it if I hadn't seen it myself. He couldn't walk for six months—his legs were paralyzed. The only way he could get around was on his ass. I was five years old at the time. I remember him fixing the fence around the house on the seat of his pants. That's the only way he could move around. He pushed himself along on his back side. He couldn't go to work, to church, nothing. The old lady—she figured this is how she would ruin him. You wouldn't believe it unless you'd seen it. Finally some people from church told him of this other woman who might be able to help him. He went to her, and she fixed him some herbs—like a tea or soup, and he drank it. And right after that he could walk like nothing ever happened. That's what changed my way of thinking about it. This old witch really could put the whammy on him. [I asked him how his father knew it was her.] She was the only person he knew of who had some grudge against him. Here he had lived so long with her, and she helped him out—and now he left. She figured she'd get even—and force him to come back. She was the only one who would be jealous of him. So he figured it must have been her. He told us she was known for being a witch already in Europe. She'd done this sort of thing to people over there before she came. She never married— who would have wanted her! It runs in families—only girls, not the boys. A mother would be a witch, then one of her daughters would be one just like her, and so on down the line. I never heard of a man putting the whammy on some-body. Just the woman—maybe they figure that you're getting it better than them, and they try to take it away. This woman, she was already in her sixties . . .

The "Deep Structure" of the Jealousy / Envy Complex

Let me now attempt to "locate" the cultural experience [16] of "jealousy" among Slovak-Americans. I have thus far enclosed "jealousy" in quotations to indicate that it is being used as a folk-term. The discussion to follow will give an analytic perspective on the folk model. If "jealousy" indeed mediates between childhood overdeterminancy and adult-cultural fear and practice of witchcraft, then the nature of the link must be explored.

In his discussion of antitherapeutic rituals, Anthony F. C. Wallace notes that one function of witchcraft is as a "general palliative for social conflict prompted by the emotional lesions left by traumatic childbrearing experiences"; furthermore, witchcraft anxiety in part reflects "neurotic guilt toward the suspected witch." [17] Robert A. LeVine similarly writes of witchcraft accusation as reflecting the use of defense mechanisms to reduce guilt feelings. [18] In their discussion of the relation between child training and adult belief, Whiting and Child postulate a high correlation between witchcraft belief and intense socialization anxiety, illness "cause," and illness explanation in three areas: oral, aggression, and dependency. As I shall discuss below, it would seem that *all* three of these components are heavily weighted in the Slovak and Slovak-American evil eye *constellation* or configuration (e.g., verbal spells or incantations, aggressive thoughts, magically introjected foreign bodies, soul loss, and spirit possession).

Warner Muensterberger writes of the ontogenetic "predisposition" to witchcraft:

> The common belief in witches tells us something about the mother's quite open ambivalence toward her children and shows a predominantly orally oriented mechanism of defense, which splits the mother image into the good, devoted mother and the dangerous, treacherous witch. . . . The belief in devouring demons is a projective manifestation of ideas which are clearly preoedipal and are very often connected with food sacrifices to deceased ancestors. This ritual is rather widespread and is an institutionalized attempt to undo oral-destructive fantasies against the retaliating mother (cf. Klein 1948). Since the struggle cannot be mastered by repression, animistic and magical concepts are created which transplant internal conflicts onto a projective, delusory antagonist. [19]

Thoughts and feelings intolerable for the maintenance of self-esteem and that may be felt as endangering one's very survival are projected outward as ego-alien and become transformed into threats from without. Early infancy is prototypic for this enduring condition, since the infant's very existence is dependent upon the mother's beneficent countenance.[20] Fantasies of biting, annihilation, devouring rage, cannibalism, and destruction intensified by the mother's ambivalence and the sharp pain of teething, create, in turn, the fantasied danger of retaliation and annihilation from the mother.[21] As a consequence of the *quality* of object relations between mother and infant, the "potential space" between them becomes injected with "persecutory material" that the infant cannot reject.[22] This "potential space" constitutes the infant's first "environment" in the social world, and the quality of relation within this potential infuses the emergent awareness of the geography and environment of the larger world with *its* meanings—the referrents of "it" being simultaneously the individual, the culture, and the environment. Out of an ambivalence-laden "dual unity" emerges what E. James Anthony has evocatively called the "deep, seething, scarifying Kleinian envy" [23] that is manifested through the dual processes of projective and introjective identification, and which produces an ego-splitting and object-splitting that is simultaneously adaptive to the world within and without. The countercathexis is the substrate for the belief in the evil eye. In this perspective the evil eye can be understood metaphorically as a *spat out introject,* an externalized, repudiated "bad self" and "bad object" that derived from the relationship with the "bad mother." Conversely, the "good self," incapable of envy, is bound up with the self-esteem derivative of the relationship with the "good mother." Recalling Freud's aphorism that "Delusions of jealousy contradict the subject," [24] one might state the transformation as follows: It is not I who envy, but he or she who envies me.

The Slovak-American data richly elucidates the tenet that "jealousy" kills, injures, paralyzes, and brings on illness. As in witchcraft accusations generally, the evil eye becomes an *explicans* for virtually anything to which one wishes to attribute it. If the referents of symbolism provide clues to its meaning, then the referents of the evil eye—discernible in rationalizations, accusation, and remedy—suggest that what the Slovak-Americans label as "jealousy" encompasses both *envy* and *jealousy.* The context of the use of the term designates its meaning. Strictly speaking, jealousy denotes one's own covetousness of what belongs to (or is a part of) another. Among Slovak-Americans, jealousy and envy operate as complements to one another. Given the "limited good" ethic, and "limited goods" in current reality and in the dimly remembered childhood experience, one *jealously* guards (i.e., suspicion) what little one has, anxious that even this will be taken away, a fear that is "reasonable" and infused with the early "ecology" of the mother-child environment; conversely, one deeply *envies* (i.e., covetousness) what another has or seems to have, again both ecologically and overdeterminedly "reasonable" given the nature of the "average expectable environment." [25] The evil eye thus encompasses and condenses into a single, reciprocal system, the *watchful guardian* and the longing, *often destructive, desire:* it is simultaneously *protection* and *projection.* In their paper on the evil eye in the circum-Mediterranean area, Moss and Cappannari have written of the

> inherent ambiguity to human interactions. The multivalence of feelings can be potentially disruptive in community interrelationships. Since the evil eye is regarded as a magical and often as an involuntary threat by its bearers, anger or retaliation can be replaced by a patterned response that provides alternatives to personal confrontation. This ambivalence is the basic social-psychological theme that underlies the evil eye belief. [26]

The magical and involuntary character of the evil eye are of equal importance in its persistence and control. Included in magicality would be the omnipotence of the wish, the magnitude of the imagined danger to oneself and another, and the equation between the thought and percept. Included in involuntariness would be the ego-alien character of the magicality, its displacement, denial, and depersonalization. Through the disqualification or disavowal of intentionality, the dangers inhering in the evil eye can be contained. Speculating into the matter of "function" and "dysfunction" of the evil eye, one might say paradoxically that the belief in the evil eye simultaneously fosters and prevents limitless strife, and its analysis reveals the delicately balanced structure of both culture and personality.

In the everyday world of the chronic but low-grade evil eye (as opposed to the flareup of witchcraft accusation), the magical potency of the evil eye is controlled and contained, not only through fear, but equally through the common consent that it is largely involuntary, that all people of good will can be struck by "attacks" of envy. Thus the danger of retaliation is controlled and lessened by a sense of common predicament, and hence empathy for the person casting the unintended spell. Compassion is due not only the one stricken by the evil eye, but equally the unfortunate who is unaware that he or she is casting it. The "preventative medicine" of spitting before uttering admiration (etc.) acts equally as a control on the spread of the evil eye.

The "endemic" only becomes "epidemic" when the "magical" over-whelms the defenses that perpetuate the sense of reality, and hence the "in-voluntary" becomes "intentional." At this point personal confrontation is infused with the anger of retaliation. For the most part, however, each acts to *protect* oneself and the others, even as one *projects* upon others one's deepest envy. Through identification, one not only protects oneself, but helps others protect themselves as well.

The concept of identification is critical for understanding the nature of witchcraft. LeVine has suggested that witchcraft belief and accusation are dependent on one's "representation of himself as mystically interdependent with his neighbors," or, in analytic terms, "symbiotic representation of the boundary and relationship between self and others":

> A person with a symbiotic representatiom of self-other relations will have devel-oped a superego in which the evaluation of actions and the activation of guilt feel-ings are primarily dependent on the maintenance of emotional and material trans-actions between himself and others; and interruption in the flow of transactions . . . that provokes ill feelings in a neighbor leads (through regression) to the judg-ment that her vengeful attitude alone—which is experienced as part of the self—is wreaking punishment upon him.[27]

I might add that the lack of distinction between self-other boundaries is isomorphic with the concomitant lack of distinction between thought and percept, or inner and outer sources of experience. Indeed, the confusion of the "mote" and the "beam" lies at the very heart of the evil eye, inten-tionally obscuring the difference between the envier and the envied.[28]

In a review of the literature essay on envy, Walter G. Joffe nicely delin-eates the parameters of the dynamics of envy, any of which can come to dominate within the clustering of elements, contingent on the nature of ob-ject-relations that underlie phenomenological structuralization.

> Envy is . . . one of a variety of responses which may occur as a reaction to the *pain* which accompanies a discrepancy between actual and ideal self. Thus envy can be conceived as a *reaction* to a painful subjective state. It is a response which may mobilize aggression, may involve hate and resentment, and may contain an element of admiration. The individual who envies develops a covetousness for that which he does not have in such a form that his narcissism and well-being is to some extent restored by the fantasy of one day possessing that which he does not have. In this sense envy may indeed be an adaptive response acting as a spur to development. However, when the component of admiration is minimal and the aggressive component is dominant, regressive and destructive consequences may occur.[29]

From the Slovak-American data, it would seem that the aggressive component predominates in the dynamics of envy, overwhelming the "component" of admiration. Through the process of idealization the bad mother/bad child introject is separated (isolated) from the good mother/good child equation, and the repressed ambivalence projected onto "witches" (sorcerers) and everyday casters of the evil eye. The evil eye thus becomes a "culturally constituted defense mechanism" [30] for handling the "return of the repressed." The evil eye becomes a *culture-syntonic* structuralization of the jealousy/envy complex of infancy, whereby a constellation of symbolism and ritual attains *relative* autonomy from its origins. [31] In response to the ever-imminent danger of the evil eye, an array of detection procedures proliferates and is followed by an equal proliferation of remedial maneuvers, during the course of which the repressed source is obscured through projection and through a concentration on divination and cure in the *outer* world.

The remedy for being striken by the evil eye betrays the oral-incorporative zonal and modal foci underlying it. Whatever the specific meaning of dropping three (or any larger odd number) hot coals or burning matches into water to determine whether they float or sink, the remedy—if the evil eye is diagnosed/divined by sinkage—is either to rub the water on the forehead of the infant or to have the infant (or adult, if the victim is an adult) drink the medicinal solution. For the child the crying, and for the adult the "eye sickness" or "headache," that is brought on by the evil eye, is assuaged, and the spell is neutralized. In its most general sense, whatever the external source of anxiety that suggests the evil eye, the remedy (whether rubbing the forehead or drinking) is always incorporative/absorptive, suggesting the oral-incorporative nature of the "problem" to which the remedy is a homeopathic solution.

In the folk idiom, "jealousy" is an act of will, secretly wanting what is not yours, wanting something you cannot have. One covetously desires to possess what one should not want; one ambivalently remembers that distant "object" one tenuously "possessed," which in turn generates a boundless rage against the ambivalent object. Thus the very act of admiration can destroy the object of admiration. The only way to neutralize the affect of "jealousy" is to spit before uttering admiration; or if you suspect someone has put the evil eye on you, to perform the flotation experiments.

The Slovak explanation holds that the first "jealousy" is wanting the mother's breast when she does not wish to give it—when it has been withdrawn. One wishes to take when one no longer is given. But one must absolutely not give in to another's will. One remains steadfast, resolute, strong. The mother's will prevails over the child's wish and pleading. The rationale: if you get what you want (even) once, you will think you can have what you want every time you want something. The child, as the mother, learns to be alternately *will-less* and *willful*.

A theme pervading Slovak socialization is the need for the child to become *strong,* and the fear that it will be *weak* and *fragile.* It is assumed that the infant is inherently weak and fragile and that it is the task of socialization to *strengthen* the child so that it will become immune to accident and harm. This is one of the purposes of swaddling, to prevent the child from injuring itself by putting its hands in its eyes; from breaking its fragile neck, back, arms and legs. To allow the child to move freely invites these disasters: for example, the baby's head must be rigidly supported lest the weight of the head break the neck. Swaddling strengthens and protects the child by forcing the bones to grow straight, preventing dreaded deformation and weakness.

Crying is another vital mechanism for strenthening the child. The *mother* knows when the child is hungry, needs a change of diaper, or is merely "crying for nothing" or crying for "attention." The mother responds always to her own needs (i.e., to give, to withhold), not to the child's evocations. Crying is good because it "builds strong lungs." When a child cries, it is left alone to cry itself out, or to cry itself to sleep.

Until the child is able to sit up by itself, it is only minimally handled by the mother for fear that she may harm it or that it may hurt itself. The swaddled baby is the secure baby. Until the infant can sit up unsupported, none of its siblings is allowed to handle it. When the infant is held, it is always held flat and in front of the person holding it: the eyes of the infant *must* always be in a position to look directly (forward) at the person. For a baby to see a person by looking backward is to invite the possibility that the infant become cross-eyed. Great care is taken that the child develop good eyes, and the mother is ever fearful that her child will develop bad eyes.

From infancy, through toddlerhood—through adulthood, for that matter— the mother is constantly on the watch lest something devastating or disastrous happen to her "child." The child is not let out of her sight, or out of the sight of a reliable surrogate. Almost constantly, the mother is snatching her toddler from disaster—after first allowing the child to get at least one foot in the abyss.

The intrapsychic structuring that underlies this "strengthening" derives from, and is an adaptation to, the frustration, rage, fear of weakness, and experience of isolation that have pervaded infancy. A central defense utilized is reaction formation, producing a hearty, resolute, "fiercely independent" personality who is forever dependent and indebted, submitting unquestioningly to authorities on Heaven and Earth. The "depressive position" characerizes the core of the personality: longing for what was never truly given, denying the wish, enraged at the one who denied early needs, guilty for the hostility and fearing retaliation, forever making unpayable reparations and resenting the eternal indebtedness—all in a vicious circle. Only through ego-splitting does *"mamička"* ("mother"-diminutive: "sweet mother") become separated from the persecutory witch.[32]

In his pioneering paper on "separation anxiety," John Bowlby offered several insights on the significance of maternal ambivalence that are directly applicable here: "the child's heightened anxiety over separation and loss of love is [a reaction] to the unconscious hostility and rejection that lies behind it or to the threats of loss of love his parents have used to bind him to them. . . . For each of these experiences—separation, threats of separation, actual rejections or expectation of rejection—enormously increases the child's hostility, whilst his hostility greatly increases his expectation of rejection and loss."[33] The repression of hostility generates further anxiety, since the need for the object coexists with a simultaneous pull away from the object and fantasied holocaust of the object. The dimly remembered source of pleasure is renounced as it is secretly sought (in magic and religion). One defends against future vulnerability, yet craves what was never given by the original object. The fear of loss vies with a fear of dependency, leading to a precocious independence and a chronic, low-grade melancholia underlying an "emotional flatness."[34] Through the cumulative experiences of swaddling, feeding, crying, weaning, efforts at evocation, autonomy, and motility, a defensive structure emerges to maximize the illusion of independence (while surrounded and engulfed by kinfolk), yet coexisting with an incapacity to be alone.[35]

In a sense, the direct association of the "bad breast" with evil eye is a case of misplaced concreteness, since the part-object is enlarged and distorted and isolated from the relational whole. The *zonal* fixation, however, reflects and is a (symbolic) condensation of the more general—and generalized—*mode* of object relation, the *quality* of mutual regulation between mother and infant.[36] Just as the *quality* of object-relations determines the nature of the experience of separation anxiety and its resolution, so equally it underlies the specific *quality* of envy and the evil eye, differentiating it from the similar constellation and relationship in other cultures, despite an underlying identity of functional prerequisites and consequences.

If ascribing the evil eye or "jealousy" to another (projective identification) reveals the projective system of the accuser, then what underlies the Slovak mother's fears that she will cause the evil eye in her infant if she nurses again after weaning? What in the mother is projected upon, located in, and eradicated from the child? I suggest that it is her wish to have more and better than she has (on her own terms), against which recognition she recoils by stamping it out in her infant. The child's "demands" reawaken her own unfulfilled cravings, which she must simultaneously repress in herself and her infant.[37] As she could not have "more," so neither will the infant have "more." As she could not have a will of her own, neither will the infant have a will of its own—which she wilfully impresses on the infant. The mother's resentment at giving (when she wants to *receive*), her resentment at being saddled with an unruly brood of children who are her justification and her torment, is repressed and transformed via reaction formation into an overgiving, overprotective domination that infuses the early mother-child relationship with hostility, even as she insists that it is all for the child's good. The child desperately wishes to "hold on" to a mother (preserve the symbiotic tie—see Mahler) whose very giving is a demand for a gratitude for what is not freely bestowed. One learns that giving with a vengeance is the essence of life; that one can only "receive" by indebting others through giving.

The oral-incorporative mode and the trauma associated with it becomes the fixated point and model for later behavior associated with wanting or admiring. Any act of admiration must be first qualified (and its latent intent, *disqualified*) by spitting—expelling as opposed to incorporating. One must do the opposite of one's wish in order to negate the envy behind one's admiring statement. Stated "reprospectively," one must reject the breast even as one wishes to have it back. Finally, one cannot actively wish for anything—one can at best accuse someone else of having gotten something through illicit means, or accuse them of being "jealous" of what little one has.

How does the evil eye come to be capable of destroying and killing? How can the very act of wanting or coveting precipitate the destruction of what is wanted? Here the interpretation at a cultural level recapitulates the interpretation at the infant-fantasy level: Having wanted "the breast" caused it to go away, and destroyed (in fantasy) the mother. To want is to alienate the very object of one's desire. One wants so ravenously that one wishes to destroy what or who one covets. Hostility is so intense that one wishes the destruction of what or whom one would possess. Not only has the mother "abandoned" the infant, which fantasy portends one's own annihilation, and which rage is projected onto the mother; but furthermore, the infant has made the mother go away by *wanting* (or having secretly ravished) her. The later spurts of autonomy, exploration, and "negativism" are responded to with horror and punishment by the mother whose projected dependency needs demand that the child-become-toddler be kept within what Mahler calls the "symbiotic orbit." Thus the mother simultaneously "abandons" the child as she with even more determination envelops it, labeling virtually all expressions of "will" (from attempts at autonomous functioning to the refusal to eliminate feces at the mother's command) the pejorative term *"fanta"*—"stubbornness."

Dependency and rage, and the vicious circle that is created, bind the infant to the mother, even as they generate a centrifugal pull away from her in order to avoid being engulfed in her ambivalent vortex. Following the establishment of a sense of guilt in the infant, adult life becomes filled with ritualized atonements for one's dimly remembered, but pervasive, badness.

The intimate connection between the evil eye of childhood and the adult struggle between dependency and independence is illustrated by the following rich episode that links orality, envy, and self-esteem through the medium of food transactions. It occurred in a second-generation Slovak-American Lutheran family at whose table I had been feasted and stuffed weekly for nearly a year. Invariably after the second or third (forced feeding?) helping, either the husband (in his early thirties) or the wife (in her mid-twenties) would come out with a last ditch warning: "If you go away from the table hungry, it's your own fault."

It was now only several days before Christmas (1971), and I had just finished feasting at their table on Slovak pastries which I greatly enjoyed. The wife then packed a half-*kolach* (nut roll) for me to take home to my wife. I started to thank them profusely, meaning every mouthful of it. Suddenly, this ever-talkative family became absolutely silent and sullen, and I felt I had done or said something wrong. Both husband and wife hung their heads. The husband then said quietly:

"You don't say thanks for food. The food's just there and you are supposed to eat it. It's there to be eaten. But you never thank someone for giving you food." His wife continued: "Not just for food, but food and flowers both. You never thank someone for flowers. They say it puts a spell on them and they'll just wither and die." I asked them if this is a Slovak tradition. The husband replied: "This is an old Slovak belief. You just never thank someone for giving you food or flowers. Why should you thank them? They didn't produce the food or the flowers. God gives us food and flowers. Therefore it's God who we owe our thanks to for these things. As far as that putting a pox on flowers goes, that's an old wives' tale, that has nothing to do with it. Flowers are from God. In the old days, everyone used to have a garden and grow flowers. If you saw a particular flower you really liked, that person would cut the flower and give it to you or would give you some of the seeds so you could grow it in your garden next year. But you never thanked them . . . you just took it." His wife added: "This isn't just Slovak. All those people from Europe believed the same way."

What had I done wrong? I had expressed unbuttoned admiration for the food by having given profuse thanks. To do so would be, according to the mythos of the evil eye, to put a curse, a pox, on it. What you are given you take and be silent about it. The only thanks that may be safely (and genuinely?) given is to God, from whom all blessings flow, a distantly, and at least in this aspect, an idealized preambivalent figure. Significantly, the husband in the above episode is a Lutheran minister; hence, the ready superimposition of the theological explanation, a post facto rationalization, upon the folk explanation.

The question arises as to how flowers and food are related. In Europe, they were often placed on the graves of parents at their funerals, at the anniversary of their death, and at ritual times during the Christian calendar.[38] In America, only the flowers continue to be put on graves. They are both (food and flowers) an offering, an attempted sacrificial placation to assuage guilt, a ritual dutifully performed.

A further, and deeper, meaning of the connection between food and flowers is that to acknowledge admiration and indebtedness for something of someone else's is to reawaken that person's own infantile dependency cravings, which he has massively repressed. Why? At the conscious level, a copious "thank you" in the above episode led to embarrassment, whose unconscious referent was the realization of their resentment at giving, which had obscured, through reaction formation, their repression of wanting. In one sense, I was paying for the "priceless"; in another sense, I was paying for the "worthless." I was attempting to repay them for something that can never be repaid, because something done out of duty is not a genuine gift. Thanking them brought out their guilt of not having wanted to give—that is, their "child side." Thanking them was perceived as my payment to them, which *reverses* their position from giving, overbearing parent, to the child who does not want to give. I was originally the "child," and they the "parents"; by *giving* thanks, I inverted the relationship, and they were now forced by virtue of the "thanks" into recognizing their guilt of not *wanting* to give, but being "forced" out of duty to give. Since the food was given out of duty, to gratify ego ideal and appease the superego, I could never eat or take enough food to satisfy them; nor could I repay them save by becoming eternally indebted to them, never able to repay the debt. Both their self-esteem and their hostility were bound up with the unspoken assumption that I do not attempt to *undo* the bind in which feeding enveloped me. Thanking did precisely that—shattered their hold on me: to which they could only respond by disqualifying my thanks and reassuming the parental prerogative.[39]

Perhaps this accounts for the above couple's sudden silence and momentary depression. Food and flowers, like sex in later life, are there for the taking. One gets "snatch" of whatever variety, and avoids getting close enough to source to feel the pangs of intimacy of indebtedness. One keeps vigilantly on guard to maintain a safe emotional distance from anyone, although one is already "swallowed up." Such pervasive mythologies as the evil eye assure that one's guard will hardly ever be let down.

Conclusion: Limited Good and its Discontents

The persistence of the jealousy/envy complex even in "limitless good" and "limitless goods" of the Slovak-American image of the American Dream attests to the vital continuity of the traditional ethos. If one's neighbor buys a new radio, one must buy one even better—and so on. Because the referents of what is "really" sought are repressed and unconscious, the cumulative gains in the real world can never be enough. To see another's gain awakens one's own deficit—and the concomitant of loss: I would hazard that this is the unconscious dimension of Foster's "image of limited good," that the pie is indeed perceived as limited, and that another can gain only at one's expense. The ubiquity of the evil eye phenomenon suggests an extension of the "limited good" ethos far beyond classical peasant society: perhaps from the tribal Nuer, to the peasant Slovaks, to the modern, conspicuously consuming Americans, whose exhibitionistic boasting merely conceals their deep sense of inferiority.[40]

The bleak existence of the Slovak peasants in the barren Tatra and Carpathian mountains, in isolated, nucleated villages prior to and under feudal Magyar rule, punctuated by invasions in their "crossroads of Europe," were productive of a hardly appetizing "pie." As in all cultural adaptation, a sense of "necessity" is elevated into "virtue," and a cultural ethos and "ethnic unconscious" was elaborated to cope with the fears from without and the anxieties from within (informed by the past as well), developing into a self-sustaining homeostasis wherein the culture became part of the anxiety-inducing and anxiety-reducing "environment." In terms of "reality testing," the existence of the evil eye reflects a worried concern for the continuity of a precarious ecological homeostasis.[41]

A Slovak worries about his oxen; a Nuer worries about his cattle. As "economics" is never merely "rational" economics, it is bound up with status, self-esteem, identity, ethos, history—and childhood. The jealous watch over one's own, and the covetous gaze at that of another, suffuse and confuse technoeconomic, interpersonal, and intrapsychic issues. Finally, within the Slovak variant on the Slavic *zadruga* [42] the subordinate and subservient role of the Slovak female in relation to the arbitrary and dominating male, her constriction within the home and to the bearing of children, produced a specific quality of hostility toward her children that became manifest in the specific quality of the Slovak evil eye. From the vast and accumulating literature on family dynamics,[43] it should be obvious that matters of role allocation and division of labor have a highly valent unconscious or latent dimension in addition to the more readily recognizable conscious or manifest dimension. The interpenetration of the two demands special attention for students of family structure.

Perhaps it is not too farfetched to link Foster's "image of limited good" with Freud's metapsychology of civilization and its discontents. Foster suggested that the image of limited good might not be limited to peasant society; and, to extend Freud somewhat, it might be suggested that "a balance of discontents" characterizes all human civilizations ("designs for living") from the most "primitive" to the most "modern." The ubiquity of the evil eye attests to the interpenetration of reality and fantasy in human cultural adaptation, to the importance of early childhood object-relations in generating anxieties, and to the role of culture (whether in the origin or in the perpetuation of a symbol system) in the resolution of these anxieties through a decisive "change of function" into the "anxiety free sphere of the ego." [44] The role of the pre-oedipal period is immense.

It is hoped that the present analysis of Slovak-American data will serve as a contribution toward elucidating the universal dynamics of the jealousy/envy complex and the evil eye in their firm rootedness in childhood and society. It is further hoped that envy will not be reified into an "essentialist" explicans in psychological anthropology, but will be investigated in a "existential" framework, as the semantic referent of a multitude of responses to varying and specifiable human conditions, and not reflecting something inherent in "the" human condition. Envy and the evil eye, like the Oedipus complex, are inextricably bound up with the vicissitudes of nature *and* nurture.

NOTES

1. This paper is based on a two-year (January 1970–December 1971) study of three- and four- generation Slovak-American families in mill town communities in western Pennsylvania. The study was supported by a fellowship in ethnicity, racism, and mental health of the Maurice Falk Medical Fund. A wider ethnohistoric and psychodynamic contextualization of issues discussed in this paper appears in Stein, "An Ethnohistoric Study of Slovak-American Identity." Thanks are extended to the several anonymous associate editors of *Ethos* for their incisive observations and criticism of earlier drafts of this paper. Finally, I would like to express my gratitude to the late Professor Stephen C. Cappannari of the Department of Psychiatry, Vanderbilt University, for his enthusiasm and encouragement in urging me to carry my analysis of the evil eye to its inexorable conclusion. His close reading of the manuscript was equally helpful to me in shredding some dross and in making the argument more tightly knit.
2. Foster, "Anatomy of Envy," p. 200.
3. See Erikson, "Identity and the Life Cycle" and *Childhood and Society*.
4. Brown, p. 188.   5. Kroeber, p. 253.
6. Erikson, *Identity*, p. 223.   7. Spiro, "Ifaluk Ghosts," p. 248.
8. For an analysis of the entire socialization-individuation process, see Stein, "Ethnohistoric Study," ch. 6.
9. See Erikson, *Childhood and Society*, pp. 72 ff.
10. See Mahler.   11. See Spiro, "Ifaluk Ghosts."
12. See ibid.; Erikson, *Childhood and Society;* Devereux, *Reality and Dream* and "Normal and Abnormal"; and Caudill.
13. See Anthony.
14. See Stein, "Ethnohistoric Study," chaps. 6 and 7.

15. Foster, "Peasant Society."   16. See Winnicott, "Location."
17. Wallace, 178–80.   18. Le Vine, p. 254 ff.
19. Muensterberger, p. 209.
20. See Erikson, "Ontogeny of Ritualization"; Winnicott, "Location"; Mahler; Guntrip.
21. See the three studies by Klein; Klein and Riviere.
22. Winnicott, "Location," p. 371.   23. Anthony, "Reactions," p. 15.
24. Freud, p. 64.   25. See Hartmann.
26. Moss and Cappannari, this volume, p. 14.
27. LeVine, p. 265.   28. See Weidman.   29. Joffe, p. 16.
30. See Spiro, "Religious Systems."   31. Hartmann.
32. See Stein, "Ethnohistoric Study," chap. 6.
33. Bowlby, pp. 107–8.   34. Rycroft, p. 48.   35. Winnicott, "Capacity."
36. Erikson, Childhood and Society, pp. 72 ff.
37. See Benedek.   38. See Muensterberger, p. 200.
39. See Wynne, et al., and Haley.
40. See Slater; also Erikson, Children and Society, chap. 8.
41. See Stein, "Ethnohistoric Study," chap. 2.
42. See ibid., chaps. 2, 6.
43. See Anthony and Benedek; Handel; Stein, "Cultural Specificity."
44. See Hartmann.

BIBLIOGRAPHY

Anthony, E. James. "The Reaction of Parents to Adolescents and to their Behavior," in Parenthood: Its Psychology and Psychopathology, E. J. Anthony and T. Benedek, eds. Boston: Little, Brown, 1970.
—— "Tustin in Kleinianland, review of Frances Tustin, Autism and Childhood Psychosis 1973," Psychotherapy and Social Science Review 7 (1973), 14–22.
—— and Therese Benedek, eds. Parenthood: Its Psychology and Psychopathology. Boston: Little, Brown, 1970.
Benedek, Therese. "The Family as a Psychologic Field," in Parenthood: Its Psychology and Psychopathology, E. J. Anthony and T. Benedek, eds. Boston: Little, Brown, 1970.
Bowlby, John. "Separation Anxiety," International Journal of Psychoanalysis 41 (1960), 89–113.
Brown, Judith. "Comments on George Foster, The Anatomy of Envy," Current Anthropology 13 (1972), 188.
Caudill, William. "Anthropology and Psychoanalysis: Some Theoretical Issues," in Anthropology and Human Behavior, T. Gladwin and W. C. Sturtevant, eds. Washington, D.C.: The Anthropological Society of Washington, 1962.
Devereux, George. Reality and Dream: Psychotherapy of a Plains Indian. 1951. Rev. ed., Garden City, N.Y.: Doubleday, 1969.
—— "Normal and Abnormal: The Key Concepts of Ethnopsychiatry," in Man and His Culture: Psychoanalytic Anthropology after Totem and Taboo, W. Muensterberger, ed. New York: Taplinger, 1970.

Elworthy, F. T. *The Evil Eye*. 1895. Reprint, New York: Julian Press, 1958.

Erikson, Erik H. *Childhood and Society*. 1950. Rev. ed., New York: Norton, 1963.

—— *Identity and the Life Cycle, Selected Papers*. *Psychological Issues*, monograph, vol. I, no. 1. New York: International Universities Press, 1959.

—— *Identity: Youth and Crisis*. New York: Norton, 1968.

—— "Ontogeny of Ritualization," in *Psychoanalysis: A General Psychology*, R. M. Loewenstein, L. M. Newman, M. Schur, and A. J. Solnit, eds. New York: International Universities Press, 1966.

Evans-Pritchard, E. E. "Some Features of Nuer Religion," *The Journal of the Royal Anthropological Institute* 81 (1951), 1–13.

Foster, George M. "The Anatomy of Envy: A Study in Symbolic Behavior," *Current Anthropology* 13 (1972), 165–202.

—— "Peasant Society and the Image of the Limited Good," *American Anthropologist* 67, no. 2 (1965), 293–315.

Freud, Sigmund. "Psychoanalytic Comments on an Autobiographical Account of Paranoia (Dementia Paranoides)," *Standard Edition*, vol. 12. London: Hogarth Press, 1957.

Goldschmidt, Walter. *Comparative Functionalism: An Essay in Anthropological Theory*. Berkeley: University of California Press, 1966.

Guntrip, Harry. *Psychoanalytic Theory, Therapy, and the Self*. New York: Basic Books, 1971.

Haley, Jay. "The Family of the Schizophrenic: A Model System," in *The Psychosocial Interior of the Family*, G. Handel, ed. Chicago: Aldine, 1967.

Handel, Gerald, ed. *The Psychosocial Interior of the Family*. Chicago: Aldine, 1967.

Hartmann, Heinz. *Ego Psychology and the Problem of Adaptation*. David Rapaport, trans. 1939. New York: International Universities Press, 1958.

——, Ernest Kris, and Rudolph Loewenstein. "Some Psychoanalytic Comments on 'Culture and Personality,' " in *Psychoanalysis and Culture*, G. Wilbur and W. Muensterberger, eds. New York: International Universities Press, 1951.

Homans, George. "Anxiety and Ritual: The Theories of Malinowski and Radcliffe-Brown," *American Anthropologist* 43 (1941) 164–72.

Joffe, Walter G. "An Unenviable Preoccupation with Envy: Review of Helmut Schoeck, *Envy: A Theory of Social Behavior, 1969*," *Psychiatry and Social Science Review* 4 (1970), 12–21.

Klein, Melanie. *Envy and Gratitude. New York: Basic Books, 1957.*

—— "Mourning and its Relation to Manic-Depressive States," in *Contributions to Psychoanalysis*. London: Hogarth Press, 1948.

—— *The Psychoanalysis of Children*. New York: Norton, 1932.

—— and Joan Riviere. *Love, Hate, and Reparation*. Atlantic Highlands, N.J.: Hillary, 1962.

Kroeber, Alfred. *Anthropology*. New York: Harcourt, Brace, 1948.

LeVine, Robert A. *Culture, Behavior, and Personality*. Chicago: Aldine, 1973.

Mahler, Margaret (with Manuel Furer). *On Human Symbiosis and the Vicissitudes of Human Individuation*. New York: International Universities Press, 1968.

Mair, Lucy. *Witchcraft. New York: McGraw-Hill, 1969.*

Middleton, John. "The Concept of 'Bewitching' in Lugbara," *Africa* 25, no. 3 (1955), 252–60.

Moss, Leonard W., and Stephen C. Cappannari. "The Mediterranean: *Mal'occhio*

Ayin ha ra, Oculus fascinus, Judenblick; the Evil Eye Hovers Above.'' Paper given at Symposium on the Evil Eye, Meetings of the American Anthropological Association, Toronto, Canada (Dec. 1, 1972.) Passage quoted includes authors' addenda to p. 14 of MS in preparation for publication; included in this volume as chapter 2.

Muensterberger, Warner. ''Psyche and Environment: Sociocultural Variations in Separation and Individuation,'' *The Psychoanalytic Quarterly* 38 (1969), 191–216.

Rycroft, Charles. *Anxiety and Neurosis.* Baltimore: Penguin, 1968.

Slater, Philip. *The Pursuit of Loneliness: American Culture at the Breaking Point.* Boston: Beacon Press, 1970.

Spiro, Melford E. ''Ifaluk Ghosts,'' in *Personalities and Cultures,* R. Hunt, ed. 1953. Garden City: Natural History Press, 1967.

—— ''Religious Systems as Culturally Constituted Defense Mechanisms,'' in *Context and Meaning in Cultural Anthropology,* M. E. Spiro, ed. Glencoe: The Free Press, 1965.

Stein, Howard F. ''An Ethno-historic Study of Slovak-American Identity.'' Ph.D. dissertation, University of Pittsburgh, 1972. Available through University Microfilms, Inc., Ann Arbor, Michigan.

Wallace Anthony F. C. *Religion: An Anthropological View.* New York: Random House, 1966.

Weidman, Hazel H. ''Anthropological Theory and the Psychological Function of Belief in Witchcraft,'' in *Essays in Medical Anthropology,* T. Weaver, ed. Southern Anthropological Society Proceedings, vol. I. Athens, Ga.: University of Georgia Press, 1968.

Whiting, John W. M., and Irvin Child. *Child Training and Personality: A Cross-Cultural Study.* New Haven: Yale University Press, 1953.

Winnicott, Donald W. ''The Capacity to be Alone,'' *International Journal of Psychoanalysis* 39 (1958), 416–20.

—— ''The Location of Cultural Experience,'' *International Journal of Psychoanalysis* 48 (1967), 368–72.

Wynne, Lyman, Irving M. Wyckoff, Juliana Day, and Stanley I. Hirsch. ''Pseudomutuality in the Family Relations of Schizophrenics,'' in *The Psychosocial Interior of the Family,* G. Handel, ed. Chicago: Aldine, 1967.

JOHN M. ROBERTS

13. CROSS-CULTURAL

Belief in the Evil Eye in World Perspective

THIS CHAPTER is designed to put the core belief in the evil eye into cross-cultural perspective and to lay the foundations for the later development of a theory of envy and the evil eye. The foregoing chapters have provided the reader with a diversity of illustrative materials, and it must be clear that the cultural patterns associated with the evil eye can be intricate and complex. Yet throughout these treatments it is clear that these cultures possess the belief that an eye is capable of inflicting injury, and this is the fundamental belief that is the concern of this chapter. Resources were not available for the cross-cultural coding of a number of relevant variables, but did permit the coding of the presence or absence of the core belief in each of 186 cultures. The cultural associations with this belief and their interpretation are the matters of concern here.

Background of the Study[1]

I first became interested in the evil eye when I speculated that one of the Ten Commandments might refer to the evil eye. Nine of the ten are either injunctions against overt behaviors or instructions for overt behaviors, but a tenth appears to refer to a covert mental state: "You shall not covet your

JOHN M. ROBERTS is Mellon Professor of Anthropology, University of Pittsburgh. He received his Ph.D. in anthropology from Yale University, has taught in Cornell and other universities, and was a Fellow in the Center for Advanced Study in the Behavioral Sciences at Stanford University. His fieldwork includes studies of the Ramah Navaho, Zuni, Omaha, and other contemporary Amerinds. He has written *Three Navaho Households: A Comparative Study in Small* neighbor's house; you shall not covet your neighbor's wife, or his manservant, or his maidservant, or his ox, or his ass, or anything that is your neighbor's'' (Exodus 20:17 RSV).

Since this commandment lists some of the familiar targets of the evil eye, and since the idea of coveting is often associated with evil eye, could it not refer to the overt behavior of casting the evil eye? What was the semantic domain of the Hebrew word translated as "covet" in the time of Moses? Consultation with Hebraicists has been inconclusive, although no one suggested that any obvious connection with the evil eye belief was implied by the word, and other inquiries have provided no answers. In the end I concluded that the inquiry should be held in abeyance until there was more scientific knowledge of the belief in the evil eye. The ancient Hebrews are included as one of the cultures in our 186-culture sample, but in no other respect does this chapter deal with the original question that prompted the inquiry.

A second line of inquiry was of more general anthropological interest. In the past the author has spent a great deal of time investigating various aspects of expressive culture, and while no single publication reviews the entire research, specific publications have dealt with expressive travel,[2] games,[3] other expressive models,[4] and other relevant topics.[5] None of these investigations, however, pertained to an expressive belief. Since there is no scientific evidence that the eye really has the power, the belief in the evil eye must contain a large expressive component. Yet it is possible that the approach developed for expressive models will also hold for expressive beliefs.

The "conflict-enculturation hypothesis of game involvement" first advanced by Roberts and Sutton-Smith [6] appears to hold for models other than games, too.[7] This hypothesis holds that there are areas of psychological conflict in the "real or nonmodel" world that are characterized by a balance of approach and avoidance attitudes, and that individuals possessing these conflicts will display curiosity about or involvement in representations of

Group Culture (1951) and *Zuni Daily Life* (1956), has coauthored four other monographs, and has written many other articles and chapters in books. He is a former president of the Society for Cross-Cultural Research.

This paper was prepared using the facilities of the Cross-Cultural Cumulative Coding Center in the Department of Anthropology at Pittsburgh University in continuation of its distinctive contribution to anthropological research.

that conflict area in a "model" world. For example a person may both want to talk and not want to talk in social situations, and if his approach attitudes toward talking are balanced by his avoidance attitudes, he can be said to be in conflict about talking. It may be the case that music is model speech; so the higher the conflict about talking, the more likely the person is to be involved in music.[8] Furthermore, there is evidence that the higher the conflict, the less representative of the "real" world the model need be in order to be expressively satisfying. Thus, a person who is in high conflict about talking should have a greater interest in instrumental music than a person with low conflict, since instrumental music appears to be less representative of speech than vocal music. It is probably the case, too, that operations within the model world result in learning that may be generalized to the real world as well, as when a poker player learns to deal with bluff and deception in ways that might be helpful in real negotiations. Sometimes this learning may affect the approaches and avoidances that define the conflict, and the involvement in the relevant models may be increased or decreased, depending upon the direction the learning takes.

The core belief in the evil eye is not a model, but the stories and the gossip about the evil eye are expressive models. It is probably the case that all learning about the evil eye occurs through the use of expressive models. Perhaps the existence of these models can be assumed, and the belief can be treated as if it were an expressive model. If this is the case, there will be no interest in the evil eye or in stories about the evil eye unless the culture fosters conflicts that make for such interest. Furthermore, within a given culture there may be differences in the strength of beliefs in the evil eye depending upon the strength of antecedent conflicts at the individual level. It is unlikely that full confirmation of this hypothesis can be obtained through the use of the cross-cultural method, but such research can lay the foundation for more exacting tests. An attempt will be made, therefore, to establish a presumptive case for the statement that the conflict-enculturation hypothesis holds for expressive beliefs as well as for expressive models.

The third line of inquiry pertains to the human ethogram, that is, the total repertoire of fixed action patterns or sequences of conditioned motor actions which do not need to be learned. The core belief in the evil eye is essentially a belief that the glance or stare of some, if not all, human beings can produce damage in other living things and even, in some instances, to material objects as well. This belief may rest, in part, on the presence of the steady stare as a signal of hostility and impending aggression in the human and even the primate ethogram. It is not difficult to see that a linkage between the hostile look and imputed hostility in others could be panhuman. Belief in the evil eye, in this sense, is potentially comprehensible to any human, even though it is culturally elaborated only in some societies. These latter cultures have made a special use of an action pattern that is available in the human ethogram. The present study, then, is an example of research that could be applied to other action patterns, such as the characteristic gestures involved in greeting behaviors. Here, though, little is done with the steady stare. It is present only by inference.

Finally, since the belief in the evil eye is commonly associated with the belief that the people casting the evil eye are motivated by envy, an understanding of the evil eye belief might constitute one avenue toward the understanding of envy. To be sure, envy may be panhuman, but societies possessing the belief in the evil eye may have more of a problem with envy. The psychological conflicts that are antecedent to involvement in the evil eye may ultimately prove to be antecedent to envy or at least related to the expression of envy.

This study, then, has the following objectives: (1) the ethnographic investigation of the belief in the evil eye as a basis for further research on the ancient Hebrew belief; (2) the testing of the applicability of the conflict-enculturation hypotheses of model involvement to an expressive belief that is probably transmitted through models; (3) a consideration of the cultural elaboration of a basic action pattern in the human ethogram; and (4) an examination of the cultural and psychological factors that may contribute to the expression of envy.

Research Design

The full design of this inquiry entails both an initial cross-cultural study and subsequent intracultural investigations. This chapter reports on the results of the initial survey, and the balance of the research will be discussed in later publications.

The cross-cultural investigation reported here is quite conventional in nature and it is not dissimilar in principle from other cross-cultural studies I have published.[9] Basically a selection from the published sources on each of the 186 cultures in the sample was read to determine whether or not the belief in the evil eye was present in each culture. The resulting two-element scale (i.e., absent and present) is presented later in this chapter. Then, the associations between this scale and other scales prepared by other scholars were determined. Most of these scales have been published, but one set of codes was obtained from the Cross-Cultural Cumulative Coding Center on a prepublication basis. Since the scales used in this study are ordinal in character, use was made of the Goodman and Kruskal "Coefficient of Ordinal Association" [10] in determining the strength of the association. Then the significant associations between the evil eye scale and the other scales were grouped on the basis of ethnographic experience. These are the findings reported later in the chapter.

At this point, though, a few cautionary statements should be made. First, statistical analyses appropriate for interval scales could not be used here. Next, while it is true that a judgment was made for the evil eye in the case of each of the 186 cultures in the sample, many of the scales taken from the published and unpublished sources contained entries for less than 186 cultures. In other words, it was not possible to code all the cultures in the sample, with the result that in extreme cases there are only entries for 80 societies or even fewer from the sample. Furthermore, the societies that are missing for one scale are not missing for another. This makes it very difficult to use a multivariate technique for data reduction. Two factor analyses were made that ignored the problems of sample size, but they must be regarded as having preliminary interest only. It would be wrong to report them in full.

Finally, the full scales are given in the presentation that follows because they are most meaningful to experienced ethnographers. They can read meaning into terse statements because they have an ethnographic background that permits them to do so. They, at least, should gain a view of the cultural context of the evil eye with little difficulty. The less experienced reader should also be able to follow the argument.

The sample of world cultures used in this study was that published in 1969 by Murdock and White, who described it as: "a representative sample of the world's known and well described cultures, 186 in number, each "pinpointed" to the smallest identifiable subgroup of the society in question at a specific point in time." [11]

The pinpointed cultures are much more specific than comparable files in the Human Relations Area Files system. The authors say they:

have "pinpointed" every society in the standard sample to a specific date and a specific locality, typically the local community where the principal authority conducted his most intensive field research, and they have eliminated from the sample all societies for which the sources do not permit reasonable accurate pinpointing.[12]

Unfortunately, in this study it was necessary to deviate from the "pinpointing" principle described above in some instances. Belief in the evil eye is not always a concern of ethnographers, and there is not always enough evidence in the literature on the pinpointed society to permit a "present" or "absent" judgment to be made. In some cases, therefore, it was necessary to cast a wider net and to deal with the larger culture in which the pinpointed society shared. Preliminary ethnographic investigation, however, suggested that if the evil eye belief is present at all, then it is generally widely distributed—it is not a belief that characteristically varies from village to village. Thus the coding given below is not as specific as Murdock and White would have liked, but little could be done about it. The sources used in this coding are listed at the end of this chapter under "Ethnographic Sources."

Even with these more liberal guidelines, the coding of the presence or absence of the evil eye was not easy. Confidence in the judgment of presence or absence varied greatly and in table 1 below it is expressed through the following scale:

1. incontrovertibly absent
2. almost certainly absent
3. probably absent
4. possibly absent
5. possibly present
6. probably present
7. almost certainly present
8. incontrovertibly present

In the analysis that follows, however, numbers 1, 2, 3, and 4 were treated as "absent" and numbers 5, 6, 7, and 8 were treated as "present."

Obviously, there were fewer errors in coding for the "incontrovertibly" absent or present and "almost certainly" absent or present categories than for the others, but there is more to be said about error than this. The belief in the evil eye is so salient in some cultures that no general ethnographer could fail to mention it but with other cultures the belief is not that salient and the ethnographer has other concerns. The myth that general ethnographers provide information on all possible topics is quite untrue; their training, competences, interests, and biases affect their descriptive efforts. A culture may well possess the belief in the evil eye and yet this fact can be ignored in those sources listed for the sample. Such an error, of course, is a serious matter for the present research.

The opposite error also occurs, but not so frequently. Some writers use the term, "evil eye," to mean sorcery or witchcraft in a loose sort of way. An ethnographer reporting the evil eye belief in an area where it is not likely to be found may be using the expression in a metaphorical sense, particularly if he provides no examples or other supporting evidence in his ethnography.

Both the false presences and the false absences tend to blur the statistical associations which will be the chief concern of this paper. When they appear as deviant cases, attention can be paid to them, but otherwise they may go unnoticed.

Use is made in this study of the Goodman-Kruskal coefficient of ordinal association [13] and the significant associations of the evil eye belief scale with other ordinal scales available in the published and unpublished sources to which the author has access are considered.

The evil eye belief code for the 186 societies in the Murdock-White sample is given in table 1 below. The number of the culture in the Murdock-White sample is given, but it must be understood that in some instances this applies to the larger culture and not to the specific community. The name of the culture and a letter designating one of the six major regions of the world are also given: A (sub-Saharan Africa—28 cultures); C (circum-Mediterranean—28 cultures); E (East Eurasia—34 cultures); I (insular Pacific—31 cultures); N (North America—33 cultures); and S (South and Central America—32 cultures). The number of the specific sampling province from which the culture was taken is presented (Murdock, in 1968, defined the 200 world sampling provinces). Finally, the entry for the belief in the evil eye scale is given along with a "present" or "absent" designation.

Sixty-seven cultures are noted in table 1 as having the belief in the evil eye present. Of these, 30 cultures were coded as having the belief "incontrovertibly present," 16 "'almost certainly present," 13 "probably present," and 8 "possibly present" category. Of 119 cultures listed as having the belief in the evil eye absent, one is cited as being "incontrovertibly absent," 45 as "almost certainly absent," 46 "probably absent," and 27 "possibly absent." Only 36 percent of the cultures in the world sample possessed the evil eye belief.

TABLE 1 *Code for Belief in the Evil Eye*

Societies of the Standard Sample	Major Region	Evil Eye Scaled Rating	Evil Eye Belief
001 Nama Hottentot	A	3	Absent
002 Kung Bushmen	A	3	Absent
003 Thonga	A	7	Present
004 Lozi	A	3	Absent
005 Mbundu	A	2	Absent
006 Suku	A	3	Absent
007 Bemba	A	7	Present
008 Nyakyusa	A	3	Absent
009 Hadza	A	2	Absent
010 Luguru	A	4	Absent
011 Kikuyu	A	7	Present
012 Ganda	A	3	Absent
013 Mbuti Pygmies	A	5	Present
014 Nkundo Mongo	A	5	Present
015 Banen	A	6	Present
016 Tiv	A	4	Absent
017 Ibo	A	4	Absent
018 Fon	A	4	Absent
019 Ashanti	A	4	Absent
020 Mende	A	3	Absent
021 Wolof	C	8	Present
022 Bambara	A	4	Absent
023 Tallensi	A	4	Absent
024 Songhai	C	4	Absent
025 Wodaabe Fulani	C	8	Present
026 Hausa	C	6	Present
027 Massa	A	4	Absent
028 Azande	A	8	Present
029 Fur	C	7	Present
030 Otoro Nuba	A	4	Absent
031 Shilluk	A	8	Present
032 Mao	A	8	Present
033 Kaffa	C	8	Present
034 Masai	A	7	Present
035 Konso	C	8	Present
036 Somali	C	8	Present
037 Amhara	C	8	Present
038 Bogo	C	7	Present
039 Kenuzi Nubians	C	8	Present
040 Teda	C	8	Present
041 Tuareg	C	8	Present
042 Riffians	C	8	Present
043 Egyptians	C	8	Present
044 Hebrews	C	7	Present
045 Babylonians	C	7	Present
046 Rwala Bedouin	C	8	Present
047 Turks	C	8	Present

TABLE 1 *Code for Belief in the Evil Eye* (Continued)

Societies of the Standard Sample	Major Region	Evil Eye Scaled Rating	Evil Eye Belief
048 Gheg Albanians	C	8	Present
049 Romans	C	7	Present
050 Basques	C	7	Present
051 Irish	C	8	Present
052 Lapps	C	5	Present
053 Yurak Samoyed	E	7	Present
054 Russians	C	8	Present
055 Abkhaz	C	8	Present
056 Armenians	C	7	Present
057 Kurd	C	8	Present
058 Basseri	E	8	Present
059 West Punjabi	E	8	Present
060 Gond	E	7	Present
061 Toda	E	7	Present
062 Santal	E	8	Present
063 Uttar Pradesh	E	8	Present
064 Burusho	E	6	Present
065 Kazak	E	6	Present
066 Khalka Mongols	E	3	Absent
067 Lolo	E	2	Absent
068 Lepcha	E	5	Present
069 Garo	E	2	Absent
070 Lakher	E	3	Absent
071 Burmese	E	3	Absent
072 Lamet	E	2	Absent
073 Vietnamese	E	3	Absent
074 Rhade	E	2	Absent
075 Khmer	E	4	Absent
076 Thai	E	2	Absent
077 Semang	E	2	Absent
078 Nicobarese	E	2	Absent
079 Andamanese	E	2	Absent
080 Vedda	E	1	Absent
081 Tanala	E	5	Present
082 Negri Sembilan	E	4	Absent
083 Javanese	I	3	Absent
084 Balinese	I	2	Absent
085 Iban	I	4	Absent
086 Badjau	I	3	Absent
087 Toradja	I	6	Present
088 Tobelorese	I	2	Absent
089 Alorese	I	2	Absent
090 Tiwi	I	2	Absent
091 Aranda	I	3	Absent
092 Orokaiva	I	8	Present
093 Kimam	I	3	Absent
094 Kapauku	I	4	Absent

TABLE 1 *Code for Belief in the Evil Eye* (Continued)

Societies of the Standard Sample	Major Region	Evil Eye Scaled Rating	Evil Eye Belief
095 Kwoma	I	3	Absent
096 Manus	I	3	Absent
097 New Ireland	I	3	Absent
098 Trobrianders	I	2	Absent
099 Siuai	I	3	Absent
100 Tikopia	I	2	Absent
101 Pentecost	I	3	Absent
102 Mbau Fijians	I	6	Present
103 Ajie	I	4	Absent
104 Maori	I	3	Absent
105 Marquesans	I	3	Absent
106 Samoans	I	3	Absent
107 Gilbertese	I	3	Absent
108 Marshallese	I	3	Absent
109 Trukese	I	3	Absent
110 Yapese	I	7	Present
111 Palauans	I	3	Absent
112 Ifugao	I	6	Present
113 Atayal	I	2	Absent
114 Chinese	E	3	Absent
115 Manchu	E	3	Absent
116 Koreans	E	2	Absent
117 Japanese	E	4	Absent
118 Ainu	E	3	Absent
119 Gilyak	E	3	Absent
120 Yukaghir	E	3	Absent
121 Chukchee	E	4	Absent
122 Ingalik	N	5	Present
123 Aleut	N	4	Absent
124 Copper Eskimo	N	3	Absent
125 Montagnais	N	3	Absent
126 Micmac	N	6	Present
127 Saulteaux	N	4	Absent
128 Slave	N	4	Absent
129 Kaska	N	4	Absent
130 Eyak	N	2	Absent
131 Haida	N	6	Present
132 Bellacoola	N	2	Absent
133 Twana	N	6	Present
134 Yurok	N	2	Absent
135 Eastern Pomo	N	4	Absent
136 Yokuts	N	2	Absent
137 Paiute	N	4	Absent
138 Klamath	N	5	Present
139 Kutenai	N	3	Absent
140 Gros Ventre	N	4	Absent

TABLE 1 *Code for Belief in the Evil Eye* (Continued)

Societies of the Standard Sample	Major Region	Evil Eye Scaled Rating	Evil Eye Belief
141 Hidatsa	N	2	Absent
142 Pawnee	N	2	Absent
143 Omaha	N	2	Absent
144 Huron	N	3	Absent
145 Creek	N	2	Absent
146 Natchez	N	4	Absent
147 Comanche	N	2	Absent
148 Chiricahua	N	5	Present
149 Zuni	N	6	Present
150 Havasupai	N	2	Absent
151 Papago	N	2	Absent
152 Huichol	N	4	Absent
153 Aztec	N	6	Present
154 Popoluca	N	8	Present
155 Quiche	S	7	Present
156 Miskito	S	2	Absent
157 Bribri	S	2	Absent
158 Cuna	S	3	Absent
159 Goajiro	S	8	Present
160 Haitians	S	8	Present
161 Callinago	S	2	Absent
162 Warrau	S	6	Present
163 Yanomano	S	3	Absent
164 Carib	S	2	Absent
165 Saramacca	S	3	Absent
166 Mundurucu	S	2	Absent
167 Cubeo	S	2	Absent
168 Cayapa	S	2	Absent
169 Jivaro	S	8	Present
170 Amahuaca	S	2	Absent
171 Inca	S	2	Absent
172 Aymara	S	4	Absent
173 Siriono	S	2	Absent
174 Nambicurra	S	3	Absent
175 Trumai	S	2	Absent
176 Timbira	S	3	Absent
177 Tupinamba	S	3	Absent
178 Botocudo	S	3	Absent
179 Shavante	S	2	Absent
180 Aweikoma	S	2	Absent
181 Cayua	S	3	Absent
182 Lengua	S	2	Absent
183 Abipon	S	3	Absent
184 Mapuche	S	2	Absent
185 Tehuelche	S	2	Absent
186 Yahgan	S	3	Absent

ASSOCIATIONS WITH THE EVIL EYE BELIEF
Geographical Distribution

The use of the world sample permits a geographical plotting of the incidence of the evil eye which has heretofore been unavailable. When the cultures possessing the evil eye belief are plotted on the maps published by Murdock and White [14] it can be seen that societies coded as "incontrovertibly" or "almost certainly" having the belief in the evil eye fall, with a few exceptions, above the equator in Africa in an arc which includes all of North Africa and much of East Africa. Similarly coded societies are found west of 60° East Longitude in West Eurasia (i.e. throughout Europe, and all of the Near East). In East Eurasia, however, such societies are found only in and around India. Elsewhere they occur sporadically: two in the Insular Pacific, two in North America, and two in South America. If the actual geographical distances between these widely dispersed cultures are ignored, the following evil-eye-belief-present cultures stand adjacent to one or more societies with a similar coding: Wolof, Riffians, Tuareg, Wodaabe Fulani, Teda, Fur, Azande, Shilluk, Mao, Kaffa, Konso, Kikuyu, Masai, Somali, Amhara, Bogo, Kenuzi Nubians, Egyptians, Hebrews, Rwala Bedouin, Babylonians, Kurds, Armenians, Turks, Abkhaz, Russians, Gheg Albanians, Romans, Basques, Irish, Basseri, West Punjabi, Uttar Pradesh, Santal, Gond, and Toda. Cultures with less certain ratings tend to lie on the margins of this central block.

The belief in the evil eye probably developed in the old world, particularly in India, the Near East, and Europe. The belief seems to have been strong in the Fertile Crescent for millennia. Within this central area throughout time, the cultures were undoubtedly linked by diffusion and cultural transmission. Elsewhere the belief either was diffused or invented independently. Somehow despite the fact that it rests on a common feature of the human ethogram, the core belief does not appear to have been readily invented independently. Even in the New World, it is likely that the authentic cases of the evil eye (there may be some errors in the coding) are the result of diffusion, although whether that diffusion was pre- or post-Columbian is another matter. The existence of this presumptive case for diffusion must be considered as essential background for the treatments of the evil eye belief that follow.

Cultural Complexity

Most experienced ethnographers carry a rough scale of cultural complexity in their heads; so they could easily see that the cultures possessing the evil eye belief fall roughly in the upper half of our sample of 186 societies as far as cultural complexity is concerned. Not all complex cultures have the belief, but those that do have it seem to fall above the median on a scale of cultural complexity.

In a article entitled "Measurement of Cultural Complexity" Murdock and Provost list ten scales that measure complexity along one dimension or another, and they present the codes for these scales for exactly the same sample. These scales listed in order of their strength of association (The Goodman-Kruskol G) with the evil eye scale are: (1) technological specialization (.487); (2) social stratification (.402); (3) writing and records (.398); (4) money (.393); (5) level of political integration (.358); (6) land transport (.287); (7) density of population (.225); (8) agriculture (.200); (9) urbanization (.093); and (10) fixity of residence (.074). The last three are nonsignificant associations, although agriculture is associated with the scale directionally.[15] The other scales, however, are important enough to warrant the detailed presentation given below in tables 2 through 11.

The ten tables dealing with Murdock's complexity scales show that there is a positive association between cultural complexity and the evil eye belief as measured by seven scales, and that two of the remaining scales can be

TABLE 2 *Technological Specialization and the Evil Eye Belief*

Scale (Murdock and Provost, "Measurement," p. 381)	Evil Eye Present	Absent
4. The society is reported to have a variety of craft specialists, including at least smiths, weavers, and potters.	20	13
3. The society is reported to have specialized metalworkers or smiths but to lack weaving and/or pottery.	25	31
2. Loom weaving is practiced but metalworking is absent or unreported.	11	20
1. Pottery is made but metalworking and loom weaving are absent or unreported.	5	22
0. Metalworking, loom weaving, and pottery-making are all absent or unreported.	6	33

$N = 186$, $G = .487$, $Z = 4.506$, $p < .01$ two-tailed.

TABLE 3   *Social Stratification and the Evil Eye Belief*

Scale (Murdock and Provost, "Measurement," pp. 382–83)	Evil Eye Present	Evil Eye Absent
4. The society exhibits a complex stratification into three or more distinct classes or castes regardless of the presence or absence of slavery.	19	11
3. The society is stratified into two social classes of freemen, e.g., nobles and commoners, or a propertied elite and a propertyless proletariat, plus hereditary slavery and/or recognized caste divisions.	7	13
2. The society is stratified into two social classes of freemen but lacks both caste distinctions and hereditary slavery.	7	12
1. Formal class distinctions are lacking among freemen, but hereditary slavery prevails and/or there are important status differences based on the possession or distribution of wealth.	21	31
0. The society is essentially egalitarian, lacking in social classes, castes, hereditary slavery, and important wealth distinctions.	13	52

$N = 186$, $G = .402$, $Z = .672$, $p < .01$ two-tailed.

collapsed into significant 2×2 tables showing the same type of association. It is probable that the scales as presented do not reflect the true complexity of the pastoral nomads, who really belong to an intricate system involving markets, relationships with town dwellers, and so on. The tables, however,

TABLE 4   *Writing and Records and the Evil Eye Belief*

Scale (Murdock and Provost, "Measurement," pp. 379–80)	Evil Eye Present	Evil Eye Absent
4. The society has an indigenous system of true writing and possesses written records of at least modest significance.	20	11
3. The society has an indigenous system of writing but lacks any significant accumulation of written records, or alternatively has long used the script of alien people.	10	2
2. The society lacks true writing but possesses significant nonwritten records in the form of picture writing, quipus, pictorial inscriptions, or the like.	3	18
1. Writing and significant records are lacking but the people employ mnemonic devices, e.g., simple tallies.	15	34
0. Writing, records, and mnemonic devices in any form are lacking or unreported.	19	54

$N = 186$, $G = .398$, $Z = 3.591$, $p < .01$ two-tailed.

TABLE 5 *Money and the Evil Eye Belief*

Scale (Murdock and Provost, "Measurement," p. 381)	Evil Eye Present	Evil Eye Absent
4. The society uses an indigenous currency in the form of metal coins of standard weight and fineness and/or their equivalent in paper currency.	16	9
3. The society uses indigenous articles of token or conventional value, such as cowrie shells, wampum, or imitation tools, as an elementary form of money.	8	19
2. The society lacks any form of indigenous money but has long used the currency of an alien people, e.g., that of its colonial rulers.	20	23
1. True money is lacking but the society employs domestically usable articles such as salt, grain, livestock, or ornaments, as a medium of exchange.	8	6
0. The society lacks any recognized medium of exchange, conducting mercantile transactions through the direct or indirect exchange of goods, e.g., barter.	15	62

$N = 186$, $G = .393$, $Z = 3.605$, $p < .01$ two-tailed.

TABLE 6 *Level of Political Integration and the Evil Eye Belief*

Scale (Murdock and Provost, "Measurement," p. 382)	Evil Eye Present	Evil Eye Absent
4. Three or more administrative levels are recognized above that of the local community, as in the case of a large state organized into provinces that are subdivided into districts.	14	15
3. Two administrative levels are recognized above that of the local community, as in the case of a small state divided into administrative districts.	15	13
2. One administrative level is recognized above that of the local community, as in the case of a petty state with a paramount chief ruling over a number of local communities. Societies that are politically completely dependent, lacking any political organization of their own and wholly absorbed into the political system of a dominant society of alien culture, are likewise coded as 2.	19	27
1. The society is stateless but is composed of politically organized autonomous local communities.	16	56
0. The society is stateless, and political authority is not centralized on the local level but is dispersed among households or other small component units.	3	8

$N = 186$, $G = .358$, $Z = 3.213$, $p < .01$ two-tailed.

TABLE 7   *Land Transport and the Evil Eye Belief*

Scale (Murdock and Provost, "Measurement," p. 381)	Evil Eye Present	Evil Eye Absent
4. Automotive vehicles, e.g., railroads and trucks, are employed extensively in land transport. Since these have commonly been introduced by foreigners in formerly colonial areas, they are indicated only where they were thoroughly integrated into the indigenous economy at the pinpointed date.	5	6
3. Animal-drawn wheeled vehicles are employed in land transport but motorized vehicles are seldom or never used.	4	7
2. Land transport is conducted to a considerable extent by means of draft animals dragging a sled, travois, or other vehicle without wheels.	1	13
1. Land transport is effected mainly by pack rather than draft animals.	29	13
0. Land transport is effected by human carriers.	28	80

$N = 186$, $G = .287$, $Z = 2.384$, $p < .01$ two-tailed.

show that a belief in the evil eye is compatible with cultural complexity. Perhaps the belief in the evil eye did not become salient in cultures until they reached a certain level of complexity, and the occurrences of the belief in the simpler societies are, in the main, either errors or special instances of diffusion that ought to be studied independently. The association of the evil eye belief with the technological specialization scale confirms the view that the evil eye becomes prominent in a culture when the society produces

TABLE 8   *Density of Population and the Evil Eye Belief*

Scale (Murdock and Provost, "Measurement," p. 382)	Evil Eye Present	Evil Eye Absent
4. The mean density of population exceeds 100 persons per square mile.	17	23
3. The density of population averages between 26 and 100 persons per square mile.	16	19
2. The density of population averages between 5.1 and 25 persons per square mile.	8	20
1. The density of population averages between 1 and 5 persons per square mile.	13	12
0. The density of population averages fewer than 1 person per square mile.	13	45

$N = 186$, $G = .225$, $p < .05$ two-tailed.

TABLE 9   *Agriculture and the Evil Eye Belief*

Scale (Murdock and Provost, "Measurement," p. 380)	Evil Eye Present	Evil Eye Absent
4. Agriculture contributes more to the society's food supply than does any other subsistence activity and is conducted by intensive techniques such as irrigation, plowing, or artificial fertilization.	28	29
3. Agriculture contributes more to the food supply than does any other subsistence activity but is not conducted by intensive techniques.	16	47
2. Agriculture yields more than 10 percent of the society's food supply but not as much as some other subsistence activity.	5	6
1. Agriculture is practiced but yields less than 10 percent of the food supply.	8	9
0. Agriculture is not practiced or is confined to nonfood crops.	10	28

$N = 186$, $G = .200$, $Z = 1.748$, $p < .05$ one-tailed.
Note: The gamma for scale type 4 as against all others is .380 ($Z = 2.302$, $p < .05$ two-tailed).

goods that can be envied and when (as the association of the evil eye belief with the social stratification scale suggests) there is an unequal distribution of these goods in the presence of social inequality. The association between money and the evil eye is particularly interesting in this connection, for if one compares the presence of true money, whether indigenous or alien

TABLE 10   *Urbanization and the Evil Eye Belief*

Scale (Murdock and Provost, "Measurement," p. 380)	Evil Eye Present	Evil Eye Absent
4. The population of local communities averages in excess of 1,000 persons.	15	9
3. The population of local communities averages between 400 and 999 persons.	10	20
2. The population of local communities averages between 200 and 399 persons.	6	27
1. The population of local communities averages between 100 and 199 persons.	15	28
0. The population of local communities averages fewer than 100 persons.	21	35

$N = 186$, $G = .093$, $Z = .818$, nonsignificant.
Note: The gamma for scale type 4 as against all others is: .558 ($Z = 2.660$, $p < .01$ two-tailed).

TABLE 11   *Fixity of Residence and the Evil Eye Belief*

Scale (Murdock and Provost, "Measurement," p. 380)	Evil Eye Present	Absent
4. Settlements are sedentary and relatively permanent.	40	62
3. Settlements are sedentary but impermanent.	4	11
2. The pattern of settlement is semisedentary.	6	14
1. The pattern of settlement is seminomadic.	5	16
0. The pattern of settlement is fully nomadic.	12	16

$N = 186$, $G = .074$, $Z = .554$, nonsignificant.

(something to be envied), with everything else, its association with the presence of the evil eye belief is remarkably strong ($G = .519$, $Z = 3.481$, $p < .01$ two-tailed). Again, the association with levels of political integration supports the social stratification finding. All in all the findings confirm the statement that the evil eye is likely to occur in the presence of unequal distribution of material goods (presumed) and in the presence of social and political inequality (confirmed). In the sections that follow these relationships will be examined in greater detail.

Technology

The strong association between the technological specialization scale and the evil eye scale (table 2) suggests that it would be profitable to examine more specific associations between the evil eye and technological activities. The data provided by Murdock and Provost show that there is a negative association between the presence of the evil eye and the presence of boat building ($G = -.421$); fishing, excluding shellfishing and aquatic hunting ($G = -.416$); and, at a directional level, the hunting of large aquatic fauna ($G = -.368$) and the gathering of shellfish and/or other small aquatic fauna ($G = -.329$). Given the geographical distribution of the cultures with the evil eye belief, this is not at all surprising. A negative association with the gathering of eggs, insects, and/or small land fauna ($G = -.502$) is not so easily explained.

The list of associations presented in table 12 below, however, is much more interesting. This table deals with the simple presence or absence of various technological activities and the presence or absence of the belief in the evil eye. The cells in the top row of a conventional two × two table are

TABLE 12   *Technological Activities and the Evil Eye Belief*

Description of the Technological Activity (Murdock and Provost, "Factors")	A (− −)	B (+ −)	C (− +)	D (+ +)	N	G	Z	p Two-tailed <
Milking	105	14	23	44	186	.870	7.434	.01
Dairy production, e.g., making butter or cheese	105	11	26	37	179	.863	6.907	.01
Tending large domestic animals, e.g., sheep, cattle, horses	64	54	13	54	185	.622	4.452	.01
Mining and/or quarrying	76	16	31	25	148	.586	3.392	.01
Metalworking, e.g., forging or casting of metal artifacts	73	41	21	45	180	.585	4.004	.01
Smelting of metal ores	91	15	35	22	163	.584	3.347	.01
Laundering	41	36	12	39	128	.575	3.146	.01
Preparation of skins, e.g., scraping, tanning	40	70	9	55	174	.555	2.970	.01
Loom weaving, excluding other techniques for making fabrics	63	46	19	43	171	.512	3.248	.01
Manufacture of leather products, exclusive of clothing	46	60	12	46	164	.492	2.729	.01
Making of clothing, exclusive of footwear and head gear	29	73	8	54	164	.457	2.108	.05
Spinning, i.e., manufacture of thread	43	56	14	44	157	.414	2.248	.05

lettered *A* and *B* (reading from left to right) and the cells in the bottom row are lettered *C* and *D*. In table 12 column *A* contains the cases where both the technological activity and the belief in the evil eye are absent; column *B* contains the cases where the technological activity is present, but where the evil eye belief is absent; column *C* contains the cases where the technological activity is absent, but where the evil eye is present; and finally column *D* contains the cases where both the technological activity and the evil eye belief are present.

The associations with milking and dairy production are particularly striking, and they suggest that there may be a linkage between the evil eye belief and that fact that milk-producing animals often go dry or stop producing milk for essentially mysterious reasons. There is a general association with large domestic animals, and everyone knows that animal husbandry at this level is uncertain and risky, for substantial amounts of capital can disappear when the animals are stolen or die. Leatherworking and weaving may be dependent upon animal husbandry, and it would be interesting to know whether or not there was an emphasis on animal fibers in evil eye cultures that spin and weave as compared with non-evil-eye cultures. Finally there is a clear association with metalworking, but this is not easy to interpret. All these associations, by the way, suggest that the belief in the evil eye gained strength after the period of domestication of large animals.

The Murdock and Provost paper also provides information on the sexual division of labor. Although there are directional findings, the only pattern of significance to be mentioned is the one pertaining to agriculture. When the nonagricultural societies are exluded from consideration, it can be seen that there is an emphasis on male activity for the evil eye societies that does not obtain for the others. Table 13 below illustrates the pattern.

In table 13 the columns are lettered *A, B, C, D,* and *E. A* refers to activities performed exclusively by males; *B* to activities performed by both sexes but predominantly by males; *C* to activities performed by both sexes with approximately equal participation or with a roughly equivalent division of subtasks; *D* to activities performed by both sexes but predominantly by females; and *E* to activities performed exclusively by females, male participation being negligible.

TABLE 13   *The Sexual Division of Labor in Agriculture and the Evil Eye Belief*

Name of Activity (Murdock and Provost, "Factors")	A	B	C	D	E	N	G	Z	p Two-tailed <
Crop planting and/or trans-planting									
Evil Eye Absent	10	19	23	21	15				
Evil Eye Present	17	16	10	5	5	141	−.431	3.510	.01
Crop tending, e.g., weeding, irrigation									
Evil Eye Absent	8	10	15	23	23				
Evil Eye Present	14	13	9	7	9	131	−.405	3.233	.01
Harvesting, including preparation for storage									
Evil Eye Absent	3	18	21	29	17				
Evil Eye Present	7	19	13	5	9	141	−.368	2.962	.01

Other ethnographic codes provide supporting evidence for the conclusions offered thus far. In the *Ethnographic Atlas* [16] there is a code indicating the "estimated relative dependence of the society" on various forms of subsistence. The code provides an ordinal scale ranging from "Zero to 5 per cent dependence" through increments of 10 percent to the tenth position of 86–100 percent dependence. The evil eye scale is negatively associated with fishing ($N = 186$, $G = -.470$, $Z = 4.268$, $p < .01$ two-tailed), gathering ($N = 186$, $G = -.470$, $Z = 3.825$, $p < .01$, two-tailed), and hunting ($N = 186$, $G = -.381$, $Z = 3.412$, $p < .01$ two-tailed). On the other hand, the evil eye scale is positively associated with animal husbandry ($N = 186$, $G = .606$, $Z = 5.795$, $p < .01$ two-tailed) and directionally with agriculture ($N = 186$, $G = .177$, $Z = 1.699$, $p < .10$ two-tailed). The evil eye societies statistically speaking, do not use fishing, gathering, or hunting as their major subsistence activities.

Table 14 below shows the distribution of domestic animals for those societies in the sample which have such animals. This distribution is taken from Murdock and Morrow.

This table shows the increasingly likelihood of the evil eye belief as the size of the domestic animals increases. The association of the evil eye scale with the presence or absence or bovine species is high ($N = 178$, $G = .575$,

TABLE 14   *Domesticated Animals and the Evil Eye Belief*

Scale (Murdock and Morrow)	Evil Eye Present	Evil Eye Absent
7. The principal domestic animals, especially with reference to their contribution to the local food supply, are bovine species, e.g., cattle, mithan, water buffaloes, or yaks.	28	18
6. The principal domestic animals are camels or related species, e.g., llamas.	3	1
5. The prinicpal domestic animals are reindeer, regardless of their contribution to the local food supply.	2	1
4. The principal domestic animals are equine species, e.g., horses or donkeys, regardless of the importance of their contribution to the local food supply.	3	11
3. The principal domestic animals are ovine species, e.g., sheep and/or goats.	12	11
2. The principal domestic animals are pigs.	28	6
1. The principal domestic animals kept locally are small species, e.g., bees, cats, dogs, fowl, or guinea pigs.	13	41

$Z = 3.589$, $p - .01$ two-tailed). Not surprisingly, the evil eye cultures are more likely to use animals in plow cultivation.

The pattern of animal utilization, shown in table 15 below, is also interesting. Again this table speaks for itself. If the entire table is regarded as an ordinal scale leading to pastoralism, the association with the evil eye scale is positive ($N = 186$, $G = .668$, $Z = 6.368$, $p < .01$ two-tailed). The relationship with milking has already been described.

A few comments should be made on the agricultural associations. Thirty-eight of the societies in the sample either had no agriculture or their agriculture was confined to nonfood crops. For the remaining societies belief in the evil eye appeared to be associated with the presence of cereal grains (e.g., maize, millets, rice, or wheat) as the principal local crop rather than vegetables, tree or vine products, or roots or tubers (see table 16). Other associations show that the evil eye belief is positively associated with intensive permanent and intensive irrigated agriculture as contrasted with other types.

Other comments could be made on technology, since the association with complexity would lead to such associations as the presence of temples,

TABLE 15   *Animal Husbandry and the Evil Eye Belief*

	Evil Eye Present	Evil Eye Absent
Scale (Murdock and Morrow)		
6. The subsistence economy is primarily pastoral, with animal husbandry contributing more to the local food supply than any other subsistence techniques. The use of dairy products is assumed in the absence of an asterisked note to the contrary.	14	2
5. Domestic animals are kept and contribute more than 10 percent of the local food supply, especially in the form of milk or dairy products, but less than one or more other subsistence techniques contribute.	17	4
4. Domestic animals are kept and contribute more than 10 percent of the local food supply, especially in the form of flesh or meat, but less than one or more other subsistence techniques contribute.	11	22
3. Domestic animals are kept and contribute to the local food supply but in an amount constituting less than 10 percent of the total food consumed.	19	47
2. Some domestic animals (at least dogs) are kept, but they do not contribute to the local food supply, e.g., are not eaten or milked.	6	36
1. No domestic animals are kept.	0	8

TABLE 16 *Principal Local Crops and the Evil Eye Belief*

Scale (Murdock and Morrow)	Evil Eye Present	Absent
The principal local crops are cereal grains.	45	51
The principal local crops are vegetables, tree or vine products, or roots or tubers.	12	40

$N = 148$, $G = .493$, $Z = 2.654$, $p < .01$ two-tailed.

churches, forts, storehouses, factories, etc., in the evil eye cultures as against cultures possessing only impressive residences or secular buildings. The principal point, however, is that the evil eye cultures emphasized milking, animal husbandry, and, in some cases, intensive agriculture.

Social Organization

Some of the features of social organization have already been given, but others warrant mention. The association between the evil eye belief and density of population has been cited. There is also an association with a size of communities larger than 1,000 ($N = 185$, $G = .597$, $Z = 2.853$, $p < .01$ two-tailed), where the evil eye is associated with the larger communities, but community size differs widely for the societies with the belief.

There is an emphasis on patrilineal descent in the evil-eye-present societies, as table 17 shows. It is not surprising that there is an emphasis on

TABLE 17 *Descent and the Evil Eye Belief*

Scale (Murdock and Wilson)	Evil Eye Present	Absent
The principal consanguineal kin groups are those based on patrilineal descent, e.g., patrilineages.	38	37
Double descent prevails, both matrilineal and patrilineal descent groups being present.	3	7
Descent is bilateral.	19	50
The principal consanguineal kin groups are those based on ambilineal descent, e.g., ramages.	1	5
The principal consanguineal kin groups are based on matrilineal descent.	6	20
Total nonpatrilineal	29	82

$N = 186$, $G = .488$, $Z = 3.256$, $p < .01$ two-tailed.

TABLE 18 *Marital Residence and the Evil Eye Belief*

	Evil Eye	
Scale (Murdock and Wilson)	Present	Absent
Patrilocal or virilocal residence, i.e., with or near the male patrilineal kinsmen of the husband.	54	64
Neolocal, ambilocal, avunculocal, matrilocal, or uxorilocal residence.	13	54

$N = 185$, $G = .556$, $Z = 3.417$, $p < .01$ two-tailed.

patrilocal marital residence, shown in table 18. There are other interesting features. For example, of the 8 societies where there is a preference for marriage with the father's brother's daughter, 7 have the evil eye belief.

Very importantly in terms of the discussion that follows, the evil eye is positively associated with modes of marriage that involve the transfer of a substantial amount of property from either the groom's or the bride's kinsmen to the kinsmen of the spouse (see table 19).

The associations with types of family and with types of household are not so clear. Apparently the evil eye belief can be found in some of the cultures possessing every type of family coded by Murdock and Wilson, and the same is true of the types of household, with the exception of the longhouse or communal dwelling pattern and the mother-child households (where the evil eye is absent), although these findings are not statistically significant. The same confusion exists with inheritance patterns, for while it is true that the evil eye belief is associated with *some* pattern of the inheritance of land

TABLE 19 *Mode of Marriage and the Evil Eye Belief*

	Evil Eye	
Scale (Murdock)	Present	Absent
Bride-price or bride-wealth, i.e., transfer of a substantial consideration in the form of livestock, goods, or money from the groom or his relatives to the kinsmen of the bride, and dowry, i.e., transfer of a substantial amount of property from the bride's relatives to the bride, the groom, or the kinsmen of the latter.	38	40
Bride service, token bride-price, gift exchange, exchange, the "absence of any significant consideration, or bridal gifts only."	27	78

$N = 183$, $G = .466$, $Z = 3.051$, $p < .01$ two-tailed.

TABLE 20   *Caste Stratification and the Evil Eye Belief*

Scale (Murdock)	Evil Eye Present	Absent
Complex caste stratification in which occupational differentiation emphasizes hereditary ascription and endogamy to the near exclusion of achievable class statutes.	5	2
Ethnic stratification, in which a superordinate caste withholds privileges from and refuses to intermarry with a subordinate caste (or castes) that it stigmatizes as ethnically alien.	2	1
One or more despised occupational groups, e.g., smiths or leather workers, distinguished from the general population, regarded as outcastes by the latter, and characterized by strict endogamy.	13	4
Caste distinctions absent or insignificant.	41	110

as against none at all ($N = 153$, $G = .459$, $Z = 2.590$, $p < .01$ two-tailed), there is no distinctive pattern associated with the belief.

We have already seen that social stratification is associated with the evil eye. Some additional information can be given on this point, for the presence of social inequality may be an important condition for the presence of the evil eye. Table 20 gives the material on caste stratification taken from the *Ethnographic Atlas*. If the first three categories are lumped so that the absence of caste stratification is compared with the presence of some form of it, the evil eye belief is associated with the presence of caste stratification ($N = 178$, $G = .713$, $Z = 4.131$, $p < .01$ two-tailed).

A similar pattern holds for the presence of slavery. Table 21 shows that the evil eye belief is associated with the presence of hereditary slavery. If the unidentified category is omitted and if the presence of hereditary slavery is contrasted with incipient and absent slavery, the evil eye belief is posi-

TABLE 21   *Slavery and the Evil Eye Belief*

Scale (Murdock)	Evil Eye Present	Absent
Hereditary slavery present and of at least modest social significance.	22	21
Slavery reported but not identified as either hereditary or nonhereditary.	4	5
Incipient or nonhereditary slavery, i.e., slave status is temporary and not transmitted to the children of slaves.	6	21
Absence or near absence of slavery.	30	68

tively associated with the presence of hereditary slavery. ($N = 168$, $G = .433$, $Z = 2.467$, $p < .02$ two-tailed).

Turning now to political variables, the societies possessing the evil eye belief tended to be politically autonomous; see table 22. The listing in this table may not be a true ordinal scale, but if the two top categories are compared with all others, the results are: $N = 184$, $G = .400$, $Z = 2.268$, $p < .05$ two-tailed. It is even better if the top three are compared with all others, and comparing the top four against the last two also gives a significant result. The evil eye belief does appear to be associated with political autonomy.

More importantly, in terms of the developing theory, the societies with belief in the evil eye tend to be those with a relative concentration of executive power; see table 23. If one contrasts the bottom row with all others, $G = .629$. Clearly the evil eye belief is associated with focused authority. Incidentally, of the 81 societies coded as selecting the executive in one way or another, societies with the evil eye belief were more likely to have a selective system where succession is hereditary and patrilineal, normally from father to son (15 societies), or where succession is the same except that a brother takes precedence over a son (2 societies; total 17). Other methods were used by 25 of the evil eye societies and 32 of the non–evil eye socie-

TABLE 22   *Political Autonomy and the Evil Eye Belief*

Scale (Tuden and Marshall)	Evil Eye	
	Present	Absent
The society or its relevant subgroup is (or was) fully autonomously politically.	13	16
The society is politically integrated with others in a pluralistic state within which it enjoys theoretically equal status.	10	6
The society pays tribute (or its equivalent) to another society with a different culture in return for which it enjoys essential autonomy in its internal affairs.	3	1
The society is politically semiautonomous, being governed by another society with an alien culture which operates largely through indigenous political institutions.	15	26
The society is theoretically subject to another society with an alien culture, e.g., to a colonial power, but is in fact essentially unadministered by the latter and thus enjoys de facto autonomy.	20	57
The society is politically dependent, being governed directly by functionaries of a dominant society of alien culture, e.g., through direct rule.	5	12

$N = 184$, $G = .298$, $Z = 2.642$, $p < .01$ two-tailed.

TABLE 23   *The Executive and the Evil Eye Belief*

	Evil Eye	
Scale (Tuden and Marshall)	Present	Absent
Supreme decision-making authority is concentrated in a single authoritative leader, e.g., a paramount chief, king, or dictator, however much he may in fact be influenced by advisors.	31	23
Supreme decision-making authority is vested in a plural executive, e.g., a committee, a dual executive, or a triumvirate.	2	0
Supreme decision-making authority is shared more or less equally by a single (or plural) executive and a deliberative body, e.g., a king, president, or prime minister and a supreme council or parliament.	9	13
Supreme decision-making authority is vested in a council, assembly, or other deliberative body with no single executive other than at best a presiding officer.	3	4
Absence of executive sovereignty, and consequently of executive functionaries, at any level above that of the local community.	20	78

$N = 183$, $G = .559$, $Z = 4.709$, $p < .01$ two-tailed.

ties. Only 7 of the non–evil eye societies, however, used the patrilineal form ($N = 81$, $G = .513$, $Z = 1.963$, $p < .05$ two-tailed).

All things considered, it is not surprising that the degree of specialization and institutionalization of police functions is positively associated with the presence of the evil eye (see table 24).

TABLE 24   *Police and the Evil Eye Belief*

	Evil Eye	
Scale (Tuden and Marshall)	Present	Absent
Police functions are specialized or institutionalized on at least some level or levels of political integration.	20	22
Police functions are assumed by the military organization.	6	0
Police functions are assumed by the retainers of chiefs.	1	3
There is only incipient specialization, as when groups with other functions are assigned police functions in emergencies, e.g., military societies at a Plains Indian annual sun dance and buffalo hunt.	0	4
Police functions are not specialized or institutionalized at any level of political integration, the maintenance of law and order being left exclusively to informal mechanisms of social control, to private retaliation, or to sorcery.	37	87

$N = 180$, $G = .348$, $Z = 2.364$, $p < .01$ two-tailed.

TABLE 25   *The Judiciary and the Evil Eye Belief*

Scale (Tuden and Marshall)	Evil Eye Present	Evil Eye Absent
Supreme judicial authority is exercised by independent hereditary functionaries.	1	0
Supreme judicial authority is independent of the political system and is vested in a priesthood or in other primarily religious functionaries.	1	0
Supreme judicial authority is vested in a functionary or functionaries who are appointed by the supreme executive and/or the supreme deliberative body but are at least relatively independent of the appointing authority.	12	11
Supreme judicial authority is exercised by the supreme executive, e.g., the king is also the supreme judge, the council is also the supreme court.	27	22
Supreme judicial authority exists at a level above that of the local community but below that of effective sovereignty.	4	2
Supreme judicial authority is lacking at any level above that of the local community.	21	82

$N = 183$, $G = .558$, $Z = 4.742$, $p < .01$ two-tailed.

The development of the judiciary presents a similar picture, although it is not so clear (see table 25).

Thus the evil-eye-belief scale is positively associated with social stratification and political integration. It is also associated with caste stratification, slavery, political autonomy, concentration of executive power, developed police, and a developed judiciary. There is also an emphasis on patrilineality and on forms of marriage involving substantial property transfer. In the aggregate these associations provide a pattern of social inequality, strong and focused authority and indications of the importance of property. These may be associated with both the evil eye and envy.

Expressive Culture

Several expressive associations are interesting and supportive of associations already described. The evil-eye-belief scale is positively associated with beliefs in high gods (i.e., strong and focused authority). See table 26.

The evil eye scale is also positively associated with the presence of games of strategy, which are known to be associated with cultural complexity.

TABLE 26 *Belief in High Gods and Belief in the Evil Eye*

Scale (Murdock)	Evil Eye	
	Present	Absent
A high god is present, active, and specifically supportive of human morality.	30	9
A high god is present and active in human affairs but does not offer positive support to human morality.	8	5
A high god is present but otiose or not concerned with human affairs.	11	36
A high god is absent or not reported in substantial descriptions of religious beliefs.	12	54

$N = 165$, $G = .669$, $Z = 5.892$, $p < .01$ two-tailed.

There are indications that involvement in games of strategy is also associated with conflict over social status and conflict over obedience (see table 27).

The distribution of prominent community ceremonials is interesting. Here there is no true ordinal scale, but the categories have been ordered in terms of the strength of the presence of the belief in the evil eye (see table 28). If the combined rites-of-passage and calendrical-ceremonies category is compared with the others, the evil eye belief has an association of $G = .403$ ($N = 179$, $Z = 2.133$, $p < .05$ two-tailed). The evil eye appears to go with forethought and planning in religious ceremonials.

Finally, although the total table is not significant, there is a hint of an emphasis on property in one form or another in the ceremonials of the societies having the evil eye belief; see table 29.

The expressive associations with the evil eye are quite consistent with the picture that is emerging. It is unlikely that there is any causal relationship among them, but they may be related to the same antecedent factors.

TABLE 27 *Games of Strategy and the Evil Eye Belief*

Scale (Murdock)	Evil Eye	
	Present	Absent
Games of strategy are present.	18	13
Games of strategy are absent, but games of physical skill and/or games of chance are present.	16	62

$N = 109$, $G = .686$, $Z = 3.572$, $p < .01$ two-tailed.

TABLE 28   *Prominent Community Ceremonials and Belief in the Evil Eye*

Scale (Murdock and Wilson)	Evil Eye Present	Absent
The most prominent ceremonies are rites of passage performed for individuals at critical points in their life cycle but normally attended by all or most members of the community, e.g., naming ceremonies, puberty initiations, weddings, funerals.	30	37
The most prominent ceremonies are calendrical, being determined by the annual cycle of economic activities (e.g., first-fruit rites, harvest ceremonies, solstice celebrations), or by a ritual calendar (e.g., saints' days).	25	37
The most important ceremonies are individually sponsored rites other than rites of passage that are normally attended by the community at large, e.g., potlatches, "feasts of merit," votive sacrifices.	4	10
The most prominent ceremonies are magical or religious rites performed on irregular occasions of individual or community concern—e.g., shamanistic curing performances, purification rituals, ceremonials before and after wars, or rites celebrating the installation of a chief—in which participation is normally by the community at large.	8	28

TABLE 29   *Ceremonial Elements and the Belief in the Evil Eye*

Scale (Murdock and Wilson)	Evil Eye Present	Absent
Distribution or exchange of property other than food.	5	5
Sacrifice (other than human), prayer, laudation, and/or other forms of propitiating spirits, deities, or ghosts of the dead, whatever their specific purpose (e.g., atonement, foretelling the future, pleas for help, thanksgiving).	23	34
Feasting and/or drinking (other than cannibalistic), including the distribution of food for subsequent consumption.	21	33
Music, dancing, games, and/or dramatic performances.	16	35
Cannibalism, human sacrifice, and/or the ceremonial killing of war captives, widows, or other victims.	2	11
Self-torture, self-mutilation, or comparable extreme masochistic behavior, not including fasting or other forms of self-abnegation.	0	1

$N = 186$, $G = .219$, $Z = 1.876$, $p < .01$ two-tailed.

Child Socialization

The most interesting associations with the evil eye belief are those that are to be found with child socialization variables. The most important associations are those to be found with child, rather than infant or early childhood, association variables, but some of the early associations should be considered. It may be important that the father is less likely to have a close association with his child in the evil eye cultures (see table 30). Societies with the evil eye belief seem to foster a later onset of motor skills than those lacking the belief (see table 31). This may reflect a certain amount of dependency. Pain, on the other hand, is certainly present (see table 32).

The societies with the evil eye belief have an early onset of modesty, in the sense that the genitals are covered (see table 33). This is compatible with sexual restraint in childhood. The evil eye societies are also more likely to have genital mutilations (see table 34).

A paper now in preparation, "Cross-Cultural Codes on Childhood" by Barry, Josephson, Lauer, and Marshall, presents a series of codes for younger boys, older boys, younger girls, and older girls. The author was

TABLE 30 *Role of the Father in Infancy and the Evil Eye Belief*

| | Evil Eye | |
Scale (Barry and Paxon)	Present	Absent
Regular, close relationship or companionship.	0	3
Frequent close proximity.	12	32
Occasional or irregular close proximity.	26	46
Rare instances of close proximity.	14	13
No close proximity.	4	4

$N = 154$, $G = -.324$, $Z = 2.383$, $p < .02$ two-tailed.

TABLE 31 *Encouragement of Motor Skills and the Evil Eye Belief*

| | Evil Eye | |
Scale (Barry and Paxson)	Present	Absent
1. Youngest onset	37	84
2. Young intermediate onset	20	26
3. Older intermediate onset	4	3
4. Oldest onset	2	0

$N = 176$, $G = .349$, $Z = 2.253$, $p < .05$ two-tailed.

TABLE 32   *Pain Infliction by Caretakers and the Evil Eye Belief*

Scale (Barry and Paxson)	Evil Eye Present	Absent
1. Absence of inflicted pain.	4	13
2. Only neonatally or very mild pain.	10	27
3. Occasional mild pain.	28	35
4. Frequent mild pain or infrequent severe pain.	11	14
5. Greater frequency of pain.	4	2

$N = 148$, $G = .306$, $Z = 2.326$, $p < .05$ two-tailed.

TABLE 33   *Ranking of Age of Onset for the Covering of Genitals and the Evil Eye Belief*

Scale (Barry and Paxson)	Evil Eye Present	Absent
1. Youngest onset	18	14
2. Younger onset	2	7
3. Intermediate onset	11	23
4. Older onset	14	31
5. Oldest onset	6	24

$N = 150$, $G = -.329$, $Z = 2.621$, $p < .01$ two-tailed.

TABLE 34   *Male Genital Mutilations and the Evil Eye Belief*

Scale (Murdock)	Evil Eye Present	Absent
Male genital mutilations absent	18	101
Male genital mutilations present	29	38

$N = 186$, $G = .621$, $Z = 4.056$, $p < .01$ two-tailed.

given access to prepublication codes and he was given permission to use the codes for the younger boys, which, in the mast majority of cases, predict quite well to the three other categories. It is possible that some corrections will be made by the authors before the publication of the paper, but it is extremely unlikely that these changes will be significant enough to affect the results given below.

One group of variables in the childhood paper consists of attributes toward which there is positive child socialization. In other words, the cultures that are high on the scales tend to foster these traits in their children, and possibly in adults as well. Some of these scales had no significant associations with the evil eye scale, and it is interesting to see that these include: fortitude ($G = .172$), self-restraint ($G = .153$), honesty ($G = -.129$), achievement ($G = .067$), self-reliance ($G = -.060$), competiveness ($G = .023$), and generosity ($G = -.008$). Note that the sign for honesty is negative.

Another group of associations was significant and important. These are given in table 35. Note that the evil eye societies are more likely to provide positive training for young boys in industry, responsibility, sexual restraint, obedience, and physical aggression and that they are less likely to provide positive training in trust. It is obvious that an adult male who was industrious, responsible, obedient, and physically aggressive would make a fine soldier if his low trust could be converted into suspicion or hatred of the

TABLE 35 *Child Training Variables and the Evil Eye Belief*

Scale (Barry, Josephson, Lauer, and Marshall)

Evil Eye Belief	12	11	10	9	8	7	6	5	4	3	2	1	n	N	G	Z	p Two-tailed <
								Industry									
Present				1	0	4	8	8	15	23	0	2	61				
Absent				0	0	1	13	6	13	61	10	3	107	168	.418	3.507	.01
								Responsibility									
Present				2	0	5	11	5	25	28	0	2	58				
Absent				0	0	3	11	1	18	46	8	9	96	154	.367	2.914	.01
								Sexual Restraint									
Present				1	0	3	19	3	10	19	3	1	59				
Absent				0	0	6	11	11	12	52	11	0	103	162	.323	2.737	.01
								Obedience									
Present	2	0	4	9	1	12	19	5	3	6	0	0	61				
Absent	1	0	0	14	2	16	32	9	8	22	3	2	109	170	.312	2.840	.01
								Physical Aggression									
Present	1	0	2	8	1	13	15	1	6	4	4	0	55				
Absent	0	0	1	6	1	15	29	6	8	22	3	1	92	147	.299	2.571	.02
								Trust									
Present	1	0	0	5	5	8	20	6	0	15	3	0	63				
Absent	1	0	3	27	7	17	24	12	7	6	4	1	109	172	-.299	2.832	.01

enemy. He might also make a good corporate employee in certain circumstances.

It is worth considering whether or not the associations mentioned above are simply linked with cultural complexity. The three measures of cultural complexity most strongly associated with the evil eye belief were technological specialization, social stratification, and writing and records. Twenty-one cultures were at the top of the scale for all of these variables; 13 had the evil eye and 8 did not. There were significant associations for two of the variables listed in table 34 for this small sample, i.e., obedience and sexual restraint, and the results were directional for two other variables (physical aggressiveness and trust). A larger sample based on other measures of cul-

TABLE 36   *Obedience, Sexual Restraint, and the Evil Eye Belief with a Sample of Complex Cultures*

Scale (Barry, Josephson, Lauer, and Marshall)

Evil Eye Belief	*Obedience*	
	Scale value of 6 or lower	Scale value of 7 or higher
Present	Romans, Irish	Uttar Pradesh, Egyptians, Babylonians, Turks, Armenians, Basques, Russians, West Punjabi, Hebrews, Aztecs
	2	10
Absent	Burmese, Javanese, Balinese, North Vietnamese, Thai, Koreans	Japanese, Chinese
	6	2

Fisher's Exact Test $p = .05$

	Sexual Restraint	
	Scale value of 4 or lower	Scale value of 5 or higher
Present	Amhara, Egyptians	Armenians, Turks, Romans, Basques, Irish, Uttar Pradesh, Aztecs, Hebrews, Russians
	2	9
Absent	Burmese, Japanese, Javanese, Balinese, Chinese, North Vietnamese, Thai	Koreans
	8	1

Fisher's Exact Test $p = .01$

tural complexity was even more productive, but table 36 will suffice to illustrate the point. It is probably not the case that the five important variables of industry, responsibility, sexual restraint, obedience, physical aggression, and trust are simply associations linked to cultural complexity and lacking direct implications for our understanding of the evil eye belief.

The Barry paper also provided data on techniques used in child socialization. The associations of these scales with the evil eye scale were nonsignificant for such techniques as gifts, praise, promises of reward, example, public opinion, lecturing, teasing and shaming, scolding, rejection, and isolation. Other techniques, however, had some interest. Table 37 provides some of the data on corporal punishment, threats of punishment, atonement, and pacification. This table appears to suggest a pattern, but only the corporal punishment scale is of any real value—the others are included only for their suggestive import.

The foregoing child training variables *must* have some sort of relationship with envy and the evil eye. It must not be concluded that they are necessarily independent variables. Industry, for example, may be closely associated with responsibility. The published paper dealing with these codes will be

TABLE 37   *Child Socialization Techniques and Belief in the Evil Eye*

Scale (Barry, Josephson, Lauer, and Marshall)

Evil Eye Belief	12	11	10	9	8	7	6	5	4	3	2	1	n	N	G	Z	p Two-tailed <
						Corporal Punishment											
Present	1	1	2	1	0	10	18	3	3	15	0	2	56				
Absent	0	0	0	2	0	10	25	8	16	22	7	8	98	154	.302	2.600	.01
						Threats of Punishment											
Present			1	5	1	2	8	1	1	1	0	0	20				
Absent			1	2	0	12	17	1	3	3	1	0	40	60	.244	1.217	nonsignificant
						Atonement											
Present				6	0	3	5	0	1	0	0	0	15				
Absent				2	0	5	7	1	3	3	0	1	22	37	.364	2.386	.01
						Pacification											
Present			0	—	0	4	10	0	2	2	0	4	22				
Absent			2	2	0	13	32	3	2	4	2	1	60	82	−.363	1.874	.10

more explicit than I can be here, for I do not want to anticipate other work. The associations support, however, a speculative theory of envy and the evil eye, which will be advanced in the discussion section that follows.

The associations as a whole, however, suggest that there are cultural environments in which the evil eye belief can flourish and that there are other cultural environments where it will not. There is a need for new research to determine causalities in this complicated picture and this will be forthcoming. The clues to understanding the evil eye belief, however, are probably among those associations already presented.

Factor Analysis

The twenty-nine scales that had the strongest associations with the evil eye scale were factor analyzed to produce some dimensions of interest. Sample overlap and missing data were simply ignored. The solution produced seven factors accounting for 88 percent of the variance. Variables with loadings of .45 or higher were used in defining the factors. Factor I appeared to be a technical specialization factor (evil eye loading of .25) with loadings on mining (.94), metalworking (.85), smelting (.84), technical specialization (.79), games of strategy (.77), loom weaving (.55), and large domestic animals (.48). Factor II (evil eye .33) was defined by laundering (.89), manufactured clothing (.89), money (.73), urbanization (.67), gathering (− .65), milking (.57), loom weaving (.57), dairy products (.56), and large domestic animals (.53), and this might be a property factor of some sort. Factor III (evil eye .23) may be a subsistence factor with grain versus tree and vine agriculture (.92), bovines (.80), large animals (.67), leather products (.47) and fishing (− .45). Factor IV had the highest loading on the evil eye (.66) and the other variables of consequence were caste (.58), dairy products (.51), and milking (.48). Factor V (evil eye .24) may have been a stratification dimension with focused authority (.78), judiciary (.78), and leather products (− .48). Factor VI had the smallest loading on the evil eye (.05) with mode of marriage (.74), urbanization (− .50), and animal husbandry (.45). Finally, Factor VII (evil eye .32) may have been some social-structural factor with marital residence (.83), descent (− .81), genital mutilation (.63), and games of strategy (.49). Clearly relatively little can be made of these dimensions, but the analysis reaffirms the close association between the evil eye and milking, for this is the factor that gives the evil eye the highest loading.

In addition 15 infancy and child training variables were factor analyzed with the evil eye. This solution provided dimensions of greater intellectual interest. The problems of sample overlap and missing data are enormous here, however, so the factor-analytic solution can only be offered as an impression. Three factors accounting for 37 percent of the variance were produced. The first (factor I) had a loading of .38 on the evil eye and the remaining loadings were .66 on sexual restraint, .54 on obedience, and − .48 on pacification. This seems to be a tough obedience factor. Factor II (evil eye .36) had loadings on industry (.77) and responsibility (.75), and it appears to be a hard work factor. Factor III had the highest loading on the evil eye (.75). Trust had a negative loading of − .59. Threats of punishment (.55) and atonement (.54) also defined what appears to be a low trust and high guilt factor. If any reliance can be placed on these data, one would say that sexual restraint, obedience, industriousness, responsibility, trust, threats of punishment, and atonement are particularly important in the evil eye complex and that they divide into the three dimensions mentioned.

There is no real justification for these factor-analytic solutions because of the data problems. They represent the kind of estimate that an experienced enthnographer might make if he were to look at the associational data. They have some value, however, in guiding future and more rigorous research.

Discussion

The associations presented in the preceding sections define in a rough sort of way the cultural environment in which the evil eye belief is likely to endure. There are numerous exceptions to any principle that might be derived from the pattern of these associations, and it would be premature to offer a theory of the belief in the evil eye on the basis of such evidence. Additional research is needed.

One direction that new research might take is the use of multivariate techniques with the cross-cultural data. There are, however, some methodological difficulties involved in using a factor analysis at this time since the samples are frequently not comparable.

It is more promising, perhaps, to initiate intracultural research designed to test hypotheses and to establish a theory. An exploratory questionnaire was given to 257 college students who were available on an opportunistic basis (no defense can be made of the sample) to show that this was feasible. This questionnaire asked the respondents to circle their level of belief in the evil eye on a scale which read: Complete disbelief −3 −2 −1 0 +1 +2 +3 Complete belief. The distribution was: −3 (127), −2 (52), −1 (14), 0 (29), +1 (23), +2 (9), and +3 (3). A few tables based on the responses to this questionnaire are given below.

Table 38 shows that students from small families are more likely to express a modicum of belief in the evil eye than students from families with four or more children. Is envy a stronger factor in small families?

The students were asked to estimate the degree to which they were responsible as children at home on a scale of 1 (low) to 7 (high). The two scales were negatively associated and table 39 below shows how a low perception of responsibility has an association with belief in the evil eye. Could it be the case that those who did not feel that they were responsible were in conflict about responsibility?

There was also a negative association between estimates of obedience as children and belief in the evil eye. Furthermore, students who said that they liked to pass at high speeds were more likely to express a belief in the evil eye. Could it be the case that they thought that the people whom they passed envied them? There was a similar finding for those who liked to drive at high speeds. All these associations were significant, but the tables will not be presented. A new intracultural study is being designed that will deal with the problem more effectively than this exploratory venture.

Some points can be considered, though, in the design of a new study dealing with the evil eye. These can be reviewed here.

TABLE 38 *Number of Children in the Family and Belief in the Evil Eye*

Belief	Three or less children	Four or more children
−3	54	63
Other	76	42

$N = 235$, $G = -.357$, $Z = 2.677$, $p < .01$ two-tailed.

TABLE 39 *Assessment of Responsibility and Belief in the Evil Eye*

Belief	Low Responsibility (1, 2, 3, 4)	High Responsibility (5, 6, 7)
−3, −2, −1	27	165
Other	19	44

$N = 255$, $G = -.450$, $Z = 2.689$, $p < .01$ two-tailed

The geographical distribution of the cultures possessing the evil eye belief supports the statement that the belief became culturally elaborated in the Near East (broadly defined). Furthermore, the cultural associations indicate that the belief became elaborated no earlier than neolithic times, when the milking of domestic animals became established. Admittedly such statements do not account for many puzzles such as the New World distribution of the evil eye belief, but they serve as working hypotheses.

If the conflict-enculturation hypothesis holds, there should be identifiable areas of psychological conflict that would lead to involvement in the expressive belief of the evil eye. One such area is that of social status and social stratification. In the presence of social inequality, there are situations conducive to the development of envy, which could then be projected to others and then made operative through the belief in the evil eye. Work with status affinity suggests that persons with distributed status affinity are more likely to be interested in games of strategy,[17] but focused status affinity may lead to envy, as in the case of a peasant who wants to be a lord but who is barred by a social system that makes that sort of mobility impossible. Social inequality is probably a precondition to any elaboration of the evil eye. Certainly numerous associations showed that the presence of the evil eye belief *is* associated with social and political inequality.

Although the principle does not appear clearly in the pattern of associations, property must be involved, too. The higher technological specialization of the evil eye societies means that property is being produced, property that can be owned and envied. If the social inequality is accompanied by an unequal distribution of material goods, the probability of an elaborated evil eye may be even greater.

The most promising areas of conflict, though, may be those indicated by the pattern of child socialization. Where one finds a premium placed on high responsibility and industry, young children must have avoidance attitudes as well as approach attitudes toward responsible work.

The pattern of conflict may be plainer when one considers the positive training toward physical aggression that is contained (in another way) by high obedience training. The person who casts the evil eye is often presumed to be hostile, envious, and not conforming to cultural codes, i.e., not obedient or responsible. Persons in conflict over aggression and obedience might well be interested in such a configuration.

Certainly there is a sexual component. The evil eye societies have high sexual restraint, and this almost certainly means conflict, for the approach attitudes to sex are easily fostered. Some of the traditional targets of the evil eye are sexual objects.

All this is accompanied by training in low trust of other people and by pain in the child socialization process. There are hints, too, of strong, focused authority that is still capricious, as in the case of the despotic ruler whose decisions are inconsistent.

The variables, then, that will be important in further work are: social status, property, focused authority, industry, responsibility, obedience, sex, physical aggression, trust, and pain. There are undoubtedly others, but these seem to be important components. The investigation of these patterns should lead to a theory of envy, and from that to a theory of the belief in the evil eye.

NOTES

1. The preliminary work for this study was done in the Human Relations Area Files at Cornell University, but all of the coding reported here was done by the Cross-Cultural Cumulative Coding Center at the University of Pittsburgh under National Science Foundation Research Grants nos. GS-2111 and GS-2998. Violetta R. Frederick was responsible for the coding, but she was aided by Edith Lauer, Lili Josephson, Catherine A. Marshall, Caterina F. Provost, and Suzanne F. Wilson. Joel Gunn and Judith T. Fine provided substantial assistance with the data processing. George P. Murdock and Herbert Barry III generously provided access to their unpublished codes and they gave other help as well. Monica Wilson and Clarence T. Maloney answered ethnographic inquiries. Isaac Rabinowitz and Jerome Rosenberg helped with the ancient Hebrew and Kevin O'Doherty aided with the religious background. Finally, the author owes a great deal to William W. Lambert with whom he has been discussing the problem of the belief in the evil eye for more than five years.
2. Roberts, Kozelka, Kiehl, and Newman; Roberts, Kozelka, and Arth; Roberts, Thompson, and Sutton-Smith; Roberts and Wicke; Hutchinson and Roberts; and Roberts, Hutchinson, and Carlson.
3. Roberts, Arth, and Bush; Roberts and Sutton-Smith, "Child Training"; Sutton-Smith, Roberts, and Kozelka; Roberts, Sutton-Smith, and Kendon; Roberts, Hoffman, and Sutton-Smith; Roberts and Sutton-Smith, "Cross-Cultural Correlates"; Sutton-Smith and Roberts, "Studies"; Roberts, Koenig, and Stark; Sutton-Smith and Roberts, "Cross-Cultural . . . Study"; Roberts, Meeker, and Aller; and Barry and Roberts.
4. Roberts and Ridgeway and Roberts and Forman.
5. Sutton-Smith, Roberts, and Rosenberg; Sutton-Smith and Roberts, "Rubric"; Roberts, "Oaths"; Roberts and Koenig; Roberts, "Expressive Aspects"; and Roberts and Gregor.
6. "Child Training and Game Involvement."

7. See Roberts and Forman, Roberts and Ridgeway.
8. See Roberts and Ridgeway.
9. Roberts, Arth, and Bush; Roberts and Sutton-Smith, "Child Training"; Roberts, Sutton-Smith, and Kendon; Roberts, "Oaths"; Roberts and Golder; Roberts and Forman; Roberts and Gregor; and Barry and Roberts.
10. See Freeman, pp. 77–88, 176–86.
11. Murdock and White, p. 329.   12. Ibid., p. 330.
13. Throughout this paper this coefficient and levels of significance have been computed in the manner described by Freeman, pp. 77–88 and 176–86.
14. Murdock and White, pp. 342–47.
15. Murdock and Provost, "Measurement," p. 10.
16. Murdock, pp. 154–55.   17. Roberts and Koenig.

BIBLIOGRAPHY

Barry, H., III, L. Josephson, E. Lauer, and C. Marshall. "Cross-Cultural Codes on Childhood." Manuscript, n.d.
—— and L. M. Paxson. "Infancy and Early Childhood: Cross-Cultural Codes 2," *Ethnology* 10 (1971), 466–508.
—— and J. M. Roberts. "Infant Socialization and Games of Chance," *Ethnology* 11 (1972), 296–308.
Freeman, L. C. *Elementary Applied Statistics.* New York: Wiley, 1965.
Hutchinson, J. W. and J. M. Roberts. "Expressive Constraints on Driver Re-education," *Psychological Aspects of Driver Behavior,* vol. 2. Netherlands, 1972.
Murdock, G. P. "Ethnographic Atlas: A Summary," *Ethnology* 6 (1967), 109–236.
—— and D. O. Morrow. "Subsistence Economy and Supportive Practices: Cross-Cultural Codes I," *Ethnology* 9 (1970), 302–30.
—— and C. Provost. "Factors in the Division of Labor by Sex: A Cross-Cultural Analysis," *Ethnology* 12 (1973), 203–25.
—— and —— "Measurement of Cultural Complexity," *Ethnology* 12 (1973), 379–92.
—— and D. R. White. "Standard Cross-Cultural Sample," *Ethnology* 8 (1969), 329–69.
—— and S. F. Wilson. "Settlement Patterns and Community Organization: Cross-Cultural Codes 3," *Ethnology* 11 (1972), 254–95.
Roberts, J. M. "Expressive Aspects of Technological Development," *Philosophy of the Social Sciences* 1 (1971), 207–20.
—— "Oaths, Autonomic Ordeals, and Power," in *Ethnology of Law,* L. Nader, ed., *American Anthropologist* 67, no. 2 (1965), 169–95.
——, M. J. Arth, and R. R. Bush. "Games in Culture," *American Anthropologist* 61 (1959), 597–605.
—— and M. L. Forman. "Riddles: Expressive Models of Interrogation," *Ethnology* 10 (1971), 509–33.
—— and T. V. Golder. "Navy and Polity: A 1963 Baseline," *Naval War College Review* 23 (1971), 30–41.

—— and T. Gregor. "Privacy: A Cultural View," in *Privacy*, J. R. Pennock and J. W. Chapman, eds., *Nomos* 13 (New York, 1971), 199–225.

——, H. Hoffmann, and B. Sutton-Smith. "Pattern and Competence: A Consideration of Tick Tack Toe," *El Palacio* 72 (1965), 17–30.

——, J. W. Hutchinson, and G. S. Carlson. "Traffic Control Decisions and Self-Testing Values: A Preliminary Note," *Traffic Engineering* 42 (1972), 42–48.

—— and F. Koenig. "Focused and Distributed Status Affinity," *The Sociological Quarterly* 9 (1968), 150–57.

——, ——, and R. B. Stark. "Judged Display: A Consideration of a Craft Show," *Journal of Leisure Research* 1 (1969), 163–79.

——, R. M. Kozelka, and M. J. Arth. "Some Highway Culture Patterns," *The Plains Anthropologist* 8 (1956), 3–14.

——, ——, M. L. Kiehl, and T. M. Newman. "The Small Highway Business on U.S. 30 in Nebraska," *Economic Geography* 32 (1956), 139–52.

——, Q. S. Meeker, and J. C. Aller. "Action Styles and Management Game Performance: An Exploratory Consideration," *Naval War College Review* 24 (1972), 65–81.

—— and C. Ridgeway. "Musical Involvement and Talking," *Anthropological Linguistics* 11 (1969), 223–46.

—— and B. Sutton-Smith. "Child Training and Game Involvement," *Ethnology* 1 (1962), 166–85.

—— and —— "Cross-Cultural Correlates of Games of Chance," *Behavior Science Notes* 1 (1966), 131–44.

——, ——, and A. Kendon. "Strategy in Games and Folk Tales," *Journal of Social Psychology* 60 (1963), 15–30.

——, W. Thompson, and B. Sutton-Smith. "Expressive Self-Testing in Driving," *Human Organization* 25 (1966), 54–63.

—— and J. O. Wicke. "Flying and Expressive Self-Testing," *Naval War College Review* 23 (1971), 30–41.

Sutton-Smith, B., and J. M. Roberts. "The Cross-Cultural and Psychological Study of Games," in *The Cross-Cultural Analysis of Sports and Games*, G. Luschen, ed. Champaign, Ill., 1970. Pp. 100–8.

—— and —— "Rubric of Competitive Behavior," *Journal of Genetic Psychology* 105 (1964), 13–37.

—— and —— "Studies of an Elementary Game of Strategy," *Genetic Psychology Monograph* 75 (1967), 3–42.

——, ——, and R. M. Kozelka. "Game Involvement in Adults," *Journal of Social Psychology* 60 (1963), 15–30.

——, ——, and B. G. Rosenberg. "Sibling Associations and Role Involvements," *Merill-Palmer Quarterly* 10 (1964), 25–38.

Tuden, A., and K. Marshall. "Political Organization: Cross-Cultural Codes 4," *Ethnology* 11 (1972), 463–64.

ETHNOGRAPHIC   SOURCES

1. Nama Hottentot of the Gei/Khauan tribe (27°30′S, 17°E) in 1860. Kolb, Peter. *The Present State of the Cape of Good Hope. 1968.* Laidler, P. W.

Magic Medicine of the Hottentots. 1928. Schapera, I. *The Khoisan Peoples.* London, 1930.

2. Kung Bushmen of the Nyae Nyae region (19°50'S, 20°35'E) in 1950. Marshall, L. "!Kung Bushmen Bands," *Africa* 30 (1960), 325–55. —— "Marriage Among !Kung Bushmen," *Africa* 29 (1959), 335–64. —— "Sharing, Talking and Giving," *Africa* 31 (1961), 231–49.

3. Thonga of the Ronga subtribe (25°50'S, 32°20'E) in 1895. Junod, H. A. *The Life of a South African Tribe.* 2d ed., 2 vols. London, 1927.

4. Lozi (14° to 18°S, 22° to 25°E) in 1900. Gluckman, M. *Essays on Lozi Land and Royal Property.* Rhodes-Livingstone Papers, no. 10. 1943. —— "The Lozi of Barotseland," in *Seven Tribes of British Central Africa,* E. Colson and M. Gluckman, eds. London, 1951. Pp. 1–93. Turner, V. W. *The Lozi People of Northwestern Rhodesia.* 1952.

5. Mbundu of the Bailundo subtribe (12°15'S, 16°30'E) in 1890. Childs, G. M. *Umbundu Kinship and Character.* London, 1949. McCulloch, M. *The Ovimbundu of Angola.* 1952.

6. Suku of Feshi Territory (6°S, 18°E) in 1920. Kopytoff, I. "Family and Lineage among the Suku," in *The Family Estate in Africa,* R. F. Gray and P. H. Gulliver, eds. Boston, 1964. Pp. 83–116. II "The Suku of Southwestern Congo," in *Problems of Africa,* J. L. Gibbs, Jr., ed. New York, 1965. Pp. 441–77. Van de Ginste, F. "Le Mariage chez les Basuku," *Bulletin des Jurisdictions Indigènes et du Droit Coutumier Congolais,* nos. 1–2 (1947).

7. Bemba of Zambia (9° to 12°S, 29° to 32°E) in 1897. Delhaise, C. "Chez les Wabemba," *Bulletin de la Société Royale Belge de Geographie* 32 (1908), 173–227, 261–83. Richards, A. I. *Bemba Marriage and Present Economic Conditions.* Rhodes-Livingstone Papers, no. 4. 1940. —— *Land, Labour and Diet in Northern Rhodesia.* Oxford, 1939.

8. Nyakyusa near Mwaya and Masoko (9°30'S, 34°E) in 1934. Wilson, M. *Good Company.* London, 1951. —— Personal communication, 1972.

9. Hadza (3°20' to 4°10'S, 34°' to 35°25'E) in 1930. Bagshawe, F. J. "The People of Happy Valley," *Journal of the (Royal) African Society* 24 (1925), 117–30. Woodburn, J. "An Introduction to Hadza Ecology," in *Man the Hunter,* R. B. Lee and I. DeVore, eds. Chicago, 1968. Pp. 49–55. —— "The Social Organization of the Hadza of North Tanzania." Ph.D. dissertation, Cambridge University, 1964.

10. Luguru around Morogoro (6°50'S, 37°40'E) in 1925. Beidelman, T. O. *The Matrilineal Peoples of Eastern Tanzania.* London, 1967. Young, R., and H. Fosbrooke. *Land and Politics among the Luguru of Tanganyika.* London, 1960.

11. Kikuyu of the Fort Hall or Metume district (0°40'S, 37°10'E) in 1920. Leakey, L. S. B. *Mau Mau and the Kikuyu.* London, 1952.

12. Ganda of the Kyaddondo district (0°20'N, 32°30'E) in 1875. Fallers, M. C. *The Eastern Lacustrine Bantu.* London, 1960. Kagwa, A. *The Customs of the Baganda.* New York, 1934. Mair, L. P. *An African People in the Twentieth Century.* London, 1934. Murdock, G. P. *Our Primitive Contemporaries.* New York, 1934. Pp. 508–50.

13. Mbuti Pygmies of the Epulu group (1°30' to 2°N, 28°20'E) in 1950. Putnam, P. "The Pygmies of the Ituri Forest," in *A Reader in General Anthropology,* C. S. Coon, ed. New York, 1948. Pp. 322–42. Turnbull, C. N. *Wayward Servants.* New York, 1965. —— *The Forest People.* New York, 1961.

14. Nkundo Mongo of the Ilanga group (0°15′ to 1°15′S, 18°35′ to 19°45′E) in 1930. Gutersohn, T. 1920. "Het economisch leven van den Mongo-neger," *Congo* 1, pt. i (1920), 92–105. Brussels. Hulstaert, G. *Le Mariage des Nkundó.* Mémoires de l'Institut Royal Colonial Belge, no. 8. Brussels, 1938. Pp. 1–520.

15. Banen of the Ndiki subtribe (4′35′ to 4°45′N, 10°35′ to 11°E) in 1935. Dugast, I. *Monographie de la tribu des Ndiki.* Travaux et Mémoires de l'Institut d'Ethnologie, no. 58, pt. ii, Paris, 1959. Pp. 1–635. McCulloch, M., M. Littlewood, and I. Dugast. *Peoples of the Central Cameroons.* London, 1954.

16. Tiv of Benue Province (6°30′ to 8°N, 8° to 10°E) in 1920. Abraham, R. C. *The Tiv People.* London, 1940. Bohannan, P., and L. Bohannan. *The Tiv of Central Nigeria.* London, 1953. East, R., ed. *Akiga's Story.* London, 1939.

17. Ibo of the Isu-Ama division (5°20′ to 5°40′N, 7°10′ to 7°30′E) in 1935. Green, M. M. *Ibo Village Affairs.* London, 1947. Leith-Ross, S. *African Women: A Study of the Ibo of Nigeria.* New York, 1939. Uchendu, V. C. *The Igbo of Southeast Nigeria.* New York, 1965.

18. Fon of the city and environs of Abomey (7°12′N, 1°56′E) in 1890. Herskovits, M. J. *Dahomey.* 2 vols. New York, 1938. Le Herissé, A. *L'ancien royaume du Dahomey.* Paris, 1911.

19. Ashanti of Kumasi state (6° to 8°N, 0° to 3°W) in 1895. Fortes, M. "Kinship and Marriage among the Ashanti," in *African Systems of Kinship and Marriage,* A. R. Radcliffe-Brown and D. Forde, eds. 1950. Pp. 252–84. Rattray, R. S. *Ashanti Law and Constitution.* Oxford, 1929. —— *Ashanti Proverbs.* Oxford, 1916. —— *Religion and Art in Ashanti.* Oxford, 1927.

20. Mende near the town of Bo (7°50′N, 12°W) in 1945. Little, K. L. *The Mende of Sierra Leone.* London, 1951. McCulloch, M. *The Peoples of Sierra Leone Protectorate.* London, 1950.

21. Wolof of Upper and Lower Salum in the Gambia (13°45′N, 15°20′W) in 1950. Ames, D. W. "Plural Marriage among the Wolof in the Gambia." Ph.D. dissertation, Northwestern University, 1953. Gamble, D. P. *The Wolof of Senegambia.* London, 1957. Gorer, G. *African Dances.* London, 1935.

22. Bambara between Segou and Bamako (12°30′N, 6°8′W) in 1902. Dieterlen, G. *Essai sur la religion Bambara.* Paris, 1951. Henry, J. 1910. *L'âme d'un peule africain: Les Bambara. Bibliothèque Anthropos* 1, pt ii. 1910. Pp. 1–240. Monteil, C. *Les Bambara du Ségou et du Kaarta.* Paris, 1924. Ortoli, J. *Coutume bambara (Cercle de Bamako).* Bougouni, 1935.

23 Tallensi (10°30′ to 10°45′N, 0°30′ to 0°40′W) in 1934. Fortes, M. *Social and Psychological Aspects of Education in Taleland.* Supplement to *Africa* 9, no. 4. London, 1938. —— *The Web of Kinship among the Tallensi.* London, 1949. Manoukian, M. *Tribes of the Northern Territories of the Gold Coast.* London, 1952.

24. Songhai of the Bamba division (16° to 17°15′N, 0°10′E to 3°10′W) in 1940. Miner, H. *The Primitive City of Timbuctoo.* Princeton, 1965. Rouch, J. *Les Songhay.* Paris, 1954.

25. Wodaabe Fulani of Niger (13° to 17°N, 5° to 10°E) in 1951. Dupire, M. *Peuples nomades.* Travaux et Mémoires de l'Institut d'Ethnologie, no. 64. 1962. Pp. 1–327. —— "The Position of Women in a Pastoral Society (Wodaabe)," in *Women of Tropical Africa,* D. Paulme, ed. Berkeley and Los Angeles, 1963. Pp. 45–92.

26. Hausa of Zaria or Zazzau (9°30′ to 11°30′N, 6° to 9°E) in 1900. Dry, E. "The Social Development of the Hausa Child," in *Proceedings of the International West African Conference* (held at Ibadan, 1949). 1956. Pp. 164–70. Greenberg, J. H. *The Influence of Islam on a Sudanese Religion.* Monographs of the American Ethnological Society, no. 10. 1946. Pp. 1–73. Olofson, Harold. Personal correspondence, 1972. Smith, M. F. *Baba of Karo: A Woman of the Muslim Hausa.* London, 1954. Smith, M. G. 1965. "The Hausa of Northern Nigeria," in *Peoples of Africa,* J. L. Gibbs, ed. New York, 1965. Pp. 119–55.

27. Massa of Cameroon (10° to 11°N, 15° to 16°E) in 1910. Garine, I.de. *Les Massa du Cameroun.* Paris, 1964. Hagen, G. von "Die Bana," *Baessler-Archiv* 2 (1912), 77–116.

28. Azande of the Yambio chiefdom (4°20′ to 5°50′N, 27°40′ to 28°50′E) in 1905. Evans-Pritchard, E. E. *Witchcraft, Oracles and Magic among the Azande.* Oxford, 1937. Lagae, C. R. *Les Azande ou Niam-Niam. Bibliotheque-Congo* 18 (1926), 1–224.

29. Fur around Jebel Marra (13°30′N, 25°30′E) in 1880. Beaton, A. C. "The Fur," *Sudan Notes and Records* 29 (1948), 1–39. Felkin, R. W. 1885. "Notes on the Fur Tribe," *Proceedings of the Royal Society of Edinburgh* 13 (1885), 205–65.

30. Otoro of the Nuba Hills (11°20′N, 30°40′E) in 1930. Nadel, S. F. *The Nuba.* London, 1947.

31. Shilluk (9° to 10°30′N, 31° to 32°E) in 1910. Oyler, D. S. "The Shilluk's Belief in the Evil Eye, the Evil Medicine Man," *Sudan Notes and Records* 2 (1919), 122–37.

32. Northern Mao (9° to 9°35′N, 34°30′ to 34°50′E) in 1939. Grottanelli, V. L. *I Mao. Missione Etnografica nel Uollaga Occidentale.* Rome, 1940. Vol. 1, pp. 1–387.

33. Kaffa (6°50′ to 7°45′N, 35°30′ to 37°E) in 1905. Bieber, F. J. *Kaffa.* 2 vols. Münster, 1920–23.

34. Masai of Tanzania (1°30′ to 5°30′S, 35° to 37°30′E) in 1900. Merker, M. *Die Masai.* Berlin, 1904.

35. Konso of the vicinity of Busc (5°15′N, 37°30′E) in 1935. Hallpike, C. R. "The Konso of Ethiopia." MS. 1969. Jensen, A. E. *Im Lande des Gada.* Stuttgart, 1936.

36. Somali of the Dolbahanta subtribe (7° to 11°N, 45°30′ to 49°E) in 1900. Puccioni, N. *Antropologia e etnographia delle genti della Somalia.* Bologna, 1936. Vol. 3, pp. 1–140. Trimingham, J. Spencer. *Islam in Ethiopia.* New York, 1965.

37. Amhara of the Gondar district (11° to 14°N, 36° to 38°30′E) in 1953. Messing, S. D. "The Highland-Plateau Amhara of Ethiopia." Ph.D. dissertation, University of Pennsylvania, 1957.

38. Bogo or Belen (15°45′N, 38°45′E) in 1855. Munzinger, W. *Ueber die Sitten und das Recht der Bogos.* Winterthur, 1859.

39. Kenuzi Nubians (22° to 24°N, 32° to 33°E) in 1900. Callender, C. and Fadwa El Guindi. *Life-Crisis Rituals among the Kenuz.* Cleveland, 1971.

40. Teda nomads of Tibesti (19° to 22°N, 16° to 19°E) in 1950. Chapelle, J. *Nomades noirs du Sahara.* Paris, 1957. Cline, W. *The Teda of Tibesti, Borku and Kawar.* General Series in Anthropology, no. 12. 1950. Pp. 1–52. Nachtigal, G. *Sahara und Sudan.* Berlin, 1879. Vol. 1, pp. 377–464.

41. Tuareg of Ahaggar (21° to 25°N, 4° to 9°E) in 1900. Holiday, G. *The Tuareg of Ahaggar*. Roodeport, South Africa, 1956. Nicolaisen, J. *Ecology and Culture of the Pastoral Tuareg*. Nationalmuseets Skrifter, Etnografisk Raeke, vol. 9. Copenhagen, 1963. Pp. 1–540.

42. Riffians of northern Morocco (34°20' to 35°30'N, 2°30' to 4°W) in 1926. Coon, C. S. *Tribes of the Rif*. Harvard African Studies, no. 9. 1931. Pp. 1–417. Westermarck, E. *Ritual and Belief in Morocco*. 2 vols. London, 1926.

43. Egyptians of the town and evirons of Silwa (24°45'N, 33°E) in 1950. Ammar, H. 1954. *Growing Up in an Egyptian Village*. London, 1954. Harris, George L. *Egypt*. Country Survey Series. New Haven, 1957.

44. Hebrews of the kingdom of Judah (30°30' to 31°55'N, 34°20' to 35°30'E) in 621 B.C. Dalman, G. *Arbeit und Sitte in Palestina*. 7 vols. Gutersloh, 1932. DeVaux, R. *Ancient Israel*. New York, 1961. Patai, R. *Sex and Family in the Bible and the Middle East*. Garden City, 1959.

45. Babylonians of the city and environs of Babylon (32°35'N, 44°45'E) in 1750 B.C. Coutenau, G. *Everyday Life in Babylon and Assyria*. New York, 1954. Saggs, H. W. F. *Everyday Life in Babylonia and Assyria*. New York, 1965.

46. Rwala Bedouin (31° to 35°30'N, 36°41'E) in 1913. Musil, A. *The Manners and Customs of the Rwala Bedouins*. New York, 1928.

47. Turks of the Anatolian plateau (38°40' to 40°N, 32°40' to 35°50'E) in 1950. Pierce, J. E. *Life in a Turkish Village*. New York, 1964.

48. Gheg Albanians (41°30' to 42°40'N, 19°30' to 20°30'E) in 1910. Durham, M. E. *High Albania*. London, 1909. Pisko, J. E. "Gebräuche bei der Geburt und Behandlung der Neugeborenen bei den Albanesen," *Mitteilungen der Anthropolischen Gesellschaft zu Wien* 26 (1896), 141–46.

49. Romans of the city and evirons of Rome (41°50'N, 13°30'E) in A.D. 110. Balsdon, J.P.V.D. *Life and Leisure in Ancient Rome*. New York, 1969. Granger, Frank. *The Worship of the Romans*. London, 1895. Paoli, Ugo Enrico. *Rome: Its People, Life and Customs*. Florence, 1958.

50. Basques of Vera de Bidasoa (43°12' to 43°20'N, 1°35' to 1°45'W) in 1940. Gallop, Rodney. *A Book of the Basques*. Reno, Nevada, 1970.

51. Irish of Kinvarra parish (53°5'N, 9°W) in 1955. Arensberg, C. M. *The Irish Countryman*. London, 1937. Browne, Charles R. "The Ethnography of Inishbofin and Inishshark, County Galway," in *Royal Irish Academy Proceedings*, 3d. ser. (1961) 317–70. Dublin.

52. Lapps of Könkämä district (68°20' to 69°5'N, 20°5' to 23°E) in 1950. Scheffer, John. *The History of Lapland*. London, 1704. Turi, J. *Turi's Book of Lapland*. New York, 1931.

53. Yurak Samoyed (65° to 71°N, 41° to 62°E) in 1894. Donner, K. *Among the Samoyed in Siberia*. New Haven, 1954.

54. Russians of the peasant village of Viriatino (52°40'N, 41°20'E) in 1955. Benet, Sula. *The Village of Viriatino*. New York, 1970. Fitzsimmons, T., ed. *RSFSR*. 2 vols. New Haven, 1957.

55. Abkhaz (42°50' to 43°25'N, 40° to 41°35'E) in 1880. Janashia, N. S. "The Religious Beliefs of the Abkhasians," *Georgica* 1 (1937): 117–53. Leningrad.

56. Armenians in the vicinity of Erevan (40°N, 44°30'E) in 1843. Elliott, Mabel E. (M.D.) *Beginning again at Arat*. New York, n.d.

57. Kurd in and near the town of Rowanduz (36°30'N, 44°30'E) in 1951. Masters, W. M. "Rowanduz." Ph.D. dissertation, University of Michigan, 1953.

58. Basseri of the nomadic branch (27° to 31°N, 53° to 54°E) in 1958. Barth, F. K. *Nomads of South Persia*. London, 1961.
59. West Punjabi of the village of Mohla (32°30'N, 74°E) in 1950. Eglar, Z. S. *A Punjabi Village in Pakistan*. New York, 1960. Honigmann, J. J. "Women in West Pakistan," in *Pakistan: Society and Culture*, S. Maron, ed. New Haven, 1957. Pp. 154–76.
60. Gond of the Hill Maria division (19°15' to 20°N, 80°30' to 81°20'E) in 1930. Grigson, W. V. *The Maria Gonds of Bastar*. London, 1938.
61. Toda of the Nilgiri Hills (11° to 12°N, 76° to 77°E) in 1900. Murdock, G. P. *Our Primitive Contemporaries*. New York, 1934. Rivers, W. H. R. *The Todas*. London, 1906.
62. Santal of Bankura and Birbhum districts (23° to 24°N, 86°50' to 87°30'E) in 1940. Mukherjea, C. L. *The Santals*. Calcutta, 1943. Orans, M. *The Santal*. Detroit, 1965.
63. Uttar Pradesh in and near Senapur village (25°55'N, 83°E) in 1945. Marriott, M. *Caste Ranking and Community Structure in Five Regions of India and Pakistan*. Poona, 1960. Wiser, Charlotte and William. *Behind Mud Walls*. New York, 1930.
64. Burusho of Hunza State (36°20' to 36°30'N, 74°30' to 74°40'E) in 1934. Lorimer, D.L.R. (Lt. Col.) *The Burushaski Language*. Oslo, n.d.
65. Kazak of the Great Horde (37° to 48°N, 68° to 81°E) in 1885. Krader, L. and I. Wayne. *The Kazakhs*. Washington, D.C., 1955.
66. Khalka Mongols of Narobanchin territory (47° to 47°20'N, 95°10' to 97°E) in 1920. Ballis, W. B., ed. *Mongolian People's Republic*. 3 vols. New Haven, 1956. Vreeland, H. H. *Mongol Community and Kinship Structure*. New Haven, 1954.
67. Lolo of Taliang Shan mountains (26° to 29°N, 103° to 104°E) in 1910. Lin, Y. H. *The Lolo of Liang Shan*. Shanghai, 1961. D'Ollone, H. M. *In Forbidden China*. Boston, 1912.
68. Lepcha of Lingthem and vicinity (27° to 28°N, 89°E) in 1937. Das, A. K. and S. K. Banerjee. *The Lepchas of Darjeeling District*. Calcutta, 1962. Gorer, G. *Himalayan Village*. London, 1938. Morris, J. *Living with the Lepchas*. London, 138.
69. Garo of Rengsanggri and neighboring villages (26°N, 91°E) in 1955. Burling, R. *Rensanggri*. Philadelphia, 1963.
70. Lakher (22°20'N, 93°E) in 1930. Parry, N. E. *The Lakhers*. London, 1932.
71. Burmese of Nondwin village (22°N, 95°40'E) in 1960. Brant, C. S., and M. M. Khaing. "Burmese Kinship and the Life Cycle: An Outline," *Southwestern Journal of Anthropology* 7 (1951), 437–54. Marshall, L. L. *The Karen People of Burma*. Columbus, Ohio, 1929. Nash, M. *The The Golden Road to Modernity*. New York, 1965.
72. Lamet of northwestern Laos (20°N, 100°40'E) in 1940. Izikowitz, K. G. *Lamet*. Etnologiska Studier, no. 17. Göteborg, 1951. Pp. 1–375.
73. North Vietnamese of the Red River delta (20° to 21°N, 105°30' to 107°E) in 1930. Langrand, G. *Vie sociale et religieuse en annam*. Lille, 1945.
74. Rhade of the village of Ko-sier (13°N, 108°E) in 1962. Sabatier, L. *Recueil des coutumes rhadées du Darlac*. Hanoi, 1940.
75. Khmer of Angkor (13°30'N and 103°50'E) in 1292. Porée, G., and E. Maspero. *Moeurs et coutumes des Khmers*. Paris, 1938.

76. Thai of the village of Bang Chan (14°N, 100°52'E) in 1955. Hanks, J. R. *Maternity and Its Rituals in Bang Chan*. Ithaca, N.Y., 1963. Phillips, H. P. *Thai Peasant Personality*. Berkeley, 1965. Sharp, L., and L. M. Hanks. "Bang Chan: The Social History of a Thai Village. "MS., n.d. Sharp, R. L., H. M. Hauck, K. Janlekha, and R. B. Textor. *Siamese Village*. Bangkok, 1954.

77. Semang of the Jahai subtribe (4°30' to 5°30'N, 101° to 101°30'E) in 1925. Schebesta, P. *Among the Forest Dwarfs of Malaya*. London, 1927. —— *Die Negrito Asiens*. Studia Instituti Anthropos. Mödling bei Wien, 1952–57. Vol. 6, pt. i; vol. 12, pt. ii; vol. 13, pt. ii.

78. Nicobarese of the northern islands (8°15' to 9°15'N, 92°40' to 93°E) in 1870. Man, E. H. *The Nicobar Islands and Their People*. Guilford, Surrey, 1932.

79. Andamanese of the Aka Bea tribe (11°45' to 12°N, 93° to 93°10'E) in 1860. Man, E. H. *On the Aboriginal Inhabitants of the Andaman Islands*. London, 1932. Radcliffe-Brown, A. R. *The Andaman Islanders*. Cambridge, 1922.

80. Forest Vedda (7°30' to 8°N, 81° to 81°30'E) in 1860. Seligmann, C. G. and B. Z. Seligmann. *The Veddas*. Cambridge, 1911.

81. Tanala of the Menabe subtribe (20°S, 48°E) in 1925. Linton, R. *The Tanala*. Field Museum of Natural History Anthropological Series, no. 22. 1933. Pp. 1–334. Ruud, J. *Taboo*. Oslo, n.d.

82. Negri Sembilan of Inas district (2°30' to 2°40'N, 102°10' to 102°20'E) in 1958. Gullick, J. M. *Indigenous Political Systems of Western Malaya*. London, 1958. Lewis, D. K. "Inas: A Study of Local History," *Journal of the Malayan Branch, Royal Asiatic Society* 33, no. 1 (1960), 65–94. —— "The Minangkabau Malay of Negri Simbilan." Ph.D. dissertation, Cornell University, 1962. Parr, C.W.C. and W. H. Macray. 1910. *Rembau. Journal of the Straits Branch, Royal Asiatic Society* 56 (1910), 1–157. Taylor, E. N. 1948. "Aspects of Customary Inheritance in Negri Sembilan," *Journal of the Malayan Branch, Royal Asiatic Society* 21, no. 2 (1948), 41–56, 115–30.

83. Javanese in the vicinity of Pare (7°43'S, 112°13'E) in 1955. Geertz, C. *The Religion of Java*. Chicago, 1960. Jay, R. R. *Religion and Politics in Rural Central Java*. New Haven, 1963.

84. Balinese of the village of Tihingan (8°30'S, 115°20'E) in 1958. Belo, J. *Traditional Balinese Culture*. New York, 1970. Covarrubias, M. *The Island of Bali*. New York, 1937.

85. Iban of the Ulu Ai group (2°N, 112°30' to 113°30'E) in 1950. Gomes, E. H. *Seventeen Years among the Sea Dyaks of Borneo*. London, 1911. Roth, H. L., ed. "The Natives of Borneo," *Journal of the Royal Anthropological Institute* 21 (1892), 110–37.

86. Badjau of Tawi-Tawi and adjacent islands (5°N, 120°E) in 1863. Nimmo, H. A. "Social Organization of the Tawi-Tawi Badjaw," *Ethnology* 4 (1965), 421–39. —— "The Structure of Badjau Society." Ph.D. Dissertation, University of Hawaii, 1969.

87. Toradja of the Bare'e subgroup (2°S, 121°E) in 1910. Adriani, N., and A. C. Kruijt. *De Bare'e-sprekende Toradja's*. 3 vols. Batavia, 1912.

88. Toberlorese of Tobelo district (1°N, 128°30'E) in 1900. Hueting, A. "De Tobeloreezen in hun denken en doen." *Bijdragen tot de Taal-, Land en Volkenkunde* 77 (1921), 217–385; 78 (1921), 137–342.

89. Alorese of Atimelang (8°20'S, 124°40 E) in 1938. DuBois, C. "The Alorese,"

in *The Psychological Frontiers of Society,* A. Kardiner, ed. New York, 1945. Pp. 101–45. —— *The People of Alor.* Minneapolis, 1944.

90. Tiwi (11° to 11°45'S, 130° to 132°E) in 1929. Barclay, A. "Life at Bathhurst Island Mission," *Walkabout* (1939). Goodale, J. C. "The Tiwi Women of Melville Island." Ph.D. dissertation, University of Pennsylvania, 1959. Harney, W. E., and A. P. Elkin. "Melville and Bathhurst Islanders," *Oceania* 8 (1943), 228–34.

91. Aranda of Alice Springs (23°30' to 25°S, 132°30' to 134°20'E) in 1896. Spencer, B., and F. J. Gillen. *The Arunta.* 2 vols. London, 1927.

92. Orokaiva of the Aiga subtribe (8°20' to 8°40'S, 147°50' to 148°10'E) in 1925. Williams, F. E. *Orokaiva Society.* London, 1930.

93. Kimam of the village of Bamol (7°30'S, 38°30'E) in 1960. Serpenti, L. M. *Cultivators in the Swamps.* Assen, 1965.

94. Kapauku of Botukebo village (4°S, 36°E) in 1955. Pospisil, L. *Kapauku Papuans and Their Law.* Yale University Publications in Anthropology, no. 54. 1958. Pp. 1–296.

95. Kwoma of the Hongwam subtribe (4°10'S, 142°40'E) in 1937. Whiting, J. W. M. *Becoming a Kwoma.* New Haven, 1941. —— and S. W. Reed. "Kwoma Culture," *Oceania* 9 (1938), 170–216.

96. Manus of Peri village (2°10'S, 147°10'E) in 1929. Mead, M. *Growing Up in New Guinea.* New York, 1930. —— *New Lives for Old.* New York, 1969.

97. New Islanders of Lesu village (2°30'S, 151°E) in 1930. Powdermaker H. *Life in Lesu.* New York, 1933.

98. Trobrianders of Kiriwina island (8°38'S, 151°4'E) in 1914. Malinowski, B. *Coral Gardens and Their Magic.* 2 vols. New York, 1935. —— *Sex and Repression in Savage Society.* London, 1927. —— *The Sexual Life of Savages in Northwestern Melanesia.* 2 vols. New York, 1929.

99. Siuai of the northeastern group (7°S, 155°20'E) in 1939. Oliver, D. L. *A Solomon Island Society.* Cambridge, Mass. 1955.

100. Tikopia (12°30'S, 168°30'E) in 1930. Firth, R. *We the Tikopia.* London, 1936. Rivers, W. H. "Tikopia," in *The History of Melanesian Society.* Cambridge, 1914.

101. Pentecost Islanders of Bunlap village (16°S, 168°E) in 1953. Lane, R. B. "The Malanesians of South Pentecost," in *Gods, Ghosts and Men in Melanesia,* P. Lawrence and M. G. Meggitt, eds. London, 1965. Pp. 250–79.

102. Fijians of Mbau island (18°S, 178°35'E) in 1840. Hocart, A. M. *The Northern States of Fiji.* Royal Anthropological Institute of Great Britain and Ireland Occasional Papers, no. 11. 1952. Toganivalu, D. *The Customs of Bau before the Advent of Christianity.* Transactions of the Fijian Society. 1911. Williams, T. *Fiji and the Fijians.* Rev. ed. London, 1884.

103. Ajie of Neje chiefdom (21°20'S, 165°40'E) in 1845. Guiart, J. *Structure de la Chefferie en Mélanésie du Sud.* Travaux et Mémoires de l'Institut e'Ethnologie, no. 66. Paris, 1963. Pp. 1–688. Leenhardt, M. *Notes d'ethnologie néo-calédonienne.* Travaux et Memoires de l'Institut d'Ethnologie, no. 8. Paris, 1930. Pp. 1–340.

104. Maori of the Nga Puhi tribe (35°10' to 35°30'S, 174° to 174°20'E) in 1820. Beaglehole, E., and P. Beaglehole. *Some Modern Maoris.* Christchurch, 1946. Best, E. *The Maori.* 2 vols. Wellington, 1924. Buck, P. *The Coming of the*

Maori. Wellington, 1949. Shortland, E. *Traditions and Superstitions of the New Zealanders.* London, 1856.

105. Marquesans of southwest Nuku Hiva (8°55'S, 140° to 10'W) in 1800. La Barre, R. W. "Marquesan Culture." MS. 1934. Linton, R. "Marquesan Culture," in *The Individual and His Society,* A. Kardiner, ed. New York, 1939. Pp. 138–96.

106. Samoans of western Upolu (13°48' to 14°S, 172°W) in 1829. Keesing, F. M. *Modern Samoa: Its Government and Changing Life.* London, 1934. Mead, M. *Social Organization of Manua. B. P. Bishop Museum Bulletin* 76 (1969). Murdock, G. P. "The Samoans," in *Our Primitive Contemporaries. New York, 1934. Pp. 48–84.* Turner, G. *Samoa.* London, 1884.

107. Gilbertese of Makin island (3°30'N, 172°20'E) in 1890. Finsch, O. *Ethnologische Erfahrungen und Belegstücke aus der Südsee* 3 (1893) 19–89. Vienna. Lambert, B. "Fosterage in the Northern Gilbert Islands," *Ethnology* 3 (1964), 232–58. —— *The Gilbert Islands: and Tenure in the South Pacific.* London, n.d. Lundsgaarde, H. P. *Social Changes in the Southern Gilbert Islands.* Eugene, Oregon, 1966.

108. Marshallese of Jaluit atoll (6N, 169°15'E) in 1900. Krämer, A., and H. Nevermann. *Ralik-Ratak. Ergebnisse der Südsee-Expedition 1908–1910,* G. Thilenius, ed. Hamburg, 1938. Vol. 2, pt. xi, pp. 1–438. Spoehr, A. *Majuro: A Village in the Marshall Islands. Fieldiana: Anthropology* 39 (1949) 1–266.

109. Trukese of Romonum island (7°24'N, 151°40'E) in 1947. Gladwin, T., and S. B. Sarason. *Truk: Man in Paradise.* Viking Fund Publications in Anthropology, no. 20. 1953. Pp. 1–655. Goodenough, W. H. Personal communication, 1972. Krämer, A. *Truk. Ergebnisse der Südsee-Expedition 1908–1910,* G. Thilenius, ed. Hamburg, 1932. Vol. 2B, pt. v, pp. 1–452.

110. Yapese (9°30'N, 138°10'E) in 1910. Müller, W. *Yap. Ergebnisse der Südsee-Expedition 1908–1910,* G. Thilenius, ed. Hamburg, 1917. Vol. 26, pt. iii, pp. 1–380.

111. Palauans of Koror island (7°N, 134°30'E) in 1873. Barnett, H. G. *Being a Palauan.* New York, 1960. Semper, K. *Die Palau-Inseln im Stillen Ozean.* Leipzig, 1873.

112. Ifugao of the Kiangan group (16°50'N, 121°10'E) in 1910. Barton, R. F. *Ifugao Law. University of California Publications in American Archaeology and Ethnology* 15, no. 1 (1919), 1–186.

113. Atayal (23°50' to 24°50'N, 120°20' to 120°' E) in 1930. Mabuchi, T. 1960. *The Aboriginal Peoples of Formosa.* Viking Fund Publications in Anthropology, nd. 29. 1960. Pp. 127–40. Okada, Y. The Social Structure of the Atayal Tribe. MS. Unpublished translation from the Japanese, Tokyo, 1949. Ruey Yih-Fu. "Ethnographical Investigation of Some Aspects of the Atayal" *Bulletin,* Department of Archaeology and Anthropology, National Taiwan University 5 (1955) 113–27.

114. Chinese of Kaihsienkung village in north Chekiang (31°N, 120°5'E) in 1936. Fei, H. *Peasant Life in China.* New York, 1946. Fried, M. *Fabric of Chinese Society.* New York, 1953. Lang, O. *Chinese Family and Society.* New Haven, 1946.

115. Manchu of the Aigun district (50°N, 125°30'E) in 1915. Shirokogoroff, S. M.

Social Organization of the Manchus. Royal Asiatic Society, North China Branch, Extra Vol. 3. Shanghai, 1924. Pp. 1–196.

116. Koreans of Kanghwa island (37°37'N, 126°25'E) in 1950. Osgood, C. *The Koreans and Their Culture.* New York, 1951. Rutt, R. *Korean Works and Days.* Rutland, 1964.

117. Japanese of southern Okayama prefecture (34°30' to 35°N, 133°40'E) in 1950. Beardsley, R. K., J. W. Hall, and R. E. Ward. 1959. *Village Japan.* Chicago, 1959. Cornell, J. B., and R. J. Smith. *Two Japanese Villages.* Ann Arbor, 1956. DeVos. G. *Social Values and Personal Attitudes in Primary Human Relations in Niiike.* University of Michigan Center for Japanese Studies, Occasional Papers. 1965.

118. Ainu of the Tokapchi and Saru basins (42°40' to 43°N, 142° to 144°E) in 1880. Batchelor, J. *Ainu Life and Lore.* Tokyo, 1927. Hilger, M. I. *Together with the Ainu.* Norman, Okla., 1971. Munro, N. G. *Ainu Creed and Cult,* B. Z. Seligmann, ed. New York, 1962.

119. Gilyak (53° to 54°30'N, 139° to 143°10'E) in 1880. Seeland, N. "Die Ghiliaken," *Russiche Revue* 21 (1882), 97–130, 222–54. Shternberg, L. *Semya i rod u narodov severovostochnoi Azii.* Leningrad, 1933.

120. Yukaghir of the upper Kolyma River (63°30' to 66°N, 150° to 157°E) in 1900. Jochelson, W. *The Yukaghir and Yukaghirized Tungus.* Memoirs of the American Museum of Natural History, no. 13. 1926. Pp. 1–469.

121. Chukchee of the Reindeer group (63° to 70°N, 171°E to 171°W) in 1900. Bogoras, W. *The Chukchee.* Memoirs of the American Museum of Natural History, no. 11. 1904–9. Pp. 1–703. Sverdrup, H. U. *Hos tendrafolket.* Oslo, 1938.

122. Ingalik of Shageluk village (62°30'N, 159°30'W) in 1885. Osgood, C. *Ingalik Material Culture.* Yale University Publications in Anthropology, no. 22. 1940. Pp. 1–500. ——— *Ingalik Social Culture.* Yale University Publications in Anthropology, no. 55. 1958. Pp. 1–289.

123. Aleut of the Unalaska branch (53° to 57°30'N, 158° to 170°W) in 1778. Bank, II, Th.P. 1953. "Botanical and ethnobotanical studies in the Aleutian Islands. II. Health and medical lore of the Aleuts," Michigan Academy of Science, Arts, and Letters, *Papers* 38 (1953) 415–32. Elliott, H. W. *Our Arctic Province.* New York, 1886. Veniaminov, I.E.P. *Zapiski ob ostrovakh unalashkinskago otdela.* St. Petersburg, 1840.

124. Copper Eskimo of the mainland (66°40' to 69°20'N, 108° to 117°W) in 1915. Jenness, D. *The Life of the Copper Eskimos. Report of the Canadian Arctic Expedition, 1913–18,* vol. 12. Ottawa, 1922. Pp. 5–227. Rasmussen, K. *Intellectual Culture of the Copper Eskimos. Report of the Fifth Thule Expedition,* vol. 9. Copenhagen, 1932. Pp. 1–350.

125. Montagnais of the Lake St. John and Mistassini bands (48° to 52°N, 73° to 75°W) in 1910. Burgesse, J. A. "The Woman and Child Among the Lac-St. Jean Montagnais," *Primitive Man* 17 (1944), 1–18. Lane, K. S. *The Montagnais Indians, 1600–1640.* Kroeber Anthropological Society Papers, no. 7. 1952. Pp. 1–62. Lips, J. E. "Naskapi Law," *Transactions of the American Philosophical Society,* n.s., 37 (1947), 379–492.

126. Micmac of the mainland (43°30' to 50°N, 60° to 66°W) in 1650. Johnson, F. "Notes on Micmac Shamanism," *Primitive Man* 16 (1943), 53–80. Le Clercq,

C. *New Relation of Gaspesia*. Publications of the Champlain Society, no. 5. Pp. 1–452. Parsons, E. C. "Micmac Notes," *Journal of American Folklore* 39 (1928), 460–85. Wallis, W. D., and R. S. Wallis. *The Micmac Indians of Eastern Canada*. Minneapolis, 1955.

127. Saulteaux of the Berens River, Little Grand Rapids, and Pekangekum bands (51°30' to 52°30'N, 94° to 97°W) in 1930. Dunning, R. W. *Social and Economic Change among the Northern Objibwa*. Toronto, 1959. Hallowell, A. Irving. *The Role of Conjuring in Saulteaux Society*. Philadelphia, 1942.

128. Slave in the vicinity of Fort Simpson (62°N, 122°W) in 1940. Helm, J. *The Lynx Point People*. *Bulletin of the National Museum of Canada* 176 (1961) 1–193. Honigmann, J. J. *Ethnography and Acculturation of the Fort Nelson Slave*. Yale University Publications in Anthropology, no. 33. 1946. Pp. 1–169.

129. Kaska of the upper Liard River (60°N, 131°W) in 1900. Honigmann, J. J. *Culture and Ethos of Kaska Society*. Yale University Publications in Anthropology, no. 40. 1949. Pp. 1–368. —— *The Kaska Indians*. Yale University Publications in Anthropology, no. 51. 1954. Pp. 1–163. Teit, J. A. "Field Notes on the Tahltan and Kaska Indians, 1912–1915," *Anthropologica* 3 (1956), 39–171.

130. Eyak (60° to 61°N, 144° to 146°W) in 1890. Birket-Smith, K., and F. de Laguna. *The Eyak Indians*. Copenhagen, 1938.

131. Haida of the village of Masset (54°N, 132°30'W) in 1875. Murdock, G. P. *Our Primitive Contemporaries*. New York, 1934. Pp. 221–63. Swanton, J. R. *Contributions to the Ethnology of the Haida*. Memoirs of the American Museum of Natural History, no. 8. 1909. Pp. 1–300.

132. Bellacoola (52°20'N, 126° to 127°W) in 1880. McIlwraith, T. F. *The Bella Coola Indians*. 2 vols. Toronto, 1948.

133. Twana (47°20' to 47°30' N, 123°10' to 123°20'W) in 1860. Eells, M. "Twana Indians of the Skokomish Reservation," *Bulletin of the United States Geological and Geographical Survey of the Territories* 3 (1877), 57–114. Elmendorf, W. W. *The Structure of Twana Culture*. Washington State University Research Studies, Monographic Supplement no. 2. 1960. Pp. 1–576.

134. Yurok (41°30'N, 124°W) in 1850. Erikson, E. H. "Observations on the Yurok: Childhood and World Image," *University of California Publications in American Archaeology and Ethnology* 25 (1943), 257–302. Kroeber, A. L. *Comparative Notes on the Structure of Yurok Culture*. Washington State University Research Studies, Monographic Supplement no. 2. 1960. —— *Handbook of the Indians of California*. Bulletins of the Bureau of American Ethnology 78 (1925), 1–97.

135. Eastern Pomo of Clear Lake (39°N, 123°W) in 1850. Freeland, L. S. "Pomo Doctors and Poisoners," *University of California Publications in American Archaeology and Ethnology* 20 (1923), 57–73. Gifford, E. W., and A. L. Kroeber. "Culture Element Distributions: IV, Pomo," *University of California Publications in American Archaeology and Ethnology* 37 (1937), 117–254. Loeb, E. M. "Pomo Folkways," *University of California Publications in American Archaeology and Ethnology* 19 (1926), 149–404.

136. Yokuts around Tulare Lake (35°10'N, 119°20'W) in 1850. Gayton, A. H. *Yokuts and Western Mono Ethnography*. *Anthropological Records* 10 (1948), 1–301. Latta, F. F. *Handbook of Yokuts Indians*. Oildale, 1949.

137. Wadadika Paute of Harney Valley (43° to 44°N, 118° to 120°W) in 1870. Park,

Willard Z. "Paviotso Shamanism," *American Anthropologist,* n.s. 36 (1934), 98–113. Whiting, B. B. *Paiute Sorcery.* Viking Fund Publications in Anthropology, no. 15. 1950. Pp. 1–110.

138. Klamath (42° to 43°15'N, 121°20' to 122°20'W) in 1860. Gatschet, A. S. *The Klamath Indians of Southwestern Oregon.* United States Geographical and Geological Survey of the Rocky Mountain Region, Contributions to North American Ethnology, no. 2. 2 vols. Washington, 1890. Spier, L. *Klamath Ethnography. University of California Publications in American Archaeology and Ethnology* 30 (1930), 1–328.

139. Kutenai of the Lower or eastern branch (48°40' to 49°10'N, 116°40'W) in 1890. Turney-High, H. H. *Ethnography of the Kutenai.* Memoirs of the American Anthropological Association, no. 56. 1941. Pp. 1–202.

140. Gros Ventre (47° to 49°N, 106° to 110°W) in 1880. Cooper, J. M. *The Gros Ventres of Montana: Religion and Ritual.* Catholic University of America Anthropological Series, no. 16. 1956. Pp. 1–491. Flannery, R. *The Gros Ventres of Montana.* Catholic University of America Anthropological Series, no. 15. 1953. Pp. 1–221.

141. Hidatsa of Hidatsa village (47°N, 101°W) in 1836. Bowers, A. W. Hidatsa Social and Ceremonial Organization. *Bulletins of the Bureau of American Ethnology* 194 (1965), 1–528. Curtis, E. S. *The North American Indian* 4 (1909), 129–72, 180–96. Matthews, W. *Ethnography and Philology of the Hidatsa Indians.* United States Geological and Geographical Survey, Miscellaneous Publication no. 7. 1877. Pp. 1–239.

142. Pawnee of the Skidi band (42°N, 100°W) in 1867. Dorsey, G. A. and J. R. Murie. *Notes on Skidi Pawnee Society,* A. Spoehr, ed. Field Museum of Natural History Anthropological Series, no. 27. 1940. Pp. 67–119. Linton, R. 1923. *Annual Ceremony of the Pawnee Medicine Man.* Field Museum of Natural History Anthropological Series, no. 8. 1923. Pp. 1–20.

143. Omaha (41°10' to 41°40'N, 96° to 97°W) in 1860. Fletcher, A. C., and F. LaFlesche. *The Omaha Tribe. Annual Reports of the Bureau of Ethnology* 27 (1911), 17–672. Mead, M. *The Changing Culture of an Indian Tribe.* Columbia University Contributions to Anthropology, no. 15. 1932. Pp. 1–313.

144. Huron of the Attignawantan and Attigneenongnahac tribes (44° to 45°N, 78° to 80°W) in 1634. Tooker, E. *An Ethnography of the Huron Indians. Bulletins of the Bureau of American Ethnology* 190 (1964), 1–183. Trigger, B. G. *The Huron.* New York, 1969.

145. Creek of the Upper Creek division (32°30' to 34°20'N, 85°30' to 86°30'W) in 1800. Swanton, J. R. *Religious Beliefs and Medical Practices of the Creek Indians. Annual Reports of the Bureau of American Ethnology* 42 (1928), 473–672.

146. Natchez (31°30'N, 91°25'W) in 1718. Swanton, J. R. *Indian Tribes of the Lower Mississippi Valley. Bulletins of the Bureau of American Ethnology* 43 (1911), 1–387.

147. Comanche (30° to 38°N, 98° to 103°W) in 1870. Linton, R. "The Comanche Sun Dance," *American Anthropologist* 37 (1935), 420–28. Wallace, E. and E. A. Hoebel. *The Comanches.* Norman, 1952.

148. Chiricahua Apache of the Central band (32°N, 109°30'W) in 1870. Opler, M. E. *An Apache Life-Way.* Chicago, 1941.

149. Zuni (35°50' to 35°30'N, 108°30' to 109'W) in 1880. Roberts, J. M. *Zuni*

276 JOHN M. ROBERTS

Daily Life. University of Nebraska Laboratory of Anthropology Monographs, notebook 3, pt. i. 1956. Pp. 1–23. Stevenson, M. C. *The Zuni Indians. Annual Reports of the Bureau of American Ethnology* 23 (1904), 1–634.

150. Havasupai (35°20' to 36°20'N, 111°20' to 113°W) in 1918. Spier, L. "Havasupai Ethnography," *Anthropological Papers of the American Museum of Natural History* 24 (1928), 81–408.

151. Papago of the Archie division (32°N, 112°W) in 1910. Lumholtz, C. *New Trails in Mexico.* New York, 1912. Underhill, R. M. *Papago Indian Religion.* Columbia University Contributions to Anthropology, no. 33. 1946. Pp. 1–359.

152. Huichol (22°N, 105°W) in 1890. Lumholtz, C. *Unknown Mexico,* vol. 2. London, 1902. Zingg, R. M. *The Huichols.* University of Denver Contributions to Anthropology, no. 1. 1938. Pp. 1–826.

153. Aztec of the city and environs of Tenochtitlan (19°N, 99°10'W) in 1520. Sahagún, B. de. 1950–57. *Florentine Codex: General History of the Things of New Spain.* Translated from the original Aztec by A. J. O. Anderson and C. F. Dibble. Monographs of the School of American Research, no. 14. Santa Fe, 1950–57. Pts. 2, 3, 4, 8, 9, 13, 14. Soustelle, J. *Daily Life of the Aztecs.* New York, 1961.

154. Popoluca around the pueblo of Soteapan (18°15'N, 94°50'W) in 1940. Foster, G. M. 1945. "Sierra Popoluca Folklore and Beliefs," *University of California Publications in American Archaeology and Ethnology* 42 (1945), 177–250.

155. Quiche of the town of Chichicastenango (15°N, 91°W) in 1930. Bunzel, R. 1952. *Chichicastenango.* Publications of the American Ethnological Society, no. 22. 1952. Pp. 1–438.

156. Miskito near Cape Gracias a Dios. (15°N, 83°W) in 1921. Conzemius, E. *Ethnographic Survey of the Miskito and Sumu Indians. Bulletins of the Bureau of American Ethnology* 106 (1932). 1–191.

157. Bribri tribe of Talamanca (9°N, 83°15'W) in 1917. Skinner, A. 1920. "Notes on the Bribri of Costa Rica," *Indian Notes and Monographs* 6 (1920) 37–106. Stone, D. *The Talamancan Tribes of Costa Rica.* Papers of the Peabody Museum, Harvard University, no. 43, pt. ii. 1962. Pp. 1–108.

158. Cuna of San Blas Archipelago (9° to 9°30'N, 78° to 79°W) in 1927. Nordenskiöld, E. 1938. *An Historical and Ethnological Survey of the Cuna Indians.* Comparative Ethnographical Studies, no. 10. Göteborg, 1938. Pp. 1–686.

159. Goajiro (11°30' to 12°20'N, 71° to 72°30'W) in 1947. Pineda, Giraldo, R. *Aspectos de la magía en la Guajiro.* Revista del Instituto Etnológico Nacional. Bogotá, 1950.

160. Haitians of Mirebalais (18°50'N, 72°10'W) in 1935. Herskovits, M. J. *Life in a Haitian Valley.* New York, 1937.

161. Callinago of Dominica (15°30'N, 60°30'W) in 1650. Breton, R. *Observations of the Island Carib.* Auxerre, 1665. Rouse, I. 1948. "The Carib." *Bulletins of the Bureau of American Ethnology* 143, pt. iv (1948), 547–65.

162. Warrau of the Orinoco delta (8°30' to 9°50'N, 60°40' to 62°30'W) in 1935. Suárez, M. M. *Los Warao.* Caracas, 1968. Turrado Moreno, A. 1945. *Etnographía de los Indios Guaraunos.* Caracas, 1945.

163. Yanomamo of the Shamatari tribe (2° to 2°45'N, 64°30' to 65°30'W) in 1965. Chagnon, N. A. 1968. *The Fierce People.* New York, 1968.

164. Carib along the Barama River (7°10′ to 7°40′N, 59°20′ to 60°20′W) in 1932. Gillin, J. 1936. *The Barama River Caribs*. Papers of the Peabody Museum, Harvard University, no. 14, pt. ii. 1936. Pp. 1–274.
165. Saramacca of the upper Suriname River (3° to 4°N, 55°30′ to 56°W) in 1928. Herskovits, M. J. and F. S. Herskovits. *Rebel Destiny*. New York, 1934.
166. Mundurucu of Cabrua village (7°S, 57°W) in 1850. Murphy, R. F. *Headhunter's Heritage*. Berkeley and Los Angeles, 1960.
167. Cubeo of the Caduiari River (1° to 1°50′N, 70° to 71°W) in 1939. Goldman, I. *The Cubeo Indians*. Illinois Studies in Anthropology, no. 2. 1963. Pp. 1–305.
168. Cayapa of the Rio Cayapas drainage (0°40′ to 1°15′N, 78°45′ to 79°10′W) in 1908. Barrett, S. A. *The Cayapa Indians. Indian Notes and Monographs* 40 (1925), 1–476.
169. Jivaro (2° to 4°S, 77° to 79°W) in 1920. Karsten, R. *The Head-Hunters of Western Amazonas*. Societas Scientiarum Fennica, Commentationes Humanarum Litterarum, no. 7. 1935. Pp. 1–588.
170. Amahuaca of the upper Inuya River (10°10′ to 10°30′S, 72° to 72°30′W) in 1960. Carneiro, R. L. The Amahuaca and the Spirit World. *Ethnology* 3 (1964), 6–11. Huxley, M., and C. Capa. *Farewell to Eden*. New York, 1964.
171. Inca in the vicinity of Cuzco (13°30′S, 72°W) in 1530. Baudin, L. *A Socialist Empire: The Incas of Peru*. New York, 1961. Cobo, B. *Historia del Nuevo Mundo*. 4 vols. Seville, 1890–95. Rowe, J. H. "Inca Culture at the Time of the Conquest." *Bulletins of the Bureau of American Ethnology* 143, pt. ii (1946), 183–330.
172. Aymara of Chucuito (16°S, 65°45′W) in 1940. LaBarre, W. 1948. *The Aymara Indians of the Lake Titicaca Plateau*. Memoirs of the American Anthropological Association, no. 68. 1948. Pp. 1–250. Tschopik, H., Jr. "The Aymara," *Bulletins of the Bureau of American Ethnology* 143, pt. ii (1946), 501–73.
173. Siriono near the Rio Blanco (14° to 15°S, 63° to 64°W) in 1942. Holmberg, A. R. *Nomads of the Long Bow*. Publications of the Institute of Social Anthropology, Smithsonian Institution, no. 10. 1950. Pp. 1–104.
174. Nambicuara of the Cocozu group (12°30′ to 13°30′S, 58°30′ to 59°W) in 1940. Lévi-Strauss, L. *La vie familiale et sociale des Indiens Nambikwara. Journal de la Société des Américanistes 37* (1948), 1–131. Paris.
175. Trumai (11°50′S, 53°40′W) in 1938. Murphy, R. F. and B. Quain. 1955. *The Trumai Indians*. Monographs of the American Ethnological Society, no. 24. 1955. Pp. 1–108.
176. Timbira of the Ramcocamecra subtribe (6° to 7°S, 45° to 46°W) in 1915. Nimuendajú, C. *The Eastern Timbira. University of California Publications in American Archaeology and Ethnology* 41 (1946), 1–357.
177. Tupinamba in the vicinity of Rio de Janeiro (22°35′ to 23°S, 42° to 44°30′W) in 1550. Métraux, A. "The Tupinamba." *Bulletins of the Bureau of American Ethnology* 143, pt. iii (1948), 95–133. Soares de Souza, G. *Tratado descriptivo do Brazil em 1587*. Revista do Instituto Histórico e Geográphico do Brazil, no. 14. 1851. Pp. 1–423.
178. Botocudo of the Naknenuk subtribe (18° to 20°S, 41°30′ to 43°30′W) in 1884. Ehrenreich, P. "Ueber die Botocudos," *Zeitschrift für Ethnologie* 19 (1887), 49–82. Saint-Hilaire, A. *Voyages dans l'interier du Brésil*. Paris, 1930–33.

179. Shavante in the vicinity of São Domingo (13°30'S, 51°30'W) in 1958. Maybury-Lewis, D. *Akwè-Shavante Society*. Oxford, 1967.
180. Aweikoma (28°S, 50°W) in 1932. Henry, J. *Jungle People*. New York, 1941.
181. Cayua of southern Mato Grosso (23° to 24°S, 54° to 56°W) in 1890. Ambrosetti, J. B. "Los Indios Cainguá del Alto Parana," *Boletín del Instituto Geográfico Argentino* 15 (1895), 661–774. Koenigswald, G. von. "Die Cayuás," *Globus* 93 (1908), 376–81. Watson, J. B. 1952. *Cayua Culture Change*. Memoirs of the American Anthropological Association, no. 73. 1952. Pp. 1–144.
182. Lengua (23° to 24°S, 58° to 59°W) in 1889. Grubb, W. B. *An Unknown People in an Unknown Land*. London, 1911.
183. Abipon (27° to 29°S, 59° to 60°W) in 1750. Dobrizhoffer, M. *An Account of the Abipones*. 3 vols. London, 1822.
184. Mapuche in the vicinity of Temuco (38°30'S, 72°35'W) in 1950. Faron, L. C. *The Mapuche Indians of Chile*. New York, 1968. —— *Hawks of the Sun: Mapuche Morality and Its Ritual Attributes*. Pittsburgh, 1964.
185. Tehuelche (40° to 50°S, 64° to 72°W) in 1870. Musters, G. C. *At Home with the Patagonians*. London, 1873. Viedma, A. de "Descripción de la costa meridional del sur," in *Coleción de obras y documentos relativos a la historia antigua y moderna de las provincias del Rio de la Plata*, P. de Angelis, ed. Buenos Aires, 1837. Vol. 6, pp. 63–81.
186. Yahgan (54°30' to 56°30'S, 67° to 72 W) in 1865. Gusinde, M. *Die Feuerland-Indianer. Vol. 2. Yamana*. Mödling bei Wien, 1937.

BRIAN SPOONER

14. CONCLUDING ESSAY 1

Anthropology and the Evil Eye

WHETHER OR NOT it may be accounted universal, the evil eye is a widespread cultural phenomenon. It is therefore interesting to consider in the conclusion to this volume why it has received relatively little attention in the literature of anthropology. After all, witchcraft, which many writers consider to be a closely related and similarly widespread concept, has received what amounts almost to obsessive attention.

As long ago as 1938 A.M. Hocart observed that:

> There is a considerable literature about the evil eye, but it does little more than add instances to instances. The fault lies in the very nature of the facts. The evil eye is known to us mainly, if not solely, as a survival; in other words the theory has disappeared and only emotional associations remain which give it vitality. We do not know how the evil eye works, because those who believe in it do not care, they only know that it works and they fear it." [1]

Forty years later, we cannot claim to have progressed very far. This is the first *anthropological* publication to be devoted to the problem.

Ideally, a volume such as this should lead to the formulation of a general theory of the evil eye within a conceptual framework that would comprehend all known occurrences. Although the chapters of this volume do little more than "add instances to instances" several of them attempt limited rationalization and explication in terms of the particular author's experience; some (see especially Reminick) link their rationalization interestingly to current theories in the literature of social anthropology that are aimed at explanation of a broader range of cultural phenomena; one (Kearney) suggests a new psychological direction in which we might proceed for the formulation of a general theory; and one (Roberts) explores statistical correlations with the occurrences of the concept of the evil eye in a worldwide, general-purpose sample of cultures. Taken all together, the explanatory hypotheses suggested in this volume are generally representative of our present state of understanding of the concept of the evil eye. The implicit separation of folk explanation from practice in Hocart's words suggests an evaluation of these hypotheses that may lead to a satisfactory synthesis.

It has been suggested that progress towards a satisfactory theory of the evil eye will only be achieved when we can assemble a range of detailed case studies. The instances reported in this volume and alluded to in references could be increased greatly by a thorough library search, to add more "instances to instances," but the very nature of these instances suggests that our desire for case studies may be misguided. So many instances have been published, and so few of these are in any useful sense cases. Perhaps the detailed case, in which a misfortune is suffered, a diagnosis is made and followed by search, accusation, and cure, though no doubt it does happen, is exceptional. This may be one reason for the general lack of interest on the part of anthropologists. "Social" processes involving the evil eye are not generally discernible, as they are, at least more commonly, with witchcraft. In the case of witchcraft this has been shown by Evans-Pritchard in words that have become classic in anthropology:

> In Zandeland sometimes an old granary collapses. There is nothing remarkable in this. Every Zande knows that termites eat the supports in course of time and that even the hardest woods decay after years of service. Now a granary is the summerhouse of a Zande homestead and people sit beneath it in the heat of the day and chat or play the African hole game or work at some craft. Consequently it may happen that there are people sitting beneath the granary when it collapses and they are injured, for it is a heavy structure made of beams and clay and may be stored with eleusine as well. Now why should these particular people have been sitting under this particular granary at the particular moment when it collapsed? That it should collapse is easily intelligible, but why should it have collapsed at the particular moment when these particular people were sitting beneath it? Through years it might have collapsed, so why should it fall just when certain people sought its kindly shelter? We say that the granary collapsed because its supports were eaten away by termites. That is the cause that explains the collapse of the granary. We also say that people were sitting under it at the time because it was in the heat of the day and they thought that it would be a comfortable place to talk and work. This is the cause of people being under the granary at the time it collapsed. To our minds the only relationship between these two independently caused facts is their coincidence in time and space. We have no explanation of why the two chains of causation intersected at a certain time and in a certain place, for there is no interdependence between them.

Zande philosophy can supply the missing link. The Zande knows that the supports were undermined by termites and that people were sitting beneath the granary in order to escape the heat and glare of the sun. But he knows besides why these two events occurred at a precisely similar moment in time and space. It was due to the action of witchcraft. If there had been no witchcraft people would have been sitting under the granary and it would not have fallen on them, or it would have collapsed but the people would not have been sheltering under it at the time. Witchcraft explains the coincidence of these two happenings.[2]

Magic had already been similarly interpreted by Frazer and Malinowski. It is a corpus of lore, assembled according to simple principles of homeopathy or contagion, that allows a folk explanation of specific occurrences. The evil eye, witchcraft, and magic may all three be simply used for explanation or applied for the attainment of a desired end. In either case they are related concepts that on the folk level aid in the patterning and therefore in the explanation of experience. They reduce what appears to be unordered or chaotic to the semblance of order. We shall return to this later. Here we must return from the concept to the practice—the instances.

In the case of the evil eye, each instance consists of one or more of the following component elements: prevention, accusation, attack, cure. Each element if studied in cross-cultural perspective may be seen to be practiced through a range of recipes and acts that can only minimally be reduced to analytical order by the use of catch-all categories such as homeopathy, attention-deflection, etc. The origins of jewelry, tattooing, and the veiling of women have been attributed to the evil eye. But the instances of the evil eye show only limited cross-cultural similarity and comparableness. The concept of the evil eye can certainly be used as an etic category in cross-cultural research, but permutations of practice do not appear to lead to a satisfactory formulation of theory. The range of types of suspect, victim, curative, and preventative depend on other factors than those that lead to the practice and the validity of the concept. They are at the level of folk rationalizations.

Four Possible Explanations

Having thus somewhat summarily disposed of the lore, we may apply ourselves to the concept. Four distinct explanations of the concept of evil eye have appeared, and each of them is represented in this volume. There is an extent to which these distinct avenues proceed to different levels of analysis.

They are therefore complementary, rather than conflicting theories. However, they are not all equally significant, since they are not all comprehensive. Further, a common failing in them is that they seek only to explain the existence of the evil eye among the repertoire of concepts in cultures where it does exist, and take no account of the equal need for an explanation for its absence in cultures where it does not exist.

The first of these theoretical orientations is concerned with tracing its origin in a particular area or areas and explaining its diffusion from its point or points of origin to the present state of distribution. Lest it be thought that this is a misguided or unworthwhile line of investigation, let me make clear immediately that I consider it only relatively less interesting than the theoretical orientations that I shall consider later, and that I am not intending to associate any particular writer exclusively with this approach. However, since I do not consider that the investigation of origins and diffusion processes can lead to a sufficient explanation of the continuing cultural validity of a concept that remains so widespread, I shall not comment further on it here except to note that such an investigation is bound to concern itself primarily with what I have set apart above as the lore associated with the evil eye, rather than with the explanation of the concept itself. Even though, therefore, it is interesting to speculate on the extreme likelihood of a major center of diffusion in ancient Mesopotamia, which would suggest that the origin of the concept is related to a combination of factors including complex societies and the interdependence of intensive advanced agriculture and pastoralism (cf. Roberts, above), this correlation cannot constitute any more than a very preliminary stage in explanation, and it is not possible to proceed further in the consideration of an extinct society.

The second approach represented in the literature is functional. There are in fact two distinct approaches that might be subsumed under this heading: one that attends to the function of the concept of the evil eye in relation to individual needs, the psychological functionalism of Malinowski already mentioned above; and another that is Radcliffe-Brownian rather that Malinowskian in that it is concerned with how the concept functions within the structure of the society to discourage individuals from exceeding the limits of their socially ascribed roles (on pain of becoming conspicuous to, and consequently struck by, the evil eye), and to encourage the golden mean in all things. Teitelbaum, who characterizes the evil eye as the "leveler," is the type representative of this approach in this volume. This is a particularly useful approach for the development of hypotheses in empirical research, and it is not coincidental that Teitelbaum received a significant part of his training in the most empiricist and behaviorist school of anthropology today at Manchester. The limitation of the approach, however, is that it cannot explain why the eye rather than any other concept (e.g., Nemesis, *jinn,* etc.) should play this role. Further, it cannot explain why it exists in some cultures and not in others.

It is this type of approach that has led to discussion of envy in the context of the evil eye, very rightly shown by Kearney to amount to a sophistication of the native model: although it is perfectly valid and necessary at one stage of analysis, the anthropologist should attempt to build models at a higher level of abstraction. Once more, of course, there is no explanation of why envy should lead to these practices in one society and not in another.

A variation of the functional approach, which might be typed "the ecological approach" is best represented in this volume in Roberts' cross-cultural paper. Roberts suggests—not as a coherent theory, but as an interpretation of the correlations that arise from his statistical study—that belief in the evil eye may be generated by one or more of the following conditions: life in a complex society, fear for fertility (in cows, children, pregnant women), fear for productivity (e.g., of lorries). Other applications of the concept would then be seen as extensions and diffusion. Once again, the same criticisms apply.

The problem of "why the eye" is fundamental, and does not seem to be solvable by a sociological approach. Let us, therefore, be content here to beg a psychological question, and note that generally "staring is an act with connotations which vary from inauspiciousness to downright rudeness, according to culture. Marçais cites 'the naturally injurious power of a strange and staring look.' " [3]

Other nonverbal means of communication (e.g., blowing, spitting, touching) tend to be value-loaded also. The *mala lingua* and the hot mouth are cited in this volume. But in these cases the values seem to be less constant cross-culturally and the concepts less well defined where they are found. Spitting, for example, may constitute the ultimate insult or may have a protective value. Touching may convey *baraka* or grace, or be associated with noisome contagion. Looking and staring have a more constant and generally better defined value, possibly because the content of such communication is better defined by the medium itself.

To summarize this discussion, the practices associated with belief in the evil eye—curative and preventative practices—though generally of homeopathic or contagious construction, are subject to cultural variation. Similarly types of persons considered likely to be responsible or vulnerable—though generally (but not always) socially conspicuous, vulnerable in good fortune and success, responsible in bad fortune or poverty—vary from one culture to another. Second, the attribution of suspicion of eye-to-eye contact, a straight look, is so widespread—and not restricted to human populations—that it does not require exaggeration to suggest that a psychological universal may explain why the concept is specifically the evil *eye*. Third, despite the common occurrence of folk explanations in terms of envy, envy is far more universal than the concept of the evil eye. Why should envy generate the concept of the evil eye in some societies and not in others? Paranoia, however (cf. Kearney), is more likely to be found as a general condition of some societies in some periods than in others.

Finally, it must be remembered that the evil eye, whatever its psychological function, is also a structural feature. We must, therefore, also eventually provide an explanation in structural terms. The evil eye is an element of the religious or symbolic system—an element that forms part of an explanation of evil.

I have not attempted to survey all the practices associated with the evil eye, or even to deal with all the theories that have been suggested. Rather I have tried to distinguish different types of theory and show the potential and the limitations of each. In conclusion I wish to emphasize that I do not consider any of the theories I have discussed to be wrong or useless. I hope to have shown that they are complementary and mutually dependent. A more detailed consideration of them and the data on which they are based may lead to a comprehensive theory of the phenomenon of the evil eye.

NOTES

1. Hocart, p. 156.   2. Evans-Pritchard, pp. 69–70.
3. Spooner, chapter 6 above.

BIBLIOGRAPHY

Evans-Pritchard, E. E. *Witchcraft, Oracles and Magic among the Azande*. Oxford: The Clarendon Press, 1937.

Hocart, A. M. "The Mechanism of the Evil Eye," *Folklore* 49 (1938), 156–57.

VIVIAN GARRISON
CONRAD M. ARENSBERG

15. CONCLUDING ESSAY 2

The Evil Eye: Envy or Risk of Seizure? Paranoia or Patronal Dependency?

IF THE CROSS-CULTURAL comparative study of a phenomenon like the evil eye, relatively unimportant in and of itself, has any significance it is because it sheds light on the nature of human behavior more generally. Most of the chapters of this book have dealt with the phenomenon of the evil eye as it exists in one culture or region at one or more points in time. Each article has proffered explanations for the existence of this belief-and-

VIVIAN GARRISON is Assistant Professor in the Department of Psychiatry, Division of Behavioral Sciences, and Staff Anthropologist, Community Mental Health Center, New Jersey Medical School, College of Medicine and Dentistry of New Jersey, and is also Senior Research Associate, Department of Anthropology, Columbia University. Her training in anthropology was at Columbia, and she has done fieldwork on religion, healing practices, and social networks in U.S. urban neighborhoods. She is author or co-author of a number of articles in the fields of anthropology and community mental health and is co-editor (with Vincent Crapanzano) of a forthcoming volume *Case Studies in Spirit Possession,* Wiley and Sons.

CONRAD M. ARENSBERG is Professor of Anthropology at Columbia University. He is author of numerous books and articles representing a broad theoretical interest in general and comparative cultural and social anthropology, in the ecology and ethnography of complex societies, and in community studies, economic anthropology, and applied anthropology. The titles relevant here include: "The Old World Peoples; The Place of European Cultures in World Ethnography" in the *Anthropological Quarterly, Special Issue on European Cultures* (1963); *Culture and Community* (with Solon Kimball) (1965); *Trade and Market in the Ancient Empires* (with Karl Polanyi and Harry Pearson) (1957); and most recently "Culture as Behavior: Structure and Emergence" in the first *Annual Review of Anthropology,* (1972) a theoretical statement of culture as processual models of interpersonal social action. He has done fieldwork in Ireland, Germany, Japan, Syria, and India.

behavior complex in the area of concern to the author. Roberts (chapter 13) has provided a cross-cultural survey of the distribution of the evil eye belief and of the traits associated with it. Maloney (Introduction) and Spooner (chapter 14) have summarized the ethnographic data and have reviewed in part the various explanations that have been proposed both here and in previous publications.

As Spooner points out, some of the authors address themselves to traditional questions or levels of explanation in anthropology: origin and diffusion (Moss and Cappannari, Maloney, Flores-Meiser), historical change processes (Appel, Swiderski), present distribution (Maloney, Roberts), social and structural functions (Mass, Swiderski, Reminick, and Teitelbaum), and psychological functions (Kearney, Stein, Reminick, Roberts). Few of the authors, however, are concerned exclusively with one of these traditional levels of explanation. Most chapters deal with the integration of the evil eye complex of beliefs and behaviors in the world view and cognitive symbol systems of the specific society under study. Several, particularly Reminick, Stein, and Kearney, attempt specifically to explain the relationships among the elements of the evil eye complex on several of these levels of analysis, particularly the relationship between psychological trait and cultural pattern, and in the case of Reminick, social structure as well.

Roberts, ignoring these traditional levels of analysis, has provided a wealth of data simultaneously considering the physical, technological, social, and psychological environment in which the evil eye beliefs are elaborated, and has further reduced these data by factor analysis. Any new hypotheses must build on his conclusions that (1) the belief has certain strong cultural associations, (2) "social inequality is probably a pre-condition to any elaboration of the evil eye," (3) "the belief became culturally elaborated in the Near East (broadly defined)," and (4) such elaboration developed only during or after Neolithic times. He, like Foster in the major theoretical statement on this subject prior to this volume,[1] considers the evil eye beliefs and behaviors as an institutionalized recognition of envy and foresees the possibility of moving toward an ecological "theory of envy and from that to a theory of the belief in the evil eye."

Spooner has reviewed and criticized the various explanations of the evil eye presented, and we need not repeat them here. We disagree, however, with Spooner's conclusion that the contributions of this volume do little more than "add instances to instances." They, in fact, provide the basic data of the distribution, associations, and processes from which a more general ecological theory of evil eye beliefs and behaviors is beginning to emerge. Spooner is absolutely right, however, when he points out that none of these chapters has singly developed a general theory of the evil eye that would account for its absence as well as its presence in different societies, for the significance of the eye specifically as the symbol of a malignant interpersonal power, or for the occurrence of those beliefs in contrast with any other forms of magic or witchcraft.

In this final chapter we will address ourselves to the problems of explanation raised by Spooner. In Part I we will examine the evidence presented in its totality and attempt the construction of a more general structural and ecological theory of the evil eye complex in the context of its distribution and statistical associations provided by Roberts. In Part II we will reexamine some of the case materials presented in this book as a partial test of this and other hypotheses, and we will attempt to show that there are homologues in the structure and process of (1) the evil eye beliefs as symbol system, (2) the social structure of the areas in which it is found, and (3) intrapsychic processes. Thus, some of the apparently competing hypotheses are, in fact, complementary as suggested by Spooner.

PART I: A STRUCTURAL HYPOTHESIS

Spooner ends his summary of the present data and existing hypotheses with a plea for a structural explanation rather than, or at least in addition to, a psychological one. This would require that we address ourselves to two further elements of a model of the evil eye not yet discussed in this book. The first concerns the nature of the evil eye complex as an "emic" (indigenously explained) belief symbolizing an "etic" (operationally modelable) social-structural or institutional process. The second would concern the fit of this structural process to the structure and conditions of the cultures within which the evil eye beliefs emerged and are perpetuated.

To establish the social process or institution putatively symbolized in the evil eye requires a method. One exists in the proposal of Arensberg [2] that a cultural form such as the one we have in the evil eye be explained as an emergent from an underlying regularity of social action best represented as a minimal-sequence model of interpersonal behaviors. He proposes that cultural forms perhaps universally emerge from the patterns created when man regularizes and sequences his social behaviors. There is much theory already in anthropology holding that symbols restate social structure. Such theory holds that symbols evolve to refer to, to recall, to evoke the sentiments of, or otherwise to render cognizable the cultural mappings of basic social and ecological relationships in human society.

Arensberg goes beyond today's "structuralist" classification of opposites in easy social categories (male/female, raw/cooked, mountain-seashore, etc.) to propose that symbol systems, like kinship nomenclatures, evolve much further and come to represent more complex, yet still quite specific, institutional minimal sequences of recurrent interpersonal action. The min-imal-sequence models of human interactive behavior constitute a structural template underlying the consciously understood folk theories or rational-izations of social behavior. The essential difference between the structural approach proposed by Arensberg and that of other structuralists is that Arensberg abstracts the interrelationship between elements in a system in the model building rather than the properties of the elements in the system. The elements (persons, roles, symbols) are variable; it is the structure and pro-cess (or interrelationships among the elements) that are relatively fixed and are repeated in many permutations and variations through the substitution of elements. As such these minimal-sequence models represent, in Chomsky's terms, "a generational grammar" of social behavior rather than a "descrip-tive grammar" in which elements are classified and the rules of permutation, substitution, and variation codified.

With this method, then, if we are successful in accurately modeling the minimal sequence of interactive behaviors involved in the evil eye beliefs, we can perhaps account simultaneously for the generation of the cultural form and for "the disputed formal and other 'deep structures of the mind' that seem to so many observers to underlie cultural behavior." [8]

The question, then, is what institution common to the region of the evil eye's distribution does the evil eye as symbol system represent, recall, or evoke?

As Spooner points out, the engagement of gaze of one person with an-other, or one animal with another, is indeed universal, and envy may well be also. But it is amply demonstrated by Roberts and Maloney that the con-figuration of the gaze, the evil eye beliefs, and their accompanying emotions and actions is substantially circumscribed in its distribution. Robert's data show it is limited, with some exceptions,[4] to complex stratified societies possessed of both milk animals (or nomadic herding populations) and grain-fields (or stable peasant agricultural communities)—in effect, to the peoples that Murdock has classified as the circum-Mediterranean cultures.[5] Histori-cally it seems to have evolved and diffused with the civilization that Arens-berg has elsewhere called "The Peoples of the Book" [6] (cf. Moss and Cap-pannari, chapter 1), and, more specifically, "The Peoples of the Plow," classified as such on the basis of the common mixed economy of agriculture and a subsistence base of bread, milk, and meat (cf. Roberts, chapter 13). The evil eye is not universal but highly specific.

The question more specifically, then, is: what institution (social configu-ration or system) common to the circum-Mediterranean civilization or to the ecology of a subsistence base of bread, milk, and meat, not found else-where, does the evil eye symbol system represent?

The answer we shall try to suggest is that the institution in question, whose sequence of interpersonal behaviors the evil eye beliefs follow, in whole or in part, is a well-known one amply reported in the circum-Mediter-ranean lands. It is personal patronage, the *personalismo* of sheikhs, land-lords, and other protectors, mediators, and sanctioners of opposing peasant and peasant-and-nomad clienteles, at work in the stratified but unstable "state societies" with tribal tributaries of the region. We shall model pa-tronage and the evil eye in parallel.

Unfortunately, we are limited in the extent to which we can accomplish either of our assigned tasks: modeling of the symbol system of the evil eye and the institution of patronage, and testing the model for fit to circum-Mediterranean civilization. The former would require more complete de-tailed accounts of the behavioral processes involved in the enactment of evil eye events than we have available. Here, as all too often, ethnography does not give us a behavioral account or any other statement of a course of events, taking refuge in secondhand accounts or in native (emic) rational-izations of what takes place. Spooner complains of how rare and how few are the accounts of detailed cases, "in which a misfortune is suffered, a diagnosis made, followed by search, accusation, and cure." This is perhaps a reflection of the inadequacy of our ethnographies, or it may be a reflection of the actual situation in the case of the evil eye beliefs and behaviors. Spooner is assuming that a detailed case would involve the sequence of events he delineates. On the basis of the extant data it appears to be other-wise; evil eye beliefs in fact rarely involve "a misfortune suffered, a diag-nosis made, followed by search, accusation, and cure." This is the process of the witchcraft event, but the evil eye appears to be, in most instances, something else. It is possible that, as suggested by Spooner in his quotation from Hocart, the evil eye is "known to us mainly, if not solely, as a survival," or that the surviving evil eye beliefs are now being used in the service of individual psychopathology or other individual and social needs that may have little or nothing to do with the origin or even with the perpetuation of the culture trait. It has also been pointed out by numerous authors here and elsewhere that such symbol systems, once they come into being, take on a vitality of their own. "If men believe a thing is real and act in accordance with that belief, the consequences of their actions are real" (Moss and Cappannari paraphrasing W. I. Thomas, chapter 1). The belief systems create their own secondary elaborations (Kearney, chapter 11). It is difficult to discern in the accounts of the evil eye as beliefs detached from the behaviors they rationalize what is fragmented "survival," what is the complete process of the evil eye, what is secondary elaboration, or what is, in fact, merely fragmentary reporting. We will try, however, in Part II to discriminate these processes.

We are also limited in our tasks by the fact that we have no complete accounts in this volume, or elsewhere to our knowledge, of a complete sequence of the enactment of an evil eye event within the core of the precise ecological and cultural area in which this complex appears to have developed (the Near East) and where it, like the ecological conditions, may be retained in most complete or nearly original form. Similarly, to test the model for fit to circum-Mediterranean civilization would require better ecological, structural, and historical cultural reconstruction of these societies than now exists. Adequate accounts of peasant and of peasant-and-nomad life in Near Eastern and European countries are just now entering the literature. Nevertheless, enough evidence of interpersonal events, or social processes, and of the broad outlines of the folk life in village and nomad culture of the circum-Mediterranean peoples of mixed milk-cattle and grain-agriculture ecology is already known so that we may hazard a minimal-sequence and processual model of the evil eye and make a preliminary test of fit.

The Social Process of the Evil Eye

First of all, about the universality of the eye contact and the behaviors linked to the gaze, enough can be said from the social ethology of primates and even of other higher animals to remind the reader that the eye-to-eye engagement is universally a first step in a train of action that further defines the interaction of gazer and gazee. On eye contact, predator and prey, or rival and rival, or lover and loved, are alerted, tensed for what may come next, and a move follows: predator or rival to the attack, lover to tactile approach, etc. The gazer moves in, or else, if the signs are against him, he moves off and away. In all events, whether the evil eye is involved or not, the eye contact and the gaze are only preliminary conditions and first behaviors in a sequence of action. The gaze initiates further action among both animals and humans, if only in the latter case clothed in belief and elaborated in culture.

Let us ask, then, if the evil eye is a characteristic social process or a drama of interpersonal action, what do the gazer and the gazee do next? What is it in the subsequent chain of events that defines this encounter as one of the "evil eye" or "envious eye" and not, for example, the "loving eye"?

To put the evil eye events and beliefs documented herein in terms of interpersonal action, the full enactment of an evil eye event appears to involve: a gazer (actual or suspected) who gazes, a gazee (actual or one who fears he may be gazed upon), who then moves to protect some possession out of his peasant-village, nomad, or urban-artisan life in family, fields, herds, or goods. The gazee specifically displays a sign of protection. The gazer or gaze is thereby averted and the possession is safe. Or, alternatively, if the possession suffers damage, the gazee moves to restore its condition through supernatural divination and cure and perhaps to retaliate.

Against what is the gazee protecting his possessions? Is the threat the power of the eye itself? Is it the power of envy motivating and projected through the eye? Or is the eye a symbol of threat from a known or unknown party (including but not limited to the possible consequences of envy)? Is the threat actual in the environment or is it an internal threat denied and projected (paranoid)? What is the protection invoked by the display of a sign? Is the sign itself a powerful magic that averts the power of the eye? Or is the sign a symbol of the protection that the gazee invokes?

The threat in emic terms is consistently a power to seize, destroy, take away, make ill or ruined, whether it is the infants of Guatemala, the pots of Indian potters, the bride and bridegroom of a Greek village, or the overproduction of cloth by the weavers of Tunisia. There are many evils and hardships, such as chronic illnesses, deformity, draughts, and famines, that do not appear to be considered consequences of the evil eye. The threats of the eye seem quite consistently to be sudden disasters of an unexpected nature that result in confiscation or destruction (by person, god, or God).

The "protection" is equally consistently an appeal to a higher person or force: saint, god, God (symbolic patron, noble, king). The action of the evil eye shows that it is not to be taken as, in Foster's term, a dyadic contract, or even "a pair of persons whose relationship is mediated or structured by an intervening property or object." [7] It involves more: minimally a pair of equals or unequals, a valued property or trait, and a conceptual superior (real or symbolic). What distinguishes the evil eye, whether motivated by envy or based in a paranoid defense, from other magic or witchcraft is this appeal against real sudden damage to possessions of concern, including women and children, to a higher force that is neither coerced nor supplicated, but merely invoked and displayed. This display, which is based neither on the principle of contagion nor that of homeopathy like much magic, is considered sufficient to avert the evil of the gaze. The evil eye seems to be different from other religious and magic symbolic behavior, then, not in the nature of the motivation, but in the behavioral chain of events it involves or supposes. The drama (symbolic or real) of the evil eye involves as a minimal sequence of interpersonal action: a gaze or suspected gaze, gazee's raising of a protection, and thereby the deflection of gazer (or his power) from seizure, expropriation, or destruction.

Nor need we consider this threat or the display of protection merely symbolic. In the circum-Mediterranean world of the Near East or its European outliers, the Sudan, and North India (but not in China with its more stable bureaucracy, its absence of feudalism, and its relative paucity of local patronage), the threat of confiscation or destruction of peasant properties (whether of produce to the tax collector, boys to the Janisaries, girls to the harems, or any valued good to the raider or corrupt official) was and is still in many places omnipresent. A gazee in a world of peasants, tribal nomads, urban artisans, landlords, prebendaries, and a "focused authority" (Roberts, chapter 13) that exacts tribute or taxes in money and goods on the basis, for example, of the "apparent style of life"—as in southern Italy to this day—is in continual jeopardy of having possessions seized or destroyed. The threat comes not only from the empowered prebendary, bureaucrat, inspector, tax collector, gendarme, or marauder, but also from the stranger, neighbor, or unfortunate that might "eye" the possession. Any gazer (whether suspect outsider or intimate) might denounce the gazee directly and deliberately, or indirectly through gossip, or merely by betrayal of emotion, to one of those having the power or the will to seize and destroy.

Further, the role of the patron, the lord, or the king in protection was and is real. A peasant in this world is protected in his possessions by his patron, landlord, sheikh, and is protected in fact not by law or custom or police but by the retaliation a patron's bullyboys can inflict upon a local raider or marauding stranger, or even upon a rapacious rival. Peasants and vassals indeed complain to their patrons, not so much for restitution as for just such protection or protective retaliation (see, for example, Vinogradov, on the Shabak) [8]—or, as in the case of envy, they themselves might also report hidden assets of a rival to a grasping tax collector official. (For example, in *The Godfather,* an undertaker whose daughter has been wronged requests exactly this kind of protective retaliation from Don Corleone.) The sign of protection raised says, in effect, "Beware, I am protected, and I or my powers, my patron, saint . . . God, will get you if you harm me." Is it not this threat of retaliation, symbolic or real, that "averts the gaze"?

The proper association of the evil eye, then, is not with its antecedent conditions, necessary but not sufficient to an explanation, but to this drama of gaze, threat or fear of seizure, appeal to protection, and threat of patronal retaliation. Symbolic or real, the *mazuza* at the door signifies God's protection of his people against rapine and extortion, just as the safe conduct stick in the desert of Arabia carried the *wajh* (face or protection) of a powerful sheikh to keep safe a lonely traveler in a world of raiders. The *mazuza,* the safe conduct stick, or the plastic evil eye charms of contemporary Italian-Americans (Swiderski, chapter 3) simultaneously symbolize the individual's placement and display whatever powers of reprisal he individually or his group collectively may command. The drama (symbolic or real), the process of the evil eye, is thus not in envious rivalry alone but in the sequence of action: gaze/seizure, gaze/appeal for protection or protective retaliation. The beliefs seem only to state this drama in supernatural terms, making an emic gloss on a real run of events, or filling in for the real drama with supernatural equivalents; to wit, symbolic patrons and their protective or retaliative powers.

The Ecology of the Evil Eye

Our second step in the development of a structural-processual hypothesis was to fit this model to the ethnographic data of the region of its primary distribution—the circum-Mediterranean. We have already given some of the characteristics of the social structure and the civilization of this region. Let us add more of that—though, of course, not exhaustively.

Among the traits associated with the evil eye belief as shown by Roberts in chapter 13 are: cultural complexity, peasant-urban economy, technological specialization including metalworking, grain agriculture, domesticated large animals, and milking or dairying. The last two have an especially strong and significant association. There is a negative relationship between the evil eye and hunting and fishing. As Arensberg has shown elsewhere, it was the "People of the Plow"—the Near East, older Europe, the Sudan, and older North India—that had exactly this ecology of mixed agriculture with a subsistence base of bread, milk, and meat. China and Southeast Asia do not use animals for milk and do not depend upon the hard grains (wheat, millets, etc.) as staples, but upon rice, involving both different patterns of management of fields and different relationships between herder and agriculturalist. The significance of milk or of large animals as regards the evil eye is not to be found in any characteristic of milk or of the large animals per se, but in the symbiosis of part-cultures (landlord, bureaucrat, agriculturalist, herder, artisan) and in the destructive effect of the nomadic herders upon settled village and state societies.

This part of the world, however, also had peasant villages with fixed fields, and at one time periodic redistribution of them, which seems to have presented exactly the situation that Foster described as an "image of limited good." [9] The wheatfields and water-rights of this world were (in Jordan until 1939, and in Iran until 1974) fixed and massed. A repartition of fields or reallocation of water rights in favor of one peasant family took fields and water away from another. This region also had the structure of periodically unstable tax-farming government (Max Weber's "prebendal bureaucracy") [10] and an unstable symbiosis between peasants and nomads in which seizures and expropriations, on receipt of information or on discovery of assets, took place. It was also characterized by a redistributive economy in which periodic scarcity in produce called for forced sales at fixed prices in a centrally controlled market, and only protected or hidden surpluses escaped arbitrary and periodic confiscation. [11] It was also a world of patronage, of sheikhs' houses, and of *personalismo*, in which protection lay less in tribal strength and stable bureaucracy than in the fluctuation of clienteles we have invoked (see Barth on the Swat Pathan).

Symbolically, this was also a world of high Gods and a multiplicity of lesser supernaturals and semidivinities: the Devil, devils, demons, Saints, folk saints, zar, jinn, spirits, etc. In popular Judaism, popular Islam, pre-Reformation Christianity and contemporary Catholicism, the high God is most often known and reached through intermediaries: prophet, Pope, priest, saint, folk saint, sayyid, pir, tzaddik, etc. These interpreters and intercessors intervene with the high God on one's behalf. The symbolic powers of good and evil are multiple and stratified. And among them there is the pattern of intercession of saints, also reminiscent of patronage relationships.

With the social conditions that emerged with the rise of civilization after the Neolithic of the Near East—a stratified society of urban officials, rural villagers, and patrons mediating between them in an "ethnic mosaic" of symbiotic "part cultures" of nomad, peasant, artisan, and tribal mountaineer—peer rivalries took a more complex form than those between fellow tribals or village equals. "Conceptual equals," again in Foster's term,[12] could no longer "fight out" their own rivalries one to one, either through direct aggression or through witchcraft, when goods were either given or taken away by a conceptual superior or taken away by one equal but different (e.g., nomad to agriculturalist) over whom there was no control but through a conceptual superior. It is not that there are no "rules of the game" for the enactment of rivalrous relationships were the evil eye is found, as suggested by Foster. It is merely that these game rules are different from those that generally obtain either in egalitarian or in industrialized societies. This situation produces a limited good, a high rate of envy, and the reliance upon patronage and patronal retaliation that is symbolized in the evil eye protection.

It is neither causal nor accidental, then, that the evil eye is associated with the veiling of women, with dissemblement of assets and hiding of displays, with, indeed so many other social structures and cultural traits of the Near East (Roberts, chapter 13). These traits are all part of a larger pattern of ecology and social structure. But it is the evil eye as social process, not the evil eye as abstract belief or psychological motive, that gives us the homologue with peasant reliance on patronage.

Belief systems, once again, are subjective renditions of social structures, not independent forces, and their character as behavioral as well as cognitive systems is clear, once we document as we have here (and more fully so) the behaviors that act them out. Certainly gaze, milk, envy, paranoia, Ethiopian caste rivalries, and the like are all scattered, and all partial associations or attributes of evil eye belief, as the chapters of this book have shown. But protection and patronage, stratified society, redistributive economy, and unstable government are equally important—or one can hazard more essential—elements.

Concomitant Variations in Ecology and Beliefs in the Evil Eye

Most interesting is the contrast between the Near East and old China. In old China milk (or symbiosis between herders and agriculturalists) and bureaucratic instability fail to appear—although other structural elements of peasant-urban civilization are the same—and both the patronage of the Near East and the evil eye belief are wanting.

In India the situation varies somewhat from that of the Near East and so do the evil eye beliefs. While India has the part-cultures of milkers and herders, agriculturalists, tribals, landlords, bureaucrats, and patrons, it has managed the herding of milk animals so there is not a distinct and separate nomadic herding population. Local government is stronger and village stability is less dependent upon either the state bureaucracy or patronal mediation. Factional disputes and rivalries are most often handled by caste or village *panchayats,* or councils of peers. Personal patronage is important only at the level of the local work team and the personal rivalries there involved—not in the mediation of caste or part-culture rivalries.

In this situation the evil eye beliefs exist, but the implied sequence of behavior is not so much gaze, appeal to protection, and threat of retaliation; it is more generally gaze and gaze deflection (a dyadic interaction). In the three behavioral sequences reported by Maloney (chapter 8) there was no appeal to the power of a human or symbolic patron to protect or retaliate against the gazer. In the first, the potters threw cow-dung flakes at gazing boys, and also propitiated the patron saint of potters to protect the pots against further damage from several causes, rain as well as the eye. This was an appeal to a symbolic patron for protection, but it was not a ritual specifically against the eye. It follows the more general pattern of the "intercession of saints," also found throughout the area of the distribution of the evil eye. In the second event, people halted the temple festival of their patron deity when a man was electrocuted and there was no appeal, only rationalization that the cause might have been the evil eye of a stranger. In the third

the reaction of fishermen suspecting the eye of the Abbé Dubois was a prag-
matic act of raising the fish and moving away. The many accounts of deflec-
tive, reflective, and curative devices provided by Maloney make apparent
the relative absence of further behaviors in the stream of action.

The ideas found in India about the psychic or interpersonal force projected
through the eye, or through the third eye, show that the evil eye belief
among Hindus is more diffuse and ambivalent than in the Near East, and
that it is made to symbolize a much larger variety of cultural traits. The principles of homeopathic and contagious magic are also more in evidence. But
in the northwestern parts of India and in Pakistan and Afghanistan, according to Maloney, both the evil eye belief and the reliance on patronage and
personalismo are closer to what one finds in the Near East. But in those
parts, as well as in southern and eastern India, the most frequent evil eye behaviors resemble simpler (and dyadic) forms of magic and countermagic.

We might speculate that the imposition of a more rigid caste-order among
the segments of Indian society has served to reduce envy (as suggested by
Foster),[13] or to reduce dependency upon patronal mediation of individual or
factional rivalries, and thereby reduce the importance of the evil eye in such
situations. We might also speculate that evil eye beliefs and symbols have
been superimposed on earlier symbolic patterns of dyadic relationship previously emically rationalized in other ways, such as witchcraft, which is not
so common in India as in Africa or Oceania, or indeed, in other areas where
the evil eye beliefs are also found.

In Africa as one moves south from the northern and coastal fringes into
central and southern Africa, stratification gives way to ranking, states to
kingdoms, and both eventually to more egalitarian tribes and bands; the evil
eye apparently also gives way to witchcraft. But in the Sahel and among the
Cushitic peoples of the East African highlands, the symbiosis between the
farming and herding components of the societies still persists along with the
evil eye. Beyond them gardeners and herders separate completely, and
witchcraft seems to prevail.

Similarly, as one moves north from the Mediterranean into central and
northern Europe, the settled agricultural populations and the distinct nomadic herding populations give way to settled agriculturalist-herders, whose
flocks are attended by an age-grade or other segment of the village population in what were and are more autonomous fiefs or villages. Here the evil
eye beliefs exist, but they are attenuated and appear most often to take the

form of what we will discuss below as "gazer prophylaxis." This is a be-havioral sequence of the evil eye (e.g., gazer makes a compliment and spits to avert the evil eye) that is dyadic, and it appears to occur principally within a homogeneous segment of a plural society, as we will see below. As far north as Finland, however, Vuorela reports extensive beliefs and behaviors surrounding the evil eye and shows a close association of these with dairying and milk products. The evil eye beliefs of northern Europe, like those of southern Europe, are fused with ideas, symbols, and processes from medieval European witchcraft.

The European evil eye beliefs and behaviors persisting today appear to show a gradation in intensity throughout the distribution that can be related to historical changes from medieval feudalism to the modern national state. In feudal Europe everyone was personally subordinated to and dependent upon landlord, noble, or king. Land was not private property, and its use for whatever purposes involved a subordination of vassal to lord. Personal and factional rivalries were then mediated by the lords or king, and sometimes courts. Personal patronage was clearly all important throughout Europe under feudalism. The manor system began to break down in England with Henry VIII and the destruction of the abbeys, and was complete with the enclosures and the advent of the modern industrial state. In France the manor system was finally destroyed with the revolution of 1789. After the French Revolution all the states of Europe gradually followed the example of France. In Slovakia (See Stein, chapter 12) the breakdown of the feudal order did not come until approximately the 1840s. In Italy the feudal land tenure system persisted until World War II. The evil eye beliefs seem to shade from least important to most important on the same gradient of time since the destruction of feudalism.

Appel (chapter 2) provides an account of the historical permutations of the evil eye belief under the impact of this changing social order in southern Italy. This account shows, we believe, the successive alterations in the beliefs with successive part-changes in the ecology and social order. In medieval southern Italy belief in the "fascination" (contracts with devils that gave people the power to curse and destroy) was held universally. With the advent of the ideas of the Enlightenment, "fascination" beliefs among the newly formed Neopolitan intellectuals came to symbolize their marginal, ambivalent position in a new myth—that of the *jettatura* (an ambivalent force within the person). And finally *jettatura* belief, in turn, sank to lodge only among peasants and marginals of today and to symbolize their marginality. The situation of both the earlier Neopolitan intellectuals and the peasants today, as Appel points out, is between two conflicting world views, one that they are powerless to change and another that they have come to value. Notice, however, the change in the theme from the opposition of powerful superior forces that are equal or nearly equal to each other (God and the Devil, patron and patron, king and king) to the conflict of good and evil within the individual. This is the big issue of the reformation—the concomitant change in the structure and symbolism of the established religions of Europe. We suggest that this change reflects a more basic conflict between autonomy and dependency that came into being as social restraints were progressively removed and replaced by a personal morality and ethic. (Compare Stein's excellent treatment of the importance of conflicts of autonomy and dependency on the intrapsychic level in the manifestation of evil eye beliefs among Slovak-Americans.) Appel attributes these changes in southern Italy to the introduction of Illuminism and Enlightenment ideas from France. We suggest that both the Illuminism and Enlightenment ideas and the changes in evil eye beliefs were emergents from the changing social structure, and the concomitant progressive freedom of the individual from the subjugation to feudal lords. But we must not forget that feudalism persisted in Italy until World War II. Taxation and law enforcement by nonresident, often corrupt inspectors and gendarmes, banditry, *personalismo,* and patronage all still persist, and so does the evil eye belief with greater force than in most of Europe.

Swiderski's chapter gives us a further historical permutation of the Italian evil eye belief system under changed ecological and social conditions. He describes how in America the concepts of evil hovering above or of evil residing in the individual gave way to a new concept of "good luck" that was transferred to the talismans traditionally worn against the "evil eye." It is easy to see how this change in beliefs came about with the change in social environment. From the hard world, if not zero-sum game, of life in southern Italy, the Italian-Americans found themselves in a world in which opportunity was the extolled value. But for the recent immigrant opportunity must often have appeared elusive, almost as far beyond one's own powers as was the poor fortune of the Old World. The windfall or sudden opportunity became the capricious fate to be invoked (in fact, the symbolic patron) while both the threat of sudden disasters resulting from the arbitrary exercise of power and the reliance on patronage as protection, while definitely not yet absent (as witness *The Godfather*), dwindled. A similar shift apparently did not occur among Slovak-Americans, a fact attributed by Stein to the "deep structure" of the evil eye beliefs in Slovak and Slovak-American personality as well as culture.

In Latin Mesoamerica, on the other hand (to which we will suppose the Near Eastern evil eye beliefs diffused, regardless of the presence or absence of preexisting, independently evolved substrate of similar beliefs or behaviors), clearly during the years following Spanish conquest peasant farmers, herding populations, and tribal tributaries were again subjugated to officialdom of the imperial bureaucracy of a fully sovereign state, but a state still using tax farming and the forced labor of children as well as adults. In Mexico and elsewhere until the land reforms of the twentieth century peasants were dependent upon the allocation of lands from *hacendados,* so that their situation resembled that of peasants in feudal Europe, particularly those living on the *latifundia* of the Mediterranean. Patronage is still strong in these parts of the New World. Governments are unstable and peasants are subjected to periodic raiding by contending segments in the national power struggles.

In this situation today the evil eye persists, but it strikes children primarily (Kearney, Cosminsky), and sometimes small animals and crops, these being the possessions that are still indisputably subject to sudden seizures by higher or arbitrary powers (God's Will, illness, weather, and raiders) to which the peasant must subordinate himself, unless, of course, his appeals to another higher power (patron, patron saint, God, or God through a saint) can be heard. In the New World at the present time the evil eye has come to be an explanation of illness that is less directly related to the environmental threat of seizure or the possible correction by patronal retaliation. It is from this situation, and not from that of the Near Eastern cradle of peasant civilization, that hypotheses of the "image of limited good" and of "envy" and "paranoia" as explanations of the evil eye have been projected.

The extension of Spanish imperial domination to the more homogeneous Tagalog of the Philippines (no milk, no specialized castes), despite the imposition of an hacienda system and an imperial bureaucracy, did not diffuse the Near Eastern form of the evil eye belief. None of Flores-Meiser's informants were aware of the Spanish concept of "evil eye," and apparently there is no appeal to a higher power in the "hot mouth" rituals reported. It is a dyadic and egalitarian interaction that is symbolized. The "hot mouth" appears to symbolize the process of "gossip" and the social control thereby exerted among peers.

In this discussion we have examined the ecological conditions under which the evil eye is found in the major areas of its distribution, and in several points in time. We have found that in all the instances where the evil eye beliefs exist so, too, do the essential elements we postulated above. Stratified, plural society, redistributive economy, unstable government, protection, and patronage exist, or at least existed until very recently. Variations in one of these elements appears to bring concomitant variations in other elements, particularly in the patronage patterns and evil eye beliefs. This discussion could be read as an argument for or a reiteration of Maloney's discussion of the origin, history, and diffusion of this complex. We intend, however, something else. We see the evil eye beliefs as a folk theory (a symbol system) rationalizing a social-structural process that has its homologue in everyday social behavior as well. Changes in the ecological conditions (including social structure) bring concomitant changes in the symbolic beliefs and behaviors. Thus we find that where patronage is confined to the local community, as in the industrialized state of Europe at the present time, the evil eye beliefs and behaviors are similarly reduced in scope. The attenuated beliefs and behaviors are not to be considered mere "survivals" of long outdated symbol systems, but rather as variants of the original beliefs now based in parts of the original complex or in newly emerged conditions and social structures.

While we are talking about diffusion, it is interesting to note that many of the symbols (charms or amulets) worn or hung against the evil eye throughout its distribution appear to invoke the specialties that emerged in the earliest circum-Mediterranean civilization, e.g., chilies, gold or iron, the *cornuto*, red or blue stones or dyes, pots, etc. They also appear to have often been trade goods. It is not unreasonable to guess that these items may have first symbolized the status of their owners, or the nature of the goods carried through a strange land in trade, and subsequently may have come to symbolize the "protection" of people of this status, whether actual patron, patron saint, devil, Devil, or God. These symbols must have predated the current patronage systems of the circum-Mediterranean and New World and the recent caste specializations of India. Specific emblems are emergents of an earlier social structure for which we have only material archeological evidence.

Summary of the Hypothesis

We have argued that evil eye beliefs and patronage relations are homologous in the drama of interpersonal action involved or implied and nearly coterminous in their distribution, and that the former is a symbolic enactment or evocation of the latter. We have said that the reliance of peasant and other specialist populations upon personal patronage is created by a system of plural, stratified, societies organized in unstable states with redistributive economies; and we have suggested that these conditions are also the ones under which the evil eye is most frequently found in Robert's cross-cultural analysis. Variations in these conditions lead, we suggest, to variations in the patterns of patronage and of the evil eye beliefs and behaviors.

We have also noted, however, a close resemblance of the pattern of action sometimes symbolized in the evil eye, witchcraft, spirit beliefs, and saint cults to the more general pattern of intercession of saints found in the institutionalized religions of the same area of distribution but with different emphases in different places. All these symbolic beliefs and behaviors have been explained at various times as the result of envy or fear of envy, paranoid mechanisms, deviance and control of deviance, rationalization of the unknown, anxiety reduction, etc. In short, they are all amenable to the same psychological and functional interpretations. Similarly all of these, and particularly the pattern of intercession of saints, in some of their instances appear to follow the same paradigm of our structural-processual model of the evil eye and patronage. Evil eye beliefs and behaviors also at times appear to follow the models of behavior and symbolism more specific to witchcraft or to other forms of magic and religion.

We have argued, however, that the evil eye differs from these other symbol systems in a number of ways: (1) its distribution is more limited; (2) it is concerned with the protection of possessions (including one's children and one's own health) against sudden disasters of the nature of seizure or destruction; (3) the contract involved is triadic in nature: gazer, gazee or gaze-fearer, and a higher power (symbolic or real) that acts upon the gazer/gaze; and (4) it does not require either coercion or supplication (in the sense of the earlier dichotomy of magic and religion) of this higher power to effect the "protection" involved, nor does it usually involve the principles of homeopathic or contagious magic. Robert's distributional and associational data has permitted us to circumscribe the evolutionary, historical, and ecological field within which the evil eye complex is found, and these very general observations of the apparent distinctiveness of the evil eye beliefs provide some clues to their uniqueness among symbolic behaviors. But we can go no further in establishing the uniqueness of the evil eye without a more thorough examination of the behavioral sequences involved in the enactment of the events of these various symbol systems within single societies where all or several are found—evidence that is not easily available in this or other publications (an exception is Dionisopoulos-Mass's chapter 4).

The structural hypothesis proposed here does not purport to invalidate the functional, psychological, and world-view hypotheses that have been proposed or any explanation of any specific instance of the evil eye beliefs and behaviors. It does seek greater generality, however, and it may not only help to explain the presence or absence of evil eye beliefs in different societies and the variations in these beliefs from one society to another, but also to assert the complementarity of these explanations, as suggested by Spooner. Some of these explanations can be subsumed within the structural model by relating them to the point in the behavioral sequence to which these hypotheses refer. The psychological explanations of envy or other motivation based on perceptions and world view refer to the motivation of the gazer at the time of initiation of action or of the gazee or gaze-fearer at the time of appeal for protection. These motivations may be relatively independent of the specific process of the evil eye. The social-functional explanations of social control, either as control of deviance or as economic leveling, refer to the consequences at the conclusion of the behavioral flow. These consequences might also be quite independent of the actual process of the evil eye drama, the consequences being realizable equally well through other processes, such as witchcraft. A psychodynamic explanation of the evil eye, however, based in subconscious processes of envy (Foster, Spooner, Roberts, Schoeck, and others), paranoid defense mechanisms (Kearney), conflicts of autonomy and dependency needs (Stein), or sibling rivalry vis à vis paternal authority (Reminick) might be homologous with the drama of the evil eye on both the symbolic and the social levels. If such a homologue is found, this would provide greater evidence for both the structural and the psychological hypotheses and would thereby elucidate the psychological and social functions. We will return to this issue in a subsequent section of this paper.

PART II: EXAMPLES AND VARIANTS—THE DATA REEXAMINED

Now let us return to an examination of some of the evil eye events reported in this volume to see if our hypothesis fits the case, lest we have strayed too far from the evidence in basing it on a behavioral stream implied in the emic accounts rather than on actual behavioral sequences. At the same time, we will attempt some further explanation of variant patterns, and also examine the fit of some of the psychological and functional hypotheses.

A large part of the evil eye beliefs and behaviors described in this volume and elsewhere are merely preventive measures in which either the gazer accompanies his gaze with a sign (blessing, spit, etc.) that he is not casting the eye, or the gazee or gaze-fearer hangs a sign of protection (amulet, cross, *gobbo,* etc.) against the possibility of "the eye." The behavioral chain is then terminated. Let us consider first these simple prophylactic measures.

There are at least three distinct sequences of interpersonal action involved in what is described emically as evil eye prevention. Each of these "partials," as we will call them, have not only a distinct sequence of action but also distinct psychodynamic implications. The first and simplest of these we will call "gazer prophylaxis," the other two "gazee prophylaxis."

Evil Eye as Gazer Prophylaxis (or Greeting Behavior)

When the gazer, either inadvertently or intentionally, engages the eye of the gazee, and gives a signal that he intends no envy or malice, this simplest of evil eye behaviors has been explained as motivated by fear of being accused of envy (Foster).[14] This may well be so in some instances, but also often enough the gazer who purportedly acts to avert gazee's possible suspicion of the evil eye has lost conscious awareness of the historic rationalization of the connection between such behaviors and envy. We would then have to suppose that the motivation was unconscious or projected envy. But if the emic connection between the behavior and the emotion has been lost, why does the unconscious envy come to take this form? It is a little far-fetched to conclude that the American who says *"Gesundheit"* when another sneezes does so because he fears that he will be accused of envying if he does not do so. Explanations of the evil eye concepts and behaviors as they presently exist must account for these persistences.

This simplest of all behavioral sequences in the evil eye complex resembles behaviors that are commonly observed in primates and still others that have been reported as "greeting behaviors" among Australian hunters and gatherers and modern man as well.

In the case of primates we know of no published accounts of this behavior, which is "common knowledge" among primatologists and monkey fanciers, but to illustrate it we will invoke anecdotal evidence, first from the experience of Byers [15] as a photographer in the rhesus colony on Cayo Santiago, and second from the experience of Garrison with two pet spider monkeys.

Byers had been told before setting off to Cayo Santiago that it would be impossible for him to take photographs, that the monkeys were far too aggressive and hostile to permit him within range to photograph. In his first contact with them they did indeed confront him with full aggressive threat behavior. He found, however, that if he averted his eyes, the threats stopped. He then found also that if he put the camera to his eyes and looked at them directly through the camera lens, there was no threat behavior. Thus it was the gaze and not the mere presence of the photographer that posed the threat that provoked the defensive threat behavior. We can guess that the gaze, as an act of engagement of two animals in an interaction, is very deep in the ethogram of our species and that it is related to biological as well as sociological and psychological responses of dominance and submission, which are also universal in the ethogram of the species. [16] It is not surprising, then, that the eye should become a symbol of a threat or potential threat.

At the same time the eye can also be "loving." Further behavior in the sequence of the interaction defines the nature of the engagement of the two individuals initiated by the gaze. For this let us look at Garrison's two spider monkeys. The young female had a badly deformed hand from the time of capture and was what is called a "cage depressed" animal. She would never initiate action with humans or her monkey companion, and she could not be engaged in eye-to-eye contact under any circumstances. The young male, on the other hand, was a healthy animal that often initiated exchanges with human, monkey, or dog. In any of these engagements he would fix the object with a steady gaze, but this gaze was accompanied by characteristically distinct behaviors that signaled different sequential behaviors. At times he screeched, jumped up and down, and shook whatever was in hand-reach, behavior that is clearly recognized as threat in primate studies. When he approached strangers he would fix them with a gaze, but he would also utter a continuing, but broken, monotonal signal (uuuuu uuuuu uuuuu uuuuu uuuuu), which some monkey fanciers call "the invitation to play." At the same time he would extend one arm outward toward them, palm down, until within range to touch. Interestingly (but we do not claim any significance for this), his next behavior in becoming acquainted with a stranger was to put his hands to their eyes, fingers extended, in a gesture that was threatening for the human stranger but not for other monkeys or familiar humans. If permitted, he would continue this sequence by stroking the closed lids of the stranger's eyes, poking his fingers into the nostrils, and eventually placing his hand in the person's mouth. Thus, the gaze was accompanied by signals on other channels (vocalizations, arm gestures, horizontal rather than vertical body movement, etc.) that defined the engagement as friendly rather than hostile.

Similarly, Australian aborigines may approach a strange camp and sit at a distance but within sight until other signals (fire sticks or sometimes mock threat behaviors) are exchanged indicating the friendly nature of the action to be expected.[17] If this is a friendly encounter the two individuals or two groups continue their sequence of action, usually with discussion of their respective genealogies, the placement of each individual or group, and the appropriate subsequent relationships between them thereby implied.

Teitelbaum, among others in this book, described specific examples of greeting behaviors (blessings and hugs) that are explained emically as evil eye prophylaxis but that do not differ in the sequence of action described etically as greeting behaviors. This gazer-prophylaxis sequence may have no relationship to the origin of evil eye beliefs. It may merely coexist or have coexisted with them, so that emic explanations were available for folk rationalization of a behavioral stream that is clearly universal. On the other hand, the common elements of the greeting behaviors and the more elaborated evil eye drama may possibly give us clues to more essential features of the evil eye event. These are engagement with the gaze, identification, and establishment of the nature of the interaction (dominance/submission, ranking).

This sequence and its resemblance to greeting behaviors may also provide clues as to why the eye came to be so elaborated as a symbol of interpersonal threat with the emergence of stratification. If the gaze is important in initiating a sequence of action of any kind for animal or man, if greeting behaviors are universal to man and the lower primates, and if both are probably related in animals and man to dominance and submission, or placement and ranking, why then was it only with stratified state societies that "the evil eye" concept came to be? We want simply to speculate that perhaps it was because the engagement of the two persons/groups was for the first time not dyadic and involved not only the actors present but a third party who was not present. This requires a "symbol," no longer only a "sign." A concept/symbol had to be evolved to communicate to a patron, "I have met with a potentially hostile encounter," and/or to communicate to the adversary that there was a patron in the picture although not visibly present. Why not the eye, or gaze? Any arbitrary symbol would do, and this one is particularly pictographic. Note that the eye is most usually only the symbol of threat (although there are exceptions to this in the eye-aversion beliefs of India, Malta, and elsewhere). Other symbols are usually used to indicate the presence of protection. These we submit are, or at least were once, symbols of placement and rank.

The point here is not the nature of the symbol as eye, rather than smell, breath, touch, mouth, etc., but that no such symbol was needed in purely dyadic interactions. Nonetheless, the relationship between evil eye beliefs, greeting behaviors, and the presence of stratification suggests other reasons why it might be the eye rather than smell, touch, etc. that assumed this function only after stratification and not before. Smell, touch, breath, mouth, etc. involve senses or organs of communication that would more likely be brought into play only at more intimate range, or, therefore, within an habitually interacting group—a homogeneous or egalitarian society or a relatively homogeneous segment of a more complex society. This is consistent with the ethnographic data on the distribution of such beliefs as the "hot mouth" among the Tagolog and the "working mouth" in Tibet, Sikkim, and Bhutan (Maloney). However, "evil breath," "black mouth," etc., are also reported by Spooner for the Middle East and by Maloney for India. It would be interesting to know whether or not the parties to the enactment of these beliefs are confined to dyadic in-group interactions.

The Evil Eye as Gazee Prophylaxis (Threat of Patronal Retaliation)

Another widely reported sequence of events in the evil eye stream, which may also seem to be partial, is that in which a gazer gazes, or gazee suspects that someone has or may have gazed, or might in the future gaze, and gazee acts to protect himself or property by raising a sign of protection. This sequence involves two distinct submodels that it is difficult, but necessary, to separate for their distinct psychodynamic implications. One involves an actual gazer who leaves fear in the gazee that "the eye" was harmful, and a gazee who next acts to protect himself or his possessions against this possible harm (see Maloney's accounts of his own experience with the potters in India and that of the Abbé Dubois with some fishermen). The other is that in which the gazee suspects that someone (not an actual gazer) has, might have, or might in the future, cast an evil eye and he acts to protect himself or his possessions against the consequences of this suspected, imagined, or projected gaze. (As a prototypic example consider the ever-present horseshoes, painted symbols, and crosses on the trulli described by Appel —protections against an equally ever-present threat in the environment that is never made clear, although it is also apparently defended against by stone walls surrounding all.)

Either of these responses on the part of gazee could be and have been interpreted as motivated by fear of envy, by a paranoid world view, or by paranoid psychodynamics. The second response, in which the threat is diffuse and unspecified, is apparently generated from within the gazee, and the individual gazee appears to have sacrificed his autonomy to an omnipotent malignant force, against which he is powerless to perform more than a magical act. It is particularly this response that supports the paranoid-worldview hypothesis (Kearney). But even more, the first submodel, in which hostile impulses are apparently projected to another, suggests paranoid symptoms to the Western psychoanalytic mind. For either of these responses, however, we would need to know more about the internal state of the gazee, the actual threats in the environment, the consequences of the action, and the gazee's awareness of the motivations and processes involved before we could make a judgment about psychodynamics. As Stein has pointed out, "we cannot automatically infer unconscious dynamics from an item of behavior." Nor can we infer unconscious dynamics from folk (conscious, socially acceptable) explanations. Let us reexamine some events in which sequence of behavior and social context are reported in the greatest detail.

Dionisopoulos-Mass reports from a Greek island, Nisi, a full chain of events involving not only the evil eye as gazee prophylaxis but other aspects of life such as gossip, magic, witchcraft, and institutionalized religion. A young couple planned to elope against the wishes of his family, who had been informed of the plan through gossip. (It is suggested that her family disapproved as well, but this is not as clear.) His family believed that their son had been bewitched by a love potion given him by someone in her household. The couple ran away to the mountains carrying not only "blue against the eye" but also "a tiny gospel to dispel evil, and scissors to 'cut the magic.' " Upon their return they were married, but the groom was unable to consumate the marriage. He became ill and was bedridden for four months. The priest was called daily to bless him and the house. Finally, a witch in Athens was consulted and the magic spell was broken. The sequence continues, but it is notable that through dishonor, illness, and divorce the evil eye was not again invoked as either explanation or protection. As Dionisopoulos-Mass points out, these are consequences of sorcery, not the eye. What then distinguishes the evil eye sequence from the sorcery sequence? It appears to be distinct both in the nature of the implied threat and in the implied solutions involved.

What was the threat against which the couple carried "the blue"? Dionisopoulos-Mass explains that the Nisi villagers believe that those who are eligible for marriage are vulnerable to the evil eye, gossip, and magic, because the usual care that is taken not to brag about one's wealth and health is put aside during the discussions of marital plans, dowry arrangements, etc. This display then makes the couple particularly vulnerable to *invidia*. But she also tells us that "The evil eye, gossip and magic, in regard to marriage, deal mainly with *philotimo* [love of honor] and *dropi* [shame]." A man's masculinity and honor are dependent both upon his own ability to seduce women and upon the chastity, fidelity, and shame of his women —wife, mother, sisters, daughters. She describes how Nisi men attempt to increase their own honor and masculinity by reducing that of another "as if masculinity were in limited supply." In a world in which masculinity is defined as dependent upon female chastity *and* upon male seduction, what must in fact be a limited good is sufficient female chastity to honor all the young males. For any generation of marriageable age in such a village the available women will not exceed greatly the number of males and any premarital liaison of one male with one of the females will, if a marriage does not result, reduce the opportunities for another male to enjoy the honor of hanging out at his marriage a properly blood-stained sheet. Further, with arranged marriages, this honor is a limited good that is apportioned among marriageable males by the senior males of the village, particularly fathers and brothers of the marriageable females. Surely the male of marriageable age is in a rivalrous relationship with other such males that will eventually be mediated by the decision of senior males. Similarly, the female of marriageable age is more vulnerable to seduction by a greedy, envious, or ambitious young man other than her approved suitor.

It is against this threat of seizure most probably that the specific prophylactic for the evil eye was carried. Why blue specifically should "protect" her or them from this seizure and destruction is unnecessary to ponder, as any agreed-upon arbitrary symbol would do; but blue or purple (indigo) were one and the same in the Near East until recently, and indigo is a traditional symbol of nobility or royalty. Regardless of the specific symbolism, it is a sign that she is "protected." And what is her "protection" in this situation? Only the retaliation of her father and brother should their "honor" be violated. The blue or other sign of protection, then, is a warning to any potential encroacher that his seizure would be followed by retaliation. In this case the symbolized protection is the possible and probable retaliation of the males to whom her chastity is important, should she be violated. It might well serve to "avert the gaze."

This is an evil eye event that may be motivated by envy in the gazer (potential seducter) and/or by fear of envy in the gazee (bride or groom), but it is unnecessary to postulate fear of envy as an intervening emotional state between the risk of seizure or loss and the act of prevention. It is also possible that the bride or the groom or both are paranoid personalities or that they have a "paranoid-like" world view as Nisi culture bearers (See Kearney, chapter 11). In order to demonstrate this, however, we would have to be able to show that there was an unconscious conflict creating fear or anxiety that was in turn denied and projected.

For Freud, the basic conflict involved in paranoia [18] was latent homosexuality. The unconscious syllogism, according to Freud, is: "I love him. No, unacceptable. I hate him. No, unacceptable. He hates me. Acceptable." Subsequent writers have challenged the idea that unconscious homosexual feelings are invariably the underlying cause of paranoid mechanisms, but the mechanism of unacceptable impulse denied and projected is generally agreed upon.[19] The groom's subsequent impotence suggests that fears for his manhood may well have been an underlying cause of both the evil eye behaviors and, more importantly, sorcery sequence. But we would be going far beyond our data to assume such a dynamic was operating. The bride and groom do exhibit "sensitiveness, suspicion, mistrust, and want of confidence in others" (Meyer quoted by Kearney), but as long as we cannot demonstrate the underlying unconscious conflict or the psychodynamics of paranoid mechanisms we have added nothing to this descriptive statement by calling the phenomenon "paranoid." In any event, we would be in error as anthropologists to "explain" our observations of cultural phenomena by borrowing and applying a descriptive label from another social science for a phenomenon that remains to be explained even within that discipline. In doing that we are only glossing the emic categories of one system with the emic categories from another, albeit more contemporary, emic system.

What is indisputably present in this instance of the evil eye enactment (as distinguished from the sorcery sequence) is rivalry between equals to be mediated ultimately by age-grade superiors or familial authorities. We will return to the discussion of the implied psychodynamics of envy below.

Dionisopoulos-Mass interprets the evil eye in Nisi society as one element in three dynamics of power (the evil eye, gossip, and magic), all of which have manifestations that have positive functions of social control while some also have negative social results. This is an interesting analysis, and as we mentioned above, it is a type of analysis that must be pursued further if we are to understand fully the unique nature of the apparently functionally interchangeable processes of gossip, witchcraft, magic, intercession of saints, and the evil eye. In the absence of more complete data from this volume on the interrelationships of these, we can go no further in generalizing the proposition put forth by Dionisopoulos-Mass.

Teitelbaum provides four more examples of evil eye behaviors as gazee prophylaxis. Teitelbaum has carefully documented the use of evil eye amulets among village weavers in Tunisia. The evil eye in this context is believed to occur between nonkin and nonaffinals who are in rivalrous relationships, and it is attributed emically to jealousy and envy. The village weavers, who are complexly interrelated by bilateral cognatic and affinal ties, are competitive in the production and marketing of cloth but also necessarily cooperative in the maintenance of the looms. Teitelbaum shows how among these weavers a standard of production is maintained at a modal 7.6 meters per day through conventions of hours of work, gossip, stereotyped joking relations, and ostracism. Certain weavers, however—specifically, handicapped slow workers, those who drink, particularly fast workers who remain in the shops, and fast workers who have moved their work into their homes—succeed in violating these sanctions and exceeding standards of hours or production by mechanisms rationalized both by them and the community in evil eye beliefs. The slow, handicapped, weavers and the very fast shop weavers are those who hang amulets as protection against the "eye," specifically fish, a symbol of pre-Islamic Christianity and of outcaste status in the Muslim world. The weavers who drink prop up their bottles (symbols of their iniquity) to view much as others hang amulets as symbols of their status. The fast workers who have moved their work into their homes are defined by the others as people who have the power to project the evil eye.

The handicapped and outcaste are by Muslim law entitled to patronage and protection for their disadvantaged status, and Allah is expected to punish those who refuse alms and protection. The handicapped and the outcaste are also often believed to be those who have the power of the evil eye (see Spooner, and examples by Moss and Cappannari and Maloney), although in this instance the handicapped are among those who hang a sign of protection and not those who are suspected of having the evil eye. Similarly, in the case of the weavers who drink, the belief is that those who drink (behavior interdicted by Muslim law) make contracts with devils. The bottle, then, becomes a symbol of that patronage and a threat of diabolic retaliation. Teitelbaum sees this as a symbolic inversion of the evil eye beliefs, which it is emically, but etically it appears to fit the same structural-processual model as the events in which the amulets are hung. Also, both of these evil eye behaviors appear contrary to the envy hypothesis—it is those who have reason to envy who are appealing for protection from envy. Using the envy hypothesis, we would have to postulate projected envy as the explanation for the use of amulets against the evil eye by the handicapped weavers who work longer hours merely in order to achieve modal production. This seems unlikely. Both instances are, however, consistent with the patronage model. Compare this account from Vinogradov on the Shabak:

> Caught between the Ottoman power and the Kurdish tribes, the Shabak were protected by their weakness. As self-declared pacifists, they carried no weapons and were known as an especially cowardly and inferior people. Thus, they avoided any involvement in the kaleidoscope of political alliances and feuds that raged around them.[20]

The Shabak are fond of telling the following story:

In 1892, the Ottoman government sent a new governor to Mosul. This governor
. . . decided to convert the Shabak to the *sunna* faith and conscript them into the
army. He therefore sent both *mullas* (religious teachers) and army officers into the
rural areas where the Shabak lived. Alarmed, the *pirs* met with their people, and
they decided on a plan. A delegation was chosen to go to the city of Mosul to try
to dissuade the governor from carrying out his plans. The delegation that made its
way to the governor's headquarters was a curious one: a score of "white
beards"—old Shabak with long hair and drooping mustaches, all riding on donkeys and playing music—followed by a jeering, heckling crowd. Attracted by the
din outside [the governor] came to the window to inquire about its cause. He was
told, "Your honor, the stupid, cowardly Shabak are here with their donkeys and
music, and the people of Mosul are teasing them, saying: 'The *wali* (governor)
must have fallen on bad times indeed to want to conscript the miserable Shabak
who have never fought a day in their lives. Doesn't he know that *Shabakstan hiya
mal dabka wtabla wzernayi?* (the Shabak nation is good only for dancing, drum-
ming and music making).' " Not wanting to become the laughing stock of the
people, . . . (the Governor) then decided that the Shabak were not really worth
bothering with after all, and he called a halt to his campaign of religious conver-
sion and military recruitment in their area.[21]

Thus both the handicapped and drinking weavers of Tunisia hang symbols
of their lowly status to secure freedom from the gossip, joking, interference
with evening-hour work, and other informal social sanctions. Together with
this freedom, however, comes ostracism as the price of this imposed or self-
defined inferior status.

The overproducing shop weavers also hang fish amulets, thereby securing
freedom to break the sanctions but also ostracism. This is an apparent exception to the patronage hypothesis, but we lack the necessary information
about the relationships in the market and actual patronage relationships that
might, in fact, protect the over-achievers. This instance, on the basis of the
information we have, is consistent with the envy hypothesis, i.e., the over-
achievers appear to fear envy. We cannot know whether they in fact *fear*
envy, but what we can know is that they are accusing others of envy by
hanging a sign of protection against envy. The emic concept of envy, then,
appears to be an essential part of the social control mechanisms involving
the evil eye. In the case of the over-achievers, it is apparently the accusation
of envy that averts the gossip, joking, and interference but also brings ostracism.

The last case, the over-achieving weavers who have moved their looms
into their homes, represent an apparent exception to both the envy and the

patronage hypotheses. Here the enviable, and not the envious, are defined as having the power of the eye. This could be interpreted as projected envy on the part of the villagers collectively, but it is easier to see it merely as the mechanism by which these nonconformists are ostracized. With respect to the patronage hypothesis, these weavers may actually have relationships outside the village, with the market perhaps, that free them of dependence upon the village, as they are freed from dependence upon the other weavers for maintenance of the looms by working in their homes and breaking the rules on segregation and division of labor between the sexes. We might also guess that they are more modernized individuals who have broken away from village traditions in a number of ways. In any event, this is not a case of "gazee prophylaxis" but one of "evil eye accusation," and it does not differ essentially from witchcraft accusation.

To summarize, then, the five cases of "gazee prophylaxis" we have reviewed from Nisi and from Tunisia all appear to involve actual peer-group rivalries symbolically mediated by a symbolic superior. Envy appears not so much as the motivating cause of these incidents but as an essential element in the symbol system that functions to effect control of such rivalries. In this respect the evil eye complex differs from witchcraft only in the concept of "protection" (and retaliation) by a superior power, which obviates further direct or indirect action by the gazee against the gazer.

The Evil Eye as Explanation of Illness and Cure

We have examples of the behavioral enactment of evil eye beliefs as explanations of illness and cure in Ethiopia (Reminick, chapter 7), southern Italy (Appel, chapter 2), India (Maloney, chapter 8), and Guatemala (Cosminsky, chapter 10), and among Slovak-Americans (Stein, chapter 12). This sequence, cast in interaction terms, involves first a gazee who is ill. Rarely if ever does a gazer or gaze precede the illness in this sequence of action. Gazee then ritually divines the cause of the illness and effects a cure, or he seeks the help of a specialist who does this. The common characteristic of each of these events (with some exceptions in the Ethiopian case) that distinguishes them from other curing and from other witchcraft events is that the divination of the cause of the disease is simultaneously the cure, and it is unnecessary to identify the gazer or to make any retaliation, symbolic or real. Thus in Guatemala (Cosminsky), if the illness was caused by the evil eye, the egg yolk turns color and the disease is removed. On Nisi (Dionisopoulos-Mass), the clove snaps from the heat and so does the spell. In Italy (Appel) the oil that does not disperse on the water is thrown out the door and the evil eye with it. In Slovakia the coals sink and the evil eye with them. Details of rituals of divination and cure also reveal that, at least in the circum-Mediterranean and Hispanic cultures, these are appeals to a source of power of good (usually God) to set the matter right. Again, the distinctiveness of the evil eye, as compared with other forms of magic and witchcraft, is in this appeal to a higher power that is merely invoked and neither supplicated nor manipulated. Search for the gazer, or even identification of the gazer, and actual retaliation are extremely rare. Thus, this sequence is gazee/illness, divination/cure, and even the sequence of evil eye as explanation of illness and cure does not involve the full sequence "in which a misfortune is suffered, a diagnosis made, followed by search, accusation and cure" assumed by Spooner. The diagnosis and cure are symbolically effected by this higher power, with search and retaliation only sometimes implied.

This use of the evil eye beliefs is probably a secondary elaboration or transfer of the evil eye beliefs to the curing system. Once the belief that the eye or the gaze can cause harm is established in the culture, it is available as a concept to be used in the rationalization of illness or other misfortune from unknown or uncontrollable sources, and particularly for the rationalization of psychosomatic complaints, anxieties, fears, or any symptoms with an immediate exciting cause in disturbed interpersonal relations. Throughout the distribution of the evil eye, however, such illnesses are also attributed to spirits or jinns, to witchcraft, to demons, and sometimes to saints who may be both the cause and the protection against the disease (see, for example, Appel, chapter 2). What distinguishes the evil eye processes from these other healing events?

It is customary in the literature of the history of psychiatry, of transcultural psychiatry, and of anthropology, to distinguish these events on the basis of the disease entity implied in the belief system. "Witches" in medieval Europe, according to many historians of medicine, were either schizophrenics or hysterics; spirit possession is also often equated with schizophrenia or hysteria. The evil eye is equated by Kearney (chapter 11) and Kiev [22] (cited by Kearney) with paranoia when an adult is affected and with phobia in the mother when a child is affected.

Garrison's recent studies of concepts of illness and cure among Hispanic, primarily Puerto Rican, populations in New York [23] indicates, however, that this approach confounds the processes of the disease entity with the coping mechanisms suggested in the curing process, and that such a simple equation of beliefs and psychiatric syndromes will work, if at all, only with otherwise identified, clinically ill populations. She has compared spiritists' evaluations, diagnoses, and treatment plans with psychiatrists' evaluations, diagnoses, and treatment plans for 50 clients drawn from a spiritist *centro* and for 50 psychiatric patients. The two samples are clearly distinct in their *use* of the culturally provided systems of explanation and cure of illness. Let us consider just paranoid ideation in this alternative belief system.

Patients in the psychiatric clinic who make extensive use of the defense mechanisms of denial and projection, or who have elaborated paranoid delusional systems (i.e., those who can be seen to have paranoid personalities or to be paranoid schizophrenics on the basis of other evidence), often report that they have had works of witchcraft performed against them. These diagnoses of witchcraft are usually self-generated; they are not grounded in an actual disturbance of interpersonal relations, and the patient believes concretely in a spirit "sent against" him or her. Similarly, clients in the spiritist *centro* who are diagnosed by psychiatrists as paranoid personalities or paranoid schizophrenics are often given diagnoses not of witchcraft but of other kinds of spirits; the clients may convert this other spiritual diagnosis to one of witchcraft in their understanding of it. For example, one diagnosed paranoid schizophrenic (formerly hospitalized) in the *centro* sample was "worked" extensively for a *causa de familia* that came with her from another lifetime and affected her whole family (one child committed suicide, one made a homicidal attempt on her, two had psychiatric hospitalizations, and three more were extremely troubled.) Interviewed after the extensive working of this *causa de familia* (the spirit was "mounted" and interrogated four times over two weeks), she said about what had been done, "Oh I had 'something' [implying witchcraft] done to me; they took it off, and I don't want to know who or why or what." In short, those who are characteristically paranoid in their defenses will use witchcraft beliefs in the service of their psychopathology. We can expect that in those cultures where the evil eye is a more popular diagnosis for adults that paranoid personalities will also use evil eye beliefs in the service of their psychopathology. But let us consider, by contrast, how the witchcraft diagnoses are used by the healer, suggested to clients, and used by those who are not paranoid.

Diagnoses of a "new witchcraft" in the *centro* are invariably related to an actual or potential disturbance of interpersonal relations, and the witchcraft diagnosis is simply a symbolic statement of that disturbed relationship. The feelings involved may be externalized, displaced, or projected by this statement, but far from being denied, they are played out and confronted. For example, a depressed woman whose husband is having an extramarital affair will be told that the other woman is doing witchcraft against her to separate her and her husband. The spirit that was sent against them by this other woman is mounted in a medium and it tells her why it is there, expressing all the anger, possessiveness, jealousy, envy, etc. that the other woman purportedly feels toward the wife. (In psychodynamic terms the wife is confronted with her projected self-recrimination.) That spirit is then convinced by the other mediums that it is in error, that the wife is a good woman who has never done it any harm, and that it should retire to the spirit world taking with it all the harm that it has been doing to the wife (fights in the home, somatic complaints, impulses to kill oneself or the husband, impulses to flee "throwing everything out the window," etc). Finally, the spirit repents and asks for pardon, and the wife is required to forgive the spirit and also the woman who sent it and to pray for the spirit's progress. Once this spirit is thus "given light" and "educated" it goes off to seek its own spiritual progress and the wife likewise. No counterwitchcraft is indicated. The wife is to say prayers, use perfumes and herb baths, and "work on her own head" and her own "protections" so that such spirits cannot affect her in the future.

Thus, the dynamics, intrapsychic and interpersonal, are very different if we look at the full process of illness and healing, and the pretreatment processes are distinct from the processes implied in the spiritist diagnosis and healing sequence. In this case the threat of loss is real, the anxiety and depression recognized, and the healing process, far from reinforcing paranoid mechanisms, may provide insight, if the person is capable of identifying with and reincorporating the psychodramatic enactment of her own projected anger at herself. If she has been using paranoid defenses, the ritual requires her to confront and forgive her own denied and projected anger. In any event, it provides a formula for coping that we can expect to be an improvement upon her prior defenses, which must have been overtaxed or she would not have presented herself at the spiritist *centro*. If this same woman were to present herself, thereafter, at a psychiatric clinic and "explain" to the examining physician that her problems were the result of another woman doing "witchcraft against her," the examining clinician would probably judge her—and most probably correctly but for the wrong reasons—paranoid.

It is this same level of fragmentary, summary information, subject to the same kind of misinterpretation, that the anthropologist is getting in the field when he accepts retrospective accounts of evil eye cures as his data on the process. Psychiatrists who study these phenomena, on the other hand, are most apt to take their observations from patients in whom the "normal" functioning of the cultural beliefs is distorted by the psychopathology. Most of the data on the evil eye as explanation and cure of illness is at this level of collection and analysis that is far too superficial for us even to begin to assess the interpersonal or intrapsychic processes involved in the illness or in the cure. Only with a number of comparative depth studies of the actual interpersonal and intrapsychic processes involved in the illness and the cure of the evil eye will we begin to be able to see the relationship between the categories of classification of the folk systems and those of modern western psychotherapy.

Evil Eye as Witchcraft in an Evolutionary Framework

Many authors here and elsewhere have noted the close resemblance between the evil eye beliefs and witchcraft. Spooner, Reminick, and Douglas elsewhere,[24] particularly argue that the evil eye is only a special case of witchcraft belief. Flores-Meiser and Maloney give a number of instances in which *bati* (evil effect from the mouth) as well as the evil eye functions like witchcraft. Reminick provides the most completely documented case of evil eye behaviors resembling witchcraft in which the sequence of action is, sometimes, a misfortune suffered, a diagnosis made, followed by search, accusation, and retaliation. He also provides a richly detailed description of the ecological context of these beliefs and a penetrating analysis of their structure and function on the cultural, social, and psychological levels. This case and Reminick's conclusions are consistent with and supported by the generalizations we have made on the basis of a review of the case materials and cross-cultural data contained in this volume. This broader cross-cultural context, however, permits us to assign slightly different orders of importance to the elements reported by Reminick and suggests an answer to the question he raises regarding the relationship between evil eye beliefs and behaviors and the typology of witches formulated by Douglas. We will not attempt a summary of this neatly presented case; we merely wish to call the reader's attention to specific points.

The Amhara of Ethiopia, settled agriculturalists and landowners, the *rega* people of "clean bone," "trace their lineages to a near relative or ancestor who had wealth and status and who was patron of many who worked the land of his estates." The *rega* people owned the land and exercised authority over the "homestead" varying "in size from that of a nuclear family to a large hamlet consisting of several related families and their servants, tenants, and former slaves." The *buda* people, craftsmen of "tainted bone" and *'ayn og,* or the power to curse and destroy, lived in an uneasy symbiotic relationship with the Amhara, who were dependent upon the *buda* for the skills that only they could master. They inhabited the lands of the Amhara, under the patronage of the same Amhara landlord who was also the patron or wealthy landed relative of the Amhara peasant; or alternatively, they inhabited the lands and lived under the patronage of a rival Amhara landlord who was also the rival of the Amhara peasant's patron. The *buda,* unlike the Amhara, who is tied to the land (if he has any) by inheritance, is free to move among rival patrons. Reminick's discussion of the fit of this case to Douglas's categories of witchcraft (witch as insider and witch as outsider) does not take this larger level of inclusion and stratification in a plural society into consideration. He points out that the Amhara-and-*buda* case is an exception to Douglas's categories in that the *buda* are both "outsiders," in terms of social definitions, and "insiders" in the sense that they live within the local group. Let us review these categories once again.

Douglas [25] classifies instances of witchcraft in accordance with the source of threat to the community and the functions of the witchcraft accusation for that community. We will try to classify the evil eye events exemplified in this volume in this system of classification (see chart 15.1).

Four salient points emerge from this attempt. One is that, as suggested by Douglas, the majority of the evil eye cases that are classifiable in this schema fall in category (b)(ii), or the witch as internal enemy, dangerously deviant, although it is necessary to redefine that deviancy as potentially envious.

The second point is that a large number of the evil eye events do not fit these categories. Categories conspicuously missing include: (1) the gazer as

CHART 15.1 *Source of Threat to Community and Function for Community of Witchcraft and the Evil Eye*

WITCHCRAFT CLASSIFICATION *	THE EVIL EYE
(a) The witch as an outsider.	(a) The gazer as an outsider.
(i) Witch not identified or punished	(i) Gazer as stranger not identified or punished. Examples: some instances from most areas.
(ii) Witch expelled. Function of accusation (i) and (ii): to redefine boundary.	(ii) Potential gazer expelled. Example: Tunisian home weavers (Teitelbaum)
(b) The witch as an internal enemy.	(b) The gazer as an internal enemy.
(i) The witch as member of a rival faction. Function of accusation: to redefine faction boundaries or realign faction hierarchy or split community.	(i) The gazer as member of a rival faction (clientage). (Our data is consistently incomplete as to what factions or clientages might be involved.) *Amhara-buda* case? (Reminick)
(ii) The witch as a dangerous deviant (dangerously powerful or rich; dangerously demanding). Function of accusation (i) and (ii): to control deviants in the name of community values.	(ii) The gazer as a dangerous deviant (the dangerously envious, the physically handicapped or deformed and the socially disadvantaged). Examples: Tunisian drinking weavers (Teitelbaum); women and beggars in the Near East (Spooner); a barren woman in India (Maloney) or Guatemala (Cosminsky). (The dangerously rich or powerful are conspicuously absent with minor exceptions, e.g., the priests in Nisi [Dionisopoulos-Mass]; a Pope [Moss.])
(iii) The witch as an internal enemy with outside liaisons. Function of accusation (iii): to promote factional rivalry, split community, and redefine hierarchy.	(iii) The gazer as an internal enemy with outside liaisons. Examples: The over-achieving shop weavers in Tunisia? (Our data is again consistently incomplete as to outside liaisons.)

* Adapted from Mary Douglas, *Witchcraft Confessions and Accusations* (London: Tavistock, 1970), pp. xxxvi–xxxvii.

internal enemy but not identified or punished. Examples are the woman with whom Dionisopoulos-Mass lived on Nisi, the woman in the market in the Guatemalan case (Cosminsky), many of the Indian examples (Maloney); (2) the gazer as internal enemy, kin or friends: examples include Iran (Barth),[26] the Toḍa (Rivers) cited by Maloney (chapter 8), neighbors in Italy and Nisi (Appel, Dionisopoulos-Mass) and elsewhere.

The third point is that information is utterly lacking on the factional divisions of these plural, stratified, unstable state societies where the evil eye beliefs are found as these divisions relate to the evil eye beliefs and enactments. We believe that the evil eye beliefs are a symbolic form of rivalry in complex societies having superordinate authorities, whereas witchcraft is a symbolic form of rivalry in less complex societies. We would therefore expect to find evil eye events in all of the categories of witchcraft, plus others specific to the more complex society; this seems to be the case.

The fourth point is that the basic division of witch as outsider or insider does not seem to work well with these data, either because of weaknesses in the data or because of the nature of the societies involved. The complex of evil eye beliefs within one society does not fit in either one or the other of these categories. Rather it seems that within each society evil eye beliefs and behaviors involve both insiders and outsiders, but possibly in different ways. Notice, for example, that among the Amhara, when they are alone out of view of the *buda* people, they engage in behaviors that we have defined as "gazer prophylaxis" and in concealment and avoidance. A compliment among Amhara, as among Slovak-Americans, is accompanied with a spit or a blessing, "May God protect you from the evil eye!" The Slovak evil eye is a specifically insider-to-insider phenomenon, and so is this same bit of behavior insider-to-insider among the Amhara. Apparently, the evil eye complex, like the complex societies within which it is embedded, has an unclear and shifting set of definitions of "insider" and "outsider" and the evil eye forms that accompany these. Reminick, Douglas, and others, have asserted that witchcraft becomes expressed at critical social disjunctions between persons who hold structurally generated enmity toward each other. It is perhaps just at the point of these fluctuating allegiances and rivalries in patron-clientage relations that the evil eye as a specific case of witchcraft is expressed.

We have suggested above that the evil eye threat is one of seizure or destruction by (1) arbitrary superior powers (outsiders in the sense of status); (2) status equals or inferiors of different specialties either within the village (insider) or in the surrounding (outsider) populations; and/or (3) status and functional equals (insiders), who might in envy or in search of self-gain denounce one to these superordinate powers or outside forces. Thus not only the action of the evil eye event is triadic, but so are the threats. We suspect that the evil eye beliefs of each society where they exist, insofar as the beliefs are fully functional, will reflect forms of (1) gazer as outsider with connections to superordinates, (2) gazer as status equal or inferior of a distinct social segment, and (3) gazer as insider, and that these will be functionally interdependent. This is consistent with the level of sociocultural complexity on which the evil eye beliefs are found in contrast to those of witchcraft. The distinction between witchcraft and the evil eye within societies where both are found may also be related to and clarified by this distinction between dyadic and triadic relationships, actual and symbolic. This we will leave for future analysts, but here we would like to recapitulate the evolutionary perspective on the evil eye that has emerged for us in this examination of the chapters of this volume.

Evolutionary stages are marked by accretions, increased elaboration, and increasing complexity of earlier institutions, and by the emergence of new forms. The earlier institutions survive within the society either as independent institutions performing the functions evolved at an earlier stage or embedded within the more complex, more evolved institutions. We submit that the "evil eye" is an elaboration of witchcraft beliefs and behaviors that emerged with stratification, the state, and patronage, and is found alternating and complexly interwined with older forms of witchcraft. *Invidia* as well we suspect, is a highly culturally elaborated definition of an emotional state. The emotional state and the rivalries to which it is attributed are probably universal. But the complex conceptualization of that state and its circumstances, as in the emic concept *invidia,* is probably not universal. It appears to have become so culturally elaborated when the good things of life not only were unequally distributed, but were unequally distributed by "right" defined by conceptually higher or lower status. Such status definitions blocked open rivalry between superiors and inferiors, and altered the nature of rivalries between equals within segments who were dependent for the "good things" upon outsider and superordinate powers. These rivalries were then necessarily mediated by superiors (patrons), or in ritual by symbolic patrons. Dyadic rivalries still occur: direct hostility, magic and countermagic, sorcery and countersorcery, or witchcraft with its appeal to community consensus and/or mob action. But added to these are the triadic patronage mediation and the symbolic patronage mediation of the evil eye and the intercession of saints.

Envy, we suspect, is particularly elaborated as a concept related to the evil eye when the rivalries occur between peers within a single segment where peers may rightfully expect equal distribution of good things. In this view, the segmentation (or "encapsulation") which Foster [27] sees as an institutional control on envy is a causal contributor to the emotional state and to the rivalries that it is also elaborated to control. Thus envy, segmentation, and the evil eye are not causally related in a linear fashion but they are functionally interrelated in a complex ecological system.

As political and social systems become even more complexly stratified and segmented, as bureaucracy becomes more efficient, and as redistribution becomes impersonal rather than personal, patronage and the evil eye both yield to other institutionalized patterns, real and symbolic, of rivalry, dominance and submission, cooperation and competition. These are, in our view, the universals of which both witchcraft and the evil eye, as well as *invidia,* sorcery, and the intercession of saints, are local, geographical, and time-limited variations.

Evil Eye as Psychodynamic Process (Envy)

There are four apparently competing explicit or implied psychodynamic hypotheses represented in this book. One of these, Kearney's paranoid hypothesis (chapter 11), has been discussed above. The other three are all variations on the psychodynamic implications of the psychological state of envy. Schoeck, following Piers, distinguishes two types of envy with distinct underlying unconscious reasoning processes. Both of these are implied in the more general interpretations of the evil eye as envy as advocated in this volume by Spooner and Roberts, and elsewhere by Foster. The first of these "is rooted in the oral aspect of sibling jealousy" and "is often suppressed or restrained by a feeling of guilt at being envious."

> The unconscious train of reasoning is more or less as follows: 'The other gets more than I. I must take it away from him or kill him.' This type of envy, as Piers remarks, is generally accompanied by resentment which may be so strong that it will colour the whole personality. This resentment resulting from impotence in the face of authority, is directed against the parents, who consciously or unconsciously, are accused of favouritism towards the sibling. Resentment can also be turned against a mere image of parental authority, ultimately against God or fate. [28]

The other type of envy Piers sees as a consequence of the maturation process and the nonoral aspects of competition with parents and siblings. This form of envy (invidious comparison)—in contrast with the other—is held in check by shame and not by a feeling of guilt. The unconscious syllogism runs: "The other is so much bigger and better than myself. I am so small. I can never be his equal." [29]

Reminick writing on the Mänze Amhara (chapter 7) suggests still another type of envy:

> *Buda* belief appears to be a function of power superiority among status equals based on the model of the eldest son as the object of envy by his less fortunate younger siblings, for it is the eldest son, in Mänz, who normally is the favored one and who inherits the lion's share of the father's land.

Stein (chapter 12) provides a very thorough documentation of the ontogony and function of both the personality trait (based on the oral aspect of sibling jealousy, or Pier's and Schoeck's first type of envy) and the cultural institutionalization of that personality trait. Reminick's account of the Mänze Amhara is an equally careful documentation of the psychological, social and cultural integration of the type of envy he describes, The cases from southern Europe, from North Africa and from the New World, however, do not fit either of these models. In these areas weaning is generally late and casual (in contrast with the Slovak oral-envy case), and equal inheritance rather than primogeniture is the general rule (in contrast with the Ethiopian case). These cultures are, however, the "shame cultures" par excellence, and therefore fit the model of the second type of envy advanced by Piers and Schoeck, that related to consequences of the later maturation process and the nonoral aspects of competition with parents (authority figures) and siblings (peers).

This nonoral envy is also consistent with the cross-cultural findings of Roberts (chapter 13): that there are no significant differences in the infant-rearing practices of societies with the evil eye present and with the evil eye absent, but that there are differences in childhood, the ontologically later training, in such matters as lack of trust, obedience, responsibility, and sexual repression.

Thus, the psychodynamics of envy appears to be homologous in structure and process with the social processes of patronage and with the symbolic structure and process of the evil eye. Further, variations in the evil eye beliefs also appear to have homologous variations in the psychodynamics of envy. The patronage hypothesis and envy hypotheses are, therefore, at least complementary, and at best homologous.

Envy, fear of envy, and projected envy, whether based in disturbances of the giving and receiving modes during the oral stage of development or in later childhood training, do not explain all of the events of evil eye belief enactment. (See discussion of Teitelbaum's Tunisian weavers and Maloney's discussion in the Introduction). We suggest that envy must be viewed as one element in the system of evil eye beliefs, rather than as the underlying linear cause. The concept of *invidia,* particularly in those societies characterized by nonoral envy, appears to function in many instances like witchcraft accusation, as a sanction against the expression or acting out of envious feelings and motives. We suggest that both *invidia*—as the elaborated, culturally defined concept that it is in these societies—and the evil eye beliefs, are emergents from behavioral processes involved in the more general categories of rivalry, cooperation, and competition in the context of dominance and submission mediated by patronage in stratified, but not yet bureaucratized, societies. Witchcraft is its equivalent in egalitarian and ranking societies, and it persists in the stratified state society concomitantly with the evil eye beliefs. Similarly, both witchcraft and the evil eye beliefs persist in the lower strata of the modern nation state (as noted by Foster),[30] where advantage and disadvantage are still controlled by conceptual superiors and mediated through *personalismo* and patronage.

In conclusion, we believe that the contributions of this volume do far more that merely "add instances to instances," as Spooner criticizes. They provide the basic data of the distribution, associations, and processes of the evil eye beliefs and behaviors from which a more general theory is beginning to emerge—a general theory that contains within it the potential to explain not only the presence of these beliefs, but their absence as well, and the variations upon the theme. Furthermore, it is a general theory that subsumes, while it does not contradict, the majority of the more specific cases and explanations.

NOTES

1. Foster, "Anatomy of Envy," p. 174.
2. Arensberg, "Culture as Behavior," pp. 1–26.
3. Ibid., p. 6.
4. In any cross-cultural research there is a smattering of aberrant cases, sometimes the result of inaccurate classification or mistaken original ethnographic reporting. Such variation is in the nature of statistical work. Therefore we will not consider

aberrant cases such as the "evil eye" reported among the Northwest Coast Amerinds, the Jivaro, the Mbute, or in Fiji or Yap, for example, until further evidence is forthcoming.

5. Murdock, p. 46.

6. Arensberg, "Old World Peoples," pp. 83 ff.

7. Foster, "Anatomy of Envy," p. 168.

8. Vinogradov, p. 216.

9. Foster, "Peasant Society," pp. 293–315.

10. Gerth and Mills, pp. 207–9   11. See Lapidus.

12. Foster, "Anatomy of Envy," pp. 170–71.

13. Ibid., p. 185.   14. Ibid., pp. 182–84.

15. Paul Byers, Associate Professor of Anthropology, Columbia University Teachers College, personal communication.

16. Chapple, pp. 96–104.   17. Peterson, pp. 60–63.

18. Here we are using the terms "paranoia" and "paranoid" loosely, as used by Kearney (chapter 11), to refer to paranoid symptoms or processes as found in the normal personality through the full range of psychopathological states to schizophrenia, paranoid type, for the same reasons given by Kearney.

19. Carr, pp. 195–99   20. Vinogradov, p. 210.

21. Ibid., p. 216.   22. Kiev, p. 173.

23. This research, the results of which are reported in small part here, was supported by U.S. Public Health Service Grant no. 1 R01 MH22563-01, "Folk Healers and Community Mental Health Programming" to Columbia University, Department of Anthropology (October 1, 1972, to June 30, 1976), Vivian Garrison and Alexander Alland, Co-Principal Investigators.

24. Douglas, p. xxx.   25. Ibid., pp. xxxvi–xxxvii.

26. Barth, *Nomads,* p. 145.

27. Foster, "Anatomy of Envy," pp. 185–86.

28. Piers as cited by Schoeck, p. 75.   29. Schoeck, p. 75.

30. Foster, "Anatomy of Envy" and "Peasant Society."

BIBLIOGRAPHY

Arensberg, Conrad M. "Culture as Behavior: Structure and Emergence." *Annual Review of Anthropology* 1 (1972), 1–26.

—— "The Old World peoples: the Place of European Cultures in World Ethnography," *Anthropological Quarterly,* 36, no. 3 (1963), pp. 75–79.

Barth, Fredrik, *Nomads of South Persia.* London: Allen and Unwin, 1961.

—— *Political Leadership among Swat Pathans.* London: Athlone Press, 1959.

Carr, Arthur C. "Observations on Paranoia and Their Relationship to the Schreber Case," in *Symposium on Reinterpretations of the Schreber Case: Freud's Theory of Paranoia,* P. M. Kitay, ed., *International Journal of Psychoanalysis* 44 (1963), 195–200.

Chapple, Eliot D. *Culture and Biological Man: Explorations in Behavioral Anthropology.* New York: Holt, Rinehart and Winston, 1970.

Douglas, Mary, ed. *Witchcraft, Confessions and Accusations*. London: Tavistock, 1970.

Foster, George M. "Peasant Society and the Image of Limited Good," *American Anthropologist* 67 (1965), 293–315.

—— "The Anatomy of Envy: A Study in Symbolic Behavior," *Current Anthropology* 13, no. 2 (1972), pp. 165–202.

Freud, Sigmud. *Psychoanalytic Notes on an Autobiographical Account of a Case of Paranoia*. 1911.

Gerth, H. H. and C. Wright Mills. *From Max Weber: Essays in Sociology*. New York: Oxford University Press, 1958.

Kiev, Ari. *Curanderismo*. New York: The Free Press, 1968.

Lapidus, Ira. *Muslim Cities in the Later Middle Ages*. Cambridge: Harvard University Press, 1967.

Murdock, George P. *Ethnographic Atlas*. Pittsburgh: University of Pittsburgh Press, 1967.

Peterson, Nicolas. Hunter-Gatherer Territoriality: The Perspective from Australia. *American Anthropologist* 77 (1975), 53–68.

Piers, Gerhart. "Shame and Guilt—A Psychoanalytic Study," in *Shame and Guilt*, by Piers, C. and M. B. Singer. New York, 1971.

Schoeck, Helmut. *Envy: A Theory of Social Behavior*. New York: Harcourt, Brace, 1966.

Vinogradov, Amal. "Ethnicity, Cultural Discontinuity, and Power Brokers in Northern Iraq: The Case of the Shabak" *American Ethnologist* 1, no. 1 (1974), pp. 207–17.

Vuorelo, Turvo. *Der böse Blick im Lichte der finnischen Überlieferung*. Helsinki: Folklore Fellows Communications, 1967.

INDEX

NOTE: For ethnic groups not listed here see pp. 230–33 and 264–78.

abortion, in animals, 50, 107, 156
accusation, 210, 290, 314; seldom done, 137–38, 182, 315; witchcraft, 320–22; *see also* Stranger
admiration: suspected, 80, 151, 216; spitting before, 201, 209; *see also* Compliment; Praise
Afghanistan, 141, 298
Africa, 234, 293, 298; sub-Saharan, xi, 87; North, xi, 63, 76; *see also* Amhara
agriculture, 239, 244–45, 282, 290, 294–96; horticulture, 144; *see also* Peasant cultures
"airs," 170, 180–81, 182–83, 188–89, 191
alcoholic drink, 72–73, 313
alum, burned, 81, 111, 137
Americas, xv, 234, 301; *see also* Latin America; Mesoamerica
Amhara, 85–100, 320, 325
amulet, 3, 64, 70, 80, 110, 118–20, 145, 302; pouch, 17; Jewish, 7–8; Mexican, 181; Italian, 17, 28; Tunisian, 70; for child, 106, 112, 121, 169; on elephant, 107
animals: associated, 243–44, 261; vulnerable, 107, 166; protected, 50, 64, 167; suspected: cat, 109, dog, 157, 165, tiger, 112; *see also* Cattle
ankh (symbol), 2–3, 9
anxiety, 180, 207, 213, 218, 311, 316
Arab, xi, 63, 76–81, 294; Arabic, xi, 115, 116
artemis (herb), 167
Āryan, 143–44
ashes, in ritual, 49, 94, 110–11, 122

baby, *see* Child
Babylon, 2, 6
Bangladesh, 113, 114, 126
bangle: conch, 119; iron, 120

Barnouw, Victor, 177
barren woman, envious, 44, 123–24
Barth, Carl, 295, 321
beads, 119; eyed, 48, 109, 143; *see also* Blue
beauty, vulnerable, 80, 90, 159
beggar, 80
bell, to distract, 125
Benedict, Ruth, 177
Bengal, 120, 121, 132, 140, 144
Berber, 63
betel leaf, 117
Bhīl tribe, 113, 138, 141
Bhutan, 130
Bible, to dispell evil, 58, 310
Bihar, 112, 138, 139
black, 31; ink, 92; rice, 110; cord, 106, 110, 112, 120; ribbon, 115, 116, 118; chicken, 163, 168; hot color, 170; forehead spot (*tilak*), 121, 127–28; blemish applied, 118, 121, 128; spots in mouth, 132
blood, "hot," 158, 165, 169
blowing, 78, 133, 153
blue, 7, 8, 11, 58, 108, 142, 310–11; eyes, 8, 80, 108, 119, 143; bead, 7, 49, 50, 57, 80; paint, 42, 50
boasting, avoided, 56, 65
boat, vulnerable, 12, 116; with eye painted, 11, 129
Brāhmaṇ, 133–34
bread, in ritual, 111, 112, 115
breasts, xiv, 54; "bad," 213–14
breath, evil, 79, 133, 153, 308
broom, in cures, 110, 111
Brown, W. Norman, 129
Buddha, protected, 124, 126; Buddhism, 109, in Tibet, 130; Buddhist, xiv, 110, 111
Burmese, xi; paranoid, 177, 190

camel, vulnerable, 64

caste, 87–88, 122, 133–35, 136; associated, 247

cattle: associated, xiv, 241–44; cured, 113; vulnerable, 98, 107, 134, 156, 198, 218; ill, 49; protected, 8, 50, 117, 127–28; see also Dairying

charcoal, in ritual, 112, 118

charity, as preventative, xiv, 121, 313

charm, xiv; Greek, 48, 51, 302; pouch, 49; plastic, 9, 30–40, 294; for spirits, 159; see also Amulet

child, 120–23, 135–36; vulnerable, 44, 64, 80, 90, 91, 98, 105, 141–56, 165–66, 175, 181, 185–86; protected, 64, 119; covered, 121, 167; hidden, 94–95, 105; left dirty, 81, 122; old clothing, 64; deprecatory names, 64, 122–23; as victim, 187; enculturation and socialization; 197–201, 212–17, 325, 253–58, 259–60, 261–62

chili: to dispell evil, 30–34, 110–13, 302; fried, 190; divination, 168

China, xi, 293, 295, 297

Christianity: evil eye in, 10–11, 12, 21–23, 34, 42, 47, 57, 107, 296; Catholic, 114, 157, 198–99, 296; Lutheran, 215–16; Byzantine, 198–99; Coptic, 86; in Near East, 77

class, social: associated with belief, 23–27, 87–88, 99, 236; status differential, 131, 134, 320

clothing: removed, 20; old, 64; dirty, 81, 122

cloves, 45–47

coconut, as preventative, 116, 121; shell, 116

complex cultures: and evil eye, xi, 144, 282, 323–24; cultural complexity, 235–40, 256

compliment: avoided, 44, 65, 91, 135–36; suspected, 107, 119, 159–60, 201, 322; not for child, 10, 121, 140, 165; affects oxen, 198; see also Admiration; Praise

corno (horn), 9, 30–35, 302

cough, 110

covering, 106; baby, 121, 167; see also Veil

cowrie shell, 80, 117, 122

crab claw, 31, 48, 49, 50

crops, vulnerable, 8, 49, 98, 107, 292–95

cross, crucifix, 48, 49, 57; painted, 18, 309; sign of, 10, 19, 45, 46, 47, 168, 171, 181

curer, 18, 51–52, 54, 58, 60, 109–12, 139;

wizard, 92; incantation, 112–13, 132; applied lotion, 155; centro, 317; see also Priest

curse, 6, 152; of God, 99; of Christ, 95

curtain, 117; before idol, 124, 125–26; see also Veil; Covering

dairying, associated, xi, xiv, xv, 121–22, 241–42, 261, 290, 299; cow dry, 50, 117; goat dry, 107

Devil, devil, 7, 50, 92, 95, 99, 170, 302; pact with, 3, 8, 84, 91, 299

Diehl, Carl, 107, 123

diffusion of the belief, xi–xv, 282, 302; to India, 140–45; to Latin America, 164, 301; to Philippines, xi, 157; to Europe, 298–300

distribution of the belief, xi–xv, 140–45, 149, 176, 187, 229–34

divination, 19–20, 81, 93–94, 110–12, 315–19; egg, 81, 163, 167–68, 185; leaves, 156; chilies, 168; water, 199; coals, 199, 211; cloves, 47; oil on water, 18, 47

dog: suspected, 157, 165; affected, 107

doting, 79, 134

Douglas, Mary, 97, 319–21

Dravidian languages, xiv; speakers, 141–44

drunk person, suspect, 165, 170

dualism, good and evil, 2, 4

Dubois, Abbé, 125, 131, 298

dung: cow, 113, 115; heap, 122

eating behavior, xv, 117–18, 146

ecological conditions, 297–302

economic leveling, 69–74, 134, 304; sharing, 205; redistribution, 295, 297

egalitarianism, 74, 134, 298

egg: symbolism, 171, in divination, 81, 163, 167–68, 185; in cure, 182, 185

Egypt, ancient, vi, xiv, 1–4, 9

electricity, analogy, 188

elephant, vulnerable, 107

England, xi

Enlightenment, 23–24

envy, vii, x, xiv, 44, 77, 130–31, 134, 179, 195–96, 210–11, 226, 261–62, 283, 284, 323–25; emic explanation of evil eye, 64–65, 133–34, 166, 283, 305, 314, 323; insufficient explanation of evil eye, viii, 14, 166, 176, 183, 211, 219, 326; by compli-

ment, 165; fear of, 98, 184–85; repressed, ix, 304, 318, 324; manifestation of, 43; *invidia*, 185, 310, 323–24, 326
epidemic, 109, 111
epilepsy, 21–22
Estonia, xi
Ethiopia, vi, vii, viii, ix, 85–100, 319–20
Etruscans, 4–5
Europe, vii, 234, 291, 298–300
evil: opposite good, viii, ix, 1, 300; evil eye independent power, vi, 14, 77, 182–83; bad luck, 32; *see also* Mouth; Breath; Face; Soul; Touch; Shadow; Tongue
exorcism, against evil eye, 20, 112, 113
eye: powerful, 14, 109, 128, 131, 133–35, 139, 146; hot, 155, 165, 170; contact, 292; contact in primates, 306–7; blue, 80, 108, peculiarity, 80, 108, 165, 166; mystique, 80, 128–29, 143; *see also* Protective eye; Loving eye; Lusting eye

face, evil, 132
factions, rival, 97, 322, 326
fascination by evil eye, 17, 21, 299; personified, 21
feces, suspected, 109
Finland, xv, 299
fire, protective, 103, 117, 125; sacred, 133; waved to protect, 112, 123, 124–26, 139; in divination, 111
fish: symbolism, 129, 142–43, 313; talisman, 70–71
fishing, not associated, 243
flowers: symbolism, 216–17; preventatives, 47, 49, 57; in cures, 111
food: symbolism, 216–17; vulnerable, 91, 106, 108, 117–18; hot and cold system, 157–58, 164
forehead, 127, 146; frontlet, 123, 126, 142, 143; spot, 126–28, 142
Foster, George, ix, xv, 61, 96, 98–99, 136, 157, 175–76, 189*n*, 194–95, 217, 296, 324
France, Brittany, xi
Freud, 100*n*, 208, 218, 311
fruits, vulnerable, 156
fumigation, 12, 80, 81, 94, 110; *see also* Incense
functionalism, 133, 282–83

garlic, in ritual, 8, 48, 49, 50, 51, 111, 163, 168, 170
gems, 119, 125, 126; as eyes, 139, 142
genitals, 46, 54, 90; to dispell evil, 10; *see also* Phallus
Germany, xi, 4
Gifford, Edward, xv
glass, to dispell evil, 119, 120
gobbo, 9, 33, 37–38
god, God, 123–26, 142; high god associated, 251, 295–96, 301; suspected, 2, 94, 108, 109; vulnerable, 108, 134
gold, protective, 39, 49, 119, 123, 126
Gond tribe, 141
gossip, viii, 43, 52–54, 56–60, 160, 202, 225, 294, 302
Greece, vi, viii, 9, 42–61, 309–11; ancient, 157
greeting behavior, 133, 306–8
Guatemala, vi, vii, viii, 163–72, 315–16
guest, treatment of, 79, 80, 117
Gujarat, 112, 117, 122, 137, 141
Gypsies, 120; feared, 10

hair, 81, 89, 94, 120
Hamitic, xiv
hand: symbol, 8; palm print, 114, 115; outstretched, 81; *mano cornuta,* 9, 33, 34–35
healer, *see* Curer
Hebrew, 3; ancient, 4, 224; incantation, 7, 8
Himalayan peoples, 121
Hindu, 121, 122, 129; cosmology, 130; beliefs, 133, 146
Hocart, A. M., 279
horn, 9, 30–31, 80; *see also* Corno
horseshoe, 10, 16, 32, 33, 35–37, 309; mule shoe, 50
Horus, god, 2, 8
hostility, 203, 213, 215, 226, 261
hot-cold system, viii, xiv, 168, 170–71, 184, 190; foods, 157–58, 164; blood, 158, 165, 169
house, vulnerable, 107, 114–15
hunchback, *see* Gobbo
Hungary, xi
hunters, belief absent, 141, 144, 243
hyena, 89, 95

idol, vulnerable, 104–5, 108, 124–26
illness, 151, 166, 315–19; causation, 14, 138–39, 171, 184
Ilocano, 151
Ilongo, 151
impotence, male, 58–60
incantation, 20, 29, 132, 153; Lord's prayer, 47
incense, preventative, 3, 125–26, 182; to cure, 111; *see also* Fumigation
India, vi, vii, viii, ix, xiv, xv, 102–46, 293, 297–98
Indo-European languages, xiv, 141–42; Āryans, 143–44
Indus Civilization, 142–44
infant enculturation, 197–201; *see also* Child
Iran, vi, xi, 76–79, 108, 117, 119, 122
Ireland, xi
iron, preventative, 10, 16, 111, 118
Islam, 63, 64, 70, 77–78, 81, 114, 115, 296, 313
Israel, ancient, vi; *see also* Jews
Italian-Americans, vi, viii, 28–40, 300
Italy, vi, viii, 8–11, 16–27, 28–29, 299–300

Jackson, A. T. M., 109, 110, 137
Japan, xi
jealousy, ix, 4, 6, 179, 201–5, 211
jettatura, 10, 23–26, 28–31, 34
jewelry, 80
Jews, 5–8, 9; Judaism, 7
jinn, 6, 78, 113, 316
Jocano, F. L., 150, 152–53

karma, 2, 105, 130, 133, 134, 137, 138
Karnataka, 118, 121, 122, 125, 131, 138
Kennedy, J., 96, 177
Kerala, 114, 131–32, 139
key, in ritual, 49
Kiev, Ari, 186–87
kin: suspected, vi, 64, 153; insider, 320–23
Kluckhohn, Clyde, 43, 61
knife blade, in ritual, 10, 113
knots in thread, 78, 110, 111, 119
Koran, 77–78; as preventative, xiv, 70, 78, 80, 119, 132; in cures, 113, 116

Lambāḍi tribe, 120
lamp, 115; *see also* Fire

lasagne, protective, 51
Latin America, belief in, xv, 157, 164, 176, 190, 301–2
LeVine, Robert, 207, 210
lice, inflicted, 91, 92
lime, in ritual, 118
limited good, image of, 43, 98, 184, 202, 208, 217–19, 295–96, 301
loving eye, 78, 106, 119, 127, 306
lusting eye, 119, 127

Maclagan, R. C., xiv–xv
magic, 54–58, 78, 281; black, 132, 136, 138; sympathetic, 77, 112, 137–38; diagram, 110, 113, 115, 119
Maharashtra, 109, 111, 115, 116, 117, 121, 137
Maldive Islands, 113, 115, 116, 131–32
Malta, 11–12, 308
mana, viii, 157
manikin, protective, 114, 116, 125
marginal people: suspect, 26, 64, 108, 116, 160, 299–300; unusual people, 78, 80; ethnic group, 87–88
Mayas, 182–83
Mediterranean, vi, xi, 1–14, 143, 176; core area, 290, 291, 302
menstruating woman, suspect, 168
mental illness, 10, 14, 113–19
Mesoamerica, xv, 190; *see also* Latin America
Mesopotamia, ancient, 282
Mexico, vi, vii, viii, xv, 175–89
Middle East, *see* Near East
milk: associated, 244–45, 296–97; vulnerable, 113, 117, 118, 164; spoiled, xiv, 107, 299; in cures, 112; weaning, 198–201; *see also* Dairying
Minakshi, goddess, 129, 142
Minturn and Hitchcock, 120, 135
mirror, deflects evil, 80, 120, 142
misfortune: blame, 79, 133, 136, 144, 292–93; 316; agent of, 172
Mithraism, 5
moon, suspect, 165–66
mouth, vii; evil, 130, 131–33, 140, 308; "black," 132, 308; "hot," 149–61, 170, 301–2; "working," 140, 308
Muensterberger, Warner, 207
mule, protected, 50

Muṇḍa tribes, 140–41, 144; languages, 141
Muslim, 24, 126, 133, 146; *see also* Islam
mustard, in cures, 110, 111, 112, 113

nail parings, 110
names, deprecatory, 64, 122–23
Near East, vi, vii, xi, 76–83, 134, 139, 297, 311; core area, xi, 143, 234, 261, 282, 287, 290
neolithic, 144, 287, 296; *see also* Peasant cultures
Nepal, vii, 129–30
nomads, and belief, 79, 144, 240, 290, 295–96
North America, Amerinds, xv, 234

object, inanimate, vii, 64; affected, 50, 107, 108, 292
obscenity, as deflector, 78; *see also* Phallus
oil, 19, 168; on water, 10, 18, 47
onion: in cures, 111; dog onion, 49, 52
Orāon tribe, 117, 121, 132, 141, 144
Orissa, 122
Osiris, god, 2, 4

Pahāṛīs, 121, 140
Pakistan, xiv, 113, 115, 116, 137, 141; prehistoric, 142, 143
Panjab, 113, 118, 120, 122, 137
paranoia, viii, 139, 175–88, 284, 301, 304, 309, 317–19
Paṭhāns, 295
patriarchal authority, 99, 101*n*, 145, 245, 262
peasant cultures, 79, 85, 98, 140, 303; association with, 144–45, 290–97, 300–1; prosperity, 134; agriculture, 239
pepper, *see* Chili
perfection avoided, 81, 120–21; by cutting ear, 122
Persia, *see* Iran
Persian, 77, 79, 141
personality, 105, 205–17; formation, 197–201, 257, 260; paranoid, 178–79, 317; *personalismo,* 290, 295, 300, 326
phallus, 78, 114, 125; *lingam,* 125; penis on manikin, 116; symbolism, 101*n*
Philippines, vi, vii, viii, xi, 148–61, 301
phobic state, 186, 316
phylacto (phylactery), 47–50

plow, associated with belief, xi, 85; *see also* Peasant cultures
Poland, xi
political systems, associated with belief, 248–50, 294–97, 299–301, 323–24
pollution and purity, viii, 106, 117, 122, 125, 133, 134–35
possession by spirit, 93, 124
pot: painted, 114, 145; eyes painted on, 143; potsherd, 115, 119; vulnerable, 102–4, 131, 139, 166, 297
potter, work vulnerable, 103–5, 166
praise, avoided, 121, 135–36, 160; *see also* Compliment
pregnancy: women suspect, 25, 165, 168; vulnerable, 80, 105–6; animal, xiv, 50; longings, 108
priest: as curer, 51, 55, 60, 93, 133; curse, 55, 131; pope feared, 10, 29; *sādhu,* 113; *pīr,* 113; *bhikku,* 111
prophylactic, 16, 305–15
protective eye, 109, 129–30
psychic projection, viii, 126–31, 146
Puerto Ricans, 317–19
pūjā, 103–4, 108, 111, 115, 123, 124–26

Quiché people, 164–72

rabbit's foot, 32
Rajasthan, 141
red: countermagic color, 8, 11, 108; sacred color, 31; paint, 8; ribbon, xiv, 7, 8, 81; yarn, 181; seeds, 167, 181; herb bag, 167; beads, 119; ink, 92; rice, 110; forehead spot, 126–28; vermillion, 125, 126; plastic, 33, 34–35, 167; "hot color," 170
rites of passage, vulnerable, 6, 60, 61, 80; postpartum, 167; *see also* Wedding
Romans, 5, 9, 28
rue: preventative, 8, 80; curative, 163, 167, 168–71
Russia, xi
Ruthenians, 197, 198

saint: cult, 21–22, 303; invoked, 114, 297
saliva, 153, 154, 181; *see also* Spitting
salt: preventative, xiv, 3, 19, 81, 110–11, 113, 181; curative, 110–12; salty eye, 77
sandalwood paste, 126

Santāl tribe, 113, 133, 140
Satan, 7; pact with, 3; *see also* Devil
Scandinavia, xi
scarification of face, 93
schizophrenia, 316–17
Schoeck, Helmut, 175–76, 189*n*, 324–25
Scotland, vii, xi, xiv, xv
Seligmann, Sigfried, xi
Semitic language group, xiv
sex roles, 80, 106, 145, 171, 218, 242; sex
    reversal, 91
sexual restraint, association with belief,
    256–57, 261–2
shadow, evil, 113, 133, 140
shaving, preventative, 90
sheep, protected, 50
shifting cultivation, 144
shoe, in cures, 111, 116
Sicily, 11, 29
Sikhs, 120
Sikkim, 140
silver: bracelet, 93; amulet casket, 110, 113
Sindh, 113, 123
sirena (mermaid), 38–39
Śiva, 129; third eye of, 127, 129, 131, 139, 142
skull, 49
Slovak-Americans, vi, vii, ix, 193–219, 300
smoke, 93, 94, 110, 156; *see also* Fumigation
snake: skin, 49, 50; stare, 80, 109, 127; cobra
    gem, 126
social control, with evil eye belief, viii, 3,
    58–60, 65, 73–74, 171, 302, 312
social inequality, a precondition, 261, 287,
    294–97, 326
soot: preventative, 49, 122; lampblack spot,
    127
sorcery: inflicting harm, 44, 51, 310; with
    gossip, 53–57; sorcerer, 55, 60–61, 197
soul, evil, 79
Southeast Asia, xi, 140; belief doubtful, 234;
    see also Philippines
Spain, xi
Spaniards, as carriers, xi, xv, 157, 164, 187,
    234, 301–2; Hispanic, 316
Spiro, Melford, 177
spitting, 94, 132–33, 283; preventative, xiv,
    81, 91, 119, 209; to cure, 110; before taking
    baby out, 121; to break spell, 199, 201;
    repudiating self, 208; *see also* Saliva

Sri Lanka, xiv, 111, 124, 126, 131–32
starfish, 49
staring, 79, 80, 155, 226, 283; gaze, 292–94,
    306–7
sterility, male, 44
stones, in curing, 111, 112, 122
stranger, suspected, 53, 64, 78–79, 88, 99,
    109, 130, 153, 165, 169, 175, 182; at
    wedding, 123; outsider as witch, 97, 320–23
string (thread, cord): in ritual, 111, 112, 113,
    119; on baby, 120–21, 122; *see also* Black
structural hypotheses, viii, x, 96–100, 135–39,
    217–19, 283–84, 288–97, 304
sun, suspect, 165–66
sweets, given, 81, 117

Tagalog, 150–53, 159, 301
Taiwan, xi
tāli (wedding symbol), protective, 123
talisman, *see* Charm; Amulet
tamarind, in cures, 111
Tamils, 102–5, 107, 108, 110–11, 114–15,
    116, 117, 119, 122; terms, 128; ancient
    literature, 142
tassles, 50, 57
tattoo, 80
tavis (amulet), 119
technology, level of, 240–45
thanks, not said, 215–16
third eye, 127, 129, 130, 131, 298; *see also*
    Śiva
Thomas, W. I., 13
thorn, in cures, 112, 113
Tibet, vii, xi, 140, 308; Buddhism, 130;
    Tibeto-Burmese languages, 141
tiger: evil look, 109, 112; nails, 118; teeth,
    118, 142, 167
tilak (forehead spot), 121, 126–28
tobacco, in cures, 163, 168, 170
Toḍa tribe, 109–10, 112–13, 121–23, 141, 322
tongue, evil, 10, 78, 79; *see also* Black
torch, 124–25; *see also* Fire
touch, 283, 308; evil, 133; not evil, 79;
    curative, 153, 181; "hot" hands, 155
trance, in cures, 93, 123
tree, vulnerable, 49, 107, 116
Trinidad, 109, 113
Trinity invoked, 19, 34, 46
Tunisia, vi, vii, viii, 63–74, 312–15

Turkey, xi
Turkic languages, xiv
Turkman, 78
turmeric: in cures, 110, 111; water poured, 123

universal, belief, 97, 279; evil eye not universal, ix–xvi, 140–45, 149, 176, 187, 229–34,
289–90
urbanization, associated with belief, xi, 145,
239, 296
Uttar Pradesh, 115, 117, 121, 135

Väddā tribe, 141
Valletta, Nicholas, 24–25
vehicles, protected, 12, 13, 32, 36, 50, 115–16
veil, 119, 296; origin, 80; *see also* Covering;
Curtain
Vishṇu, thousand-eyed, 128, 138
vulva, symbol, 8
Vuorela, Turvo, xv, 299

water: holy in cures, 18–19, 20, 46, 111, 112,
124; vulnerable, 121
weaning, 196–201, 213
wedding: vulnerable, 56, 58, 60, 123, 126,
310; newlyweds suspect, 165
White, Andrew, 3
witch, 54, 97, 112, 138, 197, 205–6, 316; not
hunted, 137–38
witchcraft, viii, xi, 2, 43–45, 96, 136–38,
186–87, 210, 298, 303; studies of, 43, 76,
97, 193–94, 279, 280–81; delusions of,
317–19; gossip of, 53–57; instead of evil eye
belief, 140, 298; evolutionary framework,
319–24
women: vulnerable, 64, 80, 106, 119, 120;
secluded, 64, 119, 171; suspect, 110, 153,
159, 165
world-view systems, viii, 1, 138–39, 146, 172,
179–83, 190, 304

Zapotec, 177 ff.
Zoroastrianism, 77